How Ottawa Spends
2002–2003

*The Security Aftermath and
National Priorities*

EDITED BY
G. BRUCE DOERN

OXFORD
UNIVERSITY PRESS

70 Wynford Drive, Don Mills, Ontario M3C 1J9
www.oup.com/ca

Oxford University Press is a department of the University of Oxford.
It furthers the University's objective of excellence in research, scholarship,
and education by publishing worldwide in

Oxford   New York
Auckland   Bangkok   Buenos Aires   Cape Town   Chennai
Dar es Salaam   Delhi   Hong Kong   Istanbul   Karachi   Kolkata
Kuala Lumpur   Madrid   Melbourne   Mexico City   Mumbai   Nairobi
São Paulo   Shanghai   Singapore   Taipei   Tokyo   Toronto

with an associated company in Berlin

Oxford is a trade mark of Oxford University Press
in the UK and in certain other countries

Published in Canada
by Oxford University Press

Copyright © Oxford University Press Canada 2002

The moral rights of the author have been asserted

Database right Oxford University Press (maker)

First published 2002

National Library of Canada Cataloguing in Publication Data
How Ottawa spends
1983-
Prepared at the School of Public Administration, Carleton University.
Publisher varies.
Continues: How Ottawa spends your tax dollars, ISSN 0711-4990.
Includes bibliographical references.
ISSN 0822-6482
ISBN 0-19-541756-9 (2002-2003 edition)

1. Canada—Appropriations and expenditures—Periodicals.
I. Carleton Univeristy. School of Public Administration

HJ7663.S6   354.710072'2   C84-030303-3

Cover design: Joan Dempsey

1 2 3 4 – 05 04 03 02

This book is printed on permanent (acid-free) paper ∞.

Printed in Canada

Contents

Preface / *v*

Chapter One **The Chrétien Liberals' Third Mandate:**
The Security Aftermath and National Priorities
G. Bruce Doern / *1*

Chapter Two **Innovation and Inclusion: Budgetary Policy,**
the Skills Agenda, and the Politics of the New Economy
Geoffrey E. Hale / *20*

Chapter Three **Inside the Perimeter:**
The US Policy Agenda and Its Implications for Canada
Michael Hart and Brian Tomlin / *48*

Chapter Four **The Neurotic State**
Luc Juillet and Gilles Paquet / *69*

Chapter Five **Toward a New Beginning?**
The Chrétien Liberals and Western Canada
Allan Tupper / *88*

Chapter Six **Being Poor in the Best of Times**
James J. Rice / *102*

Chapter Seven **Federal Spending in Health: Why Here, Why Now?**
Gerard W. Boychuk / *121*

Chapter Eight **Innovation Policy for the Knowledge-Based Economy:**
From the Red Book to the White Paper
David Wolfe / *137*

Chapter Nine **Biotechnology Policy in Canada:**
The Broadening Scope of Innovation
Markus Sharaput / *151*

Chapter Ten   **The Return of Directed Incrementalism:**
Innovating Social Policy the Canadian Way
Michael Prince / *176*

Chapter Eleven   **The Liberals' 'Reinvestment' in Arts and Culture:**
From Patron to Patronage?
Monica Gattinger / *196*

Chapter Twelve   **Getting Greener in the Third Mandate?**
Renewable Energy, Innovation, and the Liberals'
Sustainable Development Agenda
Debora L. VanNijnatten / *216*

Appendix A: Political Facts and Trends / 234

Appendix B: Fiscal Facts and Trends / 242

Abstracts/Résumés / 260

Contributors / 268

Preface

This twenty-third edition of *How Ottawa Spends* represents for the editor a trip 'back to the future'. I initiated and edited the first four editions of *How Ottawa Spends* in the 1980 to 1984 period. This was the last time a Liberal prime minister of Canada, Pierre Trudeau, had governed with a third majority mandate. So now does Prime Minister Jean Chrétien. In almost all other respects, of course, Canada's world in 2002-3 is profoundly unlike that of the early 1980s. The School of Public Policy and Administration's annual analysis of national priorities has examined these changes across the subsequent twenty-two years.

This edition was planned largely before the crucial events of September 11 and was to have focussed mainly on the Liberals' own Throne Speech innovation-led agenda. Several chapters deal with this continuing central governance and policy challenge of the early twenty-first century. But, like other Canadians, we have had to confront how agendas have changed in 'the security aftermath'.

Special thanks are owed to our contributing authors, drawn from several universities across Canada. Their willingness to contribute their time and analytical effort is crucial to providing a high-quality publication. The contributions and professionalism of Michele Morrison and Rachel Laforest in the School of Public Policy and Administration have been crucial not only technically but also in the provision of the two appendices. The excellent editorial work of Douglas Campbell is also gratefully acknowledged, as is the continued positive support of Laura McLeod and Mark Piel at Oxford University Press.

My personal thanks are also extended to my colleagues and to the secretarial staff in the School of Public Policy and Public Administration at Carleton University and to my colleagues in the Politics Department at the University of Exeter.

G. Bruce Doern
Ottawa
January 2002

The opinions expressed by the contributors to this volume are the personal views of the authors of individual chapters and do not necessarily reflect the view of the Editor or the School of Public Policy and Administration at Carleton University.

The Chrétien Liberals' Third Mandate: The Security Aftermath and National Priorities

G. BRUCE DOERN

In the first eight months of 2001, Prime Minister Jean Chrétien's theme song to himself must have included the words 'third time lucky'. He had won a third consecutive Liberal majority in the November 2000 election, an election that most of his supporters did not want him to call. His post-election Liberal mandate was crystallized in the January 2001 Speech from the Throne (SFT), and at its centre was an innovation agenda to get Canada ready to reap the rewards of the knowledge-based economy. He then witnessed with all Canadians the unbelievable implosion of the Stockwell Day-led Canadian Alliance, with the 'unite the right' effort going from two conservative parties to two parties plus a rump group of dissident former Alliance Members of Parliament. Suddenly, the Liberal party thought the unthinkable: they could actually envisage future electoral success in Alberta. As if this were not enough in the crap-shoot of political life, the Prime Minister could also pronounce immense satisfaction at the quite steep decline of the sovereigntist movement in Quebec, not only in opinion polls, but in a major set of provincial by-elections in Quebec, in which the governing Parti Québécois lost seats after making sovereignty a test-case issue.

To be sure there were some troublesome features, such as a downturn in the

dot.com economy, but even here there was the solace of the magnificent budget surplus that Finance Minister Paul Martin had stashed away under the Liberal mattress.
There was also the puzzling new American president, George W. Bush, but even this
was a plus, because the Bush presidency was born in a cloud of voting illegitimacy.
Moreover, Bush's early interest in Canada was mainly on the energy front. In a
word, Bush wanted more Canadian oil and gas, and here Chrétien was playing the
role of happy energy salesman, already hatching his new 'win Alberta next time'
strategy.[1]

But perhaps in those heady early months of 2001 Chrétien also had time to think
of the last time a Liberal prime minister was 'third time lucky'. Twenty-one years
earlier, in 1980, Pierre Trudeau had won his third (albeit not consecutive) majority
mandate, unexpectedly, as it were, the short-lived Clark minority Conservative government of 1979 having tripped over its own political miscalculations. Trudeau had
then launched three major initiatives: the Charter of Rights and constitutional
reform; the massively interventionist National Energy Program (NEP); and fiscal
policies that saw the fiscal deficit go from about $10 billion in 1979 to over $30 billion in 1982/3.[2] For the next two decades, all three were seared on the national
political memory, for good and for ill. By 1984 the Liberals were out of office. While
such policy responses can look and feel as if they are addressing the future with
confidence, two of these Trudeau initiatives, those on energy and on fiscal policy,
were not successful in the 1980s.

If Chrétien mused for long on his own earlier luck, or on that of his political men-
tor, the musing undoubtedly stopped on 11 September 2001, when terrorists struck
at both the tall buildings and the inner security of Americans. Canadians were
immediately enveloped by similar concerns, albeit interpreted through pan-
Canadian lenses. National priorities have since then been re-defined in the context
of the security aftermath. The account in this chapter of the nature and causes of
these shifts, central for the 2002–3 political, policy, and fiscal agenda, proceeds in
three steps. First, we look at the overall political context for the security-related priorities and for the politics of aligning them with what remains of the original 2001
Liberal SFT package of priorities. Next we look at the security initiatives more
closely. Third, we look at the core elements of the federal budget of 10 December
2001 and its de facto status of being both a traditional Budget Speech and the SFT II
of the third Chrétien mandate. A preview of the chapters is then presented. Three
of these chapters deal, respectively, with the larger challenges of budgeting and politics in the new economy; the Bush administration agenda and the challenges of living and working within the new North American security and economic perimeter;
and the Liberal agenda regarding western Canada. Two chapters deal with aspects
of innovation, which was, as we have seen, initially at the top of the agenda for this
mandate; one of these discusses biotechnology policy. The Liberals are seeking to
keep their innovation agenda on track, but in the December 2001 budget they re-
profiled it as strategic investments, and temporarily pruned it back. The innovation
agenda has been building for the entire last decade and remains crucial for national

policy and for economic and social prosperity.[3] Other chapters, many of which also consider different concepts and notions of innovation, deal with key ongoing issues, such as child poverty; social policy innovation; health care policy; culture and the arts; the neurotic Liberal regime and its access to information policy; and sustainable development, climate change, and innovation. Conclusions on key themes then follow.

POLITICS IN THE SECURITY AFTERMATH

The politics of national priorities in the security aftermath are basically a function of five factors and dynamics: the Chrétien leadership hegemony; the race to succeed Chrétien if and when he retires; the extent to which a one-party state is congealing at the federal level; the nature of provincial government opposition to federal policy; and the state of the economy, which in part is crucially linked to how the US Bush agenda proceeds in the short to medium term.

There is little doubt that Prime Minister Jean Chrétien stands astride the Canadian political scene without much effective opposition at the federal level. His January 2001 SFT agenda, with not a mention of security concerns, showed a political leader fashioning his legacy. Although he was at the very pinnacle of his political power, there was initially a sense that he was preparing to leave, sometime in mid-term of his third mandate. The seemingly reasonable probability of his departure necessarily sent some of his ministers and possible successors into a state of advanced preparedness for the leadership stakes. Their jockeying has undoubtedly influenced the nature, timing, and content of the post-September 11 agenda, and it undoubtedly contributed to the major cabinet shuffle that Chrétien announced on 15 January 2002, after the sudden and totally unexpected announcement by Industry Minister Brian Tobin that he was leaving politics.

Prior to September 11, the leadership race focussed on Finance Minister Paul Martin, Industry Minister Brian Tobin, and Health Minister Allan Rock. But the initial main beneficiary of the security aftermath was Foreign Affairs Minister John Manley. Previously known only as a good but stolid Minister of Industry from 1993 until 2000, Manley seized the moment of the security crisis, and became easily the most assertive Liberal minister about the need for serious action to support the United States, and about the need to re-fashion Liberal priorities. Chrétien asked Manley to head up the cabinet committee to plan Canada's security response, and thus, without doubt, Manley's star has risen rapidly in the succession race. Chrétien gave this elevation of Manley an even more personal endorsement when he named him his deputy prime minister in the 15 January 2002 cabinet shuffle. He also gave him the lead political responsibility for Ontario on Liberal party and patronage matters.

Finance Minister Paul Martin has long been the heir apparent to Chrétien, but in the early post-September 11 period was forced to take a political back seat to other ministers, whose portfolios were initially the focus of attention and scrutiny.

However, the 10 December 2001 budget restored the spotlight to Martin and allowed him to fashion and announce the full newly reworked Liberal national agenda. As shown below, federal spending has been significantly redirected to the full security package. In the forging of the budget, there is little doubt that Martin took special care to position himself particularly in relation to Brian Tobin, whose innovation agenda, including support for next-generation broadband internet facilities, had been at the centre of the earlier January 2001 SFT.

The competition between Martin and Tobin in the run-up to the December 2001 budget was initially very telling. Martin is of the same generation as Chrétien and has undoubted stature as a successful finance minister and a commanding central-Canadian politician. But the Prime Minister has never seemed enthusiastic about Martin's succeeding him as Liberal leader. Tobin represented the next generation of leadership. He was brought back to federal politics from his position as premier of Newfoundland. Chrétien, wanting him in the race, gave him the senior Industry portfolio prior to the 2000 election. It would not be difficult for Chrétien to see in Tobin the same admirable 'little guy' feistiness that Chrétien sees in himself. The fact that Tobin is not a central Canadian politician was also a potential positive factor with many Liberals and other Canadian voters. Chrétien's positive view of Tobin waned in the autumn of 2001, partly because he seemed to be too political in the post-September 11 climate, standing in stark contrast to Manley, who demonstrated a consistent *gravitas*.

The position of Allan Rock is also a part of the leadership jockeying. He is not only a next-generation leader, but also a Toronto-based one, from the Ontario Liberal heartland. However, Rock's handling of the anthrax and bio-terrorism scare, including a botched approach to patents and drug companies, has meant that, initially, Rock did not have a good war on terrorism or a good start in any possible leadership race to succeed Chrétien. In the January 2002 cabinet shuffle, Chrétien moved Rock from the health portfolio to the position of minister of Industry. He will inherit an opportunity to build his credentials as an economic minister, but on the innovation file, which is still not an easy sell to the average Canadian. Meanwhile, Chrétien has appointed Anne McLellan as the new minister of Health just as the health reform agenda escalates in 2002–3 in various provinces and in response to debate generated by the Romanow Commission, which is expected to report in this period.

In the cabinet shuffle of January 2002, Chrétien firmly re-asserted his control, after a short post-election period when he seemed to be encouraging a leadership race. The vision of a fourth consecutive term as prime minister now seems to be ascendant in the Prime Minister's mind, a vision that would put the fulfilment of Paul Martin's leadership aspirations into the 'low probability' category. The biggest single change in the Liberal cabinet since 1993, it brought 10 new faces to the cabinet table, removed seven ministers who had become political liabilities, and changed the portfolios of 13 others. Of the new appointments, the most significant and surprising was that of backbench Toronto MP Bill Graham as Minister of Foreign Affairs, one of the top five or six portfolios in the cabinet.[4]

The Chrétien agenda and the changing leadership politics of the Liberal party take on greater meaning as well because of the dismal state of the opposition parties. The notion is commonly expressed that Canada is a virtual one-party state, given the current federal political situation, and this is seen as a sad and serious weakness in Canadian democracy.[5] The Canadian Alliance may partially repair its tattered image following its own leadership race in the spring of 2002, but probably only if Stockwell Day does not succeed himself as Alliance leader. The right does not seem likely to unite, given the views and the smallish popularity gains of the Progressive Conservatives, led by Joe Clark, and his new-found parliamentary allies, the handful of dissident former Alliance Members of Parliament. In the absence of a concerted and functional 'conservative' party, with vote-splitting by conservative voters virtually guaranteed, and with a disappearing NDP vote, the Liberals would romp home again in Ontario in 2004 and hence secure most of their base for yet another Liberal victory. All of this explains why Jean Chrétien is already thinking about a fourth term.

If opposition at the federal level is problematical, the situation at the provincial level and in federal-provincial politics is less so. Key provinces will undoubtedly constitute centres of credible opposition and tension, but the key will be how issues are played out. Alberta is a source of tension, if not over energy sales then over health care and climate change policy. The sovereigntist challenge will undoubtedly reappear as the Parti Québécois government plots its next election strategy. Atlantic provinces will continue to press for Alberta-like status with respect to the treatment and use of oil and gas revenues as their energy industries reach maturity and pay-back time. And Ontario's governing Conservatives may be less easy for the Chrétien Liberals to demonize if outgoing Premier Mike Harris is replaced by a more centrist political leader.

The state of the economy is the other crucial determinant of Liberal national priorities. The downturn in the economy in 2001, first in the United States, but then obviously in Canada too, conditioned the priority-setting process in several ways. First, it caused federal revenues to decline and, as the result of some normal economy-related increases in social spending, federal expenditures to rise. And this is before one factors in the expenditures necessitated by the security package. Second, it reduced the size, and the optimistic perceptions, of the healthy fiscal surplus. Third, it raised the issue of whether a fiscal stimulus package should be mounted to boost the economy, and whether such a stimulus should be mounted even if it produces a small deficit. This latter prospect took on an added meaning when US President George W. Bush, an avowed fiscal conservative, strongly advocated and obtained a substantial fiscal stimulus package to help prime the US economy in the wake of September 11 and in the wake of the serious economic downturn in the US economy. The US stimulus produced arguments both ways. The first was that the Canadian government should do no less than the government of the United States. But the second argument was that Canada did not have to stimulate, because the US stimulus would help Canada in any event, given our economy's increasing dependence on US trade.

We revisit the state of the economy and the Martin budget below and in Chapter 2, but first we need to profile the Liberal security package. Some of its key features are clearly budgetary, but there are others that are legislative in nature and encompass moves that assert the powers and role of the federal government and profoundly affect Canadian civil liberties, and, perhaps because of this, the identity of Canadians, positively and negatively, and in ground-breaking ways.

THE SECURITY PACKAGE: A CLOSER LOOK AT NEW PRIORITIES

There is no doubt that a shift in national priorities occurred, propelled by the events of September 11 and responding to the need for Canada to be a part of the Bush-led international coalition against terrorism. In the heady and even serene period of the 30 January 2001 SFT, the Chrétien Liberals had stated that they would focus on

- building a world-leading economy driven by innovation, ideas, and talent;
- creating a more inclusive society where children get the right start in life, where quality health services are available to all, and where Canadians enjoy strong and safe communities;
- ensuring a clean, healthy environment for Canadians and the preservation of our natural resources; and
- enhancing our Canadian voice in the world and our shared sense of citizenship.[6]

But then came the post-September 11 priorities centred on the security and anti-terrorism package. The new policy, legislative, and budgetary response included several measures: anti-terrorism legislation, with new, quite draconian powers; changes to immigration law; the provision of new budgetary and personnel resources for the Department of National Defence, CSIS, and national police and border control; the heightening of attention at Health Canada regarding Canada's readiness to deal with threats such as anthrax infection and other forms of bio-terrorism; and measures to deal with airport safety and such related issues as the precarious state of Canada's airline industry, the collapse of the airline Canada 3000, and the demands of Air Canada for federal bailout funds.

Bound up in this panoply of rushed measures and responses was a need by the federal Liberals to confront their own and Canada's sense of the world and themselves. The previous Chrétien government, with Lloyd Axworthy as Minister of Foreign Affairs and International Trade, had seen the world according to a more benign vision, in which Canada lived in relative peace and security, as a principled practitioner of 'soft power'. Within days of the September 11 attack, Canada was confronting demands from the United States that it join in the construction of a North American security perimeter.[7] Some of this pressure was resisted rhetorically, but, significantly, the most hawkish of Canada's lead ministers in Canada's overall response was none other than its foreign minister, John Manley. As we have seen, Manley's political star rose markedly, because his assertiveness and his capture of the core security issues of the moment stood in contrast to the initial relative caution of the Prime Minister. But the rapid journey from 'soft power' to 'North American security perimeter' was not the only element to be faced in the confrontation of beliefs and values.

Space does not allow coverage in detail of the security package, but central to it was the federal anti-terrorism legislation, Bill C-36, tabled on 15 October 2001 and passed after the Liberals imposed closure on debate in December 2001. It too faced the Liberals and all Canadians squarely with the conflict between the need for new anti-terrorist measures and powers and the Trudeau Liberal legacy of the Charter of Rights and Freedoms; another element of the mix was another Trudeau era legacy, the memory of the invocation of the War Measures Act in 1970 during the October Crisis. A massive piece of legislation, Bill C-36 is 171 pages long and contains 146 new provisions, and changes to several pieces of related existing legislation. Central to it are provisions that under the Criminal Code would give police armed with a warrant the power to arrest and detain suspected terrorists if there were reasonable grounds to believe they were about to commit an offence. The legislation defines terrorism as an activity for political, religious, or ideological purposes that threatens the public or national security by killing, seriously harming, or endangering a person, causing substantial property damage, or disrupting an essential service or facility. The legislation also makes it an offence to knowingly participate in, contribute to, or facilitate the activities of a terrorist group. It expands police surveillance powers, strengthens anti-money laundering laws, and toughens hate-crime laws, such as those against on-line hate propaganda.

Justice Minister Anne McLellan stated confidently that the federal government believes that the new legislation, having been vetted against the Charter of Rights and Freedoms by federal lawyers, is 'charter proof', but this of course remains to be seen. Aspects of the legislation will undoubtedly be challenged in the courts and will certainly remain controversial in political debate. McLellan bowed to intense pressure from the media, opposition parties, and the Liberal caucus by announcing on 21 November 2001 that Bill C-36 would be amended to provide a sunset clause to two of its key provisions, investigative hearings and preventative arrests.[8] She also promised to amend the bill by tightening the definition of a 'terrorist act' to ensure that it does not encompass activities such as illegal strikes and native blockades and to ensure that non-violent expressions of political, religious, or ideological beliefs do not also constitute terrorist acts.

A second key piece of Liberal anti-terrorism legislation is the Public Safety Act, introduced by Transport Minister David Collenette on 22 November 2001. The legislation contains a series of anti-terrorism measures, largely created by changing 19 laws already in existence.[9] It imposes fines of up to $1 million and penalties of up to 10 years in jail for producing, stockpiling, or proliferating biological weapons or toxins. It clarifies and, in some cases, strengthens existing aviation security authorities. Its most significant change is that it enables the federal government to collect air passenger data from airlines and reservation systems and share it with foreign governments. This includes information on specific passengers or flights when it is needed for security purposes. The legislation allows cabinet ministers to issue emergency interim orders without public or parliamentary scrutiny; it also allows for the establishment of 'military security zones', when needed, to protect people and property. Powers of the latter type were severely criticized by opposition parties as a power grab and as an invasion of the privacy of passengers, and of citizens in general. The legislation was also criticized because it failed to deal with airport security and the screening of air passengers and baggage. On this latter point, there was considerable pressure to remove airport security from the control of private airlines and place it under government control. The more extensive provisions in this regard by the US Bush administration were seen as being far more decisive and more in keeping with the public mood. In the 2001 Budget Speech, a new national security authority for airports was announced.

A third string to the Liberal security bow came in the form of support for a comprehensive border agreement with the United States, announced on 3 December 2001.[10] The accord includes new joint arrangements for border policing, expanded international security teams, and coordinated immigration measures. Significantly, the Americans also announced that they would be temporarily stationing some military personnel at the border, and would be patrolling the air in selected areas. US Attorney General John Ashcroft presented this military presence as a measure to assist border officials and thus to increase cross-border traffic and commerce. He seemed to be consciously avoiding offence to the historic notion of the border between Canada and the United States as the world's longest and oldest 'undefended border', but he was also signalling to Canada the continuing strength of the view in US media and political circles that Canada's border was too porous. This perception occurred despite the fact that all of the perpetrators of the September 11 attack had been granted entry directly into the United States by US authorities and at US airports. The US view had nonetheless congealed, because of the earlier Ressam case, in which a terrorist had entered the United States from Canada, and because of the well-known debate within Canada about the porousness of the Canadian immigration and refugee regime.

Any reluctance the Chrétien Liberals may have felt about the new border regime as a security package was undoubtedly overcome by their larger concerns about ensuring continued cross-border trade and the smooth and speedy flow of goods and services. Long lines at border points in the autumn of 2001 led to the mobilization of Canadian business lobbies to ensure that *free* trade did not become *slow and secure* trade. The border measures were essentially budgetary rather than legislative; Finance Minister Paul Martin included upwards of $500 million for these measures in the 10 December 2001 budget.

The Liberals also had to make defence policy a key part of their anti-terrorism package. Defence spending and the state of Canada's defence forces were not central Liberal priorities, nor had they been for most of the Chrétien era. To support the international coalition against terrorism, Canada committed 2,000 defence personnel, but did so knowing that defence resources were thin and getting thinner. New defence spending for military deployment has been committed, but even under the best of assumptions these new commitments are small compared to other parts of the total security package.

Also emerging out of the security aftermath—but in a very different way—was the Liberal response to the crisis in the airline industry. The airline industry, in Canada and globally, suffered a major blow as a result of the terrorist attacks in the United States, but the Canadian industry had been in trouble well before that. And the struggle for a viable national airline system was in turn bound up with a series of botched Liberal restructuring efforts that had led to an Air Canada monopoly, and an airline that was still losing money. Air Canada's predatory behaviour was directed not just at its few competitors, but also at Canadian taxpayers, from whom it wanted generous handouts.

Air Canada's initial outrageous demands for federal help are ultimately an issue that goes beyond security, but this issue, with its links to the politics of security, is instructive in relation to the security package and budget. First, the amounts being sought (since pruned down) are still of the same order of magnitude as some estimates of the defence segment of the security package. Second, the airline debate, occurring as it is in a security environment, may well be reshaping related debates, such as how and on what basis Canadians think of certain industries as 'essential service industries'. The airline industry may get reconfigured because of these debates, but so also may industries, such as energy supply and pipelines, sectors that for most of the last two decades have been reformed in the name of deregulation and competitive orders, but that are really, under closer inspection, essential service networks.[11]

THE DECEMBER 2001 BUDGET AND THE SHRINKING SURPLUS

Finance Minister Paul Martin's Budget Speech of 10 December 2001 was crafted as a budget for 'securing progress in an uncertain world'.[12] In the speech itself, Martin declared that the budget does four things:

- First, it provides the necessary funding for the security measures to deal with the threats we face.
- Second, it recognizes the vital importance of an open Canada-US border to our continuing economic security.
- Third, it supports Canadians through difficult times while continuing our long-term plan to build for the future.
- And fourth, it provides Canadians with a full and open accounting of the nation's finances.[13]

In the larger Budget Plan documents, where the focus is even more explicitly fiscal and economic, the budget message is ordered somewhat differently, but still couched in notions of security that are double-edged, including as they do both physical security and economic security. Again four ways are profiled as to how the budget addresses these concerns:

- . . . it provides a timely boost to the economy at a time of global weakness and uncertainty and positions Canadians to take full advantage of the recovery expected next year;
- . . . it acts to build personal and economic security by keeping Canadians safe, terrorists out and our borders open and efficient;
- . . . it keeps the nation's finances healthy by balancing the budget this year and for the next two years; and
- . . . it fully protects the $100 billion tax cut and the $23.4 billion in increased support for health care and early childhood development.[14]

The Liberals' main initiatives are largely expenditure-oriented, and are grouped into two thematic packages: 'enhancing security for Canadians', in essence the post-September 11 agenda, with a $7.7-billion price tag over five years; and 'strategic investments: bridging to the future', in essence the Liberal effort to show some continuity with their earlier, January 2001 post-election SFT, which included the innovation agenda. The key elements under these two packages are as follows:

Enhancing Security for Canadians
- Intelligence and Policing, $1.6 billion
- Screening of Entrants to Canada, $1 billion
- Emergency Preparedness and Military Deployment, $1.6 billion
- A New Approach to Air Security, $2.2 billion (including a new federal air security authority), funded by a new Air Traveller's Security Charge
- Border Security and Facilitation, $1.2 billion

Strategic Investments: Bridging to the Future
- Investing in Health Initiatives (includes the previously announced $23.4 billion in health and early childhood development; new measures include $95 million for Canadian Institute for Health Information, and $75 million increase for the Canadian Institutes of Health Research)
- Investing in Skills, Learning and Research, $1.3 billion over three years
- Investing in Strategic Infrastructure and the Environment, $3 billion (including $2 billion for a new Strategic Infrastructure Foundation to fund large strategic projects)
- Aboriginal Children, $185 million over two years
- Furthering International Assistance, $1 billion over three years.

As Chapter 2 shows in more detail, the December 2001 budget was the Finance Minister's biggest 'spending increase' budget of his nine-year tenure. This budget is less prudent and more political leadership-tinged than his earlier ones in five ways. First, it is less transparent, in that it is difficult to know precisely how much is genuinely new spending as opposed to repackaged old spending. Second, it is couched in a set of fiscal and economic forecast assumptions that greatly reduces the contingency funds available to the federal government. Third, it fudges his earlier 1999/2000 posture as a politically right-of-centre tax-cutting minister of finance. Fourth, it hopes for, rather than confidently plans for, a non-deficit future. Fifth, it is unambiguously and highly dependent on the US stimulus package and on US economic recovery.

AN OVERVIEW OF THE VOLUME

- **Geoffrey Hale** analyses the December 2001 budget against the backdrop of earlier Chrétien and Paul Martin era budgets and draws attention to the challenges and choices involved in the effort to balance innovation and social inclusion in contemporary budgetary politics. At their core such budgetary policies are intended to facilitate the adjustment of businesses and citizens to the emerging knowledge-based or 'new' economy, which is based on the application of new technologies, business processes, and related human expertise to the development of new industries and the reinvention of many existing ones. Hale shows that politically this effort depends on the capacity of governments to balance measures intended to address the concerns of the business, professional, and academic elites who are managing the processes that lead to technological innovation and economic growth, with those aimed at ensuring that the vast majority of ordinary Canadians have the skills and opportunities necessary to participate in the benefits resulting from these changes—and the latter measures include improvements in core public services. He argues that the government's capacity to balance and sustain these initiatives over a long enough period to make them truly effective continues to depend on maintaining enough short-term fiscal discretion to accommodate unforeseen political and economic shocks and avoid a return to the fiscal overextension and chronic deficits of the past. This process lends itself to a series of incremental initiatives packaged in 'thematic budgets', which convey the impression of decisive action based on coherent priorities while leaving Finance Minister Paul Martin with enough flexibility to respond to short-term political and economic pressures.

- **Michael Hart and Brian Tomlin** examine the ways in which policy priorities in Canada are shaped, directly and indirectly, by the public policy agenda in the United States, particularly given the presence of a relatively new president, George W. Bush, and also, even more compellingly, given the events of September 11. They begin with a description of the US policy process, particularly the setting of the policy agenda and the president's role in this process, and then relate this, first, to the pre-September 11 period, when issues such as the latest round of the softwood lumber trade dispute and the Bush National Energy Plan were central to Canada-US relations. Hart and Tomlin then show the stark contrast in the period after September 11, when Canadians and their governments found themselves profoundly 'inside the perimeter'. They show that a substantial majority of Canadians now wanted their country, through their government, to stand shoulder to shoulder with the Americans in their hour of need. But the sense of being inside the perimeter took on different meanings as the months went by. If it began with concerns about physical security, it eventually became interwoven with concerns about border trade and making sure that the border continues to welcome the free flow of Canada's economic lifeblood. Hart and Tomlin argue that Canadians and the Chrétien Liberals may not yet fully understand how profoundly the world has changed since the terrorist attack on the United States.

• The chapter by **Luc Juillet and Gilles Paquet** adds a provocative and interesting new analytical dimension to the increasing debate about the centralization of power in Canada. Rather than focussing on traditional themes, such as the concentration of power in the office of the Prime Minister and the weakness of the federal opposition parties, their analysis focuses on the 'neurotic state' and the bureaucracy itself. Juillet and Paquet argue that the fast pace of socio-economic change, and a more critical citizenry, distrustful of traditional political institutions, have combined to create major challenges for the effective governance of contemporary societies.

They argue that the federal nation state has been tempted to turn inward, and has attempted to regain greater control, and shield itself from opposition and criticism, by depriving the citizenry of information about its internal decision-making procedures and operations. This neurosis, which they diagnose as paranoia, is examined in a general way and is further documented through an analysis of the tensions surrounding the interactions between stakeholders with respect to the operations of the Access to Information Act. The chapter argues that maximum openness is a sensible goal, provided that it is offset by operational principles seeking to ensure that the fundamental rights and basic interests of citizens are protected, and that the state preserves the capacity to act in the public interest. The analysis shows how paranoia has prevented the development of a workable set of arrangements, and it shows how such processes are leading to more secretiveness, a decline in public trust, centralization, conservatism, a lack of critical thinking, and the failure of government to operate as a learning organization.

- **Allan Tupper** takes up yet another crucial element of the changing power structure of Canadian politics and policy, namely the Chrétien Liberals' effort to woo Alberta and western Canada. His chapter shows that the government of Canada has paid considerable attention to western Canadian voters and interests over the last year. This is revealed through the fact that senior ministers and the Prime Minister are spending much more time in the region than heretofore, that western Canadian resource industries, especially oil and natural gas, are being defined as essential to the national interest, and that the federal government is stressing its commitment to western economic diversification, through the development of advanced research capacity and 'new economy' industries. Alberta is receiving special attention as a regional leader, a strategy personalized in Chrétien's personal approaches to Alberta Premier Ralph Klein. Tupper also argues that regionalism is weakening, as westerners shed a sense of political weakness, as their provincial governments redefine their roles, and as a new generation of western voters, especially urban voters, unimpressed by traditional regional rhetoric, assumes prominence.

- **James Rice** examines the federal government's failure to reduce child poverty significantly in Canada during the era of the 'new economy'. Rice's chapter examines how ideas regarding the new economy have influenced and shaped government decision-making. It also examines how government changes to social policies have affected the well-being of low-income families, and the consequences of these changes for their future well-being. The chapter ends with the argument that the new economy is like the old economy in that it divides workers into those who are educated and skilled and can benefit from economic change, and those who, because of a lack of education or skills, are deprived of the benefits of economic growth.

    Rice argues that Canada will continue to develop a two-tiered economy, one tier for the 'haves' and one for the 'have-nots'. Opportunities will flow to those who have the advantage of educated or well-off parents, while those with poor parents will have limited opportunities. In the old economy of white- and blue-collar jobs, there was room for upward social mobility. A young man or woman could start in the shop or the secretarial pool and work his or her way up to the front office. But with rising educational barriers, there is little or no room for an uneducated person to move from a low-paying service sector job to a well-paying job in the new economy. Although the new economy reflects only a small part of the business world, its ideas have come to have a powerful effect on the well-being of Canadians. The shift to a knowledge-based economy means that people living in poverty need financial assistance to meet the demands of daily life.

- **Gerard Boychuk** tackles the federal role in health care spending, a policy area that even in the midst of security issues was shown to be at the very top of Canadians' national priority concerns. Boychuk sets his analysis in the context of the provincial premiers' meeting in August 2001, which forcefully illustrated yet again that any indication by Ottawa of having resources available for health care was guaranteed to generate trenchant provincial demands for increases to the cash component of the Canada Health and Social Transfer (CHST). It also demonstrated that Ottawa had little hope of ever fully satisfying these demands. His chapter thus outlines the factors auguring a major federal repositioning in the field of health. Contrary to longstanding conventional wisdom regarding the federal position, Boychuk argues that there are strong incentives for Ottawa to significantly alter its commitment to the principles espoused in the Canada Health Act (CHA)—especially to relax its opposition to user fees and the private provision of health services—to allow it to pursue a more direct and more highly visible role in the field of health. If this occurs, it would be the biggest innovation in health care since the 1960s.

- **David Wolfe** also examines innovation policy, but, in contrast to the focus in Chapter Two on the skills and social inclusion aspects of innovation, zeroes in on federal support for research and development and for the concept of national innovation systems. Wolfe examines the extensive increase in federal science and technology funding and policy initiatives over the past five years, as well as numerous policy reports and documents released since 1993. He raises key questions about whether the overall framework governing the allocation of new funding is suitable for charting a course for innovation policy in the twenty-first century. His chapter reviews the government's own analyses of Canada's innovation performance, and its prescriptions to remedy the shortcomings of that performance, in the context of the innovation systems approach developed by a number of international scholars. He questions whether the deployment of new funds without a better understanding of the nature of the innovation system in this country will suffice to achieve the government's stated goals, especially those enunciated in the January 2001 SFT, the December 2001 budget, and the expected 2002 White Paper on Innovation.

- The chapter by **Markus Sharaput** also focuses on the federal innovation policy priority, but through an examination of the evolution of federal policy on biotechnology. He shows how conceptions of innovation in the biotechnology field have broadened to embrace concerns about both *economic* and *social* innovation. Early stages of the federal government's engagement with biotechnology were primarily concerned with the former potential, the role to be played by biotechnology as an enabling technology, and the necessity of maintaining a balance between invention and innovation in the innovation system that supports such technologies. Recently it has become clear, however, that the transformative impact of enabling technologies such as biotechnology requires consideration of a broader range of issues, and the incorporation of public debate into the policy process to determine the socially acceptable limits to biotechnology's transformative potential. As the controversy over GM foods indicates, not all Canadians are convinced that the potential of this technology is positive. Sharaput's chapter shows the challenges enabling technologies pose, both as a technical problem of policy management, and as a social problem of political management. The breadth of biotechnology applications and the role anticipated for the biotechnology sector in the Canadian competition strategy have led to the evolution of a policy file that is horizontal or multi-ministerial, but that nevertheless displays the characteristics of its lead coordinating ministry, Industry Canada.

- **Michael Prince**'s analysis centres on the nature of social policy innovation. He points out signs that in the late 1990s and early 2000s a style of *directed incrementalism*—setting bold goals and working toward them step-by-step over the medium to long term—is returning as a strategy for innovating social policy in Canada. Examples include the articulation of new policy visions in several policy sectors, such as disability, children and family, and Aboriginal affairs; significant changes to Canada's governance regime itself, including tax collection agreements in fiscal federalism and the approval of the Nisga'a Treaty; and new approaches to the restructuring of some major social programs, such as the partial funding of the Canada Pension Plan and the development of income-tested child benefits (provincial as well as federal) through the National Child Benefit.

  Prince argues that directed incrementalism is a style of governing and reforming that is, in its own way, politically rational, and that this becomes apparent when one considers the political benefits to policy-makers of directed incrementalism as recently practised in Canadian social policy. By staging a major reform over a number of years and budgets, this style supports federal control over financial commitments and maintains a degree of flexibility for the finance minister in managing debt reduction, tax relief, and budget surpluses. Moreover, it supports the Liberals' policy agenda of renewing social programs in response to population trends, public needs, expenditure capacity, and political priorities.

- **Monica Gattinger** examines the Chrétien Liberals' policies on the arts and culture through a close look at their Tomorrow Starts Today initiative. She argues that while the new funding is arguably a 'reinvestment' in arts and culture, that is, a re-funding of nearly a decade's worth of cutbacks, the new moneys are not simply being returned to the original points of cutback. Gattinger argues that Tomorrow Starts Today does not merely restore funding to the same program areas and agencies that sustained cutbacks during the Chrétien era. Rather, she shows that the principal beneficiary of Tomorrow Starts Today's funding is the Department of Canadian Heritage, which, in turn, raises the spectre of an undesirable degree of political influence in arts and cultural granting and in programming decision-making. Gattinger also shows that a substantial portion of the new funding supports larger Liberal policy themes, notably youth and the new economy, and that this tendency could have negative consequences for other more traditional targets of arts and cultural spending.

- **Debora VanNijnatten** examines three pillars of the Liberal green or environmental agenda. She argues that policies on innovation, sustainable development, and climate change have become increasingly intertwined over the course of the Liberals' post-1993 tenure, and that overall they suggest a more significant role for renewable energy programs. She also shows that criticism of the reliance on fossil fuel in recent debates over air quality policy in both Canada and the United States, especially within the context of binational negotiations on an 'Ozone Annex' to the Canada-US Air Quality Agreement, has encouraged governments to think twice about their energy choices. The analysis also shows that major players within the domestic energy industry have begun to invest in renewable energy developments. VanNijnatten's overall conclusion is that while the resources provided by the Liberals since 1994 have not been directly proportional to the government's policy rhetoric, support for renewable energy has increased modestly.

CONCLUSIONS

This chapter has shown that there has been a sharp change in national priorities, compelled by the events of September 11 and by the view undoubtedly held by a strong majority of Canadians about the need for solidarity with and support for the United States. None of the elements of the federal security package would have been even remotely contemplated by the Chrétien Liberals had it not been for the terrorist attack and for the need to be a part of the international coalition.

And yet, the longer-term effects of these choices are likely to be very mixed and uncertain, for Canadians and for the Chrétien Liberals. On the one hand, within Canada the package of security changes enhances the powers of the federal government and causes all Canadians to be reminded of the powers and functions of their national government as distinguished from their provincial governments. If the Liberals have longed for enhanced federal visibility, they have now secured it in spades. On the other hand, with such identity and visibility comes a new set of political searchlights. Canadians will undoubtedly have new worries about the use of anti-terrorist measures, and their potential adverse impact on civil liberties and the right of protest and political opposition, as well as, perhaps, concerns about the state of Canada's military forces. If the Canadian Alliance can ever get its act together politically, these are potentially fertile issues for it, and political proverbial 'snakes in the grass' for the Liberals.

Canadians are also likely to become more concerned about Canada-US relations than has been usual in recent decades. It is one thing to be a natural part of the US orbit or sphere of influence or even free trade area, but it is potentially quite another for Canada to be now psychologically and practically 'inside the perimeter' of a new fortress America or North America. The Bush presidency started with a form of aggressive unilateralism and selective international isolationism, but the security ethos of the post-September 11 period forced it into an international coalition-building mode. The odds suggest, however, that the Bush administration will revert to unilateralist form, and in this setting the role of the federal Liberals will become increasingly uncomfortable. The Chrétien Liberals, for domestic and international reasons, are unlikely to agree to 'blank cheque' extensions of the US list of anti-terrorist attacks and strategies. And yet it cannot afford to alienate a US administration whose power is more entrenched, with whom new softwood lumber deals must be struck, to whom it wishes to sell as much Alberta oil and gas as possible, and compared to whom it hopes to *look* but not *be* virtuous on climate change and Kyoto commitments.

These changes, possible consequences, and impending choices are also likely to affect the leadership calculus of Jean Chrétien on the one hand, and the struggle to create a viable conservative opposition out of the Canadian Alliance and the Progressive Conservatives on the other. They may also create some opportunities, albeit slim, for inroads by an otherwise demoralized New Democratic Party. In short, the security aftermath produces a political cocktail that is both interesting and somewhat uncertain for all political parties.

The likely effects in 2002–3 and beyond will of course be more than a function of the security aftermath and the extent of the 'perimeterizing' of Canada in North America. The chapters in this volume bear witness to many other underlying and continuing political, economic, and policy challenges, which can make or break governments and which can affect Canadians' own sense of themselves in a complex and shrinking world.

The debate about health care in Canada is bound to heat up as the federal government positions itself to break the rhetorical mould of how and why it defends medicare. The appointment of Albertan Anne McLellan as Health minister suggests the possibility of more openness and conciliation, and the asking of new questions about the sanctity of 1960s health care principles. This is still likely to involve some confrontations with Alberta, but it may also be a part of the general Liberal wooing of Alberta and western Canada in the face of the political weakness of the Canadian Alliance. Responses to health care are also likely to be an issue that will test the intergenerational balance of forces in the Manley and Rock versus Martin Liberal leadership race should Chrétien decide to leave office.

The innovation agenda is featured in several chapters, and has been building for a decade as various political actors have sought to characterize, deal with, and profit from the knowledge-based economy. But the closer that innovation policy and national innovation systems approach to the centre of political attention and focussed debate, the more the underlying divisions in social and economic life reappear and have to be explicitly considered. This is one of the key conclusions of this volume. The elite aspects of innovation in the form of support for research and development, universities, and knowledge industries have to be balanced or managed against the demands and needs of Canadians needing both enhanced skills and support to ensure that they are not on the wrong side of the digital divide. And as one of our chapters highlights in a telling fashion, 'being poor in the best of times' in the knowledge economy does not look or feel much different from being poor in the heydays of previous economic eras. It is a profound and persistent concern for millions of Canadians. The innovation agenda also crosses over other policy boundaries, such as those of sustainable development, climate change, and energy policy, which are increasingly driven by investments that may soon move faster than government policy ever thought possible. Even health care policy, which used to be concerned only about health care systems and medicare, now also has to be thought about and supported in terms of innovating health care *industries*, and dynamic centres of global competition and prosperity. Support for culture and the arts is also being recast, as support for an entertainment product and content industry centred on Internet and computer-based innovation. And, of course, it is clearly not beyond the capacity of Liberal spin doctors to show the intricate connection between innovation and national security technologies.

It is not at all clear that the world changed 'forever', as it was too often said to have done after September 11. Not only is forever a very long time, but too pronounced a focus on the security aftermath also seriously underplays other even more crucial long-term issues with which Canadians and other countries must grapple. National priorities did change in the security aftermath, but the longer-term agenda is also firmly present in the larger total package of spending and policy change and in the ongoing nature of numerous other policy challenges examined in this volume.

NOTES

Special thanks are owed to my colleagues, Leslie Pal and Michael Prince, for helpful and constructive comments on an earlier draft of this chapter.

1 See Bruce Doern and Monica Gattinger, 'Another NEP: The Bush Energy Plan and Canada's Political and Policy Response', in Maureen Molot, ed., *Canada Among Nations 2002: A Fading Power* (Toronto: Oxford University Press, 2002).

2 See G. Bruce Doern, ed., *How Ottawa Spends 1983: The Liberals, the Opposition and National Priorities* (Toronto: Lorimer, 1983), chap. 1.

3 See Jorge Niosi, *Canada's National System of Innovation* (Montreal and Kingston: McGill-Queen's University Press, 2000); Bruce Doern and Richard Levesque, *The National Research Council in the Innovation Policy Era: Changing Hierarchies, Networks and Markets* (Toronto: University of Toronto Press, 2002).

4 See Jeff Gray, 'PM Boosts Manley', *The Globe and Mail* [Toronto], 16 Jan. 2002, 1.

5 See Donald Savoie, *Governing from the Centre* (Toronto: University of Toronto Press, 2000) and Jeffrey Simpson, *The Friendly Dictatorship* (Toronto: McClelland and Stewart, 2001).

6 Canada, Speech From the Throne to Open the First Session of the 37th Parliament of Canada, 2.

7 See Maureen Molot, ed., *Canada Among Nations 2002: A Fading Power*, chap. 1.

8 *The Globe and Mail* [Toronto], 21 Nov. 2001, 1.

9 *The Globe and Mail* [Toronto], 23 Nov. 2001, A9.

10 *The Globe and Mail* [Toronto], 4 Nov. 2001, 1.

11 See Bruce Doern and Monica Gattinger, *Power Switch: Energy Regulatory Governance in the 21st Century* (in press).

12 See Web site: www.fin.gc.ca/budget01/speech/speeche.htm Accessed 10/12/01, 1 (of 17 pages).

13 Ibid, 2.

14 See Web site: www.fin.gc.ca/budget01/bp/bpch1e.htm Accessed 10/12/01, p.1 (of 12 pages).

2

Innovation and Inclusion: Budgetary Policy, the Skills Agenda, and the Politics of the New Economy

GEOFFREY E. HALE

Budgetary policy in Canada since the mid-1990s has focussed on the coordination of fiscal, economic, and social policies as a means of increasing Canada's competitiveness in the North American and global economies. The precise mix of policies showcased in annual budget speeches may vary with the intensity with which public opinion is focussed on particular concerns, the government's fiscal flexibility, and the internal vagaries of Liberal party politics. However, since 1998, when federal finances were brought back into balance, Paul Martin's annual budgets have sought to strike a balance between helping Canadians adapt to the continuous economic changes fostered by international competition and technological innovation, maintaining the fiscal capacity to sustain existing policy commitments, and addressing the distributive concerns of Liberal colleagues (and, more recently, prospective leadership competitors).

The government's longer-term agenda focuses on coordinating fiscal, economic, and social policies that are intended to increase Canada's competitiveness by means of major investments in basic and applied research, the development and commercialization of new technologies, and a series of measures intended to foster investments in 'human capital'—the current cliché for a well-educated, highly skilled, flexible, and adaptable workforce.

The process of continuous economic change driven by technological innovation has been a major factor in the evolution of Canadian fiscal, economic, and social policies since the early 1990s. A key part of this process has been the sustained effort on the part of governments to coordinate their policies in such a way as to help businesses and citizens adjust to the emerging knowledge-based or 'new' economy by applying new technologies, business processes, and related human expertise to the development of new industries and the reinvention of many existing ones. Politically, the process also depends on the capacity of governments to balance measures intended to address the concerns of the business, professional, and academic elites who are managing the processes that lead to technological innovation and economic growth with those that are aimed at ensuring that the vast majority of Canadians have the skills and opportunities necessary to participate in the benefits resulting from these changes—measures that include improvements in core public services.

However, the government's capacity to balance and sustain these initiatives over a long enough period to make them truly effective continues to depend on its maintaining enough short-term fiscal discretion to accommodate unforeseen political and economic shocks and to avoid a return to the fiscal overextension and chronic deficits of the past. This process lends itself to a series of incremental initiatives packaged in 'thematic budgets' that convey the impression of decisive action based on coherent priorities while leaving Finance Minister Paul Martin with enough flexibility to respond to short-term political and economic pressures. It also tends to give priority to the steady, year-by-year extension of measures intended to facilitate Canadians' adjustment to structural economic change, rather than to cyclical or short-term fiscal stimulus.

The 2001 budget cycle provides a good example of these forces at work. Since its re-election in November 2000, the Chrétien government has become more explicit in making its ongoing agenda of fostering innovation and broader participation in the 'knowledge-based economy' the centrepiece of its economic, industrial, and social policies. However, the rapid decline of economic growth since early 2001, along with the terrorist attacks on the United States of September 11, have changed both the political and the economic environments for budgetary policy. As Chapter 1 has shown, investments in national security, infrastructure investments to maintain the smooth flow of trade at Canada's congested border points, and public expectations of limited fiscal stimulus have reduced the resources available in the short term to the government's medium-term agenda of 'innovation and inclusion'. At the same time, Finance Minister Paul Martin has announced incremental extensions of existing programs that promote research and innovation, education and skills training, and other policies intended to promote 'social inclusion' in the new economy, as his cabinet colleagues jockey for a share of rapidly shrinking budget surpluses.

This chapter examines the emergence of the 'new economy' paradigm as a guiding framework for the development and coordination of economic and social

policies within the federal government, and for the 'legitimation' of Canadian economic policies in coming years. It assesses the implications of short-term political
and economic factors for the fiscal priorities of the federal government, and its
capacity to implement its innovation agenda. It also examines the government's use
of budgetary policies—specifically, Ottawa's tested techniques for adjusting to fiscal
and economic uncertainty through the use of the budget process—in the design and
incremental implementation of its innovation and skills training policies at a time
when it must adjust to unforeseen developments, such as the looming economic
slowdown and rising international security tensions.

'INNOVATION AND INCLUSION':
BLENDING WEALTH-CREATION AND SOCIAL COHESION

Federal fiscal and budgetary policies in the mid- and late 1990s were dominated by
the overriding priorities of eliminating deficits, making Canada's public services and
social policies fiscally and economically sustainable, and shifting budgetary discretion from public sector recipients of federal revenues to senior political leaders and
'their' central agencies—particularly the prime minister, the minister of finance, and
the Department of Finance.

Since balancing the budget in 1997/8, the federal Liberals have sought to coordinate fiscal, economic, and social policies within an emerging policy paradigm that
re-allocates the bulk of discretionary revenues from economic growth in general to
four major priorities. Three of these goals are directly related to Canada's adaptation to ongoing economic changes. First, Martin has announced a series of incremental initiatives intended to leverage increased public and private investment in
the emerging knowledge-based economy; second, he has announced measures to
enhance Canadians' access to the education, skills training, and upgrading that will
be necessary if they are to adapt to and benefit from ongoing processes of economic
change. Third, the budgetary run-up to the 2000 federal election allowed Martin to
showcase a series of progressive tax reductions intended, at least in part, to enhance
Canadian competitiveness in the North American and global economies.

The fourth priority allows for changes in taxation, and spending on other measures, deemed politically essential to sustain public support for the government's
main policy objectives. Overall federal spending increased by $11 billion, or 9.4 per
cent, in 2001/2, much of it driven by pre-election commitments to increase federal
transfers in support of provincial health spending, to restore previous cuts to
Employment Insurance benefits for seasonal workers, and to pay for sizable wage
increases for public sector workers. Lower- and middle-income tax relief in Paul
Martin's pre-election budgets featured reductions in the progressivity of middle-
income tax rates rather than major business and upper-income tax reduction.[1]
Heavy spending on security measures and border infrastructure announced before
the December 2001 budget and included in it was directly related to the need to

maintain relatively unimpeded movement of goods, services, and business travellers across the Canada-US border.

The government's evolving innovation strategy is linked to a broader economic paradigm in which government has a distinct, facilitative role in fostering business competitiveness in a dynamic, open economy, organizing both economic and social infrastructure, and facilitating widespread access to and participation in the benefits of the emerging knowledge-based economy. Government policies intended to enhance access to education and to improve incentives for employment-related training are critical to increasing the number of potential 'winners' and to reduce the potential 'casualties' of continuing economic and technological change. As such, they are central to the social and political consensus underlying the new economy, just as the expansion of collective bargaining and the welfare state were central to the Keynesian consensus that contributed so much to the growing prosperity and relative political stability of the generation that followed the Second World War. This agenda is being communicated and debated both at the level of the technocratic and business elites and at that of the general public.

Conceptualizing the 'New Economy'
Four major trends have influenced continuing structural changes in the economies of Canada and most other major industrial countries. Globalization and growing international competition, rapid technological innovation, structural changes in labour markets and patterns of employment, and patterns of demographic aging are changing the ways in which governments attempt to guide the process of economic change. This has resulted in a reduced emphasis on macroeconomic stabilization by means of the annual budget cycle and increased emphasis on incremental policy initiatives whose purpose is to facilitate structural economic change over the medium term.

This process has led to much discussion of a so-called 'New Economy' driven by a range of new technologies, although these technologies are also transforming production and distribution processes in traditional industries as well. The competitiveness of advanced industrialized states such as Canada is seen to depend increasingly on their capacity to sustain high levels of innovation and rapid productivity growth.[2] Central to this capacity is their ability to foster both a dynamic culture of entrepreneurship and a highly educated, skilled workforce capable of adapting to continuing change in markets, technologies, and business processes.[3] As a result, government policies must promote continuing improvements in both private and public sector productivity in order to encourage greater competitiveness, while contributing indirectly to improvements in Canadians' living standards and quality of life.

The role of governments in these processes is to facilitate economic change and opportunities for the individual citizen through the effective coordination of fiscal, economic, and social policies. Key priorities include

- maintaining fiscal sustainability by means of a competitive, efficient tax system, setting and enforcing clear priorities for public spending, and continuing to reduce Canada's debt-to-GDP ratio in order to finance the growing costs of providing social benefits to an aging population without adversely affecting competitiveness or standards of living;[4]
- providing and coordinating high quality, competitive, and cost-effective public services, often in conjunction with the non-profit and private sectors;[5]
- investing in economic and social infrastructure; maintaining and upgrading physical, technological, and social infrastructures that will reinforce both the economic and the social conditions of competitiveness, both in major urban regions and in more remote areas (significant investments in basic and applied research through the government's so-called innovation agenda have been a central part of this process); and
- fostering human capital, to produce a flexible, adaptable workforce capable of adapting to changing economic conditions with high levels of labour force participation. This goal is closely associated with flexible, responsive systems of education and skills training that span public, non-profit, and private sectors and are capable of preparing Canadians for new opportunities, while transforming research into knowledge and innovations across a wide range of endeavours.[6]

The aging of Canada's population also gives governments a compelling reason to promote innovation, opportunity, and economic growth during the next several years. Shortages of skilled labour are already looming in some sectors as Canada's dependency ratio—the ratio of seniors and dependent children to adults of working age—is rising steadily, increasing the relative cost of public services to the remaining taxpayers of working age.[7]

Implications for Budgetary Policies and Political Discourse in Canada
These principles have been central to the development of the federal government's efforts to integrate fiscal, economic, and social policies by means of a series of specific initiatives outlined in its pre-election mini-budget of October 2000, the January 2001 Speech from the Throne, and the December 2001 'security' budget. Prime Minister Chrétien has summarized the government's strategy as seeking 'innovation and inclusion . . . excellence and justice'.[8]

Key priorities for the government's innovation strategy include doubling federal research and development spending over the next decade, expanding the capacity of Canadian universities in both basic research and its commercialization, and expanding Canada's micro-electronic infrastructure.[9]

Its 'inclusion' strategy focuses on the expansion of Canada's national 'learning infrastructure', an increase in incentives and facilities for adults to improve their employment-related skills, a reduction of barriers to skilled immigrants and a recognition of their credentials, and measures to 'help families break out of the poverty trap' and address the particular challenges facing Aboriginal Canadians.[10] Proposals for government investment to provide high-speed broadband internet access for rural and remote communities, while widely criticized as an excuse for extravagant pork-barrel politics, have been packaged as a way of linking the two agendas.

The policy process intended to structure the implementation of most of these objectives has been centred on the development of a White Paper on Innovation and Skills—the 'Agenda on Innovation'—under the leadership of Industry Canada and Human Resources Development Canada. Initial drafts of the White Paper were presented to an interdepartmental committee of senior officials in June 2001. Industry Minister Brian Tobin reportedly brought another draft of the White Paper to cabinet in October.[11] At last report, the White Paper's release is scheduled for January 2002.

However, several developments have slowed this process—and have thereby reinforced the government's tendency toward progressive incrementalism rather than grand policy visions. Expectations of continued surpluses led several departments to generate innovation-oriented wish lists, sparking internal debates over which should take priority, before the economy's rapid decline in late 2001 injected a degree of fiscal realism into the process.[12]

The organization of federal action on education and skills training, and of federal-provincial co-operation in a field primarily within provincial jurisdiction, poses another challenge. Proposed initiatives include the use of federal coordinating and regulatory powers (in the recognition of skills and credentials both for immigrants and for migrants within Canada, for example), tax and grant measures to manage the challenge of student indebtedness, and a Canada Education and Skills Act that would set conditions for the use of federal-provincial transfers in this field.[13]

The economic slowdown—combined with the collapse of the high technology/ICT [Internet Communications Technology] stock market bubble—has reduced the resources available to the federal government for new spending in the short term, and raised questions as to whether its priority should be to foster large-scale expansion of high technology investment or to use existing capacity more effectively until market conditions improve. Projections of economic growth in 2001/2 dropped from 3.5 per cent in the October 2000 economic statement, to between 1.8 per cent and 2.4 per cent in May 2001, to between 0.6 and 1.1 per cent in forecasts tabled with the December 2001 federal budget.[14] As a result, Finance Minister Martin has been able to project balanced budgets only by significantly reducing the size of the contingency funds he uses as cushions against unforeseen economic circumstances (see Figure 2.1).[15]

Finally, and in the short term probably most importantly, the international conflict that has resulted from the terrorist bombings of New York City and Washington, DC, in September 2001 has further destabilized the North American and international economies, forcing the government to give priority to major new spending on security and defence, and disrupting normal budgetary processes. Pictures of trucks lining up for miles at major border crossings in the aftermath of the bombings are

Figure 2.1
The Evolution of Growth Forecasts for 2001 and 2002

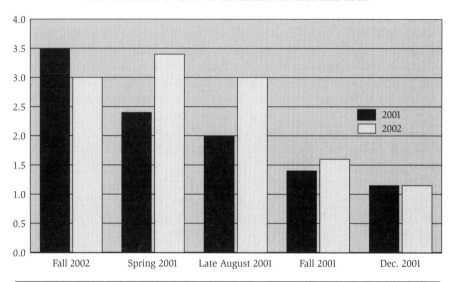

Sources: Standing Committee on Finance, *Securing Our Future* (Ottawa: House
of Commons, Nov. 2001), 6; Department of Finance, *Budget Plan, 2001* (Ottawa,
10 Dec. 2001).

but a small indication of Canada's economic interdependence with the United
States, and the linkages between physical security and economic security in cross-
border relations.

However, while short-term budgetary priorities may focus on defence and security-related issues, and on fiscal constraints resulting from the normal workings of
the business cycle, these must be balanced with longer-term structural issues of
innovation and competitiveness—and the capacity of governments and businesses
to ride the continuing wave of economic transformation.

FOSTERING A CULTURE OF INNOVATION

The new economy and the promotion of innovation have become central elements
in the policies and rhetoric of the federal government in recent years. Ottawa has
long supported private sector innovation through a range of tax incentives for
research and development, loan and subsidy programs for inventors and industry,
and direct and indirect support for basic research by government research institutions, universities, and private organizations. Figure 2.2 outlines a range of federal
policy instruments used to promote research and innovation.

Senior officials at the Department of Finance and the Department of Industry
have expressed growing concern that Canada is falling behind the United States and
other major industrial countries in the commercialization and adaptation of new

Figure 2.2
Government Agents and Programs on the Innovation Continuum

Basic Research > Applied > Technology > Production > Marketing > Research Development

⇑   ⇑   ⇑

Universities	Granting Councils	Federal Laboratories	Industrial	Technology Regional	Business Export
Canadian Foundation for Innovation (CFI)	Canadian Standards Association (CSA)	National Research Council (NRC)	Industrial Research Assistance Program (IRAP) Scientific Research and Experimental Development (SR&ED) Tax Credit	Partnerships Development Canada Agencies	Development Bank of Canada (BDC) Export Development Canada (EDC) Canadian Commercial Corporation (CCC)

Source: Commons Industry Committee (2001), Figure 4:1

technologies and processes that are considered critical to the productivity and competitiveness of Canadian industries.[16] Canada is ranked fifteenth in the world in Gross Expenditure on Research and Development (GERD), substantially behind most major industrial countries (see Figure 2.3).

While many internationally-oriented firms have been forced to upgrade technologies, production processes, and workforce skills in order to maintain their market shares, many others have been slower to adapt, or have used Canada's shrinking exchange rate against the American dollar to prop up their competitive positions.[17] The Canadian Manufacturers and Exporters, a major industry association, notes that while overall rates of growth in industrial production have parallelled those in the United States, the rate of new product commercialization by Canadian firms was only 36 per cent that of American firms between 1996 and 2000.[18]

Others have suggested that while Canada has a highly competitive Research and Development (R&D) tax environment, marginal effective tax rates that are relatively high compared to those of other industrial countries make it more attractive to commercialize the fruits of research in countries with lower corporate tax rates.[19] In 1999, Canada's gross expenditure on R&D was 1.77 per cent of GDP, well behind industrial competitors such as Japan, the United States, and Germany (see Figure 2.3). However, some observers have noted that while high levels of R&D spending can contribute to rapid economic growth, other conditions, including the extent of technology transfer and adaptation, also play a major role.[20]

Figure 2.3
GERD to GDP Ratios (1999)

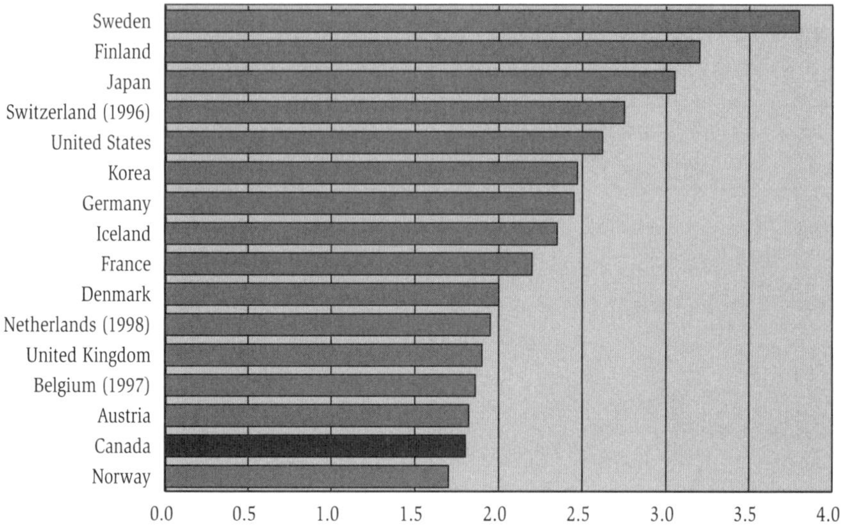

Source: Fred Gault, 'Meeting Canada's R&D Challenge: Moving from 15th to 5th in Global R&D', presentation to Research Money Conference (Ottawa: Statistics Canada, Nov. 2001).

Champions of the so-called 'productivity agenda' on the Commons Standing Committee on Finance and the Commons Standing Committee on Industry have produced a series of reports arguing for direct federal action to make productivity improvements, innovation, and industrial competitiveness key elements in Ottawa's emerging economic strategy.[21] Some of their recommendations are reflected in increased federal spending on research and innovation since 1998/9. Ottawa spent $6.3 billion on direct and indirect R&D expenditure in the 1999/2000 fiscal year—$3.3 billion in internal R&D spending and $3.0 billion on external spending, including transfers to universities, businesses, and other R&D performers. R&D tax incentives were expected to account for another $1.3 billion.[22] Federal spending on science and technology will increase to $7.4 million in 2001/2 as a result of initiatives announced in the 2000 and 2001 budgets.[23] Much of this spending is the by-product of previous budget decisions, supplemented by incremental measures after 2001.

Finance Minister Paul Martin signalled the government's shifting priorities in a series of speeches before and after the November 2000 federal election. Arguing that there is 'no room for complacency in [an] international economy subject to continuous structural, technology-driven changes', Martin argued that the quickening pace of technological change is shortening product life cycles, and this contributes to 'first mover advantages' for industries and countries that are on the leading edge of innovation. He suggested that a series of performance benchmarks be set for investments in research and innovation, to enable Canada to rise from fifteenth to the 'top 5' in R&D investment among OECD countries, that new technologies developed by Canadian universities and research institutions be commercialized, and that spending on education and skills training be increased significantly.[24]

These commitments are partly reflected in Industry Canada's budget for business and economic development subsidies, most of which are targeted to high technology industries and related infrastructure projects; this budget was projected to increase by 22 per cent between 2000/1 and 2002/3, according to figures tabled in the department's 2001/2 Estimates.[25]

The January 2001 Speech from the Throne outlined a series of initiatives to promote innovation, education, and skills training. Some of these proposals, such as major investments in Canada's micro-electronic infrastructure, had long been on the wish lists of particular cabinet ministers. However, most reflected incremental extensions of existing policies, or were couched in the vague generalities typical of such documents.

The government's innovation strategy was outlined as part of a five-part plan: to 'at least double' the current federal investment in research and development by the year 2010; 'to build on what we have already done to make Canadian universities the place to be for research excellence ([by ensuring that they have] the resources necessary to fully benefit from federally sponsored research activities'; to accelerate Canada's ability to commercialize research discoveries, and to turn them into new products and services; 'to pursue a global strategy for Canadian science and technology [so that it will be] at the forefront of collaborative international research which expands the frontiers of knowledge'; and 'to work with the private sector to determine the best ways to make broadband internet access available to all communities in Canada by the year 2004.'[26]

The latter proposal prompted considerable controversy and media criticism of the government in mid-2001 after a task force commissioned by Industry Minister Brian Tobin called for more than $1.9 billion in direct federal spending to link every community in Canada, regardless of size or market demand, to high-speed internet service over the next three years as part of Canada's 'basic telecommunications infrastructure'.[27] After media reports suggested that Finance Minister Martin had succeeded in frustrating Tobin's aggressive lobbying campaign for the broadband proposal, the Prime Minister reportedly insisted on the inclusion of a token $100 million toward start-up costs on the project in the December 2001 budget. However, this announcement took the form of a promise of funding that will begin in 2004— suggesting that the project may be subject to ongoing political and Finance Department review.[28]

However, other voices have suggested that an effective innovation strategy must be more broadly based if it is to be effective in raising overall levels of productivity and in engaging the active participation of businesses and unions from across the economy. Perrin Beatty, the head of Canada's largest manufacturing lobby group, has challenged federal priorities underlying the planned White Paper on Innovation, suggesting that it focuses too heavily on high technology megaprojects and ignores the broader challenges in the application and diffusion of new technologies for the majority of Canadian manufacturers, challenges that do not lend themselves to heavily targeted bureaucratic programs.[29] These criticisms reflect elements of the competitiveness literature that suggest that strategies based on R&D-driven innovation and those based on technology transfer are complementary rather than mutually exclusive strategies for enhancing productivity and competitiveness.[30] Moreover, they reflect a recognition that for increased government spending to be effective in generating higher levels of innovation, it must be catalytic in nature, leveraging significant volumes of private investment that are driven primarily by the likelihood of reasonable rates of return.

Significantly, one of these voices appears to be that of Paul Martin, who in March 2001 told a high technology audience that 'the role of the federal government can no longer be, if it ever could, to try and direct the economy by remote control from Ottawa. Innovation is by nature entrepreneurial, decentralized and highly dependent on a broad band of networks in communities right across the country.'[31]

The recent economic slowdown and the pressures for increased spending on defence and security that followed September's terrorist attacks on the United States have strengthened the hands of officials in the Department of Finance who prefer a more measured, incremental, and sustainable approach to new investments in research and innovation. These factors have strengthened Finance's tactical position, which is to enforce spending discipline and to match phased increases in innovation spending to the discretionary resources that remain after Ottawa has met previous fiscal commitments.

The December 2001 federal budget provided incremental increases and extensions totalling $510 million in 2001/2 and $354 million in each of 2002/3 and 2003/4 for a number of research and innovation-related initiatives announced in previous budgets. These measures included expanded funding for the Canadian Institutes of Health Research, research granting councils, regional initiatives of the National Research Council, indirect costs related to university research, and the development of a new generation of internet technology.[32]

The revised version of the White Paper on Innovation that circulated in high technology circles in Ottawa before the December 2001 budget has been described as a 'quasi-prescriptive' document; it included proposals for the incremental expansion of existing programs, an expanded venture capital investment role in selected industries for the Business Development Bank of Canada, and peer-reviewed funding for scientific research conducted by federal departments and agencies.[33]

However, an expansion of public and private spending on innovation will be of limited value if firms operating in Canada lack the kinds and levels of skilled labour necessary to expand their production, or if a substantial number of Canadians believe that economic and technological changes pose a threat to their economic security and well-being, rather than offer greater opportunities and higher standards of living. The government's emerging skills and education agenda reflects efforts to address the economic, social, and political dimensions of these concerns.

THE SKILLS/EDUCATION/ACCESS AGENDA

If we're going to have an agenda that works, people have to see themselves in that agenda.

Jane Stewart[34]

The federal government's skills and education agenda is closely linked to the governing Liberals' persistent efforts to portray themselves as the party of political and social 'balance'.

At a political level, the skills agenda is closely linked to citizens' perceptions that obtaining and upgrading education and marketable skills is vital to their own economic opportunities and security, and that of their families. The integration of economic and social policies so that they become mutually reinforcing has been a fundamental element of neo-liberal policy discourse since the report of the Macdonald Royal Commission in the mid-1980s.[35]

Concerns about growing shortages of skills in many industries, and the implications of population aging with respect to the growth of the labour force in the future, are also prompting concerns among both business and social policy groups about the need for effective federal leadership in this area.[36] These concerns are reflected in proposals to facilitate improvements in the integration of skilled immigrants into the economic mainstream, and to increase the workforce participation rates of disadvantaged groups by means of a variety of skills-related initiatives and relevant support services.

The rhetoric and the substance of the Liberals' skills agenda are consistent with the politics of triangulation that have characterized Paul Martin's post-deficit budgets. The Departments of Finance and Human Resources Development use a number of complementary policy instruments intended to combine the pursuit of specific policy goals as part of an overall strategy on the one hand, and old-fashioned distributive (or interest group) politics on the other. These include an 'elite agenda', directed to the support of university researchers and research institutions, as part of the government's broader innovation agenda, an 'access to education agenda' for the broad middle class, and a remedial access agenda for groups that have struggled to gain a foothold in the economy, old *or* new. They also include Ottawa's slowly developing Early Childhood Development Agenda, although that is beyond the scope of this chapter.

A majority of Canadians appear to have internalized the government's rhetoric that access to a 'good education' is vital to Canada's competitiveness and to their futures.[37] This is not surprising. Federal statistics show that the vast majority of jobs created during the 1990s required a post-secondary diploma or degree, while the number of jobs for workers with less than a high school education dropped by a staggering 947,000 (see Table 2.1). By 1997, Canada had the highest level of post-secondary enrolment among the 58 countries reviewed in the 2000 *Global Competitiveness Report.*[38]

However, Ottawa's ability to meet these expectations is complicated by the diversity of labour markets, the range of stakeholders whose co-operation is necessary for effective federal action, the challenges of forecasting labour market requirements in an era of continuing changes in technology and the structures of many industries, and the overriding reality of federalism.

The Canadian Opportunities Strategy, which was a major initiative in the 1998 federal budget, outlined a multi-dimensional strategy that included assistance for students by means of expanded student loans and scholarships, tax measures to assist education-related savings, investments in new research institutions, and support for universities. This approach has been consistent with the government's overall strategy of selective activism and incremental change, a strategy that generates a series of small policy initiatives, carefully targeted at particular problems or challenges identified by interest groups and government officials. These initiatives have been expanded incrementally over the past three years, notably in the 2000 federal budget and pre-election 'budget update', in the form of increased investments in research funding and expanded tax preferences for students and their families.

While the Liberals' 2000 election platform promised to 'ramp up' spending on the 'Education and Learning' agenda from an additional $315 million in 2001/2 to $810 million in 2004/5, more than 90 per cent of this figure was linked to a single initiative, the expansion of Registered Education Savings (or Learning) accounts, funded partly from HRDC's budget and partly through the tax system.[39]

This priority, while consistent with past Finance Department preferences for tax-transfer measures that enable the federal government to deal directly with individual Canadians rather than funnel transfers through third parties, has been criticized in some quarters as an excessive subsidy to the middle class.[40] Some economists and business groups have suggested a more cost-effective way of increasing the savings capacity of middle-income families with limited taxable income. A new 'retirement and education savings account', based on the tax-free accumulation of

Table 2.1

Employment Growth by Highest Level of Education Attained, 1990–9

	('000)	*(per cent)*
Post-secondary diploma or degree	2,255	155.8
High school diploma	139	9.6
Less than high school	-946	-65.4

Source: Kevin G. Lynch, 'Building a Global, Knowledge-Based Economy for the 21st Century' (Ottawa: Industry Canada, Feb. 2000), 7.

'tax-prepaid' savings (income tax refunds, for example), could be financed through the elimination of more narrowly targeted tax preferences.[41]

However, direct increases in spending on 'Human Resources Investment' over the past few years appear to have been funded primarily from within existing spending envelopes (see Table 2.2), quite possibly as a result of the pre-election scandal over poorly managed HRDC grants and contributions.

Table 2.2
HRDC 'Human Resources Investments'[1]

	1999/2000	*2000/1*	*2001/2*	*2002/3*
2000/1 Estimates	4,758.1 (f)	5,328.1 (p)	5,498.3 (p)	5,631.4 (p)
2001/2 Estimates[2]	—	4,761.6 (f)	4,732.4 (p)	4,890.7 (p)

f = forecast
p = planned

[1]The principal differences between projections of transfer payments in 2002/3 in the 2000 and the 2001 HRDC Estimates are provisions for the growth of Canada Education Savings Grants, the government's 'matching grants' under the RESP program (reduced by $541 million), and interest payments and liabilities under the Canada Student Financial Assistance Act, which have been written down by $608.4 million—even while the government is making provision for increased student lending from another envelope. Human Resources Development Canada, *Estimates: 2000–01, Part III*, 69; Human Resources Development Canada, *Estimates: 2001–02, Part III*, 73.
[2]Not including loans disbursed under Canada Student Financial Assistance Act.

Source: Human Resources Development Canada, *Estimates: 2000–01, Part III*, 27; Human Resources Development Canada, *Estimates: 2001–02, Part III*, 28.

The details of a more comprehensive federal skills agenda have been slow to emerge since the election, although the Throne Speech, Prime Minister Chrétien, and Human Resources Minister Jane Stewart have identified four major sets of initiatives that are under consideration. Three of these appear to be incremental extensions of previous government policies. They can be described as an 'access to learning' agenda, an expansion of savings vehicles for lifelong learning, student loans, and recognition of learning credentials; the 'private sector training agenda'; and the 'social inclusion agenda', intended to encourage the participation of traditionally marginalized groups in the labour force.[42] The fourth, the 'skilled immigration agenda', is a direct response to the aging of Canada's population and the prospect of serious labour shortages in many industries.

Access to Learning
Improving access to education, the 'tools of technology', and the skills to use them have been central elements in Liberal policy since the balancing of the federal

budget in 1997/8.[43] Ottawa has introduced a series of targeted policy initiatives, ranging from the 'elite' measures previously mentioned to broadly based 'access' measures intended to assist current students with the costs of education, enable families to save for future education needs, and reduce the costs of student debt. Net spending on the latter by Human Resources Development Canada increased from $888 million in 1999/2000 to the $1.4 billion projected in the main estimates for 2001/2 (see Table 2.3).

There has been an even greater increase in the estimated value of tax preferences related to education and training since 1997. Increases in education and tuition tax credits and incentives for education-related savings in the 1998 and 2000 budgets have increased the combined value of these tax preferences from $654 million in 1998 to $1.3 billion in 2001, despite the tax rate reductions contained in Paul Martin's 2000 budget and fiscal update (see Table 2.4). The December 2001 budget announced a few small extensions of education tax credits and deductions relating to apprentice training and adult education.[44]

The 2001 Throne Speech and reports of the Commons Standing Committee on Human Resources Development (HRD) and the Liberal caucus's Economic Development Committee (EDC) have suggested a number of incremental additions to these policies. These include creating 'Registered Individual Learning Accounts' to 'make it easier for Canadians to plan for and finance their learning needs'; improving loans available to part-time students to help workers 'earn while they

Table 2.3
Major Education and 'Access' Related Expenditures

($ millions)	1999/2000	2000/1 (f)	2001/2 (p)	2002/3 (p)
Canada Study Grants	103.0	120.1	120.1	130.1
Canada Education Savings Grants (RESPs)	334.1	435.0	499.0	560.0
Interest payments and loan guarantees under Canada Student Loans Act, Canada	367.2	568.5	470.7	390.9
Student Financial Assistance Act CSLA Administrative Costs	111.9	204.9	276.7	378.2
Payments to Non-Participating Provinces	126.1	138.3	195.6	191.9
Less revenues, recoveries	(154.5)	(130.0)	(148.4)	(184.5)
Total	**887.8**	**1,336.8**	**1,413.7**	**1,466.6**

f = forecast
p = planned
Source: Human Resources Development Canada, *Performance Report for the Period Ending March 31, 2000* (Ottawa, 2000), 43, 81; HRDC, *2001–02 Estimates: Part III*, 73, 94; Canada, Department of Finance, *The Budget Plan, 2001*, 134.

Table 2.4

Estimated Costs of Tax Preferences for Education, Related Savings

$ millions	1997	1998 (e)	1999 (p)	2000 (p)	2001 (p)	2002 (p)
Tuition fee credit	240	260	260	260	225	230
Education credit	77	120	120	115	200	205
Transfer of education and tuition fee credits	300	335	340	345	460	275
Carry-forward of education and tuition fee credits	—	10	75	145	255	320
Student loan interest credit	—	46	45	45	42	42
Registered Education Savings Plan (RESPs)	32	33	43	71	98	130
Partial exemption of scholarship, fellowship, and bursary income	5	6	6	27	23	23
Total*	**654**	**810**	**889**	**1,008**	**1,303**	**1,425**

e = estimated

p = projected

*Total estimated costs of tax preferences used for illustrative purposes only. Partial reductions in value of some tax preferences linked to reductions in personal income tax rates in the 2000 federal budgets. Value of carry-forwards not realized by taxpayers until claimed in future tax returns. Targeted increases in education tax credit totalling $35 million in 2002/3 introduced in December 2001 budget not included in this table.

Source: Canada. Department of Finance, *Tax Expenditures and Evaluations: 2001* (Ottawa, 1 Sept. 2001), 18.

learn', and other improvements to the Canada Student Loan Program.[45] Other proposals include measures that address concerns over student debt, including the relationship between earnings and eligibility for student loans, and provisions for debt forgiveness—perhaps linking it to length of work experience in Canada after graduation.

Both committees have suggested that the limitations on the recognition and transferability of educational and professional credentials across provincial boundaries is a problem calling for a growing federal role in the education sector. The EDC's suggestions include a greater federal role in coordinating standards for the mutual recognition of credentials, national standards for post-secondary degrees and diplomas, a federally funded National Institute of Learning to fund research into best practices on the model of the Canadian Institute for Health Information, and possibly even a National Learning Act, based on the example of the Canada Health Act.[46]

However, interviews with federal officials suggest that HRDC is firmly committed to dealing with the provinces in a collaborative way rather than attempting to use the federal spending power to micro-manage provincial or industry training priorities.

To date, the government has given little indication as to whether it is prepared to commit the resources necessary to 'buy' its way into a more significant role in defining common standards for educational achievement, let alone assume the role of policy regulator for the provinces. However, the looming prospect of labour shortages in many parts of the economy significantly increases the possibility that Ottawa will take a role in coordinating the mutual recognition of credentials, and facilitating the integration of skilled immigrants into the mainstream of Canadian economic life.[47]

Skilled Immigration Agenda

The pursuit of skilled labour and its integration into Canada's labour force is already playing a central role in the effort to protect Canada's competitiveness and its demographic capacity to sustain existing public services. It will probably play an even greater role in years to come. Immigrants accounted for 70 per cent of new entrants into Canadian labour markets between 1981 and 1995. This trend is accelerating.[48] Current demographic studies project a decline in the annual growth rate of Canada's existing labour force from an average of 1.7 per cent between 1996 and 2000 to 0.5 per cent between 2007 and 2011. Unless Canada can increase its recruitment of skilled immigrants, labour force growth is expected to shrink to zero between 2012 and 2016, and subsequently decline below its natural replacement rate—leading to a potential shortage of as many as one million skilled workers by 2020.[49]

Many immigrants face a significant challenge when they seek recognition for educational credentials and work experience gained prior to arriving in Canada. In the absence of a standardized system for the evaluation and recognition of such credentials, many universities and employers are unwilling to recognize experience from many countries of origin unless immigrants invest in extensive skills upgrading. A recent Conference Board report suggests that as many as 2.2 per cent of Canada's adult population—or 547,000 workers, 74 per cent of them immigrants—face significant barriers to economic integration and higher living standards because their credentials are not recognized.[50]

Because the federal government has a central role in the immigration process, it might have a role in coordinating processes and standards for the recognition of immigrants' skills, capacities, and achievements, in order to facilitate their integration into the Canadian economic mainstream. However, the challenges of skills recognition are not limited to new immigrants. They also apply to the training credentials and capacities of Canadians already engaged in industry or various professions. Ottawa's decision to delegate primary responsibility for skills and employment training to the provinces in recent years increases the challenge of reasserting federal leadership in this field.

A Training or 'Learning' Agenda?

Any agenda to promote the development of a flexible, adaptable labour force capable of adjusting to continuing technological and structural changes must also ensure that ongoing training and skills upgrading is available to meet these challenges. Canada ranked fifteenth, behind most of its major industrial competitors, in a recent survey of whether or not 'employee training is a high priority in companies'.[51]

The provinces have primary jurisdiction in matters of education, and have played a leading role in skills training in recent years. The federal government delegated much of its responsibility for labour market training to the provinces in the late 1990s in a series of bilateral training agreements with nine provinces. These programs channelled $891 million from federal Employment Insurance revenues toward a wide variety of provincial skills and employment training programs in 2000/1—about 43 per cent of federal spending to support EI-related 'active labour market' initiatives (see Table 2.5). Even so, since its re-election in 1997, the Liberal government has unveiled a series of initiatives to channel additional resources toward skills training and labour market development within its own jurisdiction.

However, building an active economy-wide culture of training involves more than government programs. It requires the active commitment of large and small employers and organized labour, as well as post-secondary and other training institutions. This commitment must be rooted in a management culture that recognizes that supportive public policies are not enough; that continuing business success depends upon management's making its own contribution by fostering learning and development among its employees. While government policies may encourage such cultural changes, the diverse and decentralized character of Canadian labour markets is not conducive to effective micro-management by the federal government. This reality was recognized in the December 2001 budget, where plans were announced to double financial support to industry 'sector councils' responsible for coordinating training efforts by employers and unions in 29 industrial sectors.[52]

Many employers invest in various forms of employee training, with formal training programs being more prevalent among larger employers capable of generating 'internal labour markets'. However, there are significant economic disincentives for employers to invest heavily in training in tight labour markets. Competitors may prefer to 'raid' trained employees of other companies rather than invest directly in training themselves. The growing number of 'contingent workers', including self-employed Canadians, who now account for almost 20 per cent of the private sector labour force, are another distinct group effectively beyond the reach of traditional training programs oriented toward large corporations.

Governments may promote access to apprenticeships, assist workers who choose to invest in further skills upgrading (with or without the help of employers), and enable employers to distinguish between 'skills' and 'credentials' when evaluating applicants for employment.[53] The December 2001 budget included a number of small initiatives in these areas. A recent Conference Board report strongly suggests the need for a learning recognition strategy, adapted from those used by Australia, the United States, and some European countries, to be integrated with Canada's immigration accreditation system. It also calls for the creation of a national system for 'prior learning assessment and recognition' (PLAR) capable of securing

Table 2.5

Active Labour Market Programs Financed from Employment Insurance Account

	1998/9	*1999/2000*	*2000/1 (f)*	*2001/2 (p)*
Transfers to provinces and territories	457	836	891	893
'Support Measures'*				
Employment Assistance	238	251	277	NA
Labour Market Partnerships	262	285	282	NA
Research and Innovation	11	10	15	NA
Skill development (training)	630	381	400	NA
Self-employment	108	84	88	NA
Job creation	135	73	64	NA
Wage subsidies	62	60	44	NA
Total	1,903	1,980	2,061	2,152
Provincial Transfers (as per cent of total)	24.0	42.2	43.2	41.5
Per cent of EI Benefits	16.1	17.6	17.8	17.6

f = forecast
p = planned
* Include 'Employment Assistance Services' to assist organizations in providing employment services to the unemployed; 'Labour Market Partnerships' to assist employers, unions, and communities in their capacity for labour market planning; and 'Research and Innovation Activities' to identify better ways of helping persons to prepare for or keep employment.
Source: Human Resources Development Canada, *2001–2002 Estimates: Part III: Report on Plans and Priorities* (Ottawa, 2001), 53–6; author's calculations; Labour Market Directorate, Employment Programs Branch, Human Resources Development Canada: information provided to author.

recognition from post-secondary institutions and businesses, and across provincial boundaries.[54]

However, the federal government may be able to serve only a facilitating role rather than a catalytic one in the latter area—and that only with the active co-operation of provincial governments, and sector councils that bring together employer and union representatives. An adequate response to the challenges of an aging workforce requires the conscious and coherent efforts of employers and, where relevant, unions. While these efforts may be facilitated by regulatory change, they must be incorporated into the broader human resource strategies of individual businesses in order to work effectively.[55]

Broadening the Inclusion Agenda

It is one thing to assist businesses and workers actively engaged in the economy to adapt to changing needs with respect to skills and education. It is another to bring into the mainstream of the new economy individuals and groups that were engaged only marginally, at best, in the old one. Federal studies suggest that as many as two out of five adult Canadians may lack the literacy and numeracy skills necessary to function effectively in most of the jobs the economy has created during the past decade. Other groups face disproportionate challenges in finding and retaining work.

The 2001 Throne Speech outlined a number of proposed initiatives, most of which involved 'inviting' or 'working with' the provinces to increase literacy skills, enhance labour market access for people with disabilities and Aboriginal peoples, and support young people 'staying in school' and 'getting their first job'.[56] This dimension of the 'Inclusion' strategy focuses on skills and human capital development, and is based on three main objectives: a national literacy initiative, assistance to families to 'break out of the poverty trap', and an expansion of opportunities for Aboriginal Canadians.[57] It also involves efforts to enhance the employability of disabled Canadians and to increase the job opportunities available to them. The December 2001 budget provided $185 million over two years for expanded funding for Aboriginal children's programming and an additional $10 million annually for education grants for persons with disabilities.[58] Table 2.6 summarizes current funding levels for a number of projects initiated by Human Resources Development Canada in recent years.

However, the education and skills agenda is not the only set of social policy challenges facing the federal government. Provincial governments, generally supported by public opinion, constantly clamour for more money for health care, above and beyond the escalator clauses built into the Canada Health and Social Transfer. The

Table 2.6
Financing the 'Inclusion Agenda', 2001/2 ($ millions)

Youth Employment Initiatives (including 'youth at risk initiatives')	270.3
Aboriginal Human Resources Development Strategy	235.0
Canadian-Provincial-Territorial Employability Assistance for People with Disabilities	192.0
Homelessness	
('Supporting Community Partnership Initiatives'; 'Urban Aboriginal Strategy')	165.0
Canada Jobs Fund (creating long-term jobs for people in high unemployment areas)	41.5*
National Literacy Secretariat	28.2
Opportunities Fund for Persons with Disabilities	23.8
Social Development Partnerships Program (fostering 'social non-profit sector')	16.0
Older Workers' Pilot Projects (reintegrating displaced older workers in labour force)	13.1
Total	**984.9**

* Program being wound down, effective March 2002.
Source: Human Resources Development Canada, *2001–2002 Estimates: Part III, Report on Plans and Priorities* (Ottawa, 2001), 78–86.

need to meet the social concerns of Canada's rapidly growing Aboriginal population, reinforced by a range of treaty obligations, continues to grow faster than most other areas of federal spending. As a result, the rationing and allocation of additional funding, and the choice of policy instruments used to deliver it, are subordinated to the overall demands of the budgetary process.

TRANSLATING IDEAS INTO ACTION: BIG IDEAS, LIMITED RESOURCES, AND THE POLITICS OF THE BUDGETARY PROCESS

The federal government's innovation and skills agenda may be the 'elephant in the corner'[59] that progressively makes its presence felt by shaping federal budgetary priorities and staking its claim on new fiscal resources as they become available. However, while feeding the elephant may require more than peanuts, other animals are competing for the attention of the federal zookeeper as he tends the 'four-ring circus' of the budgetary process.[60] Most recently, new spending on measures related to national security and defence is expected to add $7.7 billion to federal spending over the next five years—more than half the new spending announced in the December 2001 budget.[61]

The key to this fiscal balancing act is a disciplined fiscal framework, based on centralized control over the budgetary process, that provides the prime minister and the minister of finance with sufficient leverage to coordinate their fiscal, economic, and social policy objectives amid the pressures of an increasingly open economy subject to unpredictable external shocks and normal political competition for limited fiscal resources.

Finance Minister Paul Martin has become increasingly adept in recent years at maintaining his discretion in applying to his policy priorities a series of revenue windfalls from economic growth. This discretion has been carefully created and is protected by means of a variety of budgeting tactics, including formal contingency funds, cushions provided by prudent economic forecasts, and Employment Insurance premiums calculated at rates sufficient to generate a substantial revenue surplus, except in the event of a major recession.

Martin has usually shared a portion of his budgetary windfalls with cabinet colleagues in the form of off-budget or year-end increases for priority spending initiatives. In past years, this process has included multi-year spending announcements that provide Martin with flexibility in the timing of their implementation.[62] The existence of multiple fiscal cushions has consistently allowed him to meet or exceed public expectations—and fulfil the government's major commitments—even in the event of unforeseen economic shocks that reduce his room for manoeuvre. However, recent events have significantly reduced Martin's political and fiscal discretion.

Despite a forecast surplus of $6 billion to $8 billion in 2001/2 before any new spending initiatives, a series of unforeseen events has forced Martin to use not only his fiscal cushions, but all his political skills, to keep his pre-election budget promises of lower taxes and increased transfers, to answer urgent pressures for security-related spending in response to the events of September 2001, and to avoid a return to deficit spending in coming years.

The Economic and Political Context for the 2002 Budget

The aftermath of the September 2001 terrorist attacks on New York has contributed to a series of fiscal pressures on the federal government that place a number of unanticipated demands on Paul Martin's carefully protected fiscal cushions and contingency funds. The projected federal surplus has dwindled sharply with the decline in corporate profits and the anticipated applications for refunds of earlier instalments based on the previous year's inflated earnings. Projections of economic growth have declined from Finance's cautious economic forecast of 1.8 per cent in May 2001 to zero or a modest recession in the last three quarters of the fiscal year— and only 1.1 per cent growth in 2002.[63]

'Status quo' fiscal forecasts released in early October 2001 project 'planning deficits' in each of the next three fiscal years, based on existing commitments to increased transfers and lower taxes, before contingency and prudence factors are taken into account—even before proposed increases in spending related to defence and security are taken into account. If Martin had not used a variety of accounting tricks in his December 2001 budget, the use of previous planning frameworks would have resulted in a projected $5.5 billion deficit for the 2002/3 fiscal year.[64]

Martin initially avoided making firm statements concerning the government's willingness to return to deficit spending. This caution reflects both considerations related to international politics—notably a desire to avoid signalling a 'lack of seriousness' to NATO allies, whose defence and security commitments are generally far greater than Canada's—and Martin's determination to maintain as much political discretion as possible in balancing the spending demands of cabinet colleagues against his commitment to protect Canada's 'fiscal integrity' over the medium term.[65]

These factors argued in favour of implementing the Innovation Agenda over a longer period—as did the existence of significant surplus capacity in the high technology sector. The effectiveness of increased public investment in research and innovation largely depends on its capacity to leverage large volumes of private sector investment—something rendered even less likely if much of the high technology sector is still recovering from the massive losses of the past year. The factors also argued in favour of a medium-term effort to bring the provinces to the table for a more rational division of responsibilities with respect to skills training—possibly in conjunction with steps to implement the Romanow report on health care reform, the release of which is expected in late 2002.

Martin's pre-election tax reductions and subsequent spending increases, which continue to work their way through the economy, have already built in fiscal stimulus equivalent to at least 2 per cent of GDP during the current fiscal year. The government's current mix of monetary stimulus by means of lower interest rates set by the Bank of Canada and relative fiscal discipline responds to criticism from some economists that the opposite mix of policies during the early 1990s actually slowed

Canada's recovery compared to that of the United States.[66] Other observers suggest that falling energy prices, when linked to the economic slowdown, may add as much as $5 billion in stimulus to the estimated $6 billion effect of tax reductions announced for the current fiscal year.[67]

It is likely that, at least in the short term, HRDC's efforts to expand federal skills initiatives will have to be financed through the reallocation of existing resources rather than through major new spending commitments. As in past budgets, Martin has allocated significant resources to issues in which the Prime Minister has shown a particular interest—notably an expansion of funding for Aboriginal children's programs and a $500 million fund to finance sustainable development in Africa in anticipation of Chrétien's leadership of the 2002 G-8 conference in Alberta.[68] These and other initiatives, such as the government's new 'Strategic Infrastructure Foundation', will be financed over several years from surplus revenues, higher than anticipated economic growth, or the remains of budget contingency funds.

However, the cumulative effect of promised tax reductions, past spending increases, including those in the 2001 budget, and accounting tricks such as allowing the deferral of up to $2 billion on small business corporate tax remittances so that Martin can project a balanced budget in 2002/3, has left the government with very little fiscal discretion if it is to live up to its previous commitments. If the economy fails to meet the relatively ambitious growth target of 3.9 per cent in 2003, the government may be forced to choose between deferring existing tax or spending commitments and reverting to the deficit spending habits of the past.

A flexible, multi-year approach that outlines 'markers' for future action as economic and fiscal conditions permit allows the government to buy time as it awaits increased revenues from the normal workings of the business cycle, while taking incremental steps toward the fulfilment of its election promises. This approach would be more consistent with Martin's past approaches to economic uncertainty than the 11.5 per cent increase in general departmental spending in the 2001/2 fiscal year—followed by projections of minimal growth in subsequent years.

Budgets may contain big ideas, but their application is usually broken up into a series of discrete measures, each targeted at a specific policy objective, and implemented in instalments usually controlled by the finance minister or funded from the reallocation of other spending commitments. The government will need to retain enough fiscal discretion to meet political and economic emergencies, while limiting public expectations of major increases in transfers to the provinces for health spending following the release of the Romanow Commission and Kirby Committee reports in 2002.

Pending unanticipated policy surprises, the government will continue to make incremental changes on a number of fronts, while sending the message that it has a comprehensive 'plan' to balance continued growth with social cohesion and opportunities for the individual citizen. The timing and implementation of this plan will depend in part on fiscal considerations, levels of economic growth, the implications of proposed health care reforms, and Mr. Chrétien's decision in the coming year either to pass on the leadership baton or to stay, in the hope of matching Wilfred Laurier's record of four consecutive majorities.

NOTES

1 Geoffrey Hale, 'Priming the Electoral Pump', in Leslie A. Pal, ed., *How Ottawa Spends 2001–2002: Power in Transition* (Toronto: Oxford University Press, 2001), 29–60; Geoffrey Hale, *The Politics of Taxation in Canada* (Peterborough, Ont.: Broadview Press, 2001), chaps 10, 11.

2 Paul Martin, 'Speech to the Toronto Board of Trade', Release #2000–067 (Ottawa, 16 Sept. 2000); Thomas J. Courchene, *A State of Minds: Towards a Human Capital Future for Canadians* (Montreal: Institute for Research on Public Policy, 2001); Thomas P. D'Aquino and David Stewart Patterson, *Northern Edge* (Toronto: Stoddart, 2001).

3 Michael E. Porter, Jeffrey D. Sachs, and Andrew Warner, *Global Competitiveness Report, 2000* (Geneva: World Economic Forum, 2000); Stephane Garelli, 'Competitiveness of Nations: The Fundamentals' (Lausanne: IMD, 2001).

4 Paul Martin, 'Canada's New Economy: Winning the World Over', Speech to Canadian Society of New York (Ottawa: Department of Finance, 17 Jan. 2001).

5 Kenneth Kernaghan, Brian Marson, and Sandford Borins, *The New Public Organization* (Toronto: IPAC, 2000).

6 Canada, 'The Canadian Opportunity Strategy', in *The Budget Plan: 1998* (Ottawa: Department of Finance, 1998); Courchene, *A State of Minds*; D'Aquino and Stewart Patterson, *Northern Edge*, chap. 3.

7 Doug Bruce and Andrea Dulipovici, 'Help Wanted: Results of CFIB Surveys on the Shortage of Qualified Labour' (Toronto: Canadian Federation of Independent Business, Feb. 2001); Eric Beauchesne, 'Canada Facing Skills Shortage by 2006: Report', *The National Post*, 31 Aug. 2001, A2. The projected ratio of Canada's working-age population to retired pensioners is expected to drop by 55 per cent, from 3.6 in 1995 to 1.6 in 2050. The projected costs of public pension and health benefits as a percentage of GDP is expected to increase by 78 per cent, from 12.6 per cent in 1995 to 22.5 per cent in 2030. *Global Aging: The Challenge of the New Millenium* (Washington: Center for Strategic and International Studies, Aug. 2001), 7–8.

8 Chrétien, Hon. Jean, 'Address in Reply to the Speech to the Throne' (Ottawa: Prime Minister's Office, 31 Jan. 2001).

9 Canada, *Speech from the Throne to Open the First Session of the 37th Parliament of Canada* (Ottawa: House of Commons, 30 Jan. 2001); Chrétien, 'Address in Reply to the Speech to the Throne', Jan. 2001, 5.

10 Canada, *Speech from the Throne*, Jan. 2001; Chrétien, 'Address in Reply to the Speech to the Throne', Jan. 2001, 6–8.

11 Heather Scoffield, 'Tobin to Seek $1.5 Billion for Net', *The Globe and Mail* [Toronto], 13 Oct. 2001, A16.

12 Heather Scoffield, 'Chrétien to Address "personal" Priorities', *The Globe and Mail* [Toronto], 20 Aug. 2001, A4; Joan Bryden, 'Economy Woes Could Stall PM's Plans', *The Ottawa Citizen*, 10 Sept. 2001.

13 Canada. Standing Committee on Human Resources Development, *Interim Report: Access to Education and Training* (Ottawa: House of Commons, June 2001); Heather Scoffield, 'Chrétien to Address "personal" Priorities'; Tony Valeri, MP, 'Setting the Pace: Advancing the Skills and Learning Agenda', Report of Economic Development Committee (Ottawa: National Liberal Caucus, Aug. 2001)

14 Canada. Department of Finance, *Economic Update* (Ottawa, 23 May 2001), 42, 57; Eric Beauchesne and Shannon Kari, 'Recovery Delayed, Not Destroyed' (Toronto: TD Economics, 26 Sept. 2001), 7; Shawn McCarthy, 'Shelve Spending to Avoid Deficit, Martin Advisor Says', *The Globe and Mail* [Toronto], 11 Oct. 2001, B3; Canada. Department of Finance, *The Budget Plan 2001* (Ottawa, 10 Dec. 2001), 156.

15 Ibid. Even relatively optimistic fiscal forecasts by outside economists project 'planning deficits' between 2002/3 and 2004/5, on the basis of current spending and tax policy commitments. Don Drummond and Derek Burleton, *Report on Canadian Government Finances: Federal and Provincial Fiscal Outlooks to 2005–06* (Toronto: TD Economics, 12 Oct. 2001), 5–6; 'Planning' surpluses or deficits are based on projections of current spending and tax policies by means of econometric models linked to current economic forecasts. Because of the uncertainties of economic forecasting, the federal government also builds 'margins of error' into such forecasts by making explicit provisions for 'contingency funds' and 'economic prudence'.

16 John Manley, 'Putting People First: Productivity, Growth and Living Standards', speech to the Empire Club (Ottawa: Industry Canada, 18 Feb. 1999); Giles Gherson, 'Canada Faces Hinterland Status', *The National Post*, 31 July 1999, A1; Luiza Chwialkowska, 'Liberal Policy-makers Send Mixed Signals', *The National Post*, 1 Sept. 1999, A8; Kevin G. Lynch, 'Building a Global, Knowledge-Based Economy for the 21st Century' (Ottawa: Industry Canada, Feb. 2000).

17 Lynch, 'Building a Global, Knowledge-Based Economy', 13.

18 Canadian Manufacturers and Exporters, *Canada's Excellence Gap: Benchmarking the Performance of Canadian Industry against the G7* (Toronto, 1 Aug. 2001).

19 Canada. Standing Committee on Industry, 'A Canadian Innovation Agenda for the Twenty-First Century', Fifth Report (Ottawa: House of Commons, 2001), Figure 6.1; Jack M. Mintz, 'Reforming the Tax Cut Agenda', *Canadian Tax Journal* 48, 3 (2000): 689–709; Alberta. Alberta Business Tax Review, *Report and Recommendations* (Edmonton: Alberta Finance, 13 Sept. 2000).

20 Garelli, 'Competitiveness of Nations'; Jack M. Mintz, 'High R&D Spending Doesn't Equal High Economic Growth', *The National Post*, 4 Dec. 2001.

21 Canada. Standing Committee on Finance, 'Productivity with a Purpose: Improving the Standard of Living of Canadians', Report # 20 (Ottawa: House of Commons, 10 June 1999); Standing Committee on Finance, 'Budget 2000: New Era, New Plan' (Ottawa: House of Commons, Dec. 1999); Standing Committee on Finance, 'Security Our Future', Tenth Report (Ottawa: House of Commons, Nov. 2001); Canada, Standing Committee on Industry, 'Productivity and Innovation: A Competitive and Prosperous Canada', Fourth Report (Ottawa: House of Commons, 11 Apr. 2000); Standing Committee on Industry, 'A Canadian Innovation Agenda'; Standing Committee on Industry, 'Getting Back to Business', Sixth Report (Ottawa: House of Commons, 20 Nov. 2001).

22 For details, see Canada. Standing Committee on Industry, 'A Canadian Innovation Agenda', Table 4.1.

23 Canada. Department of Finance, *The Budget Plan 2001*, 109.

24 Martin, 'Speech to the Toronto Board of Trade'; see also Martin, 'Canada's New Economy: Winning the World Over'; Paul Martin, 'Speech to the Crossing Boundaries National Conference', Release # 2001–032 (Ottawa:

Dept. of Finance, 29 Mar. 2001); Paul Martin, 'Address to the Canadian Advanced Technology Alliance Globe Tech Conference', (Ottawa, 12 June 2001). Martin's Deputy Minister, Kevin Lynch, was also actively engaged in pep talks to business groups.

25 The 2001 estimates indicated planned increases in budgets for 'Industry Sector Development' from $668 million in 2000/1 to $817 million by 2002/3. Industry Canada, 'Transfer Payments by Business Line', *2001–2002 Estimates* (Ottawa, 26 Mar. 2001), Table 5:1.

26 Canada, *Speech from the Throne*, 30 Jan. 2001; Chrétien, 'Address in Reply to the Speech to the Throne', Jan. 2001, 5.

27 Tobin was reported to be seeking $1.5 billion over four years for his broad-band initiative in an October 2001 cabinet presentation, despite widespread criticism of the earlier proposal. Heather Scoffield, 'CME Calls for National Strategy to Boost Competitiveness', *The Globe and Mail* [Toronto], 16 Aug. 2001; Jim Brown, 'Liberal Promise of Internet Access to Cost Billions, Says Panel', *The Ottawa Citizen*, 18 June 2001; Brian Tobin, Speech to Toronto Board of Trade (Ottawa: Industry Canada, 11 May 2001); Mathew Ingram, 'Ottawa's Broadband Plan Is Dumb and Expensive', *The Globe and Mail* [Toronto], 20 June 2001, B14; 'What a Tangled Web We Fear the Feds Will Weave', *The Vancouver Sun*, 20 June 2001; Edward Greenspon, 'Minister of the Future or Minister of Yesterday', *The Globe and Mail* [Toronto], 21 June 2001, A19.

28 Heather Scoffield, 'Tobin's Budget Tactics Criticized', *The Globe and Mail* [Toronto], 21 Nov. 2001, A8; Heather Scoffield, 'Tobin's Plan Loses in Budget', *The Globe and Mail* [Toronto], 28 Nov. 2001, A1; Joan Bryden and Eric Beauchesne, 'PM Intervenes to Settle Martin, Tobin Tug of War', *The National Post*, 6 Dec. 2001, A5; Canada. Department of Finance, *The Budget Plan 2001*, 125.

29 Canadian Manufacturers and Exporters, *The Business Case for Innovation* (Ottawa, 16 Aug. 2001); Luiza Chwialkowska, 'Ottawa's Focus on Big Science Risky: Beatty', *The National Post*, 30 Aug. 2001, A6.

30 Garelli, 'Competitiveness of Nations'; Conference Board, *Performance and Potential: 2001–02* (Ottawa, 26 Sept. 2001), 38–40.

31 Paul Martin, Speech to British Columbia Technologies Association, Release #2001–025 (Ottawa: Department of Finance, 25 Mar. 2001), 3–4.

32 Canada. Department of Finance, *The Budget Plan 2001*, 115–16, 121–5, 134.

33 Jill Vardy, 'Venture Cap Funding Gets Federal Boost', *The Financial Post*, 5 Dec. 2001, FP4; industry sources.

34 Jane Stewart, 'Remarks to the Conference Board of Canada National Roundtable on Building and Sustaining a Culture of Innovation and Entrepreneurialism' (Ottawa: Human Resources Development Canada, 9 Apr. 2001).

35 Canada. Royal Commission on the Economic Union and Development Prospects for Canada, *Report*. 3 vols (Ottawa: Supply and Services Canada, 1985); Canada, *Agenda: Jobs and Growth: A New Framework for Economic Policy* (Ottawa: Department of Finance, Oct. 1994); Canada. Department of Finance, *The Budget Plan: 1998* (Ottawa, Feb. 1998); Courchene, *A State of Minds*.

36 Bruce and Dulipovici, 'Help Wanted'; Sylvain Schetagne, 'Building Bridges Across Generations in the Workplace' (Ottawa: Canadian Council on Social Development, 30 Aug. 2001); Derek Burleton and Don Drummond, 'Canada's Talent Deficit' (Toronto: TD Economics, 6 Sept. 2001); Michael Bloom and

Michael Grant, 'Brain Gain: The Economic Benefits of Recognizing Learning and Learning Credentials in Canada' (Ottawa: Conference Board of Canada, 22 Sept. 2001).

37 Earnscliffe Research and Communications, 'Pre-budget Survey Results' (Ottawa: Department of Finance, Oct. 2000); Compas Inc., 'Competitiveness and the State of the Nation: A Compas Report to the *National Post*' (1 June 2001).

38 Porter, Sachs, and Warner, *Global Competitiveness Report, 2000*, 285.

39 Liberal Party of Canada, *Opportunity for All: The Liberal Plan for the Future of Canada* (Ottawa, Oct. 2000), Addendum.

40 It has been noted that in 1998, the most recent year for which tax statistics are available, as much as one-third of RESP spending accrued to the benefit of families with incomes over $80,000. However, given that the average income of two-parent families with children in that year was $70,043, this suggests a broader criticism of middle-class entitlements delivered through the tax system rather than as subsidies to public sector institutions. Sarah Schmidt, 'Rich Families Take Advantage of Federal Education Savings Grants', *The National Post*, 3 Oct. 2001; Statistics Canada, *Income in Canada: 1998*, Catalogue # 75–202–XIE (2001).

41 This proposal, based on the so-called 'Roth IRA' provision from the US tax code, would continue the progressive shift of Canada's income tax system toward a consumption base. In contrast with existing RRSPs and Registered Pension Plans, contributions would not be tax-deductible, but investment income could be withdrawn tax free after retirement or for investment in recognized education expenses. Tax treatment of such savings plans would have to be integrated with that for existing plans. See Jonathan Kesselman and Finn Poschmann, 'A New Option for Retirement Savings: Tax-Prepaid Savings Plans', *Commentary # 149* (Toronto: C.D. Howe Institute, Feb. 2001); Thomas D. D'Aquino, 'Honing Canada's Edge: Fiscal Priorities in an Era of Global Uncertainty' (Ottawa: Business Council on National Issues, 7 Sept. 2001), 5.

42 Canada, *Speech from the Throne*, 30 Jan. 2001, 4; Chrétien, 'Address in Reply to the Speech to the Throne', Jan. 2001; Jane Stewart, 'Investing in Skills, Canadians and Canada's Future' (Ottawa: HRDC, 26 Feb. 2001); Jane Stewart, 'Remarks to Canadian Policy Research Network's National Roundtable on Learning' (Ottawa: HRDC, 19 Mar. 2001); Stewart, 'Remarks to the Conference Board of Canada National Roundtable on Building and Sustaining a Culture of Innovation and Entrepreneurialism'; Luiza Chwialkowska, 'Jobs Crisis Prompts Ottawa Plan', *The National Post*, 18 June 2001, A1.

43 Stewart, 'Remarks to Canadian Policy Research Network's National Roundtable on Learning'.

44 Canada. Department of Finance, *The Budget Plan 2001*, 117–20.

45 Canada, *Speech from the Throne*, 30 Jan. 2001, 4; Stewart, 'Remarks to the Conference Board . . . on . . . Innovation and Entrepreneurialism'; Canada. Standing Committee on Human Resources Development, 'Interim Report: Access to Education and Training' (Ottawa: House of Commons, June 2001), Chap. 2; Valeri, 'Setting the Pace'.

46 Standing Committee on Human Resources Development, 'Interim Report: Access to Education and Training', Chap. 3; Valeri, 'Setting the Pace', 14.

47 Bloom and Grant, 'Brain Gain'.

48 Stewart, 'Investing in Skills, Canadians and Canada's Future', 3; F. Denton

and B. Spencer, 'Population, Labour Force and Long-term Economic Growth,' *Policy Options* (Jan.–Feb. 1998).

49 Statistics Canada, *Labour Force Annual Average*, Cat. # 71–529 (Ottawa, 2001); Burleton and Drummond, 'Canada's Talent Deficit', 1–3; Valeri, 'Setting the Pace', 4.

50 Bloom and Grant, 'Brain Gain', 17–18.

51 Conference Board of Canada, 'Performance and Potential: 2001–02' (Ottawa, 26 Sept. 2001), 37.

52 Canada. Department of Finance, *The Budget Plan 2001*, 118.

53 Graham Lowe and Kathryn McMullen, 'Barriers and Incentives to Training', Support Document # 15 (Ottawa: Advisory Council on Science and Technology, 14 June 1999), 13–26.

54 Bloom and Grant, 'Brain Gain', 29–32.

55 William B.P. Robson, *Aging Populations and the Workforce: Challenges for Employers* (Toronto: British North American Committee, Oct. 2001).

56 Canada, *Speech from the Throne*, Jan. 2001, 4.

57 Ibid.; Chrétien, 'Address in Reply to the Speech to the Throne', Jan. 2001, 6–8.

58 Canada. Department of Finance, *The Budget Plan 2001*, 134–5.

59 Paul Wells, 'Whaddaya Mean There's Nothing New in There?', *The National Post*, 31 Jan. 2001, A9.

60 Hale, *The Politics of Taxation*, 24.

61 Canada. Department of Finance, *The Budget Plan 2001*, 144.

62 The current budget process is complicated by the government's planned shift at the end of the 2001/2 fiscal year from modified accrual accounting, which recognizes revenues as they are received in cash, to full accrual accounting. Corporate income taxes, the government's most volatile revenue source, will be attributed to the year they are earned, not when tax payments are made to the government, as in past years. The collapse of corporate profits in 2001/2 from their previous record levels is likely to result in a significant decline in the fiscal balance reported at year's end, in sharp contrast to previous years. Canada. Department of Finance, *The Fiscal Monitor* (Ottawa, 2001 [monthly]); interviews, Department of Finance.

63 Canada. Department of Finance, *The Budget Plan 2001*, 156. The volatility and uncertainty of these forecasts led Martin to schedule a second round of meetings with private sector economic forecasters in October–November 2001 in an attempt to avoid having his economic forecasts overtaken by events even before he presented a budget for 2002/3. Interviews, Department of Finance.

64 Don Drummond and Derek Burleton, *The 2001 Federal Budget* (Toronto: TD Economics, Dec. 2001), 2.

65 Paul Martin, interview, *The House*, CBC Radio broadcast, 22 Sept. 2001.

66 Pierre Fortin, 'Interest Rates, Unemployment and Inflation: The Canadian Experience in the 1990s', in Keith Banting, Andrew Sharpe, and France St-Hilaire, eds, *The Review of Economic and Social Progress: The Longest Decade: Canada in the 1990s* (Montreal: IRPP/CSLS, 2001), 119.

67 Jacqueline Thorpe, 'Falling Gasoline Prices Just the Tonic for Ailing Economy: Report', *The Financial Post*, 10 Oct. 2001, FP1.

68 Canada. Department of Finance, *The Budget Plan 2001*, 130–1.

3

Inside the Perimeter:
The US Policy Agenda and
Its Implications for Canada

MICHAEL HART AND BRIAN TOMLIN

At the start of the week of 10 September 2001, planning was underway for Canadian Trade Minister Pierre Pettigrew to convene a meeting in Vancouver on 14 September at which he would meet with the men and women who serve as Canada's Consuls General at diplomatic missions throughout the United States. The purpose of the meeting was to develop a coordinated strategy to blunt US trade remedy actions against Canadian softwood lumber exports to the United States. A countervailing duty of almost 20 per cent on softwood imports from Canada had already been applied by the US government, and an additional antidumping duty was in the works; their combined effects could cost millions of dollars in exports and thousands of jobs in Canada.[1] It is fair to say that as of 10 September, softwood lumber was at the top of the policy agenda for the Chrétien government in its relations with the United States.

The softwood lumber issue vividly illustrates the importance of policy developments in Washington in shaping the policy agenda and dialogue in Ottawa, in the case of softwood by directly affecting Canadian interests, of which trade is by far the most significant. There are other issues on which US policy is not directed at Canada in particular, but the broad impact of which still affects Canada's interests, and therefore the Canadian policy agenda. These would include such international policy issues as the refusal of the Bush administration to submit the Kyoto Protocol (to the 1992 United Nations Framework Convention on Climate Change) to the US Senate for ratification, or its determination to deploy a national missile defence system. Finally, there are issues that are largely matters of US domestic policy, but that nevertheless may spill over into the Canadian policy realm and affect the policy process indirectly, issues such as education reform, increased energy supplies, and tax cuts.

In this chapter, we examine the ways in which policy priorities in Canada are profoundly shaped, both directly and indirectly, by the public policy agenda in the United States. We begin with a description of the US policy process, particularly the setting of the policy agenda, and the president's role in this process. The policy agenda that was in development by the Bush administration prior to the terrorist attacks on New York and Washington on 11 September 2001 is described, and the immediate and medium-term implications of the attacks for that agenda are identified. The article then turns to an examination of the effects of the Bush agenda, before and after 11 September, on Canadian policy priorities, and the policy process in Canada.

Setting the US Policy Agenda

'One of the most notable resources of US presidents is their ability to influence the political agenda. More than any other actor in the US political arena, the president can focus the nation's attention—and its major political actors' attention—on a given issue.'[2] This does not mean that the president exerts the same kind of influence on the selection of policy alternatives, because in the extremely complex US policy process the presidency is but one of a large number of competing policy centres. Nevertheless, 'the ability to set the policy agenda alone gives the president considerable political leverage.'[3] We want to examine the exercise of this leverage by the Bush administration, and its direct and indirect effects on Canada, in the context of the president's role in the larger policy process.

The President and the Washington Policy Process

By the time a new president reaches office, he will have attracted a large retinue of people who share his views and have detailed ideas and proposals to offer. Throughout the campaign, they will have developed positions (at least for campaign presentation purposes) on most issues, domestic and international. The process of developing these positions is also critical to establishing who will do what in the new administration. Those whose views are most congenial to the president will form part of his personal White House staff; others will find themselves among the three to four thousand presidential appointees, who will spread throughout Washington's hundreds of departments, agencies, bureaus, and commissions to carry out the new president's program. This program will have been spelled out in considerable detail by presidential advisors, and, by the end of the administration's first summer in office, there will be people in place to carry it out. By that time, however, complementary or rival programs will also have emerged from a variety of other quarters. Both in order to get elected and in order to pursue his program, the president needs political allies, from within his own party and even from the other party. While the Democratic and Republican parties may have different values, priorities, and orientations, both are dedicated to gaining and retaining power, which means they must attract majorities of voters. By definition, therefore, each is a centrist collection of factions, with the Democrats occupying a position just to the left of centre and the Republicans a position just to the right. Within both, there are conservative and liberal wings, and much energy is devoted to building coalitions within each party and among like-minded individuals straddling the two parties.

Within the president's cabinet, and in other key positions throughout the administration, there will be people who closely share the president's perspective and his desire to implement his program. There will be others, however, who have been appointed for other reasons, and who, while they will help the president deliver his program, have programs of their own, and varying degrees of influence and power to make some progress toward implementing them. To varying degrees, these ancillary programs will form part of the administration's program, but they will not necessarily enjoy the deeply committed support of the president—or that of the coterie of White House power-brokers.

Washington's second major power centre, Capitol Hill, seethes with the ambitions of 100 Senators, 435 members of the House of Representatives, and some 20,000 staffers, all vying for a place in the sun. For some of these people, helping the president is critical to achieving their program; for others, opposing the president is their lifeblood. For most of the experienced legislators and congressional staffers, however, partisan politics is largely for show. Their days are spent performing the more important function of building issue-specific coalitions to advance their own priorities and preferences, and to slow or defeat progress on the programs and policies they oppose. Party affiliation is a factor in these activities, but not necessarily a decisive one.

Helping both legislators and administration officials in their quests are the more than 150,000 lobbyists registered with the US government, ranging from single-issue interest groups such as the National Rifle Association or the American Farm Bureau, to non-governmental public interest organizations such as the Sierra Club or Public Citizen, to the guns for hire in the many law and lobbying firms that are concentrated along Washington's K Street. Over the past thirty years, the central core of Washington has been completely rebuilt to accommodate the ever-growing army of interest groups dedicated to advancing their programs and defeating or re-shaping those of competing interest groups. In addition, there are thousands of people with ideas, proposals, and programs in think-tanks, political action committees, embassies, and other groups.[4]

It is within this cauldron of competing interests that the president attempts to establish and pursue a policy agenda for the nation. The founding fathers had in mind a system of government in which limits on the exercise of power would be accomplished through 'checks and balances' and the 'separation of powers'. As it has evolved, it has become, in the words of former Canadian Ambassador to the United States Allan Gotlieb, the sub-separation of powers. He observes,

> I see the Washington political scene as a mass or physical field or continuum in which myriad electrons or particles are constantly moving about, as in an atom, in seemingly infinite patterns and designs. Each particle is charged with power of some kind. The particle that is the president is charged, as a rule, with more power than most other particles, but the power emitted by that particle is not constant, and, in some patterns or formations, other particles may emit charges that are equally or more potent.[5]

Or, more trenchantly, it has evolved into a system where no one is in charge. The system was designed to prevent tyranny; it has worked by creating gridlock on all issues but those on which there is broad consensus.

This complex process is filtered to American, and foreign, publics and observers through the media. At one time perhaps independent of this process, the media are now very much part of it, used by all and sundry to advance their messages. The media, in turn, use this process to advance their own agendas. The cacophony created by the hundreds of electronic and print media outlets centred in Washington is marshalled and organized into the main themes favoured by the stars of the system. The principal newspaper pundits and television personalities—a relatively small group of people—shape the agenda by means of their opinions, their choices of guests, and their preference in pressing issues. Ostensibly neutral observers, many have learned that their access to both power-brokers and air time depends on their speaking the right words and emphasizing the favoured issues of the moment. Power-brokers, in turn, have learned that their agendas will not move unless they themselves get access to the media stars. Public policy is made on the basis of easily understood slogans wrapped around complex ideas, problems, and processes. Politicians and the media are each heavily involved in the business of simplifying complexity, and they need each other to succeed.

Policy Agendas and Alternatives

John Kingdon has attempted to bring some conceptual order to this complex US policy process by means of a model that is directed particularly at the explanation of agenda-setting, our principal concern here, and the development of policy alternatives.[6] Kingdon conceives the policy process as consisting of three separate streams—problem identification or recognition, the generation of policy alternatives, and politics—that flow through and around government, largely independent of one another. At certain critical times, the three streams come together, and at that juncture major policy change can occur, when policy windows—defined as opportunities to advocate particular proposals or conceptions of problems—are opened, either by the appearance of compelling problems or by happenings in the political stream. To understand how certain problems surface on the government's policy agenda, and why a particular policy alternative is selected to address the problem, we need to analyse all three process streams that flow through the public policy system: problems, policies, and politics.

Problems

It is a fact that governments pay attention to some problems while ignoring others, obliging us to ask how it is that some capture the attention of important people in and around government, and thereby obtain a place on the governmental agenda. Kingdon argues that objective indicators of the presence of a problem are important, but that they require a push from a focussing event to carry them onto a governmental agenda.[7] Such an event may arise when a crisis occurs, when a compelling symbol is created, or when a policy-maker undergoes a significant personal experience. Finally, problem identification is more likely to occur when government officials receive feedback about the inadequacy of existing policies and programs. All of these characteristics may be present, however, and a problem may still not make it onto the government's policy agenda. This is because the policy process consists of more than a stream of problems waiting to be identified; it also includes a stream of policy alternatives that must ultimately be linked to problems.

Policy Proposals

Kingdon argues that ideas about policy alternatives circulate in communities of specialists scattered through and outside government.[8] Advocates for particular proposals or ideas are policy entrepreneurs, inside or outside of government, who are defined by their willingness to invest resources (time and energy, and occasionally money) in order to secure a future return (desired policies, satisfaction from participation, or career rewards). This process of creating alternatives for policy-makers to consider proceeds independently of the process of problem identification. However, viable alternatives must exist before a problem can secure a solid position on the decision agenda. Even in this circumstance, problems and their alternative solutions exist alongside the political stream, which also exerts influence on the policy process.

Politics

In Kingdon's model,[9] the most powerful forces at work in influencing agendas are developments in the political stream. The stream is composed of elements related to the electoral, partisan, and pressure group concerns of politicians and those who serve them. An important component of the political stream is what Kingdon refers to as the national mood—gleaned from mail, media, and lobbyists, among other sources—which can provide fertile ground for certain ideas. Organized political interests are also important to those in government, insofar as the interests all point in the same direction, thus providing a powerful impetus to move on that course.

Turnover and jurisdiction in government are important as well, inasmuch as agendas are significantly affected by changes of incumbents and by turf battles.

Policy Windows

Much of the time, these three streams—problems, policies, and politics—flow through the policy system on largely independent courses. However, at certain critical times the streams come together, so that a problem is recognized, a solution is developed and available in the policy community, a political change makes the time right for policy change, and potential constraints are not severe.[10] This joining of the streams is most likely to occur when a policy window opens, and policy entrepreneurs play a critical role in what Kingdon calls the coupling of the streams, which occurs at the open window. Typically, a policy window opens because the policy agenda is affected by a change or event in the political stream, or by the emergence of a pressing problem that captures the attention of government officials.

Kingdon's model of the US policy process is derived from the garbage can model of policy choice,[11] in which organizations, including governments, are conceived as 'a collection of choices looking for problems, issues and feelings looking for decision situations in which they might be aired, solutions looking for issues to which they might be the answer, and decision makers looking for work.'[12] This conception neatly captures the realities of the Washington policy process. Certainly, before 11 September the three streams in the policy process were flowing in and around government largely independently of one another. Major change had occurred in the politics stream with the disputed election of George Bush, and this change in incumbents offered an opportunity for the administration to redefine the problems that would find a place on the governmental agenda. On most of these issues, however, no policy windows had yet opened fully, and policy entrepreneurs were still jockeying for position.

The US Policy Agenda Before September

In the world of US policy prior to 11 September 2001, the agenda being fashioned by the Bush administration had a decided domestic orientation. Top priority was assigned to securing congressional approval of a US$1.35-trillion tax cut. Although the tax cut was primarily a rate reduction rather than a reform of the tax code, it did reflect the commitment of Bush and his key advisors to fundamental change in the nature of American governance. Their aim was to create a federal government that spends less because it does less, a smaller but more accountable government that is less involved in the daily lives of ordinary citizens. As described by David Broder, 'This is a conservative government that is committed to changing the status quo. Its agenda is ambitious, and it is targeting major American institutions for overhaul.'[13] Accordingly, following the tax victory[14] the administration set out an ambitious agenda for change in the basic institutions of American life. Again according to Broder, 'Bush is out to change the way Americans educate our children, guard the nation's security, meet our energy needs, provide retirees' benefits and organize a large portion of our medical care.'[15]

The administration's agenda for education reform was focussed on the trinity of standards, testing, and accountability: standards of achievement must be raised, progress must be measured by rigorous testing, and school officials must be held accountable for student success.[16] In this plan, federal funds will be used to increase accountability through more testing and teacher training, but otherwise responsibility for education will be downloaded to lower levels of government, which in turn can ensure parents greater choice and accountability.

A national energy policy was not a critical part of the Bush campaign agenda. However, emerging supply and distribution problems on the energy front forced the administration to devote significant political resources to the development of an ambitious program of energy initiatives to stimulate exploration and the development of new sources of supply. The discussion of a national energy policy raised the hot-button issue of drilling rights in the Arctic National Wildlife Refuge (ANWR), a remote part of the North Slope of Alaska, important as the principal calving ground for the Porcupine caribou herd, which migrates between Alaska in the United States and the Yukon and the Northwest Territories in Canada. Early on, Bush let it be known that he considered drilling in a small corner of the ANWR to be an acceptable sacrifice of environmentalism in the interests of energy self-sufficiency.[17] But the issue provides a powerful symbol for proponents and opponents of drilling to rally around. For environmentalists, any drilling in any nature reserve is a serious breach of their principles, to be resisted at all costs. For the oil business in particular, and US business more generally, allowing some drilling in a nature reserve, albeit under strict control, sends a powerful signal about the limits of environmentalism. The ANWR issue seemed certain to land the administration's energy package in trouble in the Senate, where Democrats were in control.

Other aspects of the administration's domestic agenda—paying down the federal debt, modernizing and reforming the delivery of medicare, welfare, and health care, and reducing market-distorting regulations—also built on the fundamental theme of transforming the role of government. All are predicated on doing less, doing it better, and expanding the scope for private and local initiative. As Kingdon anticipated, political change in Washington had provided an opportunity to open a window for a redefinition of the US policy agenda.

On the international front, the administration identified the need for a strong military, but a military more geared to defending Americans at home than pursuing American interests abroad. The President proposed improvements in military pay, housing, and benefits, and investments in new weaponry, but the centrepiece of his defence policy was the development and deployment of a National Missile Defence (NMD) system, a sharply scaled-down version of Ronald Reagan's Strategic Defence Initiative (SDI), known by the sobriquet 'Star Wars'. Derided for the initiative by critics at home and abroad, including the European allies, Bush maintained his conviction that the United States needs a defensive system to shield it from the disastrous consequences of an attack by an adventurous rogue state.[18] The admin-istration argued that it is better to create a defensive perimeter around America's shores than to attempt to address this potential danger through diplomacy and engagement abroad.[19]

The administration's approach to foreign policy had a similar America-first qual-ity to it, leading critics to characterize it as isolationist and unilateralist. Bush was much less willing than his predecessors, including his father, to involve the United States in the affairs of other countries, particularly those that were marginal to US interests. He was unwilling to commit US prestige to efforts to resolve the problems of the world's perpetual trouble spots, whether they be the Middle East or Northern Ireland or the Balkans. Similarly, Bush was not given to what George Will charac-terized as 'the diplomacy of high-minded gestures'.[20] He made it clear that his administration would not become party to, pursue, or promote multilateral efforts that are more symbolic than real. UN conferences and programs to combat every-thing from racism to population growth would receive much more critical scrutiny than in the recent past. Nor would the United States sign on to a series of recent treaties that Bush and his advisors considered of dubious value, such as the con-vention setting up the world criminal court, the Kyoto Protocol, the land mines treaty, protocols to the 1972 Biological Weapons Convention, and more.

In response to critics, the administration denied any isolationist intent. Officials pointed to the pursuit of a Free Trade Area of the Americas, endorsement of a new round of global trade talks, and active participation in summit diplomacy as evi-dence of a commitment to an activist US foreign policy, but one attuned to results rather than gestures, to the pursuit of specific and attainable US interests rather than symbolic outcomes.[21] US Trade Representative Robert Zoellick, for example, told a congressional committee on 7 March 2001 that 'trade policy is the bridge between the President's international and domestic agendas.' A day earlier, in a press release setting out the administration's trade policy agenda, Zoellick empha-sized that 'the United States . . . must build a new consensus to promote open markets for trade in the decades to come. The Bush Administration is strongly committed to a trade policy that will remove trade barriers in foreign markets, while further liberalizing our market at home.'[22] The key to re-establishing lead-ership in these matters is for the administration to gain fast-track negotiating authority, or, in Zoellick's words, '[to re-establish] the bipartisan Executive-Congressional negotiating partnership that has accomplished so much. One of the top priorities is to re-establish trade promotion authority—based on the fast-track precedent.'[23] In April, the President sent a message to Congress formally seeking trade promotion authority.

These were the key issues on the governmental agenda that the Bush adminis-tration was establishing prior to 11 September. Political change had provided an opening for policy entrepreneurs to promote their preferred problems and solutions, and proponents of a reduced role for government had scored an early victory with the tax cut, but the battle had just been joined, and the outcome was far from certain.[24] All this would change on 11 September, and the implications for policy agendas and processes in Canada would be profound.

The US Policy Agenda After September

The horrific events of 11 September, reinforced soon thereafter by the anthrax attacks, galvanized the US policy process, and produced single-minded co-operation among key players that resulted in forceful American action against international terrorism. In the weeks following, it became clear that the attacks had decisively joined the streams in the policy process—the problem of threatened security was identified, the policy community rallied around the prospect of a war on terrorism, and the politics were right for a concerted program of action at home and abroad. That program centred on military action against Afghanistan, including the mobilization of an international coalition in support of US action, plus an array of new measures for Homeland Defence, including heightened security on US borders.

In addition, as Kingdon's model would suggest, the crisis afforded new momentum for key elements of the administration's pre-11 September policy agenda. As the terrorist attacks tipped the US economy into recession, the Bush tax cut suddenly seemed fortuitous as an economic stimulus, and more tax cuts, combined with additional spending programs, were quickly forthcoming from an aroused Congress.[25] Federal Reserve Board Chairman Alan Greenspan also moved quickly on the monetary policy agenda, with rapid and sizable interest rate cuts, bringing rates down to levels that had not been seen since the Eisenhower administration.

On the energy agenda, aggressive exploration now seemed only prudent in the face of heavy dependence on Middle East oil supplies, and the prospects for drilling in the ANWR took on new life. On the trade front, the administration drew direct links between security, prosperity, and freer trade, arguing that a more prosperous America was a more secure America. United States Trade Representative (USTR) Zoellick made the case on the Hill for trade promotion authority, insisting that freer international trade was the key to a more prosperous and secure America. At Doha, Qatar, in November, despite international jitters about holding a ministerial meeting so close to the Afghanistan war front, Zoellick took the same message to his colleagues from around the world and succeeded in launching a new round of global trade talks.[26]

Finally, the terrorist attacks reinforced the administration's resolve to press ahead with the development and deployment of a national missile defence system, despite the fact that, initially, the events of 11 September appeared to work against NMD: these attacks came from terrorists using airplanes, not a rogue state armed with ballistic missiles; the high cost of NMD would be difficult to sustain in a defence budget newly strained by the costs of prosecuting a war on terrorism; and the US determination to scrap its Anti-Ballistic Missile Treaty with Russia would not fit well with its need for Russian support in the war. However, the NMD issue demonstrates the powerful effects of the coupling of streams in the policy process, and the capacity of problems and solutions to be swept along in the combined current.

The policy window that opened on 11 September was wide indeed, and policy entrepreneurs in the United States were quick to use it to move their problems—whether energy shortages, excessive taxes, access to foreign markets, or any kind of security threat—forward on the governmental agenda, along with their preferred solutions.[27] The effects on Canadian policy priorities and on the policy process in Canada were felt immediately and with similar results.

EFFECTS ON THE CANADIAN POLICY AGENDA

The Canadian Policy Agenda Before September
As we stated at the outset, in the days immediately before 11 September softwood lumber was at the top of the policy agenda for the Chrétien government in its relations with the United States. This is an instance of policy developments in Washington shaping the policy agenda in Ottawa by directly affecting Canadian interests. In April 2001, US lumber producers launched their fourth countervailing duty complaint in 20 years against Canadian softwood exports, days after the 31 March expiry of a five-year trade agreement that placed limits on Canadian exports to the United States. The regularity of these complaints suggests that in 2001 the US industry was simply engaged in business as usual in its long-standing campaign against its Canadian competitors. However, Canadian government pleas to the Bush administration for relief were ignored, partly because the President was seeking trade promotion authority from Congress, and therefore needed to demonstrate a commitment to protect the interests of US industry.

National missile defence was another issue affecting the Canadian policy agenda prior to 11 September. In this instance, however, although US policy was not directed at Canada, as was the case with softwood lumber, its broad impact would still affect Canada's interests, and this would move the issue onto the Canadian policy agenda. As had been the case with Reagan's Star Wars in the 1980s, NMD would require Canada to take a stand on continental defence, to say whether it was a partner on the initiative with the United States or preferred to stand aside and allow the United States to take responsibility for North American defence. The Chrétien government was split on the issue, with Defence Minister Eggleton in favour of a role for Canada in the US program, and the Prime Minister and Minister of Foreign Affairs John Manley decidedly less enthusiastic. Canada had little choice but to deal with the issue, however, since the United States seemed determined to proceed.

The Bush administration's energy plan was largely a matter of US domestic policy, but its provisions were nevertheless spilling over into the Canadian policy realm, affecting the policy process indirectly. For several years, Canada had opposed proposals in the US Congress for oil and gas development in the calving grounds of the ANWR, arguing that the disruption of the caribou herd would inflict hardship on the Aboriginal Gwich'in people, who depend on the caribou for their basic needs. In the face of pressure from the Alaskan congressional delegation to proceed with development, Canada counted on President Clinton's reluctance to antagonize environmentalists by authorizing exploration in the Refuge. However, Canadian officials were uncertain, even dubious, about whether the government could count on the Bush administration to display similar restraint.

The Bush energy plan also prompted calls from a variety of US officials for a North American continental energy pact, something that appeared to affect Canadian interests directly. When the idea was first floated, in the summer of 2001, the response from Canada suggested that if Americans wanted the free movement of energy supplies, they would have to live with the free movement of softwood lumber as well. Although this linkage between the two issues was quickly disavowed by Canadian officials, the response overlooked the fact that free trade in energy had already been substantially instituted in the bilateral Canada-United States free trade agreement in 1989, including guarantees of supply for the United States in times of crisis.[28] However, Mexico had declined to adopt Canadian-type obligations on energy in the 1994 North American Free Trade Agreement, leading some to conclude that Mexico was the primary target of US proposals for a continental pact.[29]

Security on US borders was another domestic issue with the potential to directly affect Canadian interests, in a manner that would foreshadow developments following 11 September. This issue was raised initially in a proposal in the US Congress for changes in Section 110 of the Illegal Immigration Reform and Immigrant Responsibility Act (IIRIRA) that would require the documentation of every alien (including Canadians) entering and exiting the United States. Adoption of entry/exit controls at US ports of entry would seriously disrupt personal and business traffic between the United States and Canada, threatening Canada's access to the US market and causing severe cross-border congestion.[30] In the end, Canada, with the help of border-state governors such as Michigan Governor John Engler, was able to head off the implementation of controls, convincing key members of Congress that Canada was not the intended target of the legislation, and that the unintended consequences for commercial traffic would be intolerable.

However, the border issue surfaced again, in December 1999, when Ahmed Ressam was stopped while attempting to enter the United States from Canada with a car trunk full of powerful explosives. These were to be used, it was learned subsequently, in a terrorist attack on the Los Angeles international airport. Ressam had entered Canada earlier in 1999 under an assumed name, using a fraudulent Canadian passport. He was subsequently tried and convicted in a Los Angeles court. The incident was extremely embarrassing to Canada, and raised questions in US government circles about Canada's reliability as a security partner. Canada sought to reassure the United States on this count, largely by insisting on the adequacy of existing Canadian procedures, including those governing co-operation between the two countries, but few changes were made in these procedures. The effect of the Ressam affair was to open the possibility that the issue of security, largely a US domestic preoccupation, could impinge more directly on Canadian interests.

In the summer of 2001, following Ressam's conviction, US Ambassador to Canada

Paul Cellucci addressed the problem of meeting the security and political demands of the border with a minimum of economic disruption.[31] He asserted that new technologies and additional infrastructure were needed to ensure the efficient movement of people and goods across the border, while allowing officials to concentrate scarce resources on the problem cases. Beyond this, Cellucci argued that a shared continent required shared solutions, which meant not only co-operation, but also a convergence of rules and regulations. This suggested that Canada and the United States ought to be screening undesirable persons and goods not at their shared border, but at, and beyond, a common perimeter around North America. Discussion in Ottawa and elsewhere suggested a growing interest in the concept of a more open border backed up by a common perimeter approach to security issues, but not where it counts—in the Prime Minister's Office; there, the perimeter concept in particular had received a frosty reception.[32]

In broad strokes, this was the state of Canada's policy agenda, at least as it concerned the United States, in the period before the events of 11 September. While these issues were exerting their direct, broad, or indirect effects on the Canadian policy agenda, the Prime Minister let it be known in the summer of 2001 that he had his own 'personal priorities' that would be moved forward on the government's legislative agenda when Parliament resumed sitting in the autumn. These included action on climate change, support for an innovation economy, and tackling the problems of Canada's native peoples. Additionally, a number of other priority issues were receiving due attention in various policy circles. The establishment of the Romanow Royal Commission on Health Care had pushed that issue onto a slower track, and earlier musings about a national child care program and other adjustments in the social safety net seemed to have been similarly pushed off the governmental agenda.

The Canadian Policy Agenda After September

The effect of the terrorist attacks on 11 September was to expand dramatically the domain of American policy, so that the indirect effects of US policy priorities and decisions on Canada were increased to an unprecedented degree. For the United States, the security of America's borders was one of a number of key issues on a post-September policy agenda that was staggering in its magnitude: waging a multiple-front war on international terrorism, and mobilizing a domestic population in support of the sacrifices that might be required in such a war; assembling an international coalition of partners in support of the war effort, and shoring up the resolve of essential, but reluctant, partners; and dealing with the catastrophic effects of the terrorist attacks on the already slowing US economy. The anthrax attacks added further to an atmosphere of crisis and confusion. Nevertheless, the tragedy of 11 September also imposed a new single-mindedness upon US foreign and domestic policy and marginalized the trivial, providing a focus and determination that had been notably absent over the previous decade.

In Canada too the 11 September attacks produced a decisive conjunction of the streams in the policy process, as the country attempted to make its own contribution to the war effort and deal with its own economic slowdown. The border with the United States swept to the top of the governmental agenda, more particularly the challenge of convincing Americans that it was not necessary to shut down their northern border in order to protect their security. As in the United States, policy entrepreneurs were quick to use the crisis to attempt to advance their policy interests, although efforts by Health Minister Allan Rock to make use of the anxiety created by the anthrax attacks in the United States appeared to backfire.[33] Similarly, the public was quick to dismiss Air Canada's opportunistic attempt to piggyback a government bailout for its deteriorating financial situation onto the terrorist crisis; even Transport Minister David Collenette could not muster any enthusiasm for Air Canada CEO Robert Milton's demand for four billion dollars in immediate relief.[34] The terrorist threat had clearly changed the agenda, but within limits. Other issues, however, with a more direct link to the new circumstances, from refugee determination policies to military spending, would advance onto the governmental agenda.[35]

When, in the days immediately following the terrorist attacks, chaos prevailed at Canada-US border crossings, with traffic backups of up to eighteen hours, Canadian exporters pressed for immediate action to resolve the problem.[36] Although delays diminished subsequently, the problem was not about to go away. Concerns about border security persisted in Washington, and Congress passed legislation, the so-called Patriot Act, authorizing, among other things, a tripling of the number of customs, immigration, and border patrol agents for the US northern border. In addition, Congress was again considering legislation that would have the Immigration and Naturalization Service (INS) implement the Section 110 requirement to check the identity and visa status of every foreign visitor (including Canadians) moving through entry/exit controls at US ports of entry.[37] In the Executive Branch, President Bush issued a directive to begin harmonizing customs and immigration policies with Canada and Mexico, enjoining his officials to ensure maximum compatibility of immigration, customs, and visa policies, and to create a joint customs and immigration database.[38]

In the aftermath of the 11 September attacks, the US priority on Homeland Defence meant that the dominant issue on Canada's policy agenda had to be security on the Canada-US border and, by implication, on the North American perimeter. Kingdon's model suggests that, in response to a focussing event like the terrorist attacks, a major change in the governmental agenda, based especially on a reading of the national mood, should emerge from the politics stream. If this is true, then the initial reading of the mood by the Chrétien government appeared to miss the mark, as it attempted to placate the United States while still keeping its distance from American policy initiatives. Compatible policies did not mean identical policies, insisted Canadian officials: 'We're going to continue to coordinate but we are going to continue to maintain a sovereign border', said the Prime Minister's Office.[39] Perhaps, but the United States was obviously on the path to something very close to a North American security perimeter, and the concept was gaining the support of an important segment of the Canadian business establishment.[40] As Chapter 1 has shown, faced by an angry United States determined to do what was necessary to strengthen its homeland security, and an anxious Canadian business community fearful of what tighter border administration would mean for Canadian trade and prosperity, the government took steps both in legislative change and in the Budget Speech of 10 December to bring its agenda into line with the new reality.[41]

The first order of business was a hastily assembled revamping of Canadian laws governing terrorism, intelligence gathering, and law enforcement in an omnibus anti-terrorism bill. Quickly given first and second reading in the House and then hustled into both House and Senate hearings, Bill C-36 soon ran into heavy weather from civil liberties organizations alarmed at the extent of the proposed changes and the reach of new governmental police authority. Amendments flooded in and calls for a sunset clause soon became the focus of debate. The government at first seemed prepared to see the Bill amended, but then, realizing that it could lose control if it entertained too many amendments, stiffened its resolve to stay with the basic contours of its proposed legislation.

Even as Bill C-36 was wending its way through the legislative process, the government announced substantial new spending of $280 million to equip Canadian police, airports, and intelligence officials with new equipment and better resources in order to upgrade their capacity to address terrorist threats. The money would provide Transport Canada with new bomb-sniffing equipment, the RCMP with new resources to do background checks on suspected terrorists, and the Canadian Security and Intelligence Service (CSIS) with enhanced intelligence-gathering capability. The 10 December 2001 budget further increased this security package.

In order to coordinate the multi-faceted response required by the complex new circumstances, the Prime Minister appointed an ad hoc cabinet committee under the chairmanship of Foreign Minister John Manley, charged with ensuring that Canada was doing what needed to be done on the three emerging fronts: contributing to the international war on terrorism, shoring up Canadian domestic security requirements, and keeping the Canada-US border as open as possible. It soon became clear that the last front was the most pressing, but needed a credible performance on the first two if Canada was to make any headway with US officials responding to a worried population.

On the military front, again at first hesitantly but with increasing resolve, the government mobilized its forces and committed a destroyer, several frigates, and support vessels to the war theatre to assist the American-led effort with picket and other support. By the end of October, Canada's contribution to the war effort ranked third internationally, small by comparison to the US and British commitments, but psychologically important both in Canada and around the world. The mobilization, however, also cast a critical searchlight on Canada's capacity to make more than a token contribution. Decades of budget cutting had reduced military spending to the point that the physical and human resources at the government's disposal looked decidedly meagre: fewer than 60,000 men and women in uniform, using increasingly dated and worn equipment. The frigates sent to the front were new and relatively well equipped, but an important part of their mission relied on aging Sea King helicopters. The Chrétien government's 1993 decision to delay their replacement was now coming back to haunt it, as were other cost-saving measures that had looked sustainable in the immediate post-Cold War context, but now looked short-sighted.[42]

On the US front, after first resisting any overt moves to address US concerns about the security of the border and business anxieties about its openness, the government deployed a steady stream of ministers and officials to Washington to pursue a two-track strategy: convince the Americans that Canada was taking every step necessary to ensure the security of North America from terrorist and other threats; and convince them that tightening security at the Canada-US border was not the way to go. It soon became clear that the Americans required more than verbal assurances.[43] They wanted a clear plan that would be sufficient to reassure a nervous American public that the approaches to North America were secure before entertaining any ideas about calling off plans to tighten security at the Canadian border. They wanted, specifically, action to address Canadian visa and refugee policies, both of which had proved wanting in the Ressam case.

By mid-November 2001, the government was also beginning to get its mind around the business case for more open and less intrusive Canada-US border administration, particularly as it became clear that protectionist policy entrepreneurs in the United States would try to use the terrorist crisis to roll back the past decade and a half of progress in making trade freer between the two countries. While the Canadian nationalist community warned Canadians about the imminent danger to Canada's survival posed by any effort to address the US agenda, others argued that the focus on enhanced security for North America's perimeter and a more open bilateral border was a necessary response that would defend Canadian interests.[44]

Annual budgets often prove a useful guide to a government's real, rather than rhetorical, priorities. By sifting through the funds allocated to various policies and programs, one can usually divine the government's medium-term agenda more reliably than by reading throne speeches and prime ministerial pronouncements. Chapter 1 has confirmed this principle, demonstrating that the 10 December 2001 budget contained a focussed set of initiatives on four fronts: defence, police and intelligence, border infrastructure, and foreign aid. The first includes the task of refurbishing the Canadian military so that it has the capacity to contribute to the response to the new global terrorist threat; the second seeks to strengthen Canada's capacity to deal with domestic terrorist and related threats, including an increased capacity to check the backgrounds of refugee claimants; the third addresses the problem of mounting congestion at the border; and the fourth targets the building of governance and technical capacity in developing countries that are vulnerable to inroads by terrorist networks.

The budget also sends a clear signal to the United States about Canadian commitments to both perimeter security and the global war on terrorism. As Chapter 1 has shown, the budget focussed on the economic and physical security aspects of the Canada-US border issue. In the words of *The Globe and Mail*'s Edward Greenspon, this focus marks phase three of the government's response to 11 September: 'This phase largely revolves around post-Sept. 11 challenges to the economic security of Canadians and, more precisely, our ability to get our goods and people across the critical American border on a timely basis.'[45] It is likely to involve three separate but mutually reinforcing strategies: 1) efforts to make both Canadians and Americans aware of the extent to which Canada has taken, or is taking, steps to address gaps in its security, intelligence, military, refugee-determination, immigration, and visa arrangements, and related issues; 2) steps to work with the Americans in devising ways and means within existing laws and procedures to harmonize and streamline the clearance of people and goods at the Canada-US border and to coordinate the clearance of people and goods arriving from third countries; and 3) a commitment to work out with the Americans ways and means to effect a more open Canada-US border, similar to the Schengen Plan in Europe. Canadians appeared ready to take these steps soon after 11 September. The government appears now to have caught up. As Edward Greenspon argued,

> Prime Minister Jean Chrétien . . . misread the situation, jumping to the venerable but outdated conclusion that Canadians would dismiss joint initiatives with the United States as an affront to our sovereignty. Guardians of the public interest wrung their hands over the supposed incompatibility of common security and national sovereignty. . . . Canadians moderated their economic nationalist impulses over the course of the 1990s, but they didn't dispose of their nationalistic sentiments in the process. Today's nationalism is one of inclusion, not exclusion—a self-confident nationalism that allows us to pursue our own interests, without feeling the need to define ourselves as against others. That's the transformation the politicians missed on Sept. 11.[46]

CONCLUSIONS

Softwood lumber is still on the Canada-US agenda and, after a meeting between President Bush's special envoy, former Montana Governor Mark Racicot, and Trade Minister Pierre Pettigrew,[47] there was some indication that the two governments might be moving toward a resolution of the issue, at least for the time being. The breakthrough came not because either side was prepared to concede to the views of the other, but because the events of 11 September had changed the landscape of bilateral relations: neither government could afford to have this dispute continue to cast a cloud over issues that were more important to both countries. To the Bush administration, while it was unprepared to create a precedent that might come back to haunt it in relations with members of the House or Senate representing lumber interests, a softwood solution would remove this thorny issue from the agenda for the time being. For the Canadian government, the American predisposition to settle issues that might distract from their primary mission on terrorism offered an opportunity to resolve a dispute that was causing considerable economic pain, and political fallout, in Canada. In addition, resolving the issue might help create the supporting atmosphere in Washington necessary for the resolution of a potentially more damaging problem: an enlarged phalanx of more vigilant customs and immigration inspectors deployed along the full length of the Canada-US border. More than lumber trade would be placed at risk. The prosperity of the country as a whole might suffer, without necessarily addressing the security of North America.[48]

In effect, while the context and immediacy of the softwood issue had changed, the fundamentals had not. For Canada, proximity to the United States ensures that a good part of the government's policy energies must be focussed on events in Washington, either because of their direct impact on Canadian interests and priorities or because of the capacity of the American agenda to spill over and shape the Canadian policy agenda. Jean Chrétien, who prides himself on his ability to read the Canadian electorate, has pursued a cool but correct relationship with the Americans. Until 11 September that seemed to be a winning formula, given that he continued to enjoy a very high level of public approval. On the morning of 11 September, *The Globe and Mail*'s two political columnists, Jeffrey Simpson and Edward Greenspon, wrote complementary columns about Chrétien's political good fortune, the one detailing the chaos on the left and the other the chaos on the right that left the Liberals unchallenged as Parliament began a new session. Without a credible opposition to stir the creative juices, the Prime Minister was portrayed by both as presiding over a government that provided Canada with dull, complacent, but unchallenged governance.[49]

After 11 September, however, a shift in the national mood seemed to have occurred, as a substantial majority of Canadians now wanted their country, through their government, to stand shoulder to shoulder with the Americans in their hour of need. An October poll indicated a higher approval rating among Canadians for George Bush than for Jean Chrétien over the handling of the terrorist threat.[50] It took the Prime Minister more than a month to catch up to this new mood, and to set the government on a revised course. Once he had done so, however, the new direction was clear, even if the rhetoric was still couched in terms designed not to alarm nationalist sensitivities: a North American perimeter was out, but an 'outer-limit security zone' was acceptable. Whatever words are ultimately found to give expression to the new reality, the fact is that the Canadian policy agenda has been radically re-aligned by the convergence of the streams in the US policy process that occurred on 11 September, and at the top of the agenda is a fundamental redefinition of Canada-US relations, a change that might, in the end, even be sufficient to carry in its currents the perennial irritant of trade in softwood lumber.

NOTES

1 Antidumping duties averaging 12.6 per cent were imposed on 31 October 2001.

2 Lydia Andrade and Garry Young, 'Presidential Agenda Setting: Influences on the Emphasis of Foreign Policy', *Political Research Quarterly* 49, 3 (Sept. 1996): 591.

3 Ibid.

4 Overseeing much of this activity are the courts and the hundreds of quasi-judicial agencies with administrative and judicial authority independent of either the president or the Congress. The president may appoint people to these positions, often with the advice and consent of the Senate, and both president and Congress may exercise influence over their decisions through the legislative and budgetary processes, but to all intents and purposes this third branch of government pursues its own program.

5 Allan Gotlieb, *'I'll Be with You in a Minute, Mr. Ambassador': The Education of a Canadian Diplomat* (Toronto: University of Toronto Press, 1991), 31.

6 John Kingdon, *Agendas, Alternatives, and Public Policies*, 2nd ed. (New York: HarperCollins, 1995).

7 Ibid., 90.

8 Ibid., 116.

9 Ibid., 145.

10 Ibid., 165.

11 Michael Cohen, James March, and Johan Olsen, 'A Garbage Can Model of Organizational Choice', *Administrative Science Quarterly* 17 (Mar. 1972): 1–25.

12 Ibid., 2, as quoted in Kingdon, *Agendas*, 85.

13 David Broder, 'Tall Order for Reform', *The Washington Post*, 6 June 2001, A27.

14 Victory in the eyes of the President and his supporters, that is. For some others, it represented a capitulation to conservative Republicans, and eroded support for Bush among moderates. See E.J. Dionne, Jr., 'A 50 Percent Presidency', *The Washington Post*, 6 July 2001, A25.

15 Broder, 'Tall Order', A27.

16 David Broder, 'Reality Check on Education Reform', *The Washington Post*, 6 May 2001, B07.

17 In real terms, drilling in the ANWR has the potential to seriously damage the calving grounds and disrupt the herd, while having, at best, a marginal impact on US energy self-sufficiency.

18 Bush was not alone in this conviction. In 1999, the US Senate and House of Representatives had endorsed NMD by large majorities, and the Clinton administration had decided to proceed with deployment. That decision was subsequently deferred by Clinton to the new administration.

19 A Republican analyst compared the NMD debate to a theological argument: 'Republicans would be for it even if it were proven that it couldn't work. And Democrats would be against it even if it were proven that it could work.' Quoted in E.J. Dionne, Jr., 'Faith-Based Defence', *The Washington Post*, 27 July 2001, A31.

20 George Will, 'The Diplomacy of High Minded Gestures', *The Washington Post*, 5 Aug. 2001, B07.

21 In support of the administration's position, George Will states, 'Jeremy Rabkin, professor of constitutional and international law at Cornell, notes that President Clinton cavalierly signed treaties that he knew the Senate would not ratify, and hence he would not submit for ratification. The Kyoto protocol on global warming is an example of what Rabkin calls "momentary mood enhancers" that leave US diplomacy "in a fantasy land of good intentions"'. Ibid.

22 Office of the United States Trade Representative (USTR), 'USTR Trade Policy Agenda and 2000 Annual Report', Press Release 01–13, 6 Mar. 2001.

23 Ibid.

24 Especially when the Republicans lost control of the Senate with the defection in May 2001 of Vermont Republican Jim Jeffords, who left the party to sit as an Independent, giving the Democrats a one-seat edge, and control over the legislative agenda.

25 However, it did not take long for pre-September conflicts between the administration and Democrats in the Senate over the stimulus legislation to emerge again. Said Democratic Senate Majority Leader Tom Daschle, 'Democrats are proposing real help for laid-off workers, while Republicans are pushing for more tax cuts for wealthy individuals and profitable corporations.' See John D. McKinnon and Shailagh Murray, 'Jobless Data Raise Stakes in Drafting Stimulus Bill', *The Globe and Mail* [Toronto], 5 Nov. 2001, B8.

26 Noted *The Economist*, 'Well before September 11th, a new round of multilateral trade talks was urgent. Now success at Doha, in Qatar, has become part of the anti-terrorist arsenal. Robert Zoellick, America's trade representative, calls new negotiations on trade a way to "counter the revulsive destructionism of terrorism". With the world economy tipping into recession, the promise of freer trade should give a much-needed boost to confidence—even though the actual gains will be some years off.' 'High Stakes at Doha', *The Economist*, 1 Nov. 2001. However, another commentator saw Zoellick's actions differently, with 'trade being bundled (Microsoft-style) inside the with-us-or-against logic of the war on terrorism'. Naomi Klein, 'Doha's Kamikaze Capitalists and the God of Growth', *The Globe and Mail* [Toronto], 7 Nov. 2001, A21.

27 The version of the stimulus package passed by the House of Representatives included an array of tax breaks for businesses and individuals. Reflecting Kingdon's entrepreneurial behaviour principle, Barry McKenna noted that, 'Many of these tax cuts have been high on the wish-list of Washington lobbyists for years. Sept. 11 simply provided the pretext to push them through.' 'More US Government for Less Sounds Like an Oxymoron', *The Globe and Mail* [Toronto], 16 Nov. 2001, B8.

28 The government was quickly reminded of this reality by Alberta Premier Ralph Klein, following the effort by the Prime Minister and some of his ministers to link energy sales to the ongoing travails of the softwood lumber industry.

29 See 'US Ambassador Raises Energy Integration', *The Globe and Mail* [Toronto], 31 Oct. 2001, B2, and 'Why an Energy Pact?', *The Globe and Mail* [Toronto], 3 Nov. 2001, A14.

30 Some 200 million individuals cross the border every year, an average of more than half a million per day; some 30,000 trucks and 100,000 cars cross the border every day.

31 Paul Cellucci, 'Life Without Borders', *The Ottawa Citizen*, 1 Aug. 2001, A13.

32 Edward Greenspon notes that 'when the Prime Minister received his briefing books after the last election, he would have noticed the high priority that his officials placed on [the] North American integration file. They wanted him to set up a special cabinet reference group—as he has done on energy policy and aboriginals—so that his ministers could begin educating themselves on the challenges posed by our economic interdependence with the United States. But as the head of a third-term government chronically short on vision, he preferred to manage the problems in his face over the ones on the horizon.' *The Globe and Mail* [Toronto], 13 Sept. 2001, A19. For a discussion of the central and absolutely authoritative role of the prime minister, and the PMO, in the Canadian policy process see Donald J. Savoie, *Governing from the Centre: The Concentration of Power in Canadian Politics* (Toronto: University of Toronto Press, 1999).

33 See Jane Taber, 'Rock's Drug Dispute Latest in Legacy of Costly Missteps,' *The National Post*, 23 Oct. 2001, and Paul Wells, 'Rock Fried After Taking Media's Bait', *The National Post*, 31 Oct. 2001.

34 See Paul Kedrosky, 'The Bills Would Never End if Ottawa Bailed Out Air Canada', *The National Post*, 29 Sept. 2001.

35 One interesting example of what may prove to be a more successful effort to piggyback old issues onto the new circumstances is provided by Canadian customs officers. For years, they have pressed for status as peace officers with the right to bear arms. In the aftermath of 11 September, they may succeed in convincing the government of their cause. See Louise Elliott, 'Gun-toting Officers Should Replace Summer Students Staffing Borders, Says Unions', *Canadian Press*, 6 Nov. 2001.

36 The auto industry, particularly alarmed, called for a task force to identify solutions to the security-commerce dilemma. Barrie McKenna and Greg Keenan, 'Pressure Rises for Tighter Border', *The Globe and Mail* [Toronto], 20 Sept. 2001, B1. Industry spokesmen estimated that unexpected shutdowns due to the late arrival of parts can cost the industry up to $25,000 per minute. *The Globe and Mail* [Toronto], 6 Nov. 2001, B18.

37 INS Commissioner James Ziglar, in testimony before Senate and House Committees, on 3 and 11 October 2001 respectively, listed a catalogue of proposed and potential ways to enhance co-operation and coordination with Canada, but also included ominous suggestions for unilateral measures to bulk up his agency's presence at the border, and to implement Section 110.

38 Campbell Clark, 'Bush Aims to Tighten Continent's Borders', *The Globe and Mail* [Toronto], 30 Oct. 2001, A1.

39 Ibid.

40 Mike Trickey and Norma Greenaway, 'Canadian Business Leaders Push for Security Perimeter Zone', *The Ottawa Citizen*, 1 Nov. 2001, D1.

41 'As the saying goes: Then was then, and now is now. Call it expediency, or changed circumstances. Perhaps a delayed awakening. Or a new maturity. Whatever your description, the Liberals now are not the Liberals then.' Jeffrey Simpson, *The Globe and Mail* [Toronto], 17 Oct. 2001, A17.

42 'Canada pretended to support an all-singing, all-dancing military establishment, while actually turning it into an international police force, a paramili-
tary operation that was sent to patrol the lines in faraway places after the
cease-fires were securely in place. It was worthy work at much less risk and
cost, and Canada put peacekeeping on a moral pedestal compared with the
heavy-lifting military mission that fell to the Americans, our impetuous
friends. . . . [Foreign Minister John] Manley has been acknowledging some of
these realities as he looks to the future and argues that Canada needs to tem-
per its often self-serving idealism in world affairs with more credible commitments to share the burdens of war-making and prevention through
stronger counterintelligence and security establishments. Blessedly, he is not
holding on to the tired rhetoric of the little guardian angel to the north who
plays the conscience to the American man.' William Thorsell, *The Globe and
Mail* [Toronto], 15 Oct. 2001, A21.

43 *The Globe and Mail's* Washington correspondent, Barry McKenna, reported
on 19 October that 'frustrated Canadian officials continue to tell anyone willing to listen around Washington that there's "no evidence of a Canadian connection" to the Sept. 11 attacks. But their voices are being drowned out by
memories of the 1999 Ahmed Ressam case and the perception that Canada
remains a haven for terrorists and illegal aliens.' He concludes that 'the
United States appears to be opting for a state of permanent high alert at the
border: more guards, more searches and intrusive policing technology.'

44 *The Globe and Mail* editorialized that 'it falls to Canada now to offer the
Americans a strong security plan. This must be done for its own sake, to protect North America from the threat of terrorism, and to safeguard Canada's
commercial interests. Harmony should be the operative word—different
notes combining toward a mutual goal.' 'The Politics of a Secure Border', 31
Oct. 2001, A16. Writing in the *National Post*, Andrew Coyne stated, 'I do not
hold with those who see the public's rush to embrace the Americans, or their
willingness, in a crisis, to cede some degree of sovereignty in areas like
national security, as heralding the end of the Canadian nation, or a desire to
join the States. For the same surge of fellow feeling has been observed around
the world. We are, we have discovered, one people, defined by our belief in
the sanctity of human life, in freedom, in democracy, in equality.' 3 Oct. 2001.

45 'Seizing the Day on Canada–US Border Flows', *The Globe and Mail* [Toronto],
13 Nov. 2001, A21.

46 'Building the New Canadian', *The Globe and Mail* [Toronto], 10 Nov. 2001, F4.

47 See 'Ottawa Optimistic About Early Resolution of Lumber Dispute', *The Globe
and Mail* [Toronto], 7 Nov. 2001, B1.

48 The creed of North American solidarity would not prevail in all quarters in
Washington, however. Lumber's chief lobbyist in the United States warned
that Canada would have to ante up a 'realistic' offer (read increased Canadian
softwood prices) in order to get a deal. See Barrie McKenna and Peter
Kennedy, 'Legal Action on Softwood Touted', *The Globe and Mail* [Toronto],
16 Nov. 2001, B4.

49 'Why Is This Man Smiling', *The Globe and Mail* [Toronto], 11 Sept. 2001, A13.

50 'Bush Gets Higher Approval Rating in Canada than PM', *The National Post*,
29 Sept. 2001.

4

The Neurotic State

LUC JUILLET AND GILLES PAQUET

> The political community must be able to distinguish between disagreement with
> particular policies of the community and disloyalty to the community itself.
>
> *Stephen L. Carter*[1]

One of the perplexing features of Canada's political scene over the last six or
seven years has been a dramatic if silent revolution in the functioning of the federal
state. Program Review, Alternative Service Delivery, and other such initiatives have
demonstrated a clear impulse toward decentralization and privatization, but they
have also had the flavour of such good governance virtues as transparency, accountability, and integrity. Yet the net effect of these initiatives has been not only a phenomenal reconcentration of power in central agencies and in the Prime Minister's
Office (PMO), but also a shift toward a neurotic governance regime. The former phenomenon has been carefully documented and analysed;[2] we would like to examine
the latter one.

A superficial examination of these issues has led some observers to suggest
that the reconcentration of effective power at the centre is the culprit, that it has
generated the emergence of the new bunker mentality, and transformed the federal
public service into an enterprise where dissent is being subtly suppressed, where

disagreement has come to be regarded as a form of treason. But the causality also runs the other way. Mutual distrust between the citizenry and the government as well as fear of the political consequences of the disclosure of critical information about government activities contribute to a tightening of central controls. They breed organizational paranoia. One must look at the dynamics that have generated this emerging neurotic governance regime to explain the reconcentration of power and other dysfunctions that have been noted in the recent past.

At the root of these dynamics is the growing distrust of government by the citizenry. This distrust has produced added pressure for more transparency and hard accountability at a time when the turbulent environment and the accelerated pace of change would appear to require that the new governance regime be more flexible and more decentralized, that is, that agents of the state be allowed more discretion, and softer forms of accountability.[3]

While this growing public distrust is not unique to Canada, the response to it has been significantly sharper in Canada because of the fact that the Office of the Prime Minister and some other central agencies have much more formidable power bases than similar agencies in other advanced democracies. We in Canada live not in a parliamentary democracy but, in the words of Jeffrey Simpson, in a 'Prime-Ministerial Government' regime, where Parliament is ignored and Cabinet has become nothing but a 'mini-sounding-board'.[4]

One important element of this Canadian response has been a sharp decline in the willingness of governments and bureaucrats to disclose information about their operations, because it has become evident that such disclosed information is often used to fuel attacks on political and bureaucratic processes. This culture of secrecy has led in turn to greater distrust, and to more vehement requests for information, and the vicious circle continues. The ultimate result has been greater distrust on the part of the citizenry, and paranoia on the part of the state.

The main consequences of this vicious circle have been the rise of a new *raison d'État*, and the activation of a number of mechanisms that have corrupted public discourse and the governance regime. The culture of secrecy has hardened into a neurotic state, and paranoia, like a viral infection, has spread down the evolutionary ladder from one bureaucratic species to another.

Caught between the distrust of the citizens and the circling of the wagons by the prime-ministerial government, not only has the federal public service firmly sided with the government, but it has exacerbated the degree of paranoia. Middle-ranked civil servants have used this chasm between the governors and the governed as a new source of power, by claiming (as part of their refurbished burden of office) the responsibility for determining what is 'contrary to the interests of government'. This has often been done as a corollary to their indefectible commitment to saving the minister from embarrassment at all costs, but it has also increasingly become a way to immunize themselves from the citizenry's 'attacks', and to leverage their action in pursuit of policy preferences, patronage, or punishment for 'disloyalty'. As a consequence, the governed have become devoiced, their dissent generating retribution and rebuke, not only by politicians but also by faceless middle-ranked bureaucrats defending not so much the interests of 'the government' as their own particular versions of what 'the interests of the government' are.

We would like, on the basis of a series of interviews with senior officials, and an examination of documents in the public domain, 1) to identify the symptoms of this silent revolution and track down the source of the neurosis, 2) to document some of the forms it has taken, 3) to look at this dynamic at work in the access to information files, and 4) to hint at the implications it appears to hold in store for the federal public service, and for democracy in Canada.

THE SYMPTOM: A NEW *RAISON D'ÉTAT*

It is difficult to determine a precise date for the emergence of this neurotic syndrome. One may note however that this new dynamic was already in place in 1995, when Treasury Board made explicit reference to the 'public interest' as having to be defined in the light of the need for 'fulfilling federal obligations and interests'. The French version was even more ominous: 'remplir les obligations du gouvernement fédéral et en protéger les intérêts'.[5]

This is not an entirely new phenomenon. There have in the past been a number of instances where action has been taken to devoice the government's critics, but of late there has been a significant increase in the scale and importance of these efforts to suppress dissent, or to effect censorship by brandishing the phrase 'contrary to the interests of the government'.[6]

This has been nothing short of an epistemological coup, through which the state has declared that it has interests 'of its own' and that they should prevail over other interests. But it was a change more of kind than of degree. True, one had witnessed somewhat similar arrogance in the Trudeau era, but perhaps because of the very self-assured intellectual arrogance on which it was based, it had never translated into as high a degree of intimidation, exclusion, and censorship as is to be observed in the Chrétien era.

In recent years, the new arrogance has been accompanied by a sense of insecurity that has led to much double-talk, dissimulation, and deception. Autocratic intervention to suppress dissent has been routinely accompanied by sermons on openness, participation, citizen engagement, and the need to build a sensitive citizen-centred modus operandi. This mismatch between words and deeds has become a chronic feature of the new regime in many segments of the federal public service.

The pattern obviously does not apply to all agencies. Some departments and agencies have maintained a reasonable degree of effectiveness and integrity, and a good fit between words and deeds. Others have suffered from different styles of dysfunction as a result of history, circumstances, and personalities. But most federal departments and agencies have been permeated by a certain malaise, ascribable to the fact that key central agencies, which are 'définisseurs de situation' and have a major impact on the modus operandi of the whole system, have been fundamentally affected by the new mindset.

Whatever form the neurosis has taken, the result has been the discouragement of critical thinking inside the bureaucracy about any aspect of the federal apparatus and governmental processes and policies, and the emergence of a sort of self-censorship, which has prevented not only critical thinking, but also, as a consequence, any meaningful social learning.

Canada has not become a police state, of course. All these interventions have been rather subtle, and have made themselves felt indirectly, in such forms as hypersensitivity, excessive concern with hidden motives, and a sense of guarded and pervasive suspicion, all in response to a genuine loss of confidence on the part of the citizenry. But this malaise has transformed government's way of doing business.

It is easy to slip from a defensive stance such as has been described to one in which the preservation of the operating system is regarded as the central purpose of the governance regime (and its staunch defence is regarded as the dominant logic—*la raison d'État*). Indeed, this transition has occurred.

THE DISTRUST-PARANOIA VICIOUS CIRCLE

The idea of the *raison d'État* is that the state takes itself as it own end, and in so doing considers society as a mean to this end.[7] It rationalizes the use and abuse of power, and the resort to exceptional measures as a way to maintain control over the governance process, because the maintenance of control is regarded as pre-eminently important.

Checks and balances are usually in place to ensure that each sphere of the state remains within its own field of competence, and that the state does not encroach on the legitimate realm of the individual, of civil society, etc. To monitor, control, redress, and sanction such trespassing, the agencies responsible for checks and balances must have the legal authority to deal with encroachment and corruption.[8]

In many democracies over the past few years, there has been a phenomenal erosion of this delicate balance. In Canada, this problem has been aggravated by a number of idiosyncratic systems failures: the collapse of the Conservative opposition, the trivialization of the controls of the House of Commons, the transformation of Cabinet from a decision-making body into a focus group, and the effective re-centralization of power in the hands of the prime minister and his advisors. The crisis of confidence is hardly surprising.

This crisis of confidence is apparent on several fronts. First, there has been a remarkable drop in support for politicians as a group both in Canada and elsewhere.[9] A similar trend is observed in attitudes toward political parties.[10] Canadians have also shown a declining level of trust in the executive and legislative branches of government as a whole. According to 1996 surveys, only 21 per cent of Canadians trusted Parliament to represent them, a sharp decline of about 60 per cent since the mid-1970s.[11]

This decline of trust in political authorities should not be confused with apathy toward politics. Disengagement from such traditional avenues of political participation as political parties has led to the growth of alternative forms of political engagement, which tend to be more grassroots-based and confrontational vis-à-vis state agencies. It translates into a greater demand for information.[12] Recent comparative longitudinal studies of political attitudes in western democracies have found a simultaneous decline in respect for government authority and growth in support for democracy.[13]

This erosion of trust has many sources: a lack of accurate and comprehensive information about what government does, changes in the ways public institutions are evaluated, and a deterioration in the performance of public institutions (ascribable to decline either in the capacity of political agents, or in the fidelity with which political agents defend citizens' interests).[14]

The difficulty of operating transparently in a political environment of distrust and criticism is exacerbated when opposition politicians and the media use access to information provisions mainly as a tool to publicly embarrass the government. This has led to a number of paranoid reactions.[15]

THE NEUROSIS OF THE CANADIAN STATE

In our study of the emergence of this neurotic style in federal governance—as revealed by our interviews—and of the organizational dysfunctioning that it has generated, we used a simple framework proposed by Kets de Vries and Miller in 1985.[16] They examine the patterns of symptoms and dysfunction that appear to combine into syndromes of pathology, and the mechanisms through which neurotic styles and organizational behaviours would interact and lend support to one another.

Different Styles of Neurosis
Neurosis is a type of dysfunction that generates affective and emotional problems, but without disrupting the functioning of the organization. There are different styles of neurosis: paranoid, compulsive, dramatic, depressive, and schizoid. Each has its own characteristics, dominant motivating fantasy, and associated dangers. Table 4.1, borrowed from Kets de Vries and Miller, provides a broad characterization of these different styles.

All individuals have mildly dysfunctional neurotic traits, but certain dominant patterns of these traits betray a dominant neurotic style. Organizations also display such traits; they permeate or colour the functioning of the organization and its culture. And while these organizational traits may emerge as a result of various environmental forces, or shared fantasies and myths developed through the history

Table 4.1
Summary of the Neurotic Styles

	Paranoid	Compulsive	Dramatic	Depressive	Schizoid
Characteristics	mistrust hypersensitivity perceived threats	perfectionism focus on trivia dogmatism	self-dramatization narcissism exploitativeness	sense of guilt helplessness	non-involvement estrangement
Fantasy	I cannot really trust anybody; I had better be on my guard	I don't want to be at the mercy of events; I must control all things	I want to get attention from and impress people	It is hopeless to change the course of events in my life. . . . I am not good enough	The world of reality does not offer any satisfaction, so it is safer to remain distant
Dangers	distortion of reality defensive attitudes	fear of making mistakes excessive reliance on rules	overreaction to minor events actions based on appearances	inhibition of action indecisiveness overly pessimistic	bewilderment and aggressiveness emotional isolation

Source: Adapted from Kets de Vries and Miller, *The Neurotic Organization*, 24–5.

of the organization, they also depend to some extent on the personality and management style of the leader.

To psychoanalyse an organization, one must rely on interviews with members of the organization, and impressions, anecdotes, and such other data of the kind that ethnographic studies unearth. The results of such an investigation of the organizational fabric of a large concern like the federal state do not necessarily reveal a single dominant neurotic style. Different segments may indeed be associated with different styles. For instance, Statistics Canada may be associated with a compulsive style, while this need not be the case for the Privy Council Office (PCO). Some might associate Canadian Heritage with the dramatic style, Human Resources with the depressive style, Foreign Affairs and International Trade with the schizoid syndrome. Each of these hypotheses would require an extensive investigation to ascertain its validity.

Yet one may make the case that, over the past few years, as central agencies tightened their grip on the governance of the country, a particular neurotic style has permeated the whole system—as a result of signals and pressures emanating from the PCO. The results of our interviews over the last year suggest that the whole federal state has been permeated by a paranoid style of neurosis. The full verification or falsification of this hypothesis would require much more space than is afforded for this chapter. However, there is enough scope for us to sketch briefly, and in a general way, the main features of the syndrome, and to illustrate how it works and what one may expect its consequences to be.

Main Features

The paranoid organization usually emerges in the face of a dynamic environment that requires continuous scanning to detect threats and challenges.

A first characteristic of this type of organization is its managers' focus on perpetual vigilance and preparedness for emergencies, and on controlling the organization's internal operations. Indeed, the constant effort to 'uncover' organizational problems leads to tension and to an excessive sensitivity to any exposure to risk. This fosters a perceived need for constant readiness to counter threats.

A second organizational characteristic is the propensity to centralize power in the hands of top executives and their consultants. Those who feel threatened demand control over their subordinates. As they become distrustful and fearful, the locus of power shifts upward. This dynamic has an impact on junior executives, as key decision-makers tend to direct their distrust externally, and demand that their subordinates share the same sort of distrust. Indeed, those persons who do not distrust others become objects of distrust themselves if an insider suspects them. This atmosphere of distrust quickly leads to insecurity and disenchantment among lower-tier executives.

A third characteristic is extreme conservatism. Top executives cope with the situation, but they do not have a concerted and integrated strategy. Muddling through and fear lead by default to a strategy of minimized risk.

Dynamics at Work

The crucial element at the core of the paranoid organization is the pattern of confused interpersonal relationships that is generated by the core hostility. When it affects the leadership, it is a most destructive attitude. The boss sees his subordinates as malingerers and incompetents, and either tries to exert intensive control and personal supervision over them or, by adopting an overtly aggressive style, destroys their careers. This management pattern generates uncooperative behaviour, and further mistrust, suspicion, and vindictiveness.

The consequences for decision-making are important, because affective criteria replace cognitive criteria as the bases for choice. But the most destructive consequence for the organization is the constant double bind under which subordinates suffer: they are asked to be frank and to express critical thinking, but are chastised as disloyal and treasonous when they do so.

This sort of neurosis and the others mentioned in Table 1 give rise to a number of common problems that Kets de Vries and Miller have identified: improper allocation of authority, inappropriate attitude to risk, inadequate organization structures, poor distribution of information, and deficient calibre of executive talent.[17] The central challenge is to work back from these symptoms to the roots of the problems, in order to generate the requisite organizational therapy and find ways to implement it.

The central point about the neurotic state is that it is both difficult to reconstruct and almost certainly the unintended consequence of bad habits. This point has been forcefully made by Dietrich Dörner, whose analysis of 'the logic of failure' reveals that in a dynamic system crises emerge not from the action of one major culprit, but from the cumulative effect of 'complexity, intransparence, and incomplete or incorrect understanding of the system': small mistakes, bad habits, and certain mechanisms that catalyse that cumulative process.[18]

These mechanisms are studied by political psychology, but since they often work in contrary directions—as is the case, for example, in the bandwagon effect and the underdog effect in elections—they cannot be universally 'applied to predict and control social events but . . . embod[y] a causal chain that is sufficiently general and precise to enable us to locate it in widely different settings.'[19]

ACCESS TO INFORMATION POLICY
AND THE CULTURE OF PARANOIA

Recent debates about the rules regarding citizens' right to access to government information offer an interesting window on the dynamics at play within the federal bureaucracy, and illustrate the culture of paranoia in official Ottawa. Over the past few years, the relationships between the federal government (both its politicians and its bureaucrats) and the Information Commissioner have deteriorated. The implementation, interpretation, and reform of access to information legislation have been bitterly debated by the government and its critics. These developments conform in important ways to what one might expect from a para-noid organization.

The federal Access to Information Act was adopted in 1983 after decades of hes-itation and debate. Since the adoption of an access to information law by the United States in 1966, there had been active proponents of similar measures in Canada. Gerald Baldwin, the Conservative MP, an early crusader for transparency in govern-ment, first introduced a private member's bill on access to information in 1969, and reintroduced it in subsequent sessions until 1974. It was almost to no avail, though the Trudeau government adopted limited official guidelines on information disclo-sure in 1973.

Canadians had to wait for the 1979 minority government of Joe Clark to see the government table an access to information bill in Parliament. The Progressive Conservatives had promised an access to information law during the election cam-paign, and, upon taking power, introduced a bill that would have established a broad right of access to government records, a system that would have allowed some exemptions, and a review process to ensure that these exemptions were appro-priately used. Following the fall of the Clark government, the new Trudeau govern-ment introduced a modified version of the bill, which a few years later became the Access to Information Act.

The Act grants Canadians the right to access government records in any form, with some exceptions. Firstly, some classes of information, such as cabinet records, are excluded from the ambit of the legislation. The Act also allows for some exemp-tions. For example, section 14 provides for the discretionary withholding of docu-ments regarding federal-provincial affairs when disclosure would run counter to public interest.

Importantly, the Act also gives citizens the right to appeal to the Office of the Information Commissioner when they are not satisfied with the responses given to their requests. The Information Commissioner, an independent officer who reports to Parliament, can use extensive investigative powers to ensure that there has been appropriate compliance with the Act. In cases where the use of exemptions is ques-tioned, the Commissioner can review the requested documents to determine whether they were legitimately exempted. However, while he/she can make recom-mendations, the Commissioner does not have the legal authority to force the dis-closure of any records.

Over the years, the access to information legislation has been much criticized. On the one hand, MPs, journalists, Information Commissioners, and citizens have all complained that the government is adopting an excessively broad interpretation of the rules for exemptions, and that delays in responding to access requests are unrea-sonable. On the other hand, the government and public servants have complained that the demands are excessive: that they extend to parts of the government's deci-sion-making process that should remain confidential, and that compliance imposes an excessive burden on resources. Moreover, since for quite a while the Act simply served as a conduit for access to information that would 'make the government squirm',[20] the government and its public servants have become suspicious of requests, and have come to fear the consequences of transparency and information disclosure.

The Symptoms

One of the most serious effects of the ensuing climate of distrust is the change in the way that many civil servants work. In the interviews conducted for this project, several public servants told us that they are increasingly reluctant to write down anything that could be construed as remotely controversial, since it might well make its way to the public domain through the access to information rules. One experienced manager with the Department of Fisheries and Oceans told us that in the units where he worked the unspoken rule had become 'You don't write down anything important about issues that could become controversial.' Another interviewee spoke of someone who confided in her that she now worried about forgetting important things about her work, because she was reluctant to take comprehensive notes during meetings.

This attitude appears to be fairly prevalent within the public service. The Information Commissioner recently noted that the attitude toward information management in the public service has truly become 'Why write it, when you can speak it? Why speak it when you can nod? Why nod, when you can wink?'[21] Many high-level committees in government, his office has found, have ceased the practices of 'creating agendas, keeping minutes and tabling briefing notes and papers to assist discussion'.[22] In the words of Alasdair Roberts, it has come to the point where one may speak of a 'shadow government'.[23] This severe aversion to the risks of information disclosure has also led senior management and central agencies to tighten internal decision-making processes regarding disclosure. One such attempt to strengthen its control from the centre is the recent decision of the Privy Council Office (PCO) to rescind an agreement with the Information Commissioner's Office about the refusal to disclose sensitive material. This protocol, which had been in place since 1984, allowed the Commissioner to ask the Clerk of the Privy Council to provide a certificate attesting that certain records claimed to be cabinet confidences—which were consequently being kept secret despite an access to information request—were indeed confidences. The PCO now claims that the issuance of such certificates is not necessary.

The PMO has also recently decided to contest the right of the Information Commissioner to review its records to determine whether it has grounds for refusing their disclosure. It claims that the PMO falls outside the purview of the access to information law, and it is now engaged in a series of fifteen lawsuits with the Commissioner's Office to deny it the right to examine some requested documents concerning the Prime Minister's agenda.

Clear evidence that the desire of members of the senior bureaucracy to increase their control over internal processes in order to limit their exposure to risk also comes from experiences at Transport Canada. In response to the perceived risk created by compliance with access to information requests, the department has installed a centralized approval system, in order to give senior management more control. According to data from the Information Commissioner's Office, more than 40 per cent of access requests are now personally reviewed and approved by the deputy minister.[24]

The 'grants and contributions scandal' at Human Resources Development Canada has also led the government to tighten central controls over the disclosure of information. In two memoranda issued in February 2000, the Treasury Board Secretariat (TBS) asked departments to file with TBS copies of all access requests for internal audits, copies of all audit reports to be released, copies of all audit reports that have not been requested under the access law, and any departmental plans of action for dealing with the informal or formal (i.e., those in response to access requests) release of audits. The Secretariat eventually withdrew its request for copies of all access requests, but continued to demand all other material.[25]

There is also evidence that middle-ranking civil servants are directly affected by the attitudes communicated from the centre. One experienced civil servant interviewed for this project clearly thought that his work as an internal auditor had become more difficult over recent years as a result of the new climate of distrust and paranoia about the consequences of information disclosure. He complained of receiving frequent phone calls from his minister's office asking for advance notice of what his audit reports would contain, and of being regularly reminded of the potential political consequences of his findings.

A final example of the government's desire to keep tight control over information disclosure issues is its reaction to the amendment of the Access to Information Act adopted in 1998. The amendment, which took the form of a private member's bill, added a subsection to the law that prohibits the destruction, concealment, or falsification of records for the purpose of avoiding disclosure. In 1999, the TBS published a new directive to departments forbidding anybody in a department other than the deputy minister to notify the Information Commissioner's Office about allegations of such violations of the access law. In the face of such allegations the deputy minister was instructed to conduct an internal investigation and, depending on its results, decide whether to notify independent law enforcement agencies.[26]

The Information Commissioner's campaign

As might be expected, the Information Commissioner has responded sharply to the government's poor compliance with the letter and spirit of the access law. However, in doing so he has adopted a confrontational approach that seems to support the view of the government and civil servants that they are the objects of sustained unreasonable attacks, and that they are generally considered 'enemies' by the Commissioner and parts of the citizenry.

The confrontational approach of the Commissioner is well captured in his latest report to Parliament. The first section of the report, entitled 'Access: A Right Under Siege', began with the following statement:

Last year . . . the government was put on notice: There would be a 'zero-toler-
ance' policy for late responses to access requests; a new, pro-openness approach
to the administration of the Access Law would be expected and, most important,
the full weight of the Commissioner's investigative powers would be brought to
bear to achieve these goals.[27]

These are uncharacteristically tough words for an officer of Parliament, whose
authority to 'put the government on notice' seems questionable at best. But the tone
is indicative of the aggressive and uncompromising character of recent exchanges
between the Commissioner's Office and the public service. The Information
Commissioner may have publicly complained that civil servants have been 'circling
the wagons' as a result of his inquiries, but he himself has clearly gone to war.

A Manichean language, pitting citizens against government, outsiders against
insiders, is common in the documents penned by the Information Commissioner's
Office. In his last report, the Commissioner wrote, 'For too long, the whiners and
complainers inside the system have had their causes taken up by TBS; it is the turn
of the citizens on the outside and the access law to have the designated minister
become their champion.'[28]

The practice of issuing annual 'report cards' to rate the performance of departments in responding to access to information requests in a timely fashion is also
illustrative of the hard-nosed, confrontational approach of the Information
Commissioner's Office. Under its grading scheme, any department that fails to
answer 20 per cent or more of the access requests it receives within the statutory
deadline is assigned an 'F'. In the 1998/9 annual report, the six departments
reviewed were ascribed the failing grade. In the 1999/2000 report, five of the eight
departments featured also received an 'F'. While the Commissioner acknowledges
that the PCO deserved praise for moving from an 'F' to an 'A' in just one year (by
cutting the percentage of requests it answered outside the statutory deadline by 90
per cent), he nevertheless severely condemns it for leading an 'attack upon the very
foundation of the Commissioner's role'.[29]

The tone and nature of these exchanges are obviously affecting the attitudes of
some senior civil servants. Frustrated by a perceived lack of co-operation from
senior bureaucrats, the Commissioner has resorted to issuing subpoenas to force
deputy ministers to explain, on the record and under oath, the reasons for departmental delays in answering access to information requests. This aggressive use of
investigative powers is only confirming the senior bureaucrats in their view that the
Commissioner's office is 'out to get them'. In memory of these encounters, one
deputy minister, we were told by one interviewee, has had his subpoena framed and
installed on the wall of his office.

The Review Process and the Bryden Committee
For the past few months, the Information Commissioner has not been alone in his
battle with the Liberal government and the public service on the issue of access to

information. In June of 2001 a group of backbench MPs led by Liberal member John Bryden took the highly unusual step of creating an unofficial ad hoc committee to study the reform of the access to information legislation. The creation of the committee, which is composed of MPs from most parties and is holding meetings within the parliamentary precinct, but which has not been mandated or created by Parliament, came about in direct response to the government's handling of the Act's official review process.

In 2000, the Liberal government finally decided that the time had come to make changes to the access to information rules. The President of the Treasury Board appointed a task force to study options and recommend specific changes; it was composed exclusively of civil servants. While the task force created an advisory committee composed of outsiders, it nevertheless drew heavy criticism for being too close to the government and to the viewpoint of the public service.[30] Some MPs, including John Bryden, were especially displeased by the limited role elected officials, who frequently use the access law, would get to play in the review process. Moreover, the task force, which received submissions and briefs from some stakeholders, was also condemned for not sufficiently consulting Canadians. The government, it was claimed by critics, was making sure that the review process would lead to a curtailment of the scope of the legislation.[31]

The Bryden committee was meant to be a response to this process. The committee would work more independently from the government and consult more widely than the task force. However, as could be expected, the government failed to collaborate with the independent-minded members, and it actively impaired the committee's ability to conduct a full review by forbidding civil servants to appear before it.[32] The government's official position was that civil servants could be held liable for comments that they might make before the committee, since it was not an official creation of Parliament. Moreover, the government House Leader argued, confusion might arise, which would be detrimental to the official review process, if civil servants' testimony were to be taken out of context, especially by the media.[33]

While Bryden repeatedly tried to gain the collaboration of the government House Leader and the Clerk of the Privy Council in this regard, he was thoroughly unsuccessful. Moreover, officials from Crown corporations such as NavCan and Canada Post, after having agreed to appear before the committee, decided to backtrack when they saw the government boycotting the committee's work. As a result, the committee heard from advocacy groups and experts, but was forced to table its report without the benefit of having talked to government officials. According to Bryden, some information experts also decided to abstain from participating in the committee's work for fear of reprisals and the loss of government contracts.[34] As a result, the committee's witness list was reduced by two-thirds, and two Liberal backbenchers decided to leave the committee.[35]

The government's position and tactics only fuelled the critical fire of those of who believed that it simply sought to control the scope of the Act. Mike Gordon, chairman of Open Government Canada, a coalition of groups concerned about access to information, described the government's response in this way:

> This is an extremely hostile act by the cabinet and they are essentially putting the leash back on MPs. The [government] is saying that we, the cabinet, do not want to allow any public review; we want to control the Access Act and our little closed task force will be adequate to that effect.[36]

Some Liberal MPs associated with the committee also used unusually harsh language about the government. For example, Reg Alcock, a Liberal backbencher, said that the Chrétien government had become blinkered and elitist over its years in power, and displayed, like its bureaucrats, a natural desire to conceal information that might be embarrassing.[37] Less surprisingly, the Opposition also used the opportunity to send a similar message. Grant McNally, a Democratic Representative Caucus member, said, 'There's a clear message there that the Prime Minister likes the culture of secrecy around the Access to Information Act. That should be a concern to all Canadians.'[38]

Government and bureaucrats have also used every opportunity to extend their power to take files out of reach of the Access to Information Act. The anti-terrorism bill introduced in Parliament in October 2001 suggests that when the bill becomes law the minister of justice will have the authority to issue a certificate prohibiting the disclosure of information for the purpose of protecting international relations, national defence, or security. This decision will leave the Information Commissioner with no authority to inspect records to determine whether the new power is reasonably applied, the federal court will have no authority to review the decision of the minister, and the citizenry will not even have access to the certificate itself. This has been sharply criticized by the Information Commissioner and other observers as unjustified.[39]

Overall, recent debates about access to information suggest that a vicious dynamic is at play: distrust of government leads citizens to seek disclosure aggressively, and to see in delays and exemptions clear signs of authoritarianism; in turn, citizens, members of parliament, and the Information Commissioner publicly attack the government and the public service for failure to comply with the Act. Mutual distrust and paranoia are natural reactions.

CONSEQUENCES

The recent debates on access to information are symptomatic of a general organizational paranoia that has crystallized in some parts of the public service. One may reasonably ask what consequences can be expected from such a development. There are at least three areas where there is cause for concern. The first has to do with the capacity of the public service to truly become a learning organization and to contribute actively to social learning in Canada. For an organization to learn, information sharing, the tolerance of risks in seeking new ways of doing things, and the ability to openly discuss performance and past failures are essential. To the extent that an organizational culture of paranoia leads to a tightening of central controls over experimentation, as well as restrictions on the disclosure of information about considered options and past failures, organizational learning is stunted.

The second area of concern stems from the fact that in the new knowledge-based society, not only is information a public good, it is also a public resource. Some analysts have even talked about an 'informational commons'.[40] While in earlier periods information might reasonably have been rationed on a need-to-know basis without much consequence, in the new information society access to information is a basic necessity. In this context, a culture of secrecy and adverse attitudes about information disclosure are tantamount to self-imposed restrictions on the availability to citizens of some of our most valuable resources. This can only dramatically weaken the capacity for citizen engagement.

Most importantly, perhaps, the culture of paranoia, fuelled by the adversarial dynamics surrounding access to government information, is threatening the health of our democracy. Democratic governments have to accept some responsibility for ensuring that their citizens have access to the information required for their full, informed participation in governance processes. This is all the more important since the state is the largest repository of information in society, and often the only source of some unique data of great relevance for understanding our contemporary social and natural environment, and therefore needed for meaningful political participation by the citizenry.

However, there is no indication that things are about to change. As the Information Commissioner himself pointed out recently, 'Securing compliance with the Access to Information Act will be a highly adversarial struggle for some time to come.'[41] Moreover, while clearly identifying the adverse reaction to his aggressive campaign against the public service, the Information Commissioner does not appear to realize that his approach may be part of the problem. In his last annual report, the Commissioner notes that a side effect of recent battles about access to information rules has been that many civil servants have stopped adequately documenting their daily work and decisions. But, interestingly enough, this observation leads him to advocate further stringent regulation about information management; he goes so far as to advocate a new law requiring civil servants to make and produce records in the course of their work.[42] The vicious circle is at work.

CONCLUSION

The fast pace of socio-economic change, which creates the need for continual adaptation by public and private actors, the increase in uncertainty, and a more critical citizenry that is distrustful of traditional political institutions and more skilful at opposition and challenge have combined to create major challenges for the effective governance of contemporary societies. In looking for a response to these challenges, national states are tempted to turn inward in an attempt to regain control and shield themselves from opposition and criticism by depriving the citizenry of information about their internal operations and their decision-making processes. Such a course of action has been characteristic of the Canadian response, but, given the phenomenal power of the state apparatus in Canada, governmental reaction has been stronger than elsewhere. It has generated a neurotic regime.

This disquisition is only meant to whet the reader's appetite and to suggest the heuristic power of an approach to organizational effectiveness that is based on neurotic styles. In this short chapter, we have used a simple classification scheme to examine the dynamics that has led to this neurotic state. The neurosis has probably taken different forms in different segments of the Canadian state. But behind these diverse styles, one may detect the dominant neurotic flavour: paranoia.

We have documented the tensions surrounding the interactions between stakeholders with respect to the operations of the Access to Information Act. In this context, maximum openness is a sensible goal, provided that it is offset by operational principles that seek to ensure that the fundamental rights and basic interests of citizens are protected, and that the state preserves the ability to act effectively in the public interest. We have shown how paranoia has prevented the materialization of a workable set of arrangements.

While the Access to Information case is illustrative of this drift toward the neurotic state, it is not an oddity. We intend that the hypothesis we propose, the neurotic state, underpin a program of research that attempts to make sense of a variety of instances that might otherwise be regarded as insignificant anomalies. In other segments of the Canadian state we have found other forms of neurosis, which are not documented here. They have generated the same cumulative causation process that has led to more secretiveness, a decline in public trust, centralization, conservatism, a lack of critical thinking, and the failure of government to operate as a learning organization.

Nothing short of a cultural revolution can reverse the tendencies that underpin these different forms of neurosis. Democratic accountability and social learning will be best served by a widely shared culture of openness and transparency in government and the public service, and by the creation of a reasoned dialogue among public servants, politicians, and citizens. Such a culture of openness and reasoned dialogue will not emerge unless we can restore greater trust in government.

NOTES

1   Stephen L. Carter, *The Dissent of the Governed* (Cambridge: Harvard University Press, 1998), 17.
2   Donald Savoie, *Governing from the Centre* (Toronto: University of Toronto Press, 1999); Jeffrey Simpson, *The Friendly Dictatorship* (Toronto: McClelland & Stewart, 2001).
3   Luc Juillet, Gilles Paquet, and Franscesca Scala, 'Gouvernance collaborative, imputabilités douces et contrats moraux', *Gouvernance* 2, 1–2 (2001): 85–95.

4 Simpson, *The Friendly Dictatorship*, 63.

5 Treasury Board Secretariat, *Framework for Alternative Program Delivery* (Ottawa, 1995); for an analysis of this evolution, see Gilles Paquet, 'Alternative Service Delivery: Transforming the Practices of Governance', in Richard Ford and David R. Zussman, eds, *Alternative Service Delivery: Sharing Governance in Canada* (Toronto: KPMG/IPAC, 1997), 31–58.

6 This is not the place to record a comprehensive list of such abuses. In our interviews, they have been presented as ranging from subtle forms of rebuke of dissent, to chronic discouragement of any sort of critical attitude vis-à-vis any aspect (even the most trivial) of government policies, to explicit exclusion of any dissonant voice in publicly sponsored forums, to the outright banning or sanitizing of public discourse on sensitive issues. Very often, at first, these abuses pertained to minor issues, but they helped establish a climate of suspicion and self-censorship that has become over the years a new mindset that often has persisted after the departure or retirement from an institution or agency of those persons who had been instrumental in injecting it into the agency's daily life.

7 Chantal Millon-Delsol, *L'État subsidiaire* (Paris: Presses Universitaires de France, 1992), 29.

8 Guillermo O'Donnell, 'Horizontal Accountability in New Democracies', *Journal of Democracy* 9, 3 (1998): 112–26.

9 Susan Pharr and Robert D. Putnam, eds, *Disaffected Democracies* (Princeton: Princeton University Press, 2000).

10 R.C. Carty, William Cross, and Lisa Young, *Rebuilding Canadian Party Politics* (Vancouver: UBC Press, 2000).

11 L. Leduc, 'Citizens' Revenge', in Paul Fox and Graham White, eds, *Politics: Canada*, 8th edn (Toronto: McGraw Hill Ryerson, 1995), xxx; Harold D. Clarke et al., *Absent Mandate* (Toronto: Gage, 1995).

12 Neil Nevitte, *Citizens' Values, Information and Democratic Life: Report to the Access to Information Review Task Force* (Ottawa, 2001).

13 Ronald Inglehart, 'Postmodernization Erodes Respect for Authority but Increases Support for Democracy', in Pippa Norris, ed., *Critical Citizens* (Oxford: Oxford University Press, 2000), 236–56.

14 Pharr and Putnam, *Disaffected Democracies*, 22–6.

15 Public discourse has been sanitized, suspicion has come to prevail in a general way, and a garrison mentality has emerged in various segments of the federal public household. This has led to various whimsical knee-jerk reactions when any critical discussion of any initiative of the government has materialized—a decision by the Canadian Centre for Management Development's (CCMD) authorities not to publish a series of studies on the general restructuring of government in the mid-1990s that CCMD had funded and that had been peer-reviewed and assessed as excellent even though not uncritical of government; the explicit control of the pulpit at CCMD by the top authorities and the development of an informal blacklist of persons not to be invited to lecture there; the sanitization of the content of courses to ensure that they are purged of any critical content and focus entirely on machinery of government issues; explicit censorship of *Optimum: The Journal of Public Management* by officials of Consulting and Audit Canada because articles were published suggesting that the ill-fated Universal Classification System

implementation process might be gender-biased, etc.—but, most importantly, it has translated into various forms of self-censorship and subservient behaviours, and a culture of courtesanship and deception in higher places.

16 Manfred F.R. Kets de Vries and Danny Miller, *The Neurotic Organization* (San Francisco: Jossey-Bass Publishers, 1985).

17 Ibid., 171–2.

18 Dietrich Dörner, *The Logic of Failure* (Reading, Mass.: Addison-Wesley, 1997), 37.

19 Jon Elster, *Political Psychology* (Cambridge: Cambridge University Press, 1993), 5. We will not describe all such mechanisms that may be of use in our discussion, but a few of them will illustrate our argument: a tendency to apply an overdose of established measures when under pressure; groupthink; intuitive rather than analytical reaction; a tendency to ascribe responsibility to the other party; symbolic and tactical reforms that inflame the opposition; cognitive dissonance; self-reinforcement.

20 Jeffrey Simpson, *The Friendly Dictatorship*, 57.

21 Ibid., 59.

22 Office of the Information Commissioner of Canada, *Annual Report 1999–2000* (Ottawa, 2000), 22.

23 Alasdair Roberts, 'Protecting Your Right to Information', Talk to the Founding Conference of Open Government Canada, Toronto, 11 Mar. 2000.

24 Office of the Information Commissioner of Canada, *Annual Report 1999–2000*, 15.

25 Ibid., 17.

26 Ibid., 24.

27 Ibid., 9.

28 Ibid., 14.

29 Ibid., 9.

30 See, for example, Alasdair Roberts, 'Reform of the Access to Information Act', Working Paper, Campbell Public Affairs Institute, Syracuse University, August 2001, 1–4; Ian Jack, 'Liberals in "clear conflict", Hearing Told', *The National Post*, 30 Aug. 2001, A6.

31 Ian Clark, 'Ottawa Blocks MPs' Access to Civil Servants: Will Not Let Them Appear Before Openness Committee', *The National Post*, 7 Aug. 2001, A1.

32 Ibid.; Ian Clark, 'Critics Blast Silencing of Civil Servants' Openness Committee: Boudria's Refusal to Allow Testimony Called Undemocratic', *The National Post*, 8 Aug. 2001, A6.

33 Valerie Lawton, 'Bureaucrats Crucial to Hearings: Bryden', *The Hamilton Spectator*, 13 Aug. 2001, A2.

34 Ian Jack, 'Pressure from Top Stalls Hearings: Boudria's Silencing of Civil Servants Sends a Message: 'Fear of political repercussions' Blamed as Witnesses Cancel on Access Committee', *The National Post*, 20 Aug. 2001, A1.

35 Ian Jack, '"Defiant" Backbencher to Go Ahead with Report: MPs to Call for Reform of Access to Information Act', *The National Post*, 28 Aug. 2001, A6.

36 Jen Ross, 'House Leader Slams Access Act Overhaul: Boudria Warns Ad Hoc Group's Review to Be 'incomplete and unsatisfactory', *The Ottawa Citizen*, 11 Aug. 2001, A3.

37 Ian Jack, 'Pressure from Top'.

38 Ian Jack, 'Five of Eight Liberals on Committee Miss Hearing', *The National Post*, 29 Aug. 2001, A6.

39 Aladair Roberts, 'The Department of Secrets: The Chrétien Cabinet is Using Fears of Terrorism to Further Restrict Public Access to Information', *The Ottawa Citizen*, 18 Oct. 2001, A19; J. Aubry, 'Expert Doubts Access Fears', *The Ottawa Citizen*, 17 Nov. 2001, A7.

40 Alasdair Roberts, 'The Informational Commons at Risk', in Daniel Drache, ed., *The Market and the Public Domain: Global Governance and the Asymmetry of Power* (London: Routledge, 2001), 175–201.

41 Office of the Information Commissioner of Canada, *Annual Report 1999–2000*, 29.

42 Ibid., 22.

5

Toward a New Beginning?
The Chrétien Liberals
and Western Canada

ALLAN TUPPER

This chapter examines the relationship between the Liberal government of Prime Minister Jean Chrétien and Canada's four most westerly provinces. Once an area of strength, the Canadian west has been barren electoral terrain for the federal Liberals since the 1960s. For example, in the general elections of 1993, 1997, and 2000, the Liberals won only 56 of the 262 seats in Manitoba, Saskatchewan, Alberta, and British Columbia. Of the 56 Liberal seats, 23 were in Manitoba. Since 1993 the Liberals have won only 25 of the 178 seats available in the prosperous provinces of British Columbia and Alberta. In Alberta, Liberal fortunes have been very bleak. Since 1968, the party has won only 12 of Alberta's 224 seats. The Liberals were shut out in Alberta for the six general elections between 1972 and 1988 inclusive.

Observers of Canadian politics note how the 'first past the post' electoral system shapes the composition of party caucuses and, more generally, voters' images of the parties. Western Liberals often maintain that the electoral system understates their party's western strength. But in the 2000 general election, the Liberals' popular vote dropped in each western province. This result was disappointing, in that Ottawa was running a budgetary surplus, the regional economy was robust, and federal-provincial relations were, by Canadian standards, harmonious.

The modern Canadian west's estrangement from the governing Liberals profoundly shapes Canadian politics, government, and public policy. It raises such fundamental issues as the continuing distinctiveness of western-Canadian political attitudes and practices, competing provincial, regional, and national identities, and the long-term implications of western Canada's modest electoral representation in successive Liberal governments.

This chapter probes the government of Canada's evolving position within western Canada. Its themes—that western regionalism is in decline and that Liberal prospects in western Canada are better than they have been for decades—differ from received regional and national wisdom that asserts growing 'western alienation'. My aims are to provide a different perspective and to stimulate thought about a changing western Canada in the larger context of federal budgeting and priority-setting. The debate about the west's status in Canadian government is unlikely to recede. The Liberals are likely to remain the 'government party' for the foreseeable future.

My ideas are fleshed out by first noting the classic themes of western-Canadian political economy. Second, a thumbnail sketch of modern western Canada is provided. This quick portrait reveals a changing region whose identity is in flux. Third, the chapter examines the Chrétien Liberals' 'western strategy' in the aftermath of the 2000 general election. It notes Ottawa's efforts to build alliances with western-Canadian leaders in major resource and technology sectors, to woo urban voters, and to give evidence that western interests and aspirations matter in Ottawa. A remarkable anchor of this nascent plan is the efforts to build links with the Alberta Conservative government of Premier Ralph Klein. Fourth, I argue that the Liberal strategy has appealing elements that build on changing relationships between western Canadians and their provincial governments and changing western attitudes about the region's place in Canada. Finally, the chapter evaluates the possibility of a new era in centre-periphery relations in Canada.

THE REBELLIOUS CANADIAN WEST

The scholarship and politics of western Canada are dominated by such themes as resentment of external control, unrealized economic potential, and powerful political regionalism. A central proposition is that the Macdonald-Laurier National Policy made the emerging Canadian west subordinate to a dominant central-Canadian metropolis. As D.V. Smiley put it, 'Yet in the acquisition and subsequent development of the vast area between the Great Lakes and the Rockies the national policy was mercantilist, and it is characteristic of this form of political and economic organization that the hinterland develops a pattern of interests contrary to those of the metropolitan centre'.[1] From this basic proposition emerged a litany of western economic grievances, including federal tariff and commercial policy, inequities in transportation policy, and, more recently, the maldistribution of federal expenditures. Until 1930, the prairie provinces resented their subordinate position as provinces that lacked constitutional authority over natural resources and Crown lands. As the west developed, complaints of systematic exploitation were supplemented by the idea that regional interests and ambitions were ignored by the federal government and overwhelmed by national majorities. A more modern complaint is that the country's culture and tastes, by virtue of the mass media's concentration in Toronto, are poured into a central-Canadian mould.

Economic subordination and hinterland status led to a political regionalism rooted in a sense of newness, ethnic distinctiveness, and geographic separateness from the metropolitan centre. The theme of newness reflects the rapid emergence of provincial communities in sparsely populated frontiers, especially in Alberta and Saskatchewan. Immigrants from Ontario, the Maritimes, the United States, Britain, and various European countries filled these provinces. Ethnic diversity is a revered idea in western regionalism. The Prairies' self-image is that of an ethnically diverse region that differs markedly from central Canada. Vast distances between major urban centres and pronounced geographic differences reinforce and shape economic tensions, the sense of newness, and ethnic diversity.

The image of an aggrieved western Canada has seldom been challenged, although a few scholars have chipped away at icons. Ken Norrie, an economic historian, argues that western economic grievances are principally quarrels with a market economy rather than with a discriminatory national government.[2] Western laments are typical of sparsely populated hinterlands that are powerless against broader economic forces. By the same token, Doug Owram notes that the National Policy was not obviously conceived as an instrument of regional economic subordination: '[T]he idea of an agricultural region fed by a metropolitan one did not, in itself, imply an inferior standard of living or economic influence for the former.'[3] David E. Smith has also observed that the Liberal party and the government of Canada were, until the 1950s, generally capable of accommodating western ambitions.[4]

Western-Canadian politics are notoriously unorthodox. They have spawned new political parties, notably the Progressives and, recently, Reform/Canadian Alliance. Provincial governments noteworthy for periods of political radicalism are also evident. Alberta Social Credit, the CCF in Saskatchewan, the Alberta Conservatives since 1971, and British Columbia's centre-right coalitions illustrate the region's restlessness. Since the Second World War, many western voters have supported parties other than the Liberals. John Diefenbaker made the once-despised Conservatives the choice of many western voters. Reform/Canadian Alliance achieved regional prominence after displacing the Conservatives in 1993.

W.L. Morton notes three distinct periods of western-Canadian political protest.[5] The first period is one of 'colonial protest', during which western Canada sought autonomy and provincial status. The second period, 'agrarian protest', is characterized by powerful farmers' parties, whose members wanted to gain political power in order to alter their inferior status. Finally, Morton discerns 'utopian politics' in the 1930s, when new options such as Social Credit and CCF were embraced by westerners as harbingers of new social orders. More recently, Tom Flanagan has characterized western-Canadian politics as dominated by a resentment of external power blocs, by discontent with parliamentary government, and by a 'thirst for fundamental solutions'.[6] Flanagan's third theme echoes Morton's notion of utopian politics. It refers to a desire for radical reform that will move the country, not merely western Canada, to a higher plane. Flanagan sees Social Credit, farmers' parties, CCF, and Reform as western-Canadian political movements inspired by a desire for fundamental change.

Since the 1970s, aggressive provincial governments have shaped western Canada. Led by Alberta, such governments have diversified their economies, demanded more responsive federal policies, and called for greater provincial powers. They have also worked to create and solidify provincial identities and to build deeper links between citizens and provincial governments. Such efforts were easily undertaken, given a succession of national Liberal governments without substantial western representation. Under these circumstances, the provincial governments have been convincing in their claim to represent the provincial will.

THE CHANGING CANADIAN WEST

In his analysis of modern western Canada, Gerald Friesen portrays a complex area whose self-image is increasingly at variance with its economic and sociological realities. At the same time, the rest of Canada also clings to outdated ideas about the west. As he puts it, 'Canadians' understanding of one another is becoming out of date. The country is changing rapidly, right along with the rest of the world. In this increasingly global age, the inherited explanations of each region are lapsing into meaninglessness. They must be refurbished or replaced.'[7]

What has changed about modern western Canada? Is it still a hinterland? Friesen sees a single Canadian west that has replaced longstanding divisions between prairie and coastal wests. Common interests in resource industries, economic diversification, growing Aboriginal communities, and urbanization characterize the new west. In Friesen's view, economic diversification has profoundly altered western Canadians' mindsets. The regional economy is relatively stable and western Canadians are losing their fear of economic stagnation. More orthodox politics may follow.

Friesen's analysis is contentious. For example, it might well be argued that the dichotomy between the prairies and coastal British Columbia has been replaced by a cleavage between Alberta and British Columbia on the one hand, and Saskatchewan and Manitoba on the other. In this view, Vancouver and Calgary are metropolitan centres in their own right. A single west is hard to discern when the two most westerly provinces overpower the other two in terms of population and economic prowess. Moreover, the west lacks an overarching sense of regional identity or common purpose. It may share an interest in economic diversification, but it lacks a clear sense of itself. In fact, Friesen's evidence about a single west is more suggestive of the region's integration into a pan-North American culture of suburban living, mall shopping, and mass entertainment.

That said, Friesen does highlight some essential characteristics of modern western Canada, notably a more diversified economy and more complex regional politics. Western Canadians are hard-pressed to see themselves as an exploited people with external foes when their own conflicts of interest are increasingly visible. Moreover, urbanization is shaping western-Canadian attitudes and politics. It is not crude determinism to note that urban life shapes a common political agenda. Transportation, civic infrastructure, economic development, and crime concern Torontonians, Haligonians, Calgarians, and Winnipeggers. The new Canadian west is strikingly urban.

On the other hand, Friesen also sees western Canada as comprising four distinct provincial societies. In other words, western Canada is confronting its own internal heterogeneity. As a region, it has long-standing urban/rural tensions, social class cleavages, and deep ethnic, religious, and linguistic divisions. Since the 1970s, economic change has made diversity more evident. The prairies no longer share the unity that flowed from wheat, its once undisputed staple. Oil, natural gas, and many 'upstream linkages' now drive Alberta. Calgary has a burgeoning research sector and substantial capacity in financial services, particularly as they relate to oil and gas. British Columbia is heavily dependent on its forestry and extractive resource industries, while wheat, agricultural research, and other products power Saskatchewan's economy. Manitoba has the most diversified industrial structure of the four western provinces. More subjectively, each province has its own style, its own set of dominant political issues, and its own urban/rural issues. Western-Canadian provinces now differ substantially with respect to per capita income: Alberta soars, once-dominant British Columbia lags, and Saskatchewan and Manitoba struggle in relative decline.

In its efforts to rebuild a western base, the government of Canada confronts new challenges. The region now partakes in a common North American life style. Its agrarian heritage and agrarian political economy have been replaced by specialized provincial economies, with links to other parts of Canada, North America, and the world. Western Canada's sense of separateness and distinctiveness has been reduced, although certainly not eliminated, by urbanization. Westerners are more aware of the differences within their region than heretofore.

In some fundamental ways, western Canada is now more like other parts of Canada. At the same time, it is more complex, more internally diverse, and, as a result, more difficult to predict.

THE CHRÉTIEN LIBERALS AND WESTERN CANADA

The causes and consequences of the federal Liberals' unpopularity in western Canada are seldom analysed. The personal attitudes and public policy priorities of Pierre Trudeau assume pride of place in some westerners' demonology. Trudeau was allegedly indifferent to the region, perplexed by its politics, and unwilling to take western discontent seriously. Even charitable westerners assumed that his priorities were the resolution of Quebec's place in Canada, the promotion of pan-Canadian identities, and the assertion of a greater role for the government of Canada. The National Energy Program's efforts to shift oil and gas production from Alberta to the Canada Lands controlled by the government of Canada and to increase federal power led to intense federal-provincial conflict. It caused Liberals to be seen as hostile to Alberta's dominant industry.

To see Trudeau as personally responsible for the Liberal demise is woefully simplistic. The decline in Liberal power in the west began in the 1950s and clearly preceded his arrival in national politics. Those who vilify Trudeau should remind themselves of the hostile western-Canadian reaction to the alleged sins of the Mulroney Conservatives. Many westerners felt that the 1984 Mulroney government, with western Canadians in important cabinet positions, would lead to a happy new era. Federal-provincial conflict continued, and westerners expressed shock over the CF-18 maintenance contract that awarded lucrative work to a Montreal firm even though a Winnipeg firm was apparently better qualified. Reform quickly captured this resentment and by 1993 had displaced the Conservatives as western Canada's dominant federal party.

David E. Smith has carefully analysed the Liberals' western demise.[8] He sees it as reflecting major changes in Canada's political economy, governmental institutions, and political party system. A key factor was the Liberal party's increasingly technocratic approach to agricultural policy, which, in contrast to its traditional stance, saw agriculture as an economic sector, not a way of life. Moreover, the elevated role of executive federalism in Canadian government both caused and reflected the growing separation between federal and provincial politics in Canada. The federal-provincial divide hamstrung the Liberals. As well, the Liberals, after devastating losses to the Diefenbaker Conservatives, concluded that party organization was outdated and to blame for defeat. The practice of appointing dominant provincial ministers as the centrepieces of Canadian Liberalism beyond Ottawa was discredited, and the party moved to radical ideas about participatory democracy. Westerners found themselves left out of Ontario-dominated Liberal party councils, whose message was modern, technocratic, and alien. Over decades, such forces conspired to place the Liberals in dire straits in western Canada.

The disappointing 2000 general election results in western Canada have made the region a high Liberal priority. Certainly the Liberal government's policy priorities since 1993 had accorded no special status to western-Canadian issues, nor had it shown any special concern for them. Government messages, which have been well probed in previous issues of this volume, have expressed a pan-Canadian theme. Ottawa has stressed the need to embrace a 'new economy', the need to make federalism work better, and the imperatives of fiscal prudence, tax reform, and debt repayment. Neither the west nor any other region has been deemed a focus for concerted policy attention. Moreover, the Liberals fared poorly in western Canada in

1993 and 1997. After those general elections, they were not moved to action. Events may have been propelled by the unexpected crisis of the Canadian Alliance, or by a deeper conviction that sooner or later Alberta and British Columbia, given their size and economic strength, would have to be embraced.

Since the general election of 2000, the Liberal government has paid considerable attention to western Canada, although it remains to be seen whether the momentum will be maintained. Four themes clearly dominate the government's response to date: a quest for enhanced visibility for the government of Canada, an emphasis on western resource industries as sources of national economic prowess, recognition of the region's 'new economy', and the deliberate construction of an alliance with the government of Alberta.

1. The Quest for Federal Visibility

Since the 2000 general election, Ottawa has increased its visibility and presence in western Canada. Mr Chrétien has made major addresses about energy in Calgary, the federal government was visible at the World Track and Field Championships in Edmonton, and the Minister of Intergovernmental Affairs, Stephane Dion, and other senior ministers have frequently visited western Canada.[9] Seasoned Liberals with strong western-Canadian connections have been given roles in the Prime Minister's Office as evidence of the government's interest and commitment.[10] The Liberal caucus met in major western cities during the summer of 2001.

Critics are quick to dismiss such greater Liberal visibility as an opportunistic substitute for serious policy reform. But heightened Liberal interest in western Canada both reflects and responds to the region's claim that it is ignored and misunderstood. Indeed, an inescapable theme in western-Canadian political debate is a desire to be properly recognized and acknowledged, to be consulted, and to be taken seriously in Ottawa. As David E. Smith put it, western Canadians have long sought a vote of confidence from federal Liberal governments.[11]

2. Western Canadian Resource Industries

The Liberals are aggressively supporting western-Canadian resource industries as contributors to national prosperity. Mr Chrétien has stressed federal interest in accelerated development of western hydrocarbons and greater continental integration of energy markets, especially given the Bush administration's controversial concerns about supply shortages. In expressing strong support for western-Canadian resource industries, the Prime Minister has emphasized the need to develop resources through 'an unswerving commitment to competitive markets and fair regulation'.[12] Such remarks highlight Liberal desires to distance the party from the National Energy Program, which remains a notorious symbol of Liberal hostility and heavy-handed statism. The Prime Minister and other federal spokespersons have stressed that they see strong western resource industries as sources of national economic prosperity. As Mr Chrétien said in April 2001, 'A strong energy sector is not only a pillar of the Alberta economy, it is absolutely fundamental to Canadian prosperity. In 2000, the industry made $21 billion of capital investments. That number could reach $25 billion this year. The industry is also responsible for almost 50 per cent of Canada's trade surplus.'[13]

Common interests between federal and provincial governments, between Canada and the United States, and between resource producers and resource consumers are easier to assert than to demonstrate. Nevertheless, Liberals are trying to overcome lingering perceptions of hostility and indifference among western voters

3. The New Economy and Western Canada

A third dimension of Liberal strategy is recognition of the region's 'new economy', a dimension that itself has two strands. The first strand acknowledges the economic importance of new western-Canadian firms and industries. Federal spokespersons highlight western-Canadian capacity in fuel cells, notably in British Columbia, in advanced medical and health sciences, especially in Alberta, and in bioscience research in Saskatchewan. Ottawa has stressed its major policy initiatives in advanced university research. The Canada Foundation for Innovation, the fledgling program of research chairs and new initiatives in health sciences, is promoted as evidence of federal concern for economic diversification and advanced research in western Canada. Such federal initiatives appeal to western Canada's emerging self-image as a source, not merely of raw products, but also of economic innovation. Ottawa's stress on the commercialization of university research builds common interests between university researchers, western business, and the government of Canada.

The 'knowledge economy' theme also identifies western Canada's primary resource sectors as important components of the new economy. In line with Ottawa's stress on industrial innovation, western resource industries are seen as research-based knowledge industries. Bruce Doern and Monica Gattinger note Natural Resources Canada's efforts to advance this view in federal policy-making and, especially under Ralph Goodale's leadership, to break down stereotypes of an Ontario-centred knowledge economy flanked by a prosperous western hinterland and a lagging Atlantic Canada: 'At the insistence of both its current minister and key parts of its resource industries, NRCan has sought to reassert that the natural resource industries have always been innovative (and global) and have always been underpinned by long-standing first-class earth sciences capacity.'[14] Such federal actions and words appeal to western-Canadian elites, who see themselves as important participants in a dynamic economy.

In 1975, D.V. Smiley noted the government of Canada's growing interest in a new 'national policy' based on scientific innovation, federally sponsored alliances between universities and businesses, advanced research capacity, and economic diversification.[15] Such federal initiatives are now evident in Ottawa's emphasis on innovation, support for advanced research, and the modernization of Canadian industry. Smiley predicted that Ottawa's new 'national policy' would founder on the shoals of western-Canadian resentment and the opposition of determined westerners, who favoured strong provincial governments in order to achieve economic diversification. But since Smiley wrote, major changes have occurred in Canadian federalism and the role of government. Early in the 2000s, western-Canadian governments and public opinion appear more receptive to federal overtures.

4. Alberta: A New Federal Ally?

A final thread is an emphasis on effective intergovernmental relations and the designation of Alberta, and its present premier, Ralph Klein, as the province and regional leader whose co-operation is essential to a Liberal renaissance. A stress on intergovernmental co-operation is the legacy of the failed constitutional negotiations of the 1980s and 1990s and public pressures for efficient government in the face of growing public sector deficits and debts. It also reflects Mr Chrétien's conviction that fundamental institutional reform and constitutional change are no longer priorities for most Canadians. In western Canada, good federal-provincial relations help erase the legacy of past struggles over energy and the constitution.

The embrace of Alberta and Ralph Klein, its unconventional leader, indicates an interesting federal assessment of changes within western Canada. Klein is perceived as a 'new wave' western premier, who harbours little memory of past injustice and who seldom invokes the rhetoric and symbols of western alienation. He is open-minded about Quebec, unimpressed by radical decentralization of federalism, and willing to co-operate with the government of Canada where necessary. His successful deficit/debt elimination strategy and tax reductions have made him popular in Alberta and well known beyond it. Mr Chrétien and senior federal ministers routinely stress Alberta's newfound role as a voice of moderation in intergovernmental circles and a province whose support is apparently essential to the success of Ottawa's intergovernmental initiatives. Ottawa's present course—to employ surpluses to reduce taxes, pay debt, and increase expenditures in priority areas—is comparable to Alberta's 'post deficit' strategy, although Alberta has stressed debt payment more heavily than Ottawa has.

An instructive episode occurred in January 2001, when *The National Post* gave prominent coverage to an 'Alberta Agenda', prepared by well-known Albertans, including Stephen Harper, a former Reform MP, and Tom Flanagan, a University of Calgary professor and former research director for Reform.[16] Prepared as an 'open letter' to Mr Klein, the Alberta Agenda complained about the Chrétien government's manifest hostility to Alberta. The authors called for a 'firewall' around Alberta that was to be achieved by a vigorous prosecution of provincial powers, including Alberta's withdrawal from the Canada Pension Plan, provincial collection of all major tax revenues, the creation of a provincial police force, and enhanced provincial control over health care. The 'Alberta Agenda', having eliminated a hostile national majority from Alberta public affairs, would usher in a benign era of provincial democracy in Alberta.

In a carefully crafted response, presented as a provincial general election loomed,

Klein dismissed the Alberta Agenda.[17] He acknowledged friction with Ottawa over health care policy and expressed a general interest in an Alberta pension plan. But on the general matter, he sounded more like a Liberal prime minister than a western-Canadian premier. He described 'firewall' ideas as 'defeatism', and saw intergovernmental friction as a fact of life in a sprawling country. Klein implied that public opinion in Alberta was indifferent to radical provincialism and that Albertans wanted to contribute to a strong Canada. In addition, the 'Alberta Agenda', despite the province's reputed provincialism, was received with deafening silence by Alberta elites, a fact that was undoubtedly noted in Ottawa.

REGIONALISM IN RETREAT?

Given the tepid response to the 'Alberta Agenda', a careful reconsideration of cherished stereotypes about western-Canadian politics is necessary. My claim is that western-Canadian alienation is noticeably weakening. The region is developing a new image of itself and redefining its relationships with other parts of Canada. A decline of regionalism will not necessarily lead to a resurgence of Liberal electoral fortunes, but it certainly raises the possibility, in a way that was unthinkable even a decade ago.

Many forces underpin this major change. First, western Canada is slowly shedding its sense of weakness in national politics. Westerners, who campaigned for free trade in the 1980s, see free trade with the United States and now NAFTA as protection against a predatory national government and a guarantee that such regionally hostile initiatives as the National Energy Program will be much harder to mount. Regional self-confidence is buoyed by growing awareness that Alberta exercised a major influence on the constitutional settlement of 1982 and that some western concerns about federal policy, admittedly through the efforts of Reform under Preston Manning, have been heard in Ottawa. The continuing prosperity of the two most westerly provinces and their growing urban populations belie hinterland status.

At the same time, and with the exception, until 2001, of British Columbia, the governments of Canada and the western provinces share broadly similar interests in the reduction of governments' direct role in the economy, the restraint of public expenditures, and the reform of health care. Governments have generally abandoned, at least for the medium term, the interventionist strategies that led to intense conflict in the 1970s and early 1980s. To the degree that 'post deficit' politics are occurring, governments tend to share common interests in the disposition of modest budget surpluses.

Alienation is also diminishing as a result of changes in the roles of western provincial governments. Many observers assert that the role and influence of the government of Canada, and national governments in general, are being reduced, as a result of major economic changes. An apparent shift in power toward supranational bodies on the one hand and regional governments and large cities on the other is allegedly squeezing national governments. Tom Courchene cites such 'glocalization' as a potent force.[18] Powerful pressures unleashed by the dramatic events of 11 September 2001 demand reconsideration of this claim, but it was suspect on other grounds already.

The role of western-Canadian provincial governments as defenders of provincial interests in the face of an unrepresentative Liberal federal government is commonly noted. However, provincial governments' capacity to perform this role has been altered by their own actions in the 1990s. A principal outlet for western grievance and resentment is thus lost. Since the mid-1980s, provincial governments have reduced their economic roles, restructured their operations to achieve greater efficiency, and reduced public expenditures. They have tried to reduce citizens' expectations about governments' capacity to shape society and to deliver social services.

Such changes in provincial governments' roles have major consequences for provincialism and regionalism. First, provincial politics are more competitive and conflictual. They increasingly focus on competing ideas about the role of government. Scant attention is now paid to once-dominant questions about relations with other parts of the country, constitutional change, and federal-provincial relations. Intraprovincial debates about the role of government heighten provincial citizens' awareness of intraprovincial differences. In turn, citizens become resistant to claims about an overarching provincial interest.

Western-Canadian governments have changed their roles in the eyes of their citizens. To many, they are now cautious vehicles of fiscal restraint rather than visionary province-builders. Western provincial governments have distanced themselves from citizens by restructuring government. In each province, privatization, contracting out, and various forms of 'alternative service delivery' have the common consequence of removing citizens from direct contact with their provincial governments. This trend is increased by widespread use of new administrative agencies, notably semi-autonomous health care authorities, whose role it is to 'buffer' provincial governments from direct responsibility for restructuring. For these reasons, the provincial governments confront complex provincial agendas of their own making, and citizens who now see provincial governments in less positive ways than heretofore. As western-Canadian provincial governments have been downsized, they have become neutered as voices of regional and provincial complaint.

Other signs reveal weakening western alienation. For many younger westerners, western Canada is as Friesen depicts it: urban, relatively affluent, and distant from the legacy of depression, agrarian populism, and the National Energy Program. The notion of 'hinterland' is unlikely to engage a young Calgarian who sees a booming city populated by headquarters of major Canadian corporations, or an ambitious Vancouverite whose city is now a major North American centre. The regional economy now provides unprecedented, although not unlimited, employment opportunities in 'new economy' industries. Younger western Canadians live in large cities with diverse populations whose very heterogeneity mocks notions of common provincial and regional identities. Moreover, political identities are complex: region, province, and nation vie for status with gender, social class, race, and ethnicity.

Younger western Canadians, although less provincialist in orientation than their elders, are not necessarily imbued with a strong sense of Canadianism or an emotional attachment to the government of Canada. Yet they are obvious targets for future Liberal appeals and probably the basis for the party's longer-term hopes for a renaissance.

Finally, as Roger Gibbins argues, increased use of advanced communications technology, such as the Internet, will shape Canadians' identities and probably erode the political significance of territory.[19] Within federal states, provincial identities will probably decline in importance. Except in the minds of some Quebeckers, Canada as a nation will continue to play a role and will remain a prime source of citizen identification. Local governments will also become more prominent, as citizens develop new needs and interests related to their immediate environs. In Gibbins's words, 'Conventional regional conflict can be expected to diminish as provincial governments become less important in the general scheme of things. . . . This should be particularly so outside of Quebec, where federal values have more instrumental roots and also shallower roots than they do there. Regional conflict should also subside as ICTs [Internet Communications Technology] erode the very notions of centre and periphery; if there is no centre to the digital world, can there still be regions and regional marginalization? Can there be a periphery without a centre?'[20]

In summary, the government of Canada has paid considerable attention to western-Canadian voters and interests over the last year. Ottawa's words and deeds are driven by several themes. Senior ministers and the Prime Minister are spending much more time in the region than heretofore. Western-Canadian resource industries, especially oil and natural gas, are being defined as essential to the national interest. The federal government is stressing its commitment to western economic diversification through the development of advanced research capacity and 'new economy' industries. These efforts are buttressed by an emphasis on traditional western industries, especially mining, oil and natural gas, and agriculture, as 'knowledge industries' that use advanced technologies, manifest remarkable productivity gains, and employ skilled personnel. Finally, Ottawa has tried to build good relations with western-Canadian provincial governments. Alberta is receiving special attention as a regional leader.

My argument is that such initiatives may bear fruit. Regionalism is weakening as westerners shed a sense of political weakness, as their provincial governments redefine their roles, and as a new generation of western voters, unimpressed by traditional regional rhetoric, assumes prominence.

CONCLUSIONS: WILL IT WORK?

Can the Liberal party renew itself as an electoral force in western Canada? Is western regionalism declining? My tentative answer to the first question is 'possibly' and to the second question 'probably'. Critical readers will argue that westerners remain skeptical of Liberal motives, resistant to Liberal appeals, and committed to strong provincial governments. For such critics, the west remains foreign territory for federal Liberals, a unique region that marches to a different ideological drummer. They note the angry western response to Mr Chrétien's casual remark in Edmonton in August 2001 that Alberta's resource wealth might have to be shared. In other words, my argument badly underestimates the continuing vigour of western alienation.

A different criticism is that the Liberals are embracing a narrow strand of western-Canadian opinion. Their emphasis on advanced technology, new economy brainpower, and partnerships between universities and industry appeals to a small, urban elite. It will not root the party or the government of Canada in a strong, long-term relationship with western voters. In the same vein, the Liberals' embryonic western strategy fails to embrace the region's uniqueness. It merely forces western interests into a precast pan-Canadian template. Moreover, good relationships with western-Canadian provincial governments may have been given exaggerated importance by Liberal planners. For example, Liberal electoral fortunes have generally declined in western Canada in the 1993–2000 period despite good intergovernmental relations.

At a deeper level, critics may claim that I wrongly equate the decline of regionalism with the embrace of a deeper nationalism. The error is important, because diminished regionalism may simply be seen as evidence of Canada's fragmentation. Regionalism declines as Canadians, in the face of continental economic integration, share fewer bonds and fewer common interests. With respect to this basic point, I do not think that attenuated western regionalism necessarily implies strengthened nationalism. No reading of Canadian history points to such a conclusion, although forecasts of imminent national demise in the face of continental integration are themselves well rehearsed. Second, my analysis simply highlights trends in western Canada that receive scant attention. Government decisions, actions, and rhetoric reflect and shape citizens' attitudes, policy options, and partisanship. Western Canada may remain indifferent to the Liberals. But this state of affairs is not preordained. Politics, policy, and events all matter. The west's status remains an open question, as it has been for decades.

NOTES

1 D.V. Smiley, 'Canada and the Quest for a National Policy', *Canadian Journal of Political Science* 8, 1 (Mar. 1975): 43.
2 Kenneth H. Norrie, 'Some Comments on Prairie Economic Alienation', *Canadian Public Policy* 2, 2 (Spring 1976): 211–24.
3 Doug Owram, 'Reluctant Hinterland', in R.S. Blair and J.T. McLeod, eds, *The Canadian Political Tradition: Basic Readings* (Toronto: Nelson Canada, 1989), 105–6.
4 David E. Smith, *The Regional Decline of a National Party: Liberals on the Prairies* (Toronto: University of Toronto Press, 1981).
5 W.L. Morton, 'The Bias of Prairie Politics,' in A.B. McKillop, ed., *Contexts of*

Canada's Past: Selected Essays of W.L. Morton (Toronto: Macmillan, 1980), 149–60.

6 Tom Flanagan, 'From Riel to Reform: Understanding Western Canada', Working paper for the Fourth Annual Seagram Lecture, 26 Oct. 1999.

7 Gerald Friesen, *The West: Regional Ambitions, National Debates, Global Age* (Toronto: Penguin/McGill, 1999), 183.

8 Smith, *Regional Decline*.

9 Dion has spoken widely in western Canada in the last year. For an example of his common themes see Hon. Stephane Dion, 'The West and the Liberal Government at the Beginning of the New Mandate: The Need to Work Better Together', Saskatchewan Institute of Public Policy, University of Regina, 6 Mar. 2001.

10 Robert Fife, 'Two Advisors to Provide Western Perspective', *The Globe and Mail* [Toronto], 30 Mar. 2001, 6.

11 Smith, *Regional Decline*.

12 Rt. Hon. Jean Chrétien, 'Notes for an Address by Prime Minister Jean Chrétien', Canadian Association of Petroleum Producers, Calgary, 6 Apr. 2001.

13 Ibid., 5.

14 G. Bruce Doern and Monica Gattinger, 'New Economy/Old Economy? Transforming Natural Resources Canada', in Leslie A. Pal, ed., *How Ottawa Spends 2001–2002: Power in Transition* (Don Mills, Ontario: Oxford University Press, 2001), 230.

15 Smiley, 'Canada and the Quest for a National Policy'.

16 'Open Letter to Ralph Klein', *The National Post*, 26 Jan. 2001, A14.

17 'Klein Responds to "firewall" Proposal', *The Edmonton Journal*, 9 Feb. 2001, A17.

18 Thomas J. Courchene, 'A Mission Statement for Canada,' *Policy Options* 21, 6 (July-Aug. 2000): 6–14.

19 Roger Gibbins, 'Federalism in a Digital World', *Canadian Journal of Political Science* 33, 4 (Dec. 2000): 667–90.

20 Ibid., 685.

6

Being Poor in
the Best of Times

JAMES R. RICE

The purpose of this chapter is to examine the federal government's failure to reduce child poverty in Canada significantly during the emergence of what many have called the 'new economy'. It examines how ideas regarding the new economy have influenced and shaped government decision-making. It also examines the effects of the government's changes to social policies upon the well-being of low-income families, in the past and the future. The chapter ends with the argument that the new economy, like the old economy, continues to divide workers into those who are educated and skilled and can benefit from economic change and those who, because of a lack of education or skills, are left out of the benefits of economic growth.

Many social policy analysts and community watchers were buoyed in 1989 when the House of Commons promised to end child poverty by the year 2000.[1] They looked forward to the day when there would be no Canadian children living in poverty. This idea was not new. Papers and reports had been written about poverty before 'the promise', and continued to be written afterwards, and there were a number of proposals in circulation. In 1987 the National Council of Welfare prepared *Welfare in Canada: The Tangled Safety Net*, an important report that made 55 recommendations, dealing with simplification, accessibility, equity, adequacy, and due process in the social welfare system. A few years later the Economic Council of Canada wrote a crucial document entitled *The New Face of Poverty*, which set out a number of recommendations, including the creation of an integrated continuum of support for working aged people, and for families with children. At about the same time the Standing Committee on Health and Welfare, Social Affairs, Seniors, and the Status of Women presented its report, *Towards 2000: Eliminating Child Poverty*, which called for new ways to measure poverty, particularly an 'Indicator of Income Inadequacy'. Other reports asked for help with child care and dental care, and increased support for social assistance programs, and there was some talk that the federal government would step in and introduce a guaranteed annual income.

While the reduction of child poverty stood as an enormous challenge to any government, realization of the goal seemed on the edge of possibility. The federal government had been working hard to eliminate poverty among the elderly, and by 1989 there were fewer Canadians over the age of 65 living in poverty than ever before. The federal government had also focussed on families, with the result that family poverty had been reduced from a high of 18.2 per cent in 1983 to a low of 13.6 per cent in 1989. Policy analysts thought that similar efforts could lead to a deep reduction in child poverty.

When the House of Commons made 'the promise' in 1989, 1,016,000 children— 15.3 per cent of all children—were living in poverty. These children came from 506,000 families, of which 264,000 had two parents and 242,000 had only one.[2] Many of these parents were working full-time and many others part-time, but neither group earned enough to get out of poverty. The task of reducing child poverty was daunting. The government would need to find a way of committing approximately $11.2 billion annually if it wanted to eliminate poverty among children.[3]

The National Council of Welfare was very concerned about the fate of children; it knew that the elimination of child poverty would be an enormous challenge for the federal and provincial governments.[4] The 1990 federal budget was already calling for a freeze on social assistance support for three of Canada's wealthiest provinces, and the Council knew that this did not bode well for children. It pleaded with the government that this was 'no time for cuts', and that any cuts would directly affect poor children.

The government appears not to have heeded these calls. Although 'the promise' was made, things did not turn out well for poor children, and the federal government did not eliminate child poverty. In fact, in six out of the eight years in which the United Nations voted Canada 'the best place in the world to live', child poverty grew. Child poverty rates grew from 15.3 per cent in 1989 to 19.2 per cent in 1998, reaching a high of 21.6 per cent in 1996. These years can be thought of as bitter years for children. While the rest of the economy was growing, and people in the general population were prospering, children from poor families were living increasingly desperate lives.

THE NEW ECONOMY

Many business editorials and newspaper articles describe the emergence of a 'new economy', in which there will be endless economic flexibility and high rates of growth. As Charles Handy points out, for a while 'the relentless growth of the American economy, boosted by developments in the new technologies, seemed to support [these] ideas.'[5] The idea of a new economy is based in part on the argument that all industrial countries are converging toward new, common ways of organizing economic activities. The argument posits that convergence is the consequence of an increasing flow of information and knowledge across national boundaries, and a move by governments to deregulate their economies in an effort to gain economic advantages. Suzanne Berger claims that the ideas about convergence reflect new 'conceptions of the importance of international competition, globalization, regional integration, and the deregulation of domestic economies on national structures.'[6]

Peter Drucker contends that knowledge is the foundation of the new economy, and that there is a major shift from muscle power to brainpower in the production of goods and services.[7] He is not alone. An Organization for Economic Co-operation and Development (OECD) report asserts that 'knowledge is now recognised as the driver of productivity and economic growth. As a result, there is a new focus on the role of information, technology and learning in economic performance.'[8] The new focus on communications technology has changed the way companies do business. All forms of transactions, from ordering products to managing the production process, getting loans, or talking with the stockbroker, have changed since the introduction of personal computers, modems, fax machines, cellular phones, and the Internet. All of these forms of communication use digital processing, which makes information flow more easily. Businesses related to information technology have grown in the past 10 years to become one of the major contributors to economic growth. Stephen B. Shepard claims that information technology boosts productivity, reduces costs, cuts inventories, and facilitates electronic commerce. It is, in short, a transcendent technology, like railroads in the nineteenth century and automobiles in the twentieth.[9]

Whether the claims of a new economy are premature or not, a set of ideas related to the new economic thinking is dramatically reshaping the way governments make social policies. These ideas reflect a growing belief in market forces, freer trade, and widespread deregulation. At the heart of the belief in a new economy is the idea that governments must get out of the way so that businesses can create economic growth. Governments must open boundaries, remove trade barriers, and free markets from constraints. It is argued that this new economy will produce economic growth, and thereby improve the lives of everyone. The first order of business in the new economy is to eliminate deficits by cutting government expenditures. The second order of business is to level the playing field by removing policy hindrances to economic growth. Before Gordon Thiessen, Governor of the Bank of Canada, left office he was claiming that 'in order to have a vibrant, dynamic economy, we count on the business community to take the initiatives that increase productivity and competitiveness so that we, as a nation, can benefit from rapidly changing technologies and increasingly open global markets.'[10] An old but powerful idea has regained acceptance in most political arenas: economic growth will solve most social problems—or, as John F. Kennedy said, 'a rising tide lifts all boats.'

THE EFFECT OF A CHANGING ECONOMY ON POOR CANADIANS

The critical question for this chapter is 'What impact is the new economy having on the well-being of the poor?' To answer this question, we must select measures of poverty that reflect the changes brought about by the economy, and the government's response to them. Canadians have traditionally thought in terms of two types of poverty: *relative* poverty, defined on the basis of a comparison between one person's means and those of other people, and *absolute* poverty, defined in terms of a person's ability to obtain the necessities of life. *Relative* poverty is measured using a poverty line, and *absolute* poverty is measured by determining the cost of a list of necessities and designating as 'poor' those who cannot afford the items on the list. The differences between these two ways of measuring poverty have led to the development of at least eight different measures for determining who lives in poverty. Some of these measures rely on the creation of a line, and others focus on a basket of goods. The National Council of Welfare argues that all poverty lines are imperfect; that is, they misrepresent the number of people living in poverty. This is because they are relative (they change with changing expectations), they are arbitrary (they are dependent upon a cultural interpretation), and they measure the incomes of groups rather than individuals.[11]

Table 6.1 lists the eight poverty lines that have been proposed for a family of four living in a large city. The most generous is that of the Community Social Planning Council of Toronto, which in 1998 was set at $41,098. The Sarlo (Fraser Institute) line, in contrast, was set at $20,014 for the same year. One might wonder how two poverty lines could be so different. The first line is based on a basket of the consumer goods that one would need in order to live according to an inclusive standard of living, and the other is based on the minimum it takes to stay alive.

The National Council of Welfare has traditionally used the Statistics Canada Low Income Cut-offs (LICOs) as its measure of poverty. The LICO is a complicated determination of the percentage of income spent on the necessities of life. Although Statistics Canada has always stressed that as far as it is concerned the LICOs are not poverty lines, they are the most widely used measure of poverty in Canada. Thirty-five individual lines have been drawn, reflecting living conditions for different-sized families living in different-sized communities. In 1998 they ranged from approximately $11,000 for one person living in a rural setting to over $40,000 for a seven-person family living in a city of over 500,000 people.[12] The National Council of Welfare uses these lines to produce an annual poverty rate, a measure of how many Canadians live in poverty.

Table 6.1

**Poverty Lines and Basic Social Assistance for a Family of Four
Living in a Large City, 1998**

Community Social Planning Council of Toronto	$41,098
Pre-Tax Low-Income Cut-off	$32,706
Low-Income Cut-off Post-Tax	$28,862
Pre-tax Low-Income Measure	$27,172
Market Basket Measures (Toronto)	$25,835
Montreal Diet Dispensary	$23,454
Low-Income Measure Post-Tax	$22,814
Sarlo (Fraser Institute)	$20,014

Source: National Council of Welfare, *Poverty Profile 1998* (Minister
of Public Works and Government Services Canada, Autumn 2000), 6.

Figure 6.1 presents the poverty rates for all persons, for working-age persons, and
for children under 18. In all three cases poverty rose between 1989 and 1997, with
some small bumps in between, and fell in 1998 (these are the most recent figures
available). The figures are substantially higher than those in the period immediately
before the 1990–1 recession. The National Council of Welfare reports that over 4.9
million people in Canada, including 1.3 million children, were living in poverty in
1998.[13]

Poverty lines are an important measure of the general impact of the economy and
of government decisions upon low-income families. However, they hide the depth

Figure 6.1
Poverty 1989–1998

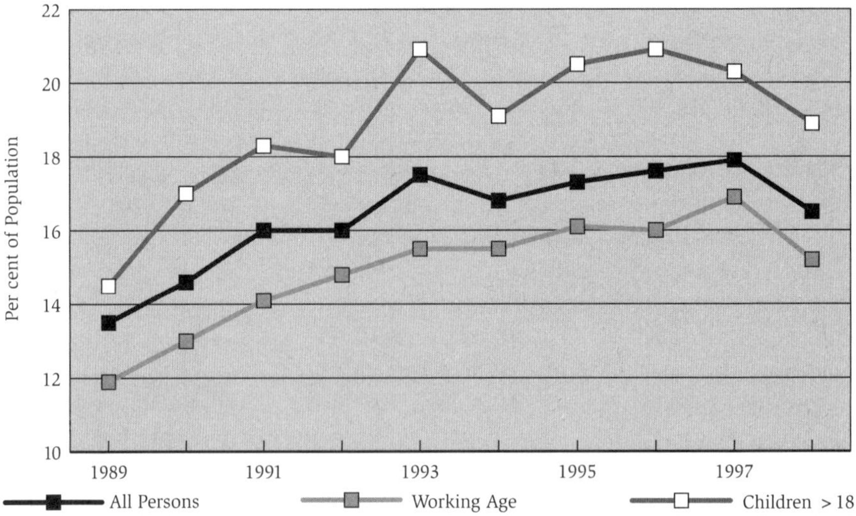

Source: National Council of Welfare (2000), 10–12.

of poverty, and do not measure the impact of the economy upon those living below the poverty line. One way to investigate the effect of economic changes on those living below the poverty line is to examine how deeply people are in poverty. The distance between the official poverty line and the actual income of the poor is called the poverty gap. If the poverty line is $24,000 and a household earns $18,000, then the poverty gap is $6,000. In order to close the poverty gap this household would need $6,000 in additional income each year. The total poverty gap in Canada is the amount of income that it would take to bring all Canadians up to the poverty line.

Figure 6.2 demonstrates that the amount of money it would take to close the poverty gap has increased, rather than decreased, over the last eight years. In 1989 the government would have had to spend $11.2 billion to close the gap. By 1998 the amount was $18 billion. Different types of households have different poverty gaps. In 1998 the average gap for unattached women under 65 was $7,038, for men in the same category it was $6,803, for couples (under 65) with children (under 18) it was $8,772, and for single-parent mothers (under 65) with children (under 18) it was $9,230. The larger the gap the worse the overall state of poverty. Figure 6.2 shows that the gap widened by 62 per cent between 1989 and 1998. The combination of a rising poverty rate (Figure 6.1) and a widening gap (Figure 6.2) demonstrates the magnitude of the problem of poverty for low-income families.

While these poverty measures provide important insights into the number of people living below the poverty line, and the depth of their poverty, they treat everyone the same. When policy-makers find that the economic or policy changes they

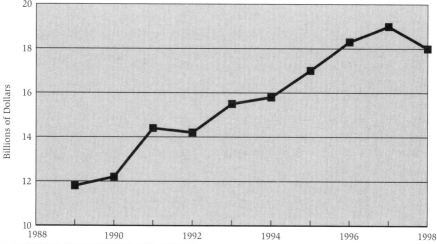

Figure 6.2
Total Poverty Gap
(Constant 1998 Dollars)

Source: National Council of Welfare (2000), 60.

introduce for the benefit of the worst off in our communities seem to have little or no effect on the poverty rate as recorded in poverty tables, they become frustrated.[14] In response to this problem, Lars Osberg advocates the use of the Shorrocks, Sen, and Thon (SST) poverty measure, which combines the poverty rate with the depth of poverty to create a poverty intensity index.[15] Because this index registers income changes below the poverty line, it makes it possible to see the impact of the new economy or of government policy changes on low-income families. Figure 6.3 shows how poverty intensity declined between 1980 and 1990, with one large bump in 1982–4, and then began to rise again in the 1990s.

Figure 6.3 shows that during one of the best economic periods in recent times, a time when the government was able to pay down its deficits and amass surpluses, poverty intensity was rising, not falling. Either the economic benefits of the new economy were not getting to those living below the poverty line, and/or the government was cutting support for poor Canadians more quickly than they could earn income. We will return to these issues in the next section, but first we will look at two other indexes, to see the effect of this rise in poverty intensity.

Osberg and Sharpe have combined a wide array of information to produce two very interesting indexes.[16] The first is an index of economic security. To calculate this index Osberg and Sharpe used data regarding a number of risks: unemployment, illness, single-parent poverty, and old age. They then calculated the prevalence of the combined risk by determining the proportion of the population it affects. Figure 6.4, which shows the index of economic security from 1988 until

Figure 6.3
Poverty Intensity Index

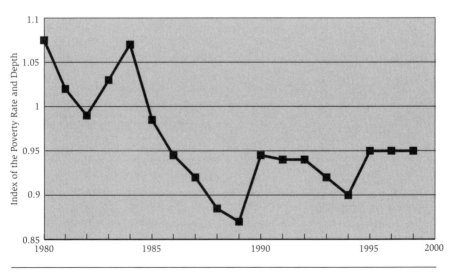

Source: Lars Osberg and Andrew Sharpe, *An Index of Economic Well-Being for Canada* (Human Resources Canada, 1998), 29.

Figure 6.4
Index of Economic Security

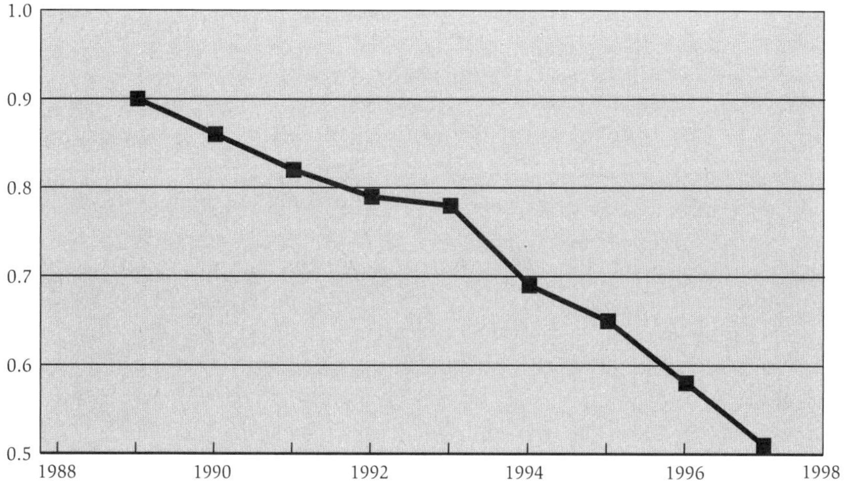

Source: Lars Osberg and Andrew Sharpe, *An Index of Economic Well-Being for Canada* (Human Resources Canada, 1998), 45.

1998, indicates that there has been a decline in economic security. According to Osberg and Sharpe, the decline in security is the result of changes in unemployment levels, reductions in unemployment insurance coverage, an increase in the number of single parents (who have high poverty rates), and increased private expenditures on health.[17]

In their second index, which measures Canada's overall economic well-being, Osberg and Sharpe have combined information about consumption flows, wealth stocks, equality, and economic security.[18] This index is sensitive to the weight given each cluster of variables, and therefore caution must be taken in interpreting the results. The two authors compare their well-being index with the GDP per capita from 1971 to 1997. The measures move together in the early 1970s and then begin to diverge. As the GDP goes up, the well-being index starts to go down, and remains low for the entire period of prosperity. Osberg and Sharpe point out that 'over the 1971–97 period, real GDP was up 58.3 per cent, nearly 10 times the rate of advance of the index of economic well-being (6.7 per cent).'[19] This was important news for policy-makers: a growing GDP does not foretell economic well-being for the entire community. The divide between the two factors appears to be growing.

We can divide the four components of the well-being index into two sub-groups: consumption flows and wealth stocks, which reflect elements such as level of personal income, investments, and commodity prices, are related to upper- and middle-income groups, whereas equality and security relate more to low-income groups. Measures of consumption flows and wealth stocks levels are above the well-being index, and measures of equality and security are below.[20] The overall well-

being index is pulled down by the steep decline in economic security, which is influenced by the rising number of financially vulnerable households, such as single-parent families. The well-being index would be much more consistent with United
Nations statements about Canada's being the best country in the world if low-income
Canadians had not suffered such a loss in economic security over the past 10 years.

Figure 6.5 presents the overall well-being index for the period from 1980 to 1997.
It shows a general increase in well-being during the 1980s and a decline that starts
in 1989 and lasts until 1997. The indexes of economic security and overall well-
being draw our attention to the failure of the economy to maintain the economic
position of low-income families relative to that of other income earners. The two
indexes support the broader evidence provided by the Statistics Canada LICOs, but
they allow us to see the changes taking place below the poverty lines. The decline
in the equality and economic security measures reflects how long it takes for
changes in the economy to affect the incomes of people living in poverty, and the
impact changes to welfare programs are having on the poor as governments shift
responsibility for economic well-being away from themselves and onto families and
individuals. Ross, Scott, and Smith point out that 'a heavier reliance on the marketplace begs the question of whether the private sector can actually deliver enough
jobs, with adequate earnings, to provide security for all families.'[21] The evidence in
the three indexes suggests that the market and government programs have failed to
provide low-income Canadians with economic security, especially during the 1990s.
Ross, Scott, and Smith provide similar evidence when they show that the number
of working-poor families increased by 65.9 per cent between 1981 and 1997, and the

Figure 6.5
Total Economic Well-Being Index

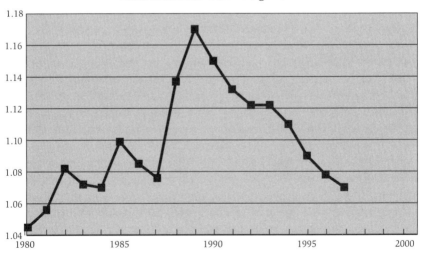

Source: Lars Osberg and Andrew Sharpe, *An Index of Economic Well-Being for
Canada* (Human Resources Canada, 1998), 45.

number of working-poor unattached individuals by 152.5 per cent, with the greatest increase occurring between 1989 and 1997.[22]

Ross, Scott, and Smith were also interested in the market activities of poor Canadians. They examined whether the labour market is providing adequate employment at decent wages. Their study shows that if only market income is considered, 21.9 per cent of Canadian working-age families were poor in 1997, compared with 15.9 per cent who remained poor after government transfers were factored in. There has been a growth in market poverty over the past twenty years. The Ross, Scott, and Smith study shows that 14.7 per cent of working-age families faced market poverty in 1981, 16.5 per cent in 1989, and 21.9 per cent in 1997.[23] The rise in market poverty has been the result of low wages, periods of unemployment, and periods of time when people were not in the labour force. The authors point out that as it currently functions, the marketplace 'is unlikely to be able to generate enough well-paying jobs for those who are poor. . . . It seems unlikely that families that are now market poor will have any real hope of becoming more self-reliant in the future.'[24] Real GDP grew by an average of 3.5 per cent during the 1990s, while at the same time poverty rates rose by an average of .08 per cent.[25]

A combination of the evidence provided by Osberg and Sharpe with that provided by Ross, Scott, and Smith indicates that low-income families have faced two problems. The market has not provided them with good jobs or good wages, and the government has reduced their benefits, so that their income has fallen during the rising tide of the new economy.

GOVERNMENT INTENTIONS AND RESPONSES
TO A CHANGING ECONOMY

The Liberal government has failed to respond adequately to the needs of poor Canadians. It has cut financial support to the provinces, ravaged the unemployment insurance program, and spent a large portion of the surplus on deficit reduction and tax cuts. Only one new program, the Canada Child Tax Credit, has been introduced, and it has begun very modestly. To understand the factors that affected this failure we need to turn to the Liberal government's record.

Since 1993, in preparation for the last three elections, the Liberals have written three Red Books. While these books are full of hyperbole and promises, they provide us with an insight into how the Liberals were thinking about solving social problems. In the first Red Book, entitled *Creating Opportunity: The Liberal Plan for Canada*, the party set out a basic plan for improving the lives of Canadians. It describes programs for education, training, apprenticeship, literacy, health care, safe communities, and equity in employment.[26] This first Red Book points out that to rely on market forces alone to solve social problems or create economic growth is folly. It claims that 'jobs, health care, safe and sustainable environment, equality for women and men, care for the very young and the aged, and the alleviation of poverty are societal issues that cannot be addressed simply by having each individual aggressively pursue immediate, narrow self-interest.'[27] This reflects the older welfare position, that the role of the government is to provide programs that protect the most vulnerable in society. The Liberals had criticized the Conservatives for their tendency to 'focus obsessively on one problem, such as the deficit or inflation, without understanding or caring about the consequences of their policies in other areas such as lost jobs, increased poverty, and dependence on social assistance.'[28] This Red Book held out considerable hope for low-income families—they would not be lost in the restructuring of the economy.

The second Red Book, *Securing Our Future Together*, shifted the government's focus. Now more voice was given to the role of economic growth in solving social problems. The Liberals now claimed that the government had to intervene less in the economy and instead offer people tools and opportunities so that they can take advantage of the 'new economy'.[29] While in this second Red Book the Liberals recognized that people living in poverty face greater challenges than others and that low-income families with children have sacrificed more than almost anyone else, they did not offer any new programs. Rather they relied on the collaborative activities of the provinces to develop programs to meet the needs of children living in poverty.

The third Red Book was a slim 30-page volume called *Opportunity for All: The Liberal Plan for the Future of Canada*. In this book the Liberals spent most of their time talking about the good things they had done in the previous seven years. They pointed out that they had 'eliminated the deficit, put a lid on inflation, lowered interest rates, and balanced the budget.'[30] They also made debt repayments that totalled $28.7 billion and hoped to introduce the biggest tax cuts in Canadian history. The Liberal agenda was to 'vault Canada into the new economy', by investing in education, jobs training, and scientific research and development.

The three Red Books began with a commitment to deal with social problems and shifted to concerns about deficits, and economic growth. These policy shifts were reflected in the policy choices that the Liberals made while governing the country. Their actions spoke louder than the promises made in the Red Books. Over the last nine years, the Liberal government has dramatically altered the basic foundation of welfare in Canada. Even though the provinces have fundamental responsibility for social welfare (as mandated by the British North America Act), the federal government has historically come to share these responsibilities in two ways. First, it has taken major responsibility for social security programs such as Employment Insurance, Old Age Security, the Guaranteed Income Supplement and Spouses' Allowance, the Canada Pension Plan, child benefits, and veterans' benefits. Second, it has provided the provinces with financial assistance to help them pay for health care, post-secondary education, social assistance, and social services. It did this in the beginning with categorical programs aimed at particular groups, such as the disabled or the elderly, and later with the development of the Canada Assistance Plan (CAP) and the Established Programs Financing Act (EPF).

These two programs, CAP and EPF, were the bedrock of the welfare system in

Canada. Developed in 1966, the CAP provided essential financial support to the provinces to help them develop their social assistance programs. The federal government paid half the costs of welfare payments and social services. The provinces took advantage of the CAP program to develop a wide range of programs designed to meet the needs of the poor. One of the fundamental goals of these new social programs was the 'elimination of poverty'.[31] This financial arrangement allowed poorer provinces to develop the same welfare systems as richer provinces, and both poor and rich were able to develop systems they could not have afforded without federal support. The net result was that the government of Canada, by sharing the financial burden with the provinces, built a welfare state that protected most citizens from the risks inherent in a modern industrial society. In return for its financial support, the federal government asked that all Canadians, when in need, be given access to an adequate amount of welfare, that they not be required to work for welfare, that they be given the right to appeal a welfare decision, and that they not be required to meet residency requirements in order to be eligible.

The federal government introduced EPF in 1977, eleven years after CAP. This legislation provided cash and tax transfers to the provinces and territories in support of health care and post-secondary education. The federal government linked its support for EPF to the rate of growth in the economy, but set a revenue floor as a way of protecting the provinces from dramatic declines in GDP. Gradually, limits were put on the growth of EPF, and finally, in 1990, a freeze was placed on the payments. Although there was constant tension between federal and provincial governments regarding the financing of EPF, the program had grown considerably in the 18 years since its inception. By 1995, its last year, the provinces and territories received $22.0 billion total EPF entitlements (cash and tax), 71.2 per cent of which was intended for health care and the rest for post-secondary education.

In 1994 the Liberal government set out to redesign the social welfare system. It asked Lloyd Axworthy, Minister of Human Resources, to lead a review process. The government set two goals for this review: first, to remove disincentives to work while securing income support for people who have lost their means of earning income, a goal that reflects the growing shift to a 'new economy' ideology, and second, to reduce child poverty—a renewed commitment to an old pledge. While the review started optimistically, by 1995 it was in a state of collapse. Axworthy could not get agreement from the Bloc Québécois or the Reform party regarding the recommendations, and the Liberal government itself was no longer interested in the findings in the review.

Instead, the Liberals made a number of critical decisions. Led by the Department of Finance, they set a path that not only did not redesign the social welfare system, but fundamentally altered the ability of the federal government to meet the needs of low-income Canadians. On 1 April 1996 they scrapped the CAP and the EPF. They replaced these acts with the Canada Health and Social Transfer (CHST), which combined all expenditures into one block fund and removed the four conditions contained in the earlier legislation. At the same time they reduced the size of their support by some $6 billion over a three-year period.[32]

The impact of these changes reverberated throughout all of the provinces' social assistance programs. Some provinces cut benefits, others raised eligibility requirements, and still others shifted from social assistance to workfare. The cuts made by the government of Ontario represent the worst of these actions. When the Conservative government came to power in 1995 it cut welfare support by 21.6 per cent, driving children in families receiving welfare support into deeper poverty. As Krissa Fay points out, as of 2001, families receiving social assistance in Ontario have 27.5 per cent less income, given the rise in the cost of living, than they did before the 1995 cuts.[33]

The shift from CAP and EPF to the CHST means that provinces no longer need to provide support to people 'in need' regardless of their category. They can now decide to provide benefits to some groups and not to others. Many provinces have tightened their regulations regarding single unemployed males. Some have tightened their regulations regarding mothers with children. Others have introduced the requirement that applicants meet mandatory work conditions before receiving social assistance. Some provinces have changed the way that 18-year-old adults are treated, making them dependent upon their parents for support. Provinces want to introduce literacy tests and drug tests or other more draconian requirements. All of these changes have come about as a result of the federal government's dropping its requirement that provinces support people 'in need'.

Many of these changes are based on the new economy idea that poor people must be forced to become more self-sufficient. This notion reinforces the idea that poor people do not seek self-sufficiency themselves and must be driven to it by such measures as workfare. It reminds us of the old ideas expressed at the time of the reform of the English Poor Law: '[H]unger will tame the fiercest animals, it will teach decency and civility, obedience and subjection, to the most perverse. In general it is only hunger which can spur and goad them (the poor) on to labor.'[34] Government programs are designed to make people less 'dependent' upon existing programs. What this really means is that the government is prepared to increase the risks that poor people face. The result has not been a freeing of these people from the disincentives of social assistance, but rather a deeper fall into poverty. The market does not seem to have met the needs of these people who need to be 'spurred and goaded' into labour.

Similarly, the training and work readiness programs have not helped remove people from poverty. It is true that everyone can benefit from learning better job search skills or how to write a better resumé. And it is equally true that skills development and academic upgrading will help people find jobs. But those who have received these new techniques and skills have not been helped to rise out of poverty. At the time of the greatest economic growth in many years we see an increase in poverty, not a decrease. Osberg provides evidence that indicates 'the absolutely low probability of moving from low wage employment to income self-sufficiency.

Overwhelmingly, low wage jobs are "dead end" jobs.'[35] He goes on to say that 'given the empirical evidence on the importance of the demand side, it may be considered odd that Canadian social policy reforms have concentrated on improving worker motivation and training—i.e. on increasing the effective supply of labour.'[36]

On the darker side, the Caledon Institute has pointed out many times that the failure of governments to index or partially index social assistance has represented a cut in welfare benefits each year by the cost of inflation. Ken Battle coined the term 'social policy by stealth' to describe this type of policy change.[37] It allows government to erode or diminish programs quietly and steadily without having to tell the public that it is doing so. In a recent report Battle shows that in many jurisdictions, between 1989 and 1999, these cuts reduced support for single employable people, single disabled people, and single parents.[38]

While the federal government was reconstructing the foundations of the welfare system it was also making deep cuts in the unemployment insurance program. In 1990 the Conservative government increased the qualification period from 10–14 weeks to 10–20 weeks, depending upon the jobless rate in the local region. In 1994 the Liberals increased the qualification period to 12 weeks for those living in areas with 13 per cent unemployment. This meant that the federal government shifted the base rate by requiring two additional weeks of work before a person could receive unemployment insurance. In 1996 the government started calling the program Employment Insurance. It wanted Canadians to know that it was encouraging people to be part of the new economy. One of the changes that was introduced at the time of the change of name was a shift in the means of calculating the qualification period from number of weeks worked to number of hours worked. People applying for maternity or sickness benefits needed to work 700 hours before they could receive these benefits. Another regulation made it mandatory that new workers (the most vulnerable) and people returning to the work force (except parents) work 910 hours before they can apply for benefits.

While the government was increasing the number of days a person had to work before becoming eligible for benefits it was also diminishing the value of Unemployment Insurance. In 1993 it reduced benefits from 60 per cent of insurable earnings to 57 per cent, and in 1994 to 55 per cent. In 1996 it introduced a new rule, which imposed a penalty of one per cent for every 20 weeks in which benefits are received, to be applied to the next period of unemployment. This meant that unemployment income could be reduced to 50 per cent of eligible earnings.

Ken Battle points out that in preparation for the 2000 election the Liberals rescinded the intensity rule and removed some of the clawback mechanisms that were intended to reduce the benefits the government paid to recipients. He claims that 'the percentage of the unemployed receiving regular unemployment benefits fell from 83 per cent in 1989 to just 45 per cent in 1998.'[39] One of the compounding problems is that qualifications for the other work-related benefits, such as maternity leave and parental leave, are related to qualifications for unemployment insurance. Workers who do not meet the basic qualifying conditions for the latter are not eligible for the other programs. This means that part-time workers and the long-term unemployed will find it more difficult than before to obtain benefits.

The Liberal government's decision to fundamentally alter the welfare system was based on the 'new economy' assumption that economic growth would raise people out of poverty. But this did not turn out to be the case. While the income of some poor families did rise, that of others fell. While the wealthy were experiencing substantial increases in their wages, the poor saw only marginal increases. Life was getting better for those who had money and worse for those who did not. And the government was standing aside and allowing the burdens of economic growth to fall on the shoulders of the least advantaged. Lars Osberg believes that increases in poverty in Canada over the last few years can be directly attributed to policy changes in unemployment insurance and social assistance.[40]

When we pull back the analytical camera and look at the last 10 years we see a particularly bleak picture for children. Only one government initiative was directed toward children during this period. The National Child Benefit (NCB) Supplement was introduced in 1998. The federal government redesigned the Child Tax Benefit/Working Income Supplement into the Canada Child Tax Benefit (CCTB) as its share in the building of the new system. The CCTB has two components: the NCB Supplement, which is available to families with incomes of $32,000 or less, and the CCTB base benefit for low- and middle-income families. As of July 2001, the maximum annual benefit will be $2,372 for the first child, $2,172 for the second child, and $2,175 for each additional child. The CCTB base benefit will increase in July of every year to keep pace with inflation. Provinces are allowed to adjust their social assistance programs by the amount provided by NCB and use these savings for other programs and services for low-income families with children.

The CCTB is the first policy initiative in a number of years. The program is designed to reduce child poverty in Canada, to promote labour market attachment, and to reduce overlap and duplication between federal and provincial programs. More than 80 per cent of Canadian families, which includes 5.9 million children, will receive the Canada Child Tax Benefit in 2001/2.[41] Policy analysts hold out considerable hope that the federal government will use this program to deal with poverty in general, and child poverty in particular. The big question is whether the government will stay the course or, finding the new economy too stressful, feel the need to cut back again on programs for low-income families.

CONCLUSION

The basic argument in this chapter is that the development of a 'new economy' has divided the world into two groups: those with high skill levels, who benefit from economic growth, and those with low skills, who do not.[42] We have a growing economy, for which workers are required who possess certain skills, including higher levels of competence in mathematics, communications, interpersonal relations, and the use of computers. These requirements exclude from the economy a growing number of people, who have poor mathematics and literacy skills and lack a high school diploma. Projects intended to make people more 'employable', such as job-finding clubs, resumé-writing classes, and work readiness support programs, have only limited success. While they may encourage people to find a job, the job does not provide enough income to raise these workers out of poverty.

It appears that the new economy is having the same effect as the old economy had: it is polarizing work and income into good jobs and bad jobs. This means that Canada will continue to develop two economies, one for the haves and one for the have-nots. Opportunities will flow to those who have the advantage of educated or well-off parents, while those with poor parents will have limited opportunities. In the old economy of white- and blue-collar jobs, there was room for upward social mobility. A young man or woman could start in the shop or secretarial pool and work his or her way up to the front office. But in the new economy, with its rising educational barriers, there is little or no opportunity for an uneducated person to move from a low-paying service-sector job to a job that pays well.

Although the new economy represents only a small part of the business world, its ideas have come to have a powerful effect on the well-being of Canadians. The shift to a knowledge-based economy has meant that people living in poverty need financial assistance in order to meet the demands of daily living. They need protection from adjustments in the labour market, including effective unemployment insurance and social assistance programs. Put very simply, the working poor need adequate income support.

The federal government must find ways to overcome the deeply divisive nature of the new economy. The challenge is to find ways to engage those who have low skills in meaningful re-education. It appears that the only way to encourage people to go back to school is to pay them to do so, by means of some form of refundable tax credit. Learners could use retraining expenses, including living expenses, as deductions against their taxes, perhaps as a refundable tax credit.

The federal government has a powerful instrument in the Employment Insurance program. It can use this program to forge a new sense of social security in the country. The government can rethink the limits it has put on the system and reopen eligibility and benefit criteria. The evidence that markets fail to lift people out of poverty means that the government must provide programs that protect people from falling into poverty.

The federal government also has a powerful instrument in the Canada Child Tax Credit. It can use this instrument to deal with child poverty. By increasing benefits and shifting more of these benefits to people outside of the workforce, the federal government can take a large step toward meeting the needs of poor families, particularly poor children.

At the broader level, the federal government needs to provide leadership regarding the basic well-being of Canadians. We have seen that well-being, as expressed in the Osberg/Sharpe well-being index, has declined. The federal government has the power to authorize payments directly to individual Canadians. It needs to use

this power to expand national programs that provide unifying social security benefits for all Canadians.

We are facing unstable economic times. The first wave of the new economy has
come and gone. Technology, computers, the Internet, and mass communications are
not going to end the cycle of economic ups and downs. Markets have not produced
the security many hoped they would. World events have clearly indicated that governments need to return to the active social role they have played in the past, pro-
ducing public policies that will help to create and maintain communities that are
safe and secure—not only physically, but economically as well.

NOTES

1 In November 1989 the House of Commons unanimously passed an all-party
   resolution to eliminate child poverty by the year 2000. This motion came
   about in response to Ed Broadbent's retirement speech in Parliament. The key
   message was that governments could work together to eliminate child
   poverty. This set a benchmark against which to measure government commitment and activity.
2 National Council of Welfare Reports, *Child Poverty Profile, 1998* (Summer
   2001).
3 For a full discussion of the poverty gap from 1980 to 1990 see National
   Council of Welfare, *Poverty Profile, 1980–1990* (Minister of Supply and
   Services Canada, 1992).
4 National Council of Welfare, *The Canada Assistance Plan: No Time for Cuts*
   (Minister of Supply and Services Canada, 1991).
5 Charles Handy, *The Elephant and the Flea: Looking Backwards to the Future*
   (London: Random House, 2001), 89.
6 Suzanne Berger, Introduction, *National Diversity and Global Capitalism*,
   Suzanne Berger and Ronald Dore, eds (Ithaca: Cornell University Press,
   1996), 5.
7 Peter Drucker, 'The Age of Social Transformation', *The Atlantic Monthly* 274,
   5 (Nov. 1994): 53–80.
8 Organization for Economic Co-operation and Development, *The Knowledge
   Based Economy* (Paris, 1996), i.
9 Stephen B. Shepard, 'The New Economy: What It Really Means', *Business
   Week*, 17 Nov. 1997. See Web site: www.businessweek.com/1997/46/
   b3553084.htm
10 Gordon Thiessen, Governor of the Bank of Canada, Remarks to the Kelowna
   Chamber of Commerce, Kelowna, British Columbia, 15 June 2000.
11 National Council of Welfare, *A New Poverty Line: Yes, No or Maybe?* (Minister
   of Public Works and Government Services Canada, Winter 1998–99), 1.
12 National Council of Welfare, *Poverty Profile 1998*, 5.
13 Ibid., 9.
14 J. Myles and G. Picot, 'Poverty Indices and Policy Analysis', *Review of Income
   and Wealth* (forthcoming).
15 Lars Osberg, 'International Trends in Poverty: How Rates Mislead and
   Intensity Matters', Paper presented to the Canadian Economic Association
   Annual Meetings, McGill University, Montreal, June 2000.

16 Lars Osberg and Andrew Sharpe, *An Index of Economic Well-Being for Canada* (Human Resources Canada, 1998).

17 Ibid., 41.

18 Ibid., 45.

19 Ibid., 49.

20 See Chart 3 in Osberg and Sharpe, *An Index of Economic Well-Being*, for a detailed description.

21 David Ross, Katherine J. Scott, and Peter J. Smith, *The Canadian Fact Book on Poverty* (Ottawa: Canadian Council on Social Development, 2000), 83.

22 Ross, Scott, and Smith define the working poor as non-elderly households whose adult members have, between them, at least 49 weeks of either full-time or part-time work during the year. For a further discussion of the working poor see Ross, Scott, and Smith, *Canadian Fact Book*, chap. 5.

23 Ibid., 90.

24 Ibid., 101.

25 Statistics Canada, *Canadian Social Trends, Social Indicators* (Autumn 2001), 23.

26 Liberal Party of Canada, *Creating Opportunity: The Liberal Plan for Canada* (Ottawa, 1993), 11.

27 Ibid., 12.

28 Ibid., 10.

29 Liberal Party of Canada, *Securing Our Future Together: Preparing Canada for the 21st Century* (Ottawa, 1997), 13.

30 Liberal Party of Canada, *Opportunity for All: The Liberal Plan for the Future of Canada* (Ottawa, 2000), 3.

31 Canada, Parliament, House of Commons, *Debates*, 5 Apr. 1965, 5.

32 For a fuller discussion of the implications of these changes see James J. Rice and Michael J. Prince, *Changing Politics of Canadian Social Policy* (Toronto: University of Toronto Press, 2000), or James J. Rice, 'Redesigning Welfare: The Abandonment of a National Commitment', *How Ottawa Spends 1995–96: Mid-Life Crises*, ed. Susan Phillips (Ottawa: Carleton University Press, 1995), 185–207.

33 Krissa Fay, 'Ottawa Has Broken Promise to End Child Poverty', *The Hamilton Spectator*, 20 Apr. 2001, A11.

34 Quoted in Karl Polanyi, *The Great Transformation: The Political and Economic Origins of Our Time* (Boston: Beacon Press, 1957), 113.

35 Lars Osberg, 'Social Policy and the Demand Side', a paper prepared for presentation at the Canadian Employment Research Forum workshop on Income Support, Ottawa, Ontario, September 1993, 32.

36 Ibid., abstract.

37 Ken Battle, 'The Politics of Stealth: Child Benefits Under the Tories', in Susan Phillips, ed., *How Ottawa Spends 1993-94: A More Democratic Canada . . .?* (Ottawa: Carleton University Press, 1993), 417–48.

38 Battle, Ken, *Relentless Incrementalism: Deconstructing and Reconstructing Canadian Income Security Policy* (Caledon Institute of Social Policy, 2001), 27.

39 Ibid., 23.

40 Lars Osberg, *Poverty in Canada and the USA: Measurement, Trends and Implications*, Presidential Address to the Canadian Economic Association, 3 June 2000.

41 News release on the Social Union Web site: http://socialunion.gc.ca/news/ 071701_e.htm

42 For a full discussion of these ideas see Robert Haveman and Johnathan Schwabish, *Macroeconomic Performance and the Poverty Rate: A Return to Normalcy*, University of Wisconsin Institute for Research on Poverty, Discussion Paper DP 1187-99. Evidence from the 1980s has led policy analysts to believe that economic growth does not necessarily benefit low-income families. This evidence indicates that economic growth during the 1970s and 1980s led to increased wealth for those at the top of the income scale, while those at the bottom did not fare as well as before. Haverman and Schwabish believe that the most recent data show a return to a relationship between economic growth and poverty reduction.

7

Federal Spending in Health: Why Here? Why Now?

GERARD W. BOYCHUK

In September 2000, Allan Rock, the federal minister of health, noted that he had been asked repeatedly, '*Why* exactly is Ottawa *now* trying to get involved in the health sector?'[1] Formal constitutional debates having faded from the Canadian political agenda, health care has filled the vacuum as the main focus of intergovernmental interaction, thus significantly raising the stakes of this intergovernmental 'political football game'. In early 2000, favourable federal fiscal fortunes clearly set the stage for a major federal initiative, although, ultimately, the federal 'plan to save Medicare' did not succeed. While the federal fiscal situation now appears somewhat less bright, other strategic factors continue to contribute to a situation conducive to major federal repositioning in this field. The recent electoral endorsement of an activist stance on the part of Ottawa vis-à-vis the provinces in the health care field has been followed by sustained public demand that Ottawa focus its attention on health care issues. Considering the dismal state of the parliamentary opposition and the early point in the electoral cycle, the governing Liberals currently enjoy significant political freedom.

While Ottawa has been eager to exercise leadership in health care, federal spending in this area has been considerably constrained, largely by conditions of its own creation. Certainly there have been a number of small but important and innovative federal initiatives in this area. However, recent federal attempts at major initiatives, such as Rock's home care plan of early 2000, have failed, largely because of provincial recalcitrance. The annual meeting of provincial premiers in August 2001 forcefully illustrated yet again that any indication by Ottawa of having resources available for health care is guaranteed to generate trenchant provincial demands for increases to the cash component of the Canada Health and Social Transfer (CHST), transfers that provide little direct political benefit to Ottawa either electorally or vis-à-vis the provinces. Coming less than a year after the signing of the Health Accord in September 2000, the premiers' demands also clearly demonstrated that Ottawa has little hope of ever fully satisfying the provinces. Recent federal moves, including, most notably, the appointment of the Romanow commission in March 2001, presage a major shift in federal strategy.

The chapter outlines the factors auguring a major federal repositioning in the field of health, examines the initiatives undertaken by Ottawa to date, and then examines the reasons why the federal government has not yet been successful in significantly refashioning its role. The chapter attempts to understand recent federal moves by considering the various political incentives faced by Ottawa. Contrary to longstanding conventional wisdom regarding the federal position, there are strong incentives for Ottawa to significantly alter its commitment to the principles espoused in the Canada Health Act (CHA)—especially for it to relax its opposition to user fees and private provision of health services—in order to allow it to pursue a more direct and more highly visible role in the field of health.

FEDERAL INTERVENTION . . . WHY HERE? WHY NOW?

Why Here?
Federal intervention in health care is driven primarily not by its limited constitutional responsibilities in the field, but, rather, by political concerns.[2] A significant and widely recognized role for Ottawa has developed in this field. Consequently, health care has become central both to partisan electoral competition at the federal level and to intergovernmental political jockeying. The federal government would abandon this turf to its political and intergovernmental rivals at its own peril. Even after two 'health care' elections, there is little evidence of the Canadian public's becoming fatigued about the issue. Health care remains at the top of the list of the public's concerns: 'The public's demand for Ottawa to focus its attention on health care over the next five years has increased in recent months, eclipsing taxes, the debt and unemployment as the most pressing issue.'[3] The Liberals' own polls continue to confirm this—a fact of which the Liberal caucus has been repeatedly reminded.[4]

The federal government maintains its presence in this field primarily through the federal spending power, by which it makes block-funding transfers to the provinces under the CHST for health, post-secondary education, and social assistance.[5] The CHA, adopted in 1984, applied to the cash component of health transfers of the block-funds then under the Established Programs Financing (EPF) a set of principles that 'the provinces must respect in the functioning of their health care systems: public administration of health insurance, comprehensiveness of benefits, universality of coverage, portability across provinces, and equal access to services.'[6]

As a result of its political popularity and the continued federal reluctance to broach constitutional issues, health care has become the central focus of intergovernmental interaction in Canada—displacing the pride of place formerly enjoyed by constitutional issues. Antonia Maioni describes the politics of health care as an increasingly sophisticated 'political football game', which is 'played by professional state-builders in a charged atmosphere in which the political and financial stakes are considerably higher than they were in the past.'[7] Interestingly, the Health Accord of September 2000, described in more detail below, was the product of top-level interprovincial negotiations and was signed by first ministers themselves. Arguably, twenty years ago this would have been a matter for ministers responsible for health. As Maioni notes, all players 'recognize the extent to which disputes about health care involve struggles over economic and political space in the federation.'[8]

The importance of health care has been magnified as a result of its symbolic significance: '[I]f you stop a Canadian on the street and ask them that most difficult question about self-definition—what is the Canadian identity—nine times out of ten, they'll refer to our health care system.'[9] This imbues the federal government's role in health, in particular, with considerable symbolic significance:

> [T]he federal government can claim to have 'nationalized' health care and promoted 'equal citizenship' among Canadians and guaranteed health benefits to all. In debates about provincial autonomy, national unity, or constitutional renewal, this is of enormous significance: the federal government has no constitutional role in health care but can claim to defend the 'integrity' of the popular features of the 'Canadian' health care model. The federal government achieves clout without the headache of administering and budgeting for health care services.[10]

However, as pressures on provincial health care systems mount, these claims appear increasingly tenuous, and the attendant political capital appears to have been diminishing rapidly.

As a result of its complex and, at times, paradoxical role in health care, the federal government's strategy has three delicately balanced elements: it portrays the health care system as being in crisis; it carefully denies any responsibility for this crisis; and, simultaneously, it ensures that Ottawa will have a central role in any remedial prescriptions—preferably going beyond simply providing greater transfers to the provinces. These contradictory imperatives are evident in Rock's statements when he unveiled the federal plan to save medicare: '[A]s we look at the problems around us and the difficulties confronting medicare, we have to act to fix it. And if we don't fix it, we're going to lose it. And fixing it means not just more money, but doing things differently. Making the kind of structural changes within the principles of the *Canada Health Act* to enable us to have a public health system that's sustainable into this coming century.'[11] The clear emphasis is on a strong federal role: 'Because it's a *Canadian* project it belongs to all of *Canada* and that's why it's so important to have the Government of *Canada* continue as the custodian of its *national* principles.'[12]

Why Now?

Throughout 2000, Rock was repeatedly asked why the federal government was *now* trying to intervene in the health sector. A number of factors prior to the 2000 election augured increased federal intervention in the field, and the political context, though now different, continues to be conducive to a major federal repositioning. In early 2000, these factors included Ottawa's much improved fiscal position, the spectre of a pending election under reinvigorated opposition leadership, and the eagerness of an ambitious minister (with his own leadership aspirations) to put his personal stamp on a high-profile and popular policy initiative.

By mid-2001, both Chrétien and Martin were warning that economic slowdown would require 'some government belt-tightening'.[13] Martin's projections predicted that the federal surplus 'will virtually disappear by 2002–2003, thanks to tax cuts already announced, scheduled increases in transfers to the provinces, rising costs in areas such as seniors' benefits and the economic slowdown.'[14] Martin is reported to have told the Liberal caucus that '[o]ver the next five years, Ottawa "will not be able to respond to all the pressures" it faces in its own areas of jurisdiction, let alone transfer significant new money to the provinces.'[15] This message was aimed at provincial premiers as much as at anyone else.[16] At the same time, Ottawa posted a record-breaking surplus. The events of 11 September 2001 generated new budgetary demands, raised the spectre of a deeper and more protracted recession, and, as a result, added a further level of complexity to the significantly mixed budgetary messages emanating from Ottawa.[17]

The political context, though now changed, is still conducive to a major repositioning of Ottawa in the health care field. The focus on health care in the last election has translated into continuing support among the Canadian public for federal intervention in this area: 'The 2000 election can be interpreted as an endorsement of an activist stance by the federal government with respect to provincial areas of jurisdiction such as health care.'[18] In addition, the Liberals enjoy relative political freedom, given the implosion of the parliamentary opposition and the early stage in the electoral cycle.

It is not likely to matter whether or not the federal government has significant new resources to devote to the health care field. When it has had money to spend the federal government has been attracted to the health care field because it has been an area with significant potential electoral benefits; in tighter financial circumstances similar attention has been paid and will continue to be paid to health care, because this has been an area in which significant federal spending is to be found.

CHALLENGES FACING FEDERAL INTERVENTION

The primary challenges to new federal initiatives arise from the limits to Ottawa's jurisdiction in the field. Federal proposals are traditionally met with objections from the provinces that they constitute intrusions into provincial jurisdiction. This fundamental difficulty in fashioning a federal leadership role in health care has been seriously compounded by a condition of the federal government's own creation—strong insistence on the principles enshrined in the CHA despite dwindling federal financial contributions.

Total federal transfers for health, post-secondary education, and social assistance declined sharply in the mid-1990s, and, even with recently announced federal increases, have only just returned to the total value of transfers at their peak in 1994/5 (see Figure 7.1).[19] Cash transfers in 2002/3 will still be $2 billion less (in real dollars) than they were in 1993/4. At the same time, provinces have been facing sharply increasing health care costs. All the while, the federal government has been adamant in its opposition to provinces' making recourse to user fees or privatized health service delivery to ease their financial burdens.

Figure 7.1
Federal Transfers (EPF/CAP and CHST), 1993–2003
(Cash and Tax Points in Constant Dollars)

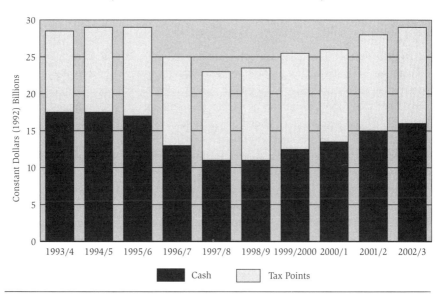

Sources: Edith Boucher and Arndt Vermaeten, 'Changes to Federal Transfers to Provinces and Territories in 1999', in Harvey Lazar, ed., *Canada: The State of the Federation, 1999/2000* (Kingston: Institute of Intergovernmental Relations, 2000), 135; Department of Finance, 'A Brief History of the Canada Health and Social Transfers (CHST)' [see Web site: http://www.fin.gc.ca/fedprov/hise.html].

The politics of this paradoxical federal approach played out powerfully in the demise of the federal plan to save medicare. In January 2000, Rock announced a new plan to save Canada's health care system. The plan included a major new matching cost-sharing initiative for home care, reform of primary care, and the implementation of national standards for the delivery of health services.[20] The inclusion of a major program initiative was not surprising, given the federal government's fortunate fiscal position and the fact that public opinion polling suggested that home care enjoys very strong public support.[21]

Rock's plan was reported in the national media to have been greeted with 'scorn' by various provinces.[22] Ontario, the most vociferous of the provincial critics, accused the federal government of 'blatant hypocrisy'.[23] Quebec accused Ottawa of 'wanting to be the Santa Claus of health care',[24] and argued that the plan was tantamount to 'a robber trying to gain control over its victims.'[25] Alberta simply stated that it was 'not interested in the federal government establishing new programs.'[26] British Columbia reacted with concern as to whether the federal plan would infringe on provincial jurisdiction.[27] New Brunswick demanded that the federal government first restore transfers.[28] Thus it was not surprising that by July 2000 the home care plan was officially dead.[29] The failure of the plan was rooted in the politics of the CHST. Past cuts have placed the federal government on tenuous ground in resisting provincial demands that reinvestment in the field be automatically channelled into restoring transfers. Virtually all provinces, even those that supported the plan, agreed that Ottawa would first have to restore CHST funding. However, the restoration of CHST funding would provide little in the way of political visibility for the federal government.

As the spectre of an election loomed, the federal Liberals were increasingly pinched between the electoral pressure to do something about health care and their own inability to manoeuvre in the field, given the demands of the provinces. In September 2000, the federal and provincial governments reached an agreement on funding for health care that provided an increase of $23.4 billion over five years. In addition to a $21.1 billion increase over five years to the CHST, the federal government committed $1 billion of transfers to the provinces for the purchase of diagnostic equipment (including MRI machines and CAT scanners), $500 million for the development of information technology, and $800 million of transfers for primary care reform.[30] The Health Accord included a statement of support for the principles of the CHA, a commitment to share information as well as to report to Canadians on 'health status, health outcomes, and the performance of publicly funded health services', a strengthened commitment to investment in home care and community care, and a commitment to work together to develop common strategies regarding assessment of pharmaceuticals.[31] According to some observers, the Accord is best seen not as a shift in the federal approach to intergovernmental relations, but as a 'one-off agreement keyed to the 2000 federal election campaign'.[32] Gibbins argues that: '[b]oth SUFA [the Social Union Framework Agreement of February 1999] and the Health Accord were products of their times, the results of a particular set of political circumstances confronting the federal and provincial/territorial govern-ments. Many of those circumstances have now changed, in some cases quite dra-matically.'[33] Despite the federal government's bold intentions, the plan to save medicare and introduce home care was, in the end, largely reduced to an initiative to partially restore CHST transfers, driven largely by the immediate imperatives of the pending election.

The federal government has enjoyed success in fashioning a more direct leader-ship role for itself only in much more limited initiatives, which, while both impor-tant and innovative, are unlikely to provide the political payoff that might have been expected from a big-ticket program reform such as a national home care or phar-macare program. The Health Transition Fund, established in 1997, was designed to support pilot and evaluation projects in areas identified collaboratively by both lev-els of government. In June 2000, the federal government launched the Canadian Institutes for Health Research (CIHR), which was announced in the 1999 budget and would replace the Medical Research Council of Canada.[34] The CIHR initiative, whose research budget is scheduled to be double that of the Medical Research Council of Canada within three years, will create a series of virtual institutes that will link researchers in new and innovative ways across different areas of health research. More recently, Rock has proposed a federal-provincial initiative to change the drug approval process to include considerations of cost-effectiveness in addition to those of safety and efficacy.[35] However, these initiatives do not have the political visibil-ity of a federal plan to save medicare through major new programs.

The Health Accord and the brief entente with the provinces that it signalled con-tributed significantly to the federal Liberals' ability to undercut any immediate elec-toral threat from other parties on the issue of health. The election victory to which the health deal contributed now allows the federal government considerable politi-cal latitude to reposition itself aggressively vis-à-vis the provinces.

HEALTH CARE, POST-ELECTION:
OTTAWA'S TACTICAL REPOSITIONING

A number of events occurred in 2001 that appeared to presage a major effort by the federal government to reposition itself in the field of health: the Liberals' appoint-ment of the Romanow commission in March, Chrétien's musings regarding user fees in June, the public release in August of Liberal polls purportedly showing support for user fees and privately provided health services, and the release of the interim report of the Senate committee headed by Michael Kirby in September.

Ottawa faces significant incentives to relax the CHA. The removal of prohibitions on user fees and the acceptance of some privatized services would likely have sev-eral effects: they would weaken the legitimacy of provincial demands for increased transfers (based on the claim that Ottawa constrains provinces in their ability to fund health care while simultaneously failing to provide commensurate compen-satory transfers); they would sow dissension among the provinces, because some provinces are much stronger advocates of trading funding for conditionality; and they would dull public support for increased transfers of weakened conditionality relative to more direct federal initiatives, which, in turn, produce the biggest benefits for Ottawa both electorally and intergovernmentally. These benefits may accrue to the federal position regardless of whether the provinces pursue these policy alternatives, which, of course, remain their prerogative alone.

The Romanow Commission

In April 2001, the federal government announced the appointment of the Commission on the Future of Health Care in Canada, headed by former Saskatchewan premier Roy Romanow. In March 2000, Rock had stated unequivocally, '[W]e've had enough studies, we've had enough reports, we've had enough commissions. We're now at the stage where by working together we can move from recommendation to action.'[36] Not surprisingly, after the appointment of the commission he faced tough questioning in Question Period: '[A]fter three years of study and $12 million in spending, the national forum on health submitted its exhaustive report to the Prime Minister. Most of the provinces have done studies or established commissions on the health care system. The other House is working on this very issue. Despite all this, the government is setting up a commission of inquiry. Why? . . . Why on earth by creating this commission is the government making official its immobility for at least 18 months?'[37] The appointment of the commission just months before the Senate Committee on Social Affairs, Science and Technology, chaired by Michael Kirby, which had been studying the health care system since December 1999, was to release its interim report on issues and options for health care raises the question of the Liberals' motives for the appointment, as well as its timing.

The conventional wisdom regarding royal commissions is that governments appoint them when they do not know what else to do. This conclusion was stated forcefully in regard to the Romanow commission by Marjory LeBreton, the deputy chair of the Senate committee: '[I]t's just buying time, a stop-gap to figure out what they are doing. What other conclusion can you come to?'[38] Certainly the timing of the appointment of the commission had the benefit of providing the Chrétien government with solid ground from which to rebuff provincial demands for enriched transfers, which could be clearly anticipated to emerge from the annual premiers' conference scheduled for the summer.

However, there are other more credible explanations for the federal decision to strike a commission. Given Rock's public comments regarding the absolute lack of any need for further study, what seems more likely is that the federal government knows what it would like to do, and that, in the words of Frank Graves, one of Canada's leading pollsters, 'Romanow can sell the public a prescription for change.' Graves continues, 'Romanow has a lot of moral authority with the public, high trust levels. A Royal Commission of this sort will be far more credible than anything authored by the Senate.'[39] Subsequent events are strongly suggestive of a clear preference in Ottawa for one particular prescription for change.

The Liberal Shift on User Fees

In a presentation to the Kirby committee, a noted Canadian economist argued early in June 2001 that 'we will never have a rational debate about user fees in Canada. The concept of user fees has become a symbol in the federal-provincial jostling over power in health policy. We are all better off giving up on the idea of user fees for physician services and hospital service.'[40] Certainly this seemed a reasonable interpretation, considering that the federal government had long used its opposition to user fees (and private provision of health services) as *the* major justification for its role in health care. Strongly in keeping with the conventional federal stance, Chrétien repeatedly stated his opposition to user fees during the election campaign of 2000: 'The Liberal party has a very clear position on user fees. We're not studying it at all. We're opposed to that.'[41] Less than six months later and only two months after announcing the appointment of the Romanow commission, Chrétien publicly mused about the possibility of user fees: 'We don't have [user fees] and the people are not asking for it, but it's good to look into that.'[42] It is not surprising that notable observers of health care policy such as the Canadian Federation of Nurses have become suspicious that the federal government is complicit in, if not leading, a move toward user fees.[43]

In part as a result of Chrétien's comments, the Romanow commission will not be able to avoid dealing with issues such as user fees and the private provision of health services, and by dealing with them, it will contribute, willingly or unwillingly, to their becoming firmly fixed upon the public agenda: '[T]here seems to be no avoiding a debate that will challenge entrenched positions on whether Canada needs to accept some commercialization of medicare. Mr. Chrétien himself . . . assured that . . . when he mused aloud about the possibility of adopting user fees for health care services.'[44] The day after Chrétien's musings were made public, Romanow acknowledged that he would have to consider user fees 'in order for the commission to have continued credibility'.[45] By mid-August Romanow had stated that, despite his strong doubts that they would work, he would 'keep an open mind about the growing talk of imposing health user fees'.[46] For his part, when asked if he favoured amending the CHA to allow for user fees, Rock stated, 'The issue of user fees is better left to the royal commission that we've asked to look into the design of the health care system.'[47]

Many observers were surprised by what seemed to be a significant reversal of federal policy—some might say a 'major flip-flop'—on the part of the federal Liberals. One interpretation might be that Chrétien is now willing to cede one of the federal government's central symbolic weapons in its jostling with the provinces over health policy. An alternative interpretation is that the federal Liberals have come to see such conditions as no longer central to their position in the field or, even more strongly, as undermining the federal position.

To date the federal government has been constrained by a condition largely of its own creation—its insistence on vigorously defending the principles of the CHA while decreasing its financial contribution to health. Federal conditions themselves underpin the legitimacy of provincial claims: Ottawa constrains provinces in their ability to fund health care while simultaneously failing to provide commensurate compensatory transfers. A relaxation of the CHA, removing prohibitions on user fees and allowing some privatized services, would likely have several effects: the legitimacy of provincial demands for increased transfers would be weakened; dissension would be sowed among the provinces, given that some provinces are much stronger advocates of trading funding for conditionality than are others; and public support would be dulled for an increase in transfers of weakened conditionality relative to more direct federal spending initiatives, which, in turn, produce the biggest benefits for Ottawa both electorally and intergovernmentally.

A final political consideration is how the relaxation of CHA principles would play in terms of the relationship between Ottawa and individual provincial governments—most notably the Klein government in Alberta. Health care has been a major source of tension between the two governments, and federal resistance to user fees and privatized service delivery has been a major irritant in their relationship.[48] Assuming that federal Liberals wish to improve their electoral standing in Alberta as well as their relationship with the Klein government, a loosening of the CHA principles would serve to ease tensions considerably.[49]

Coming just weeks before the routine media buildup to the annual premiers' conference, Chrétien's comments may have been calculated to generate tension among the provinces. Alberta and Ontario both welcomed what they perceived to be a significant shift in federal policy, while the government of Quebec stated that user fees were 'totally out of the question' and that the federal government would have no power to introduce them—a reaction that is not surprising, considering Quebec's well-established resistance to such fees.[50]

The possibility that Chrétien's comments were merely off-the-cuff musings or part of a short-term political calculation to forestall a consensus among the provincial premiers at their annual meeting was laid to rest with the public release in August of the Liberals' own private polls showing 'strong' public support for user fees and privatization. The polls were released a week after Romanow, in a speech to the Canadian Medical Association (CMA), 'all but dismissed user fees as a solution to Canada's medicare crisis', and two weeks after a survey commissioned by the CMA reported that 'Canadians appear willing to allow a greater role for the private sector in medicare but only if it doesn't involve user fees.'[51] In the public relations battle over user fees, the federal government now appears to be firmly onside with the proponents—including, most recently, the Kirby committee.

The Kirby Committee

In September 2001, the Kirby committee released the issues and options instalment of its interim report. While ostensibly an open-ended discussion document, the report implicitly endorses the adoption of user fees and privatized service delivery in order to expand health care coverage under new programs entailing significant federal involvement in such areas as national pharmacare, home care, and the provision of health technology. Clearly, the report provides considerable support for the type of federal repositioning outlined above.

One of the main thrusts of the report is the adoption of user fees. The report warns that 'if Canadians do not agree to explore new sources of financing, then some reduction in services is inevitable', while largely ruling out increasing health care spending using existing tax revenues.[52] The report offers a number of arguments that favour user fees over alternative means of increasing individual contributions to health care financing, such as higher premiums: 'User charges can be valuable in diverting demand from high cost services to those which are less expensive without diminishing access to medically necessary services.'[53] Arguments countering potential criticisms of user fees constitute a major element of the report. The example of Sweden is used to demonstrate how user fees can be implemented without impeding access, and also to demonstrate that even a very 'socialized' country can rely on user fees.[54]

The report's discussion of what services and what citizens should be covered by public health insurance focuses mainly on a broadening of coverage, including proposals for home care, pharmacare, and a long-term federal program for financing the acquisition and operation of health care technology.[55] The report outlines a range of funding and design options for expanding public coverage for pharmacare and home care—the two services areas for which, it notes, 'there appears to be the greatest public demand for coverage expansion'.[56] The options range from provincial provision of services, with federal contributions being made through the CHST, to new cost-shared programs. For both home care and pharmacare, the report outlines an option for the direct federal delivery of benefits through the tax system.

The report is very sensitive to the weaknesses of block-funding, especially as perceived from the federal perspective. The report notes that the current funding arrangements suffer from 'three major weaknesses: a lack of federal visibility, a lack of federal and provincial accountability, and a lack of stability in federal funding.'[57] Significant consideration is given to the visibility of the federal contribution: 'A major issue with regard to the CHST relates to the impossibility of determining the exact federal contribution to health care. This problem could be solved by designating a notional portion of the CHST for the purpose of health care as was done under EPF. This would ensure recognition of federal funding, while not affecting provincial flexibility.'[58] The implication is that the main problem is not a matter of policy, but rather the political problem of ensuring federal visibility.

For precisely these reasons, the federal government is unlikely to be overly enthusiastic about new block-funding programs. At the same time, it is also unlikely, in the current context, to be very enthusiastic about new cost-sharing initiatives. The decision rules of the SUFA regarding intergovernmental transfers 'appear to constrain the federal government more than do the rules in respect of direct transfers.'[59] The provisions of the SUFA suggest that under new conditional transfers 'the conditions would be general and provinces would have played a large role in shaping them.'[60] As a result, '[i]n many situations, provinces will prefer this kind of intergovernmental transfer to a direct transfer.'[61] However, the failure of the home care plan of 2000 provides little reason to be sanguine on this score. Not only is there more visibility for Ottawa in direct transfers but more flexibility and latitude. It is not surprising that, in general, the provinces 'suspect Ottawa is tempted to make greater use of direct transfers than intergovernmental transfers.'[62] On the other hand, perhaps provinces would be more accommodating if they believed that the federal government was ready to proceed with direct transfers for home care or pharmacare through the tax system, one of the scenarios envisioned by the Kirby committee.

Undoubtedly, the timing, content, and tone of the Kirby committee report will generate considerable pressure on the Romanow commission. Media reaction has been that the Kirby committee put user fees squarely on the agenda.[63] The reaction in various provinces was clear; for example, the day after the release of the report, '[p]eople in Alberta [were] being told that they may soon have to pay directly for health care.'[64] Kirby himself has put direct pressure on the commission: 'Romanow has already effectively rejected notions like user fees and a second, private tier for health care.' According to Kirby, Romanov's rejection highlights the differences in the agendas of the two inquiries: 'We're in a different space in the sense that we are looking at much deeper significant structural change.'[65] Whether accurate or not, the perception that Romanow has ruled out user fees *a priori* on ideological grounds has already resulted in the characterization of the Romanow commission by one of Canada's leading news columnists as predictably thinking 'inside the box', while the Kirby recommendations are portrayed as a bolder approach based on thinking 'outside the box'.[66]

The Kirby report insists that 'responsible public planning requires' a discussion of additional funding, and implies that the discussion must go beyond a consideration of simply increasing government funding out of existing tax revenue; it needs to include an exploration of ways to raise additional funds. It notes that a refusal to consider ways to generate additional funding for health care, such as user fees, allows one to 'skirt the most controversial health care issues'.[67] It is unlikely that the Romanow commission will be able to do so, given the Kirby committee's interim report and, presumably, its final report, which is due in 2002, just months before that of the Romanow commission.

CONCLUSIONS

The federal government's intervention in the area of health has been limited to important and innovative, but nonetheless politically unrewarding initiatives. Its bolder moves have been blocked by recalcitrant provinces, which derive much of the legitimacy for their claims from Ottawa's own actions in the health care field. However, recent federal moves suggest the possibility of a major shift in federal strategy and federal spending in the health care field. Given the incentives that the federal government faces, it would not be surprising if it were to abandon its commitment to the prohibition of the provincial use of user fees and privatized service delivery in order to increase its latitude for new initiatives, such as a national home care or pharmacare program delivered in a more direct manner to individual Canadians—perhaps through the tax system. With the release in 2002 of the Kirby committee's final report and of the report of the Romanow commission, the debate concerning how Ottawa spends in the health care field will certainly rise again to the top of the national agenda.

NOTES

1 Allan Rock, 'Speaking Notes for Address to the Chambre du Commerce et l'Industrie, Thérèse-De Blainville', Sainte-Thérèse, Sept. 2000. See Web site: www.hc-sc.gc.ca/english/archives/speeches/21sept2000mine.htm
2 Federal jurisdiction in the provision of health care is limited to care provided to specific classes of persons, including Aboriginal people, federal inmates, and members of the armed forces. See Antonia Maioni, 'Health Care in the New Millennium', in Herman Bakvis and Grace Skogstad, eds, *Canadian Federalism: Performance, Effectiveness, and Legitimacy* (Don Mills: Oxford University Press, 2002), 101.
3 Justine Hunter, '36% Back Two-tier Health: Poll', *The National Post*, 7 July 2001, on-line edition.
4 Shawn McCarthy, 'Tax Cuts Divide Chrétien, Martin', *The Globe and Mail* [Toronto], 24 Aug. 2001, on-line edition.
5 In 1996, the Canada Health and Social Transfer (CHST) replaced block-funding for health and post-secondary education under the Established Programs Financing (EPF) program and matching conditional funding for social assistance under the Canada Assistance Plan. The principles of the Canada Health Act (CHA) continue to apply to transfers under the CHST as they did to transfers under EPF.
6 Maioni, 'Health Care in the New Millennium', 89.
7 Ibid., 87.
8 Ibid., 88.
9 Allan Rock, 'Speaking notes for address to the Canadian Medical Association's 134th Annual General Meeting', Quebec City, Aug. 2001. See Web site: www.hc-sc.gc.ca/english/archives/speeches/13aug2001mine.htm
10 Maioni, 'Health Care in the New Millennium', 100.
11 Allan Rock, 'Speech delivered to the British Columbia Association of Infant Development Consultants', Vancouver, 28 Jan. 2000.
12 Rock, 'Speaking Notes for an Address to the Canadian Medical Association' (emphasis added).
13 McCarthy, 'Tax Cuts Divide Chrétien, Martin.'
14 Ibid.
15 Ibid.
16 Shawn McCarthy, 'Cautious Martin Pleads Poverty', *The Globe and Mail* [Toronto], 27 Aug. 2001, on-line edition.

17 'Federal Budget Under Pressure with Fears of Deficit', *CBC Newsworld*, 18 Sept. 2001, on-line edition; Shawn McCarthy, 'Ottawa Logs $17.1-billion Surplus; Debt Drops', *The Globe and Mail* [Toronto], 19 Sept. 2001, on-line edition; Robert Fife and Peter Morton, 'Recession and War Pushing Liberals Toward Budget Deficit', *The National Post*, 20 Sept. 2001, on-line edition.

18 Roger Gibbins, 'Shifting Sands: Exploring the Political Foundations of SUFA [Social Union Framework Agreement]', *Policy Matters* 2, 3 (July 2001): 9.

19 Federal transfers for health are a combination of a cash component and transfers of tax points.

20 Camille Bains, 'Provinces Greet New Federal Health Care Proposals with Cynicism', *Canadian Press Newswire*, 27 Jan. 2000.

21 PricewaterhouseCoopers' *Health Insider* reported that 80 per cent of Canadians 'believe that home care should be a free, universal health care program' and that 83 per cent 'felt public coverage for prescription drugs should be expanded (up from 73% in 1998).' PricewaterhouseCoopers, *Health Insider*, 2000.

22 Anne McIlroy, 'Scorn Greets Rock's Health Plan: Ontario and Quebec Say Ottawa's Cutbacks Caused the Problems', *The Globe and Mail* [Toronto], 28 Jan. 2000, A1.

23 Office of the Premier of Ontario, News release of open letter to Right Honorable Jean Chrétien, 27 Jan. 2000, *Canada Newswire*. See Web site: www.newswire.ca/releases/January2000/27/c3734.html

24 Bains, 'Provinces Greet New Federal Health Care Proposals with Cynicism.'

25 McIroy, 'Scorn Greets Rock's Health Plan.'

26 Bains, 'Provinces Greet New Federal Health Care Proposals with Cynicism.'

27 Gerard Young, 'BC Health Ministry Is Concerned About Whether a Federal Plan to Overhaul the Health System Could Cut into Provincial Jurisdiction', *Canadian Press Newswire*, 27 Jan. 2000.

28 'New Brunswick Not Ready to Accept Federal Health Care Proposal', *Canadian Press Newswire*, Jan. 28, 2000.

29 Anne McIlroy, 'Liberals Dump Homecare Plan in Try for Deal: Billions at Stake as Health Ministers Begin Meeting to Address Canada's Ailing System', *The Globe and Mail* [Toronto], 19 July 2000, A4.

30 Finance Canada, *Economic Statement and Budget Update 2000*. See Web site: www.fin.gc.ca/ec2000/ecch1e.htm

31 Canadian Intergovernmental Conference Secretariat, *First Ministers Meeting: Communiqué on Health*, news release, 11 Sept. 2001. See Web site: www.scics.gc.ca/cinfo00/800038004_e.html

32 Gibbins, 'Shifting Sands', 12.

33 Ibid., 8. However, the federal Minister of Health continues to refer to the Health Accord as the central plan guiding developments in the field, and claims, regarding the plan, that 'we're actively pursuing it.' Allan Rock, 'Speaking Notes for an Address to the Canadian Medical Association.'

34 Health Canada, 'Health Minister Launches Canadian Institutes of Health Research', news release, 7 June 2000. See Web site: www.hc-sc.gc.ca/english/archives/releases/2000/cihre.htm

35 Mark Kennedy, 'Rock Poised to Limit Drug Spending', *The Ottawa Citizen*, 11 Aug. 2001, on-line edition.

36 Allan Rock, 'Canada's Health Care System,' Speech delivered to the University of Calgary, Faculty of Medicine, Calgary, Mar. 2000

37 House of Commons, *Hansard*, 6 Apr. 2001. Question from André Bachand (Richmond-Arthabasca, PC).

38 Justine Hunter, 'Medicare Commission a Waste: Tory Senator', *The National Post*, 27 June 2001, on-line edition.

39 Frank Graves, president of EKOS Research Associates, Inc., quoted in Justine Hunter, 'Romanow: Ottawa's Spoonful of Sugar', *The National Post*, 7 July 2001, on-line edition.

40 Åke Blomqvist, quoted in Senate Standing Committee on Social Affairs, Science, and Technology, *Committee Proceedings*, 13 June 2001, on-line. See Web site: www.parl.gc.ca/37/1/parlbus/commbus/senate/Com-e/soci-e/22ev-e.asp?Language = E&Parl = 37&Ses = 1&comm_id = 47

41 Justine Hunter, 'Crack the Medicare Mould: Kirby', *The National Post*, 3 July 2001, on-line edition.

42 Justine Hunter, '36% Back Two-Tier Health: Poll.'

43 Canadian Press, 'Critics Warn of Plot to Approve User Fees', *The Globe and Mail* [Toronto], 26 Sept. 2001, on-line edition.

44 Justine Hunter, 'Romanow: Ottawa's Spoonful of Sugar.'

45 Robert Remington, 'Pressure Builds for User Fees: Romanow Says He'll Have to Look at Them; Two Provinces Welcome PM's Turnaround', *The National Post*, 23 June 2001, on-line edition.

46 Aaron Derfel, 'User Fees Deter the Poor, Romanow Tells Physicians', *The National Post*, 15 Aug. 2001, on-line edition.

47 Canadian Press, 'Critics Warn of Plot to Approve User Fees.'

48 Health Canada, 'Health Minister Responds to Bill 11', news release, 11 May 2000. See Web site: www.hc-sc.gc.ca/english/archives/releases/2000/2000_46e.htm

49 See Allan Tupper, 'Toward a New Beginning? The Chrétien Liberals and Western Canada', chapter 5 of this volume.

50 Robert Remington, 'Pressure Builds for User Fees: Romanow Says He'll Have to Look at Them; Two Provinces Welcome PM's Turnaround', *The National Post*, 23 June 2001, on-line edition; 'Quebec Vows to Block Planned X-Ray User Fees', *The National Post*, 27 July 2001, on-line edition.

51 Aaron Derfel, 'User Fees "Outlawed for Good Reason": Romanow Says Health Charges Would Only Punish the Poor', *The Ottawa Citizen*, 15 Aug. 2001, on-line edition; Mark Kennedy, 'Public Open to Larger Private Health Role', *The Ottawa Citizen*, 9 Aug. 2001, on-line edition.

52 Senate, Standing Committee on Social Affairs, Science and Technology, *The Health of Canadians: The Federal Role: Volume 4: Issues and Options* (Sept. 2001), 69. See Web site: www.parl.gc.ca/37/1/parlbus/commbus/senate/com-e/soci-e/rep-e/repintsep01-e.htm

53 Ibid., 67.

54 Ibid., 62.

55 While the report briefly considers arguments for delisting services, such an option is quickly dismissed on the grounds a) that there is little agreement on which services to delist or on the process that would determine such delisting, b) that delisting may not generate substantial savings, and c) that 'there is a real danger that this option would lead to making decisions about what

services should be covered based more on economic considerations than on medical necessity.' Ibid., 69.

56 Ibid., 53.

57 Ibid., 56.

58 Ibid., 58.

59 Harvey Lazar, 'The Social Union Framework Agreement and the Future of Fiscal Federalism', in Harvey Lazar, ed., *Canada: The State of the Federation 1999/2000: Toward a New Mission Statement for Canadian Fiscal Federalism* (Kingston: Institute of Intergovernmental Relations, 2000), 121.

60 Ibid., 122.

61 Ibid.

62 Harvey Lazar, 'In Search of a New Mission Statement for Canadian Fiscal Federalism', in Harvey Lazar, ed., *Canada: The State of the Federation 1999/2000*, 30.

63 Brian Laghi, 'Senate Health Committee Puts User Fees on Agenda', *The Globe and Mail* [Toronto], 18 Sept. 2001; Valerie Lawton, 'Consider User Fees: Senator', *The Toronto Star*, 18 Sept. 2001, on-line edition.

64 'Alberta Health Minister Suggests Health Care User Fees Not Far Away', *CBC Newsworld*, 18 Sept. 2001, on-line edition; Darcy Henton, 'Rising Costs Rekindle Alberta Debate on Health-Care User Fees', *The Globe and Mail* [Toronto], 20 Sept. 2001, on-line edition.

65 Ibid.

66 Jeffrey Simpson, 'Our Future Health Care: Kirby or Romanow?' *The Globe and Mail* [Toronto], 7 Sept. 2001.

67 Senate Committee, *The Health of Canadians*, xvii.

8

Innovation Policy for the Knowledge-Based Economy: From the Red Book to the White Paper

DAVID A. WOLFE

The need to accelerate Canada's transition to a knowledge-based economy and society (KBE/S) and to increase our investment in research and development (R&D) has been a prominent theme of the Liberal government since the election of 1993. Commencing with the original Red Book, *Creating Opportunity: The Liberal Plan for Canada*, the government has highlighted the importance of federal support for R&D as a key policy priority. It reaffirmed this commitment in the Speech from the Throne on 30 January 2001: 'To secure our continued success in the 21st century, Canadians must be among the first to generate new knowledge and put it to use.'[1] The Throne Speech committed the government to a doubling of current federal investment in R&D by 2010. However, the progress toward realizing this commitment has been successively undermined, originally by the priority placed on achieving a balanced budget during the first mandate, and more recently, in the current budget, by the priority attached to the new security agenda (outlined in the Introduction to this volume). The early priority on fiscal probity was symbolized by the major expenditure cuts in the 1995 budget, including many to key programs that support R&D. The return to a stronger fiscal position that coincided with the second mandate in 1997 was followed by the introduction of programs of new spending on R&D. Among the initiatives introduced in the past five years are the establishment of the

Canada Foundation for Innovation (CFI), increased funding for the research granting councils and the National Research Council (NRC), the formation of the Canadian Institutes for Health Research (CIHR), increased support for the Networks of Centres of Excellence (NCE) and for Technology Partnerships Canada (TPC), stable funding for the Canadian Space Agency, the creation of the Canada Research Chairs, and the formation of Genome Canada.

Whether these individual measures add up to an effective 'innovation policy', and whether they can deliver on the government's promise to make Canada one of the top nations for the generation and use of new knowledge, is open to question. Despite the new initiatives, and the increases in federal funding (part of which merely compensated for the budget cuts imposed in 1995), the government's own spokesmen have indicated that Canada continues to lag significantly in its performance in the area of R&D. In a widely quoted speech to the Toronto Board of Trade in September 2000, Minister of Finance Paul Martin pointed out that Canada ranks fifteenth among Organization of Economic Co-operation and Development (OECD) countries in the ratio of its R&D spending to Gross Domestic Product, and said quite simply, 'That is not good enough.' Our goal should be to rank in the top five.[2] The commitment to move Canada from fifteenth to fifth emerged as a central plank in the Liberal platform, *Opportunity for All*, in the federal election of 2000. The Red Book asserted, 'A new Liberal government will help Canada move by 2010 to the top five countries for research and development performance by at least doubling federal expenditures on R&D.'[3] The cost of this promise was projected to be a minimum of an additional $1 billion in federal funding by fiscal year 2004/5.

The widely anticipated Innovation White Paper is expected to outline the government's approach to the implementation of this policy priority, but preliminary versions leaked in the press suggest that it too may fall short of what is expected.[4] Both the significant new investments in R&D over the past five years and the numerous policy reports and documents released since 1993 raise questions about whether the overall framework governing the allocation of new funding is a suitable means of charting a course for innovation policy in the twenty-first century. This chapter reviews the government's analyses of Canada's innovation performance and its prescriptions to remedy its shortcomings, in the context of the innovation systems approach developed by a number of international scholars. It evaluates the effectiveness of the current policy mix and questions whether the deployment of new funds without a better understanding of the nature of the innovation system in this country will suffice to achieve the government's stated goal.

POLICY REVIEW AND BACKGROUND

The federal government's role in R&D has been subject to considerable strains since the election of the Liberal government in 1993. That election generated high expectations, based on the Liberal platform, for science and technology (S&T) policy. The Red Book recognized that Canada was undergoing a transition to a global and knowledge-based economy. It argued that this new economy requires a greater capacity for adjustments and innovation, which in turn must build upon the capacity of private and public institutions to become learning organizations. It stressed the dynamic role of small and medium-sized enterprises (SMEs) in a growing economy; the need to revitalize the manufacturing, resource, and service industries and to enhance the idea-based sectors of the economy; and the importance of supporting the communities in which these businesses are grounded. It identified the need to move research from the laboratory to the marketplace more effectively and to help Canadian business adopt and use new technology more effectively.

The Red Book called for new initiatives by the government to facilitate the adoption and diffusion of ideas in the innovation process and for measures to create a national system of innovation in Canada. It advanced the objective of doubling Canada's contribution to R&D spending. Among the explicit measures it spelled out were the provision of an additional $1 billion in federal funding for R&D over the next four years, as well as the creation of a new Canadian Technology Network (CTN) linking universities, industry associations, and governments to improve the dissemination of information to SMEs on new technology developments, to be run by the NRC's Industrial Research Assistance Program (IRAP). The Red Book also called for measures to improve technology partnerships between universities and/or government research institutions and private firms, and to ensure stable funding for the three federal granting councils and the federal NCEs.[5]

A related theme of the strategy was the need to build clusters of economic activity in different regions of the country, in order to create value-added jobs. As Paquet and Roy argued in an earlier edition of *How Ottawa Spends*, this approach focussed on a bottom-up strategy of creating prosperity through the formation of clusters at the local and regional level.[6] It maintained that strong regional economies were the building blocks of Canada and that the federal government had a responsibility to encourage local and regional governments to co-operate with a range of private sector actors in charting their own economic directions. Communities themselves take the responsibility for promoting the growth of clusters and related industries within their regions in order to create jobs and greater economic prosperity. The principle means for realizing this goal was the fostering of an entrepreneurial spirit and the development of forums for economic co-operation and networking at the local and regional level. However, Paquet and Roy saw little demonstration of commitment on the part of the federal government to implement this approach over the following few years. As we shall see below, this problem has continued to bedevil the federal government during the latest round of program initiatives and policy reviews.

Agenda: Jobs and Growth

In the fall of 1994, the government released a series of policy documents as part of the 'Agenda: Jobs and Growth'. The overview document, *A New Framework for Economic Policy*, saw innovation policy as one of the four pillars of its economic agenda: 'Since productivity growth depends on working smarter—for example, mastering the economics of "ideas"—Canada must position itself to be at the fore-front of *innovation* in the products and services we create; in the ways we organize economic and social activity; and in the ways we govern ourselves.'[7] A companion document, *Building a More Innovative Economy*, placed the government's proposed S&T initiatives within the context of its broader economic agenda. Policy initiatives were to be pursued in four key areas: trade, infrastructure, technology, and the climate of the marketplace. In the area of infrastructure spending, the government intended to support the information highway through its commitment to regulatory reform in the area of telecommunications policy, through its efforts to extend the CANARIE network with capital spending, and through its support for linking all schools and libraries in the country to the Internet through the SchoolNET program. With respect to technology, it outlined the key issues to be addressed in the formal S&T Review (launched as part of a more comprehensive process of program review): a more systematic approach to the commercialization of R&D, the creation of a strong scientific culture in Canada, the need to establish which scientific and technological developments Canada should pursue, the need to ensure that federal laboratories play an effective role in the commercialization of technology, and the promotion of the rapid diffusion of technology to industry.[8] It translated the campaign commitment to create partnerships from a process of fostering community-based networking and co-operation into one designed to help small business by cutting red tape, increasing loan guarantees to small business, and providing better support for exports.[9]

The Science and Technology Review
The high expectations raised by the Red Book and sustained through the 'Agenda: Jobs and Growth' were shattered by the federal budget of February 1995. It signalled a major change in policy away from the themes of the election and toward a priority on deficit reduction. Without awaiting the outcome of the S&T Review, it levelled major cuts at program spending that were especially severe in the area of S&T. The S&T Review was left to carry on to a painful conclusion, despite the lack of fiscal room for any of the anticipated new initiatives. The results of the review were widely anticipated in the S&T research community, given the very inclusive nature of the consultation process that was conducted. In addition, four interdepartmental committees each produced an internal report, and another was prepared by the National Advisory Board on Science and Technology. The inclusiveness of the process sustained the belief that the government still intended to pursue the policy goals articulated in the campaign platform of 1993.[10]

After two years of work, the S&T Strategy, released in March 1996, articulated its goal:

> to create in Canada world centres of excellence in scientific discovery; to build a broad base of scientific enquiry; to foster Canadian participation in all major fields of science and technology; and to ensure that new knowledge can be acquired and disseminated widely, from Canadian sources and from around the world.[11]

The Strategy identified the need for the government to establish clear priorities for spending in light of the continuing pressure to reduce its fiscal deficit. As a result of the reductions already underway, the report underlined the need for public spending to focus on core activities in the S&T policy area. The principal means for improving the efficiency of delivery mechanisms was the use of partnership arrangements between government departments and agencies and other key components of the innovation system. The core S&T activities of the federal government were identified as 1) funding research that supports the mandates of federal agencies, 2) providing research support to universities, the Centres of Excellence, and other non-governmental research institutes, 3) supporting private sector research and development, and 4) disseminating knowledge, building information networks, and acting as an information analyst. Despite the rhetoric of the strategy document, the action plans announced were widely perceived as a disappointment. In the eyes of one commentator, '[I]t took too long to deliver and resulted in a feeling that the policy leadership developed by the government was lost.' [12]

The Knowledge-Based Economy/Society

Although the S&T Review landed with something of a thud, efforts by the federal policy apparatus to formulate new ideas on how to facilitate Canada's transition to a knowledge-based economy continued. The underlying ideas of the knowledge-based economy and society drew heavily on work done by the OECD. According to the OECD, most industrial economies are rapidly becoming knowledge-based economies. These are economies in which the production, use, and distribution of knowledge and information are becoming more critical for economic growth and development—'more science-intensive via the better use of existing stocks of scientific knowledge, more technology-intensive via the diffusion of advanced equipment, as well as more skills-intensive in terms of managing the increasingly complex knowledge base related to productive activities'.[13] The knowledge-based economy highlights the production of knowledge in new, networked institutional settings and the ability to distribute that knowledge to the relevant components of society.

The locus of thinking on this question shifted to the Policy Research Committee (PRC), an initiative launched by the Clerk of the Privy Council in the aftermath of the 1995 budget cuts to focus the government's policy-making capacity on key issues that cut across a wide range of government departments. Chaired by two assistant deputy ministers from Human Resources Development Canada (HRDC) and Health Canada, the PRC undertook a number of initiatives, not the least of which was the research pilot project on the KBE/S. The feasibility study submitted to the PRC Steering Group in 1997 outlined a thematic approach to the issues to be addressed in a study of the KBE/S, as well as a proposal for implementation of the project. The Report by the KBE/S Working Group argued,

Powerful forces are transforming fundamentally the nature of the economy and the whole of society. Ideas, invention and innovation are the lifeblood of a new 'knowledge-based economy and society'. . . . To survive and prosper in this environment requires continuous innovation and adaptation by all actors. . . . [I]t introduces a new set of transitions and adjustment challenges for governments, firms and individuals.[14]

The report identified a number of key challenges that must be met if successful adjustment is to occur: the acquisition by individuals of the appropriate skills for a KBE/S; the effective creation and management of knowledge on the part of firms; the ability to adopt new technology in order to enhance firm performance; the implementation of organizational structures and human resource practices appropriate to the KBE/S; the capacity of firms to innovate; and the ability of the institutional structures of the society as a whole, such as the financial system, the legal and regulatory framework, the industrial relations system, and the educational sector, to make the adjustments needed to facilitate the overall transition to a KBE/S.

PROGRAMS AND POLICY INITIATIVES

Despite the wide range of ideas presented in the various policy reviews between 1993 and 1997, the actual initiatives introduced over the period have largely been of an incremental nature, supporting or expanding existing programs, or have concentrated on the funding of research. While the government has paid lip service to the concept of a national innovation system, its actual initiatives reveal little understanding of the implications of such a system for the policy framework. The federal budget for 1994 announced funding for the CTN (promised in the Red Book), additional funds for the NRC, and stabilized funding for the NCEs and the Research Granting Councils. The purpose of the CTN, run by the NRC's IRAP, was to provide firms with access to a suite of different services, including relevant government and private sector services and programs, benchmarking, managing technology, training, financing, standards and regulations, and assessment and evaluation of technologies. Each CTN member has specialties in certain sectors or technologies, or business expertise; members also act as networking agents, putting parties in touch with the skills and expertise needed to address their concerns.

This positive start suffered a severe setback, as noted above, with the expenditure reductions imposed in the budget of 1995. The Industry portfolio, including most of the relevant S&T programs, was particularly hard hit, suffering a 42-per cent reduction in its program spending over a two-year period, including most of its industrial subsidy programs, such as the highly regarded Defence Industry Productivity Program (DIPP). The situation began to turn the following year after the release of the S&T Strategy, when the government introduced the TPC program in order to provide support to private sector partners, such as those in aerospace, in their efforts to commercialize high-technology products and processes. The aerospace industry was hardest hit by the cancellation of the DIPP in 1995, and its firms had protested strongly to the federal government. Although TPC differs in important ways from its predecessor, it went a long way toward satisfying the concerns of the industry. Originally funded at $150 million per year, it was to increase to $250 million per year by 1998/9. Its unique feature is that successful projects are repayable to the federal government; it is hoped that the program will be 50 per cent self-financing.

In the years since, the steady improvement in the government's fiscal position, combined with a growing concern over the importance of innovation and the transition to the KBE/S, has led to a number of new program and spending initiatives in the S&T policy portfolio. First among these was the CFI, established in 1997 with an initial allocation of $800 million over a period of five years. The CFI provides funds on a matching basis to the provinces and universities for the modernization of research facilities in the natural sciences, engineering, and health sciences at universities, colleges, research hospitals, and non-profit research institutions. Contributions by the CFI cover up to 40 per cent of the total cost of infrastructure projects, leveraging a total of $2 billion in new infrastructure funding. CFI funding includes expenditures for the acquisition of state-of-the-art equipment, the establishment of computer networks and communication linkages, and the creation of significant research databases and information-processing capabilities.[15] In addition, the 1997 budget made the NCE program permanent, with stabilized annual funding of $47.4 million—achieved largely by reallocating money from the budgets of Industry Canada and the granting councils. Finally, funding for the popular and successful IRAP, run by the NRC, was stabilized.

These measures to boost Canada's R&D capacity were further enhanced in the 1998 budget. A budget document, *The Canadian Opportunities Strategy*, spelled out several new commitments, including the restoration of funding levels for the three federal granting councils—the Natural Sciences and Engineering Research Council (NSERC), the Medical Research Council (MRC), and the Social Sciences and Humanities Research Council (SSHRC)—to their 1994/5 funding levels. The councils were promised that in future years their budgets would grow once again, so that they would receive an additional $400 million by 2000/1.[16]

The budget of February 1999 further boosted Canada's S&T capability. The budget allocated an additional $200 million to the CFI to help it meet the growing demand for research infrastructure in the areas of health, the environment, science, and engineering. It allocated a further increase of $75 million over three years to NSERC, as well as $15 million to SSHRC. It promised $90 million of new funding over three years to the NCE to create up to eight new networks. It also allocated $16 million over three years to the NRC to invest in advanced equipment, as well as $15 million to support national and regional research goals. The budget added $55 million in spending over three years to current federal investments in biotechnology research and development by science-based departments and agencies. The Canadian Space Agency was provided with additional resources of $430 million over three years and was promised that its budget would be stabilized at $300 million annually. An additional $150 million was provided to TPC over the period from 1999 to 2002.[17]

The budget also included a major restructuring of federal support for medical research with the replacement of the existing MRC by the CIHR. The objective of the CIHR is to accelerate the discovery of cures and the prevention of disease; to foster collaboration across a wide range of health research disciplines; and to help bring new health products and services to the market. The budget set aside $65 million for the first year of operation, 2000/1, with an increase to $175 million in its second year.[18] In total, the 1999 budget added $1.8 billion for the current year and for the next three years to federal government spending on the creation, dissemination, and commercialization of knowledge.

The last budget before the 2000 election saw a further increase in spending on the S&T portfolio. It promised $900 million of federal funding over five years to create 2,000 new Canada Research Chairs, as well as a further $900 million to the CFI, raising the federal government's total commitment to the CFI to $1.9 billion. Following on the creation of the CIHR in the previous budget, the government announced the establishment of the Genome Canada project—with a commitment of $160 million to five centres across the country to provide laboratory facilities for researchers from universities, government, and the private sector. The budget also included the announcement of a Sustainable Development Technology Fund, to foster innovation by helping companies develop new technologies in areas such as clean burning coal and new fuel cell developments and bring them to market.[19]

The combined impact of the four budgets from 1997 through 2000 represented one of the most significant federal investments in S&T spending in many decades. In light of this increase in federal spending, it is puzzling to hear key government leaders, such as the Minister of Finance and the Prime Minister, saying that Canada's performance in R&D is inadequate and that we are lagging behind our major competitors. Yet a closer examination of the current situation reveals the basis for their concern.

The latest figures from Statistics Canada indicate that Canada's total spending on research and development rose significantly during the decade, from $12.992 billion in 1993 to $18.288 billion in 2000 in constant 1997 dollars. Expenditures on R&D as a percentage of Gross Domestic Product rose from 1.67 per cent in 1993 to 1.81 per cent in 2000, largely as a result of the enormous boom in the high technology sector. The proportion of R&D expenditure funded by business enterprises rose slightly, from 41.3 per cent to 42.6 per cent, while the proportion funded by government declined from 25.9 per cent in 1993 to 18.2 per cent in 2000, despite the substantial increases contained in the federal budgets between 1997 and 2000.[20] One explanation for this discrepancy is that many of the announcements made by the government, especially for the CFI and the Canada Research Chairs, involve multi-year commitments that stretch out over the course of the current decade, while other spending initiatives, such as those for the granting councils and the NCE, largely compensate for the stagnation of federal funding and the serious cutbacks suffered in the 1990s. The reality is that well into its third mandate, after three successive Red Books and three consecutive electoral victories, the Liberal government is still struggling to deliver on the promises of the first electoral platform. The current commitment to increase federal spending by $1 billion by 2004/5 sounds remark-ably similar to the one contained in the original Red Book!

THE THRONE SPEECH COMMITMENT

With a sense of déjà vu, the Throne Speech of January 2001 takes us back to the situation of 1993. Even the rhetoric used in the Speech and the Prime Minister's Response to the Speech sounds similar to that of the original Red Book. In his speech, the Prime Minister maintained that

> Canada must have one of the most innovative economies in the world. A key ele-ment in getting there is to ensure that our research and development effort per capita is amongst the top five countries in the world.
>
> To achieve this objective, the government has a five-part plan.
>
> First, to at least double the current federal investment in research and devel-opment by the year 2010. The government over the course of its mandate will increase its investment in the Granting Councils. It will do more for Genome Canada and the Canadian Institutes of Health Research. And for research within government. . . .
>
> Second, to build on what we have already done to make Canadian universities the place to be for research excellence. And a place where the best and the bright-est want to come. The government will work with the university community to assist our universities so that they have the resources necessary to fully benefit from federally sponsored research activities.
>
> Third, to accelerate Canada's ability to commercialize research discoveries, and to turn them into new products and services.
>
> Fourth, to pursue a global strategy for Canadian science and technology. Canada must be at the forefront of collaborative international research which expands the frontiers of knowledge.
>
> Fifth, to work with the private sector to determine the best ways to make broad-band internet access available to all communities in Canada by the year 2004.[21]

The Prime Minister's commitment to make Canada fifth in the world in per capita spending on R&D represents a subtle shift from the electoral promise, given that we currently rank higher on this measure than on the ratio of R&D expenditures to GDP. Regardless of which indicator is used, a move to fifth position by the end of the decade will represent a massive challenge for the government. The challenge is made more difficult by the fact that with respect to its international standing in R&D intensity, Canada has been leapfrogged in the past decade by several of the smaller industrial countries, including most of the Nordic countries. According to the Conference Board of Canada's *Second Annual Innovation Report*, released in 2000, just to improve our R&D intensity ratio to the OECD average would require an invest-ment of about $6 billion in current dollars, with about half the increase coming from business and half from government. This represents a substantially greater increase than the government has promised and would still not move Canada to the fifth rank among the OECD countries.[22]

The budget brought down on 10 December 2001 provided an opportunity for the government to deliver on its Throne Speech commitment. Yet, just as the original Red Book promise was sidetracked by the 1995 fiscal crisis, the recent commitment suffered a similar fate as a result of the security agenda (as outlined in Chapter 1). While the government announced a number of new measures to support R&D, they fall far short of meeting the challenge outlined above. Among the measures related to innovation that were included in the budget was a one-time expenditure of $200 million for the universities and research hospitals, to offset the indirect costs associated with federal funding of research activities. The government made a further commitment to provide ongoing support for the indirect costs of research in a way that is predictable, affordable, and incremental to existing support for direct costs. This responded to a long-standing complaint of the universities, but fell short of the more permanent solution they were looking for. The government also allocated additional funds to the base budgets of the granting councils—$36.5 million to NSERC, $7.5 million to SSHRC, and $75 million to CIHR.

The budget expanded on a set of new initiatives by the NRC that had been provided support following the 2000 budget. In year-end 2000/1, the government granted the NRC $110 million over the next five years to support cluster-based research centres in Atlantic Canada. The 2001 budget provided an additional $110 million over three years to support similar initiatives in other parts of the country, including a National Institute for Nanotechnology in Alberta, the Advanced Aluminum Technology Centre in Quebec, a new research program in the Plant Biotechnology Institute in Saskatoon, fuel cell research in British Columbia, and the Canadian Photonics Fabrication Facility in Ottawa. The budget accelerated several internet-related issues by allocating $600 million to the implementation of the Government On-Line Strategy by 2005, $110 million to build CA*net 4, the next generation of Internet broadband architecture, linking all research-intensive institutions in the country, and an additional $35 million a year to support the existing SchoolNET and Community Access Programs in place of the far more ambitious broadband strategy sought by the Minister of Industry.[23] The largely incremental nature of the spending initiatives, with the exception of the NRC's new cluster approach, and the limited amount of funding, fell far short of realizing the ambitious agenda laid out in the Throne Speech.

A final opportunity for the government to deliver on its Throne Speech commitment rests with the Innovation White Paper, expected in January 2002. However, a preliminary leak of its contents, and the limited funding announcements included in the budget, suggest that the innovation agenda has been deferred in favour of other priorities. The leaked copy of the White Paper contained a number of recommendations already announced in the 10 December budget, including payment to the universities for the indirect costs of research, increased funding to the granting councils, the development of CA*net 4, and the expansion of the NRC's Atlantic

Innovation Strategy. However, the draft White Paper also contained additional recommendations that did not receive mention in the budget. These included measures to leverage the commercialization potential of publicly funded academic research, a new program modelled on the NCEs to promote collaboration between government research institutions, universities, and the private sector, additional funding to enable IRAP to expand into international joint ventures and allow firms to access global technology, measures to increase the supply of venture capital through the Business Development Bank, a doubling of the number of Master's and Doctoral fellowships and scholarships, the establishment of a National Academy of Sciences to advise government on the formation of science-based frameworks and priorities for new investments, the launching of a sustained investment branding strategy to attract foreign and domestic investment, and the provision of smaller communities with funding to develop innovation strategies with the participation of local leaders from private, public, and academic sectors.[24]

The question still remains whether these measures, taken as a package, are sufficient to realize the Throne Speech commitment. Its realization depends on the answers to two critical questions: is it feasible to move Canada to fifth in the world in per capita R&D spending, and even if this objective were achieved, would it automatically make Canada 'one of the most innovative economies in the world'? An exclusive focus on one indicator, such as R&D intensity, may prove to be more misleading than helpful as a means of improving Canada's innovative capacity in the knowledge-based economy. An established body of research casts doubt on the value of 'benchmarking' industrial countries against each other on the basis of broad and indiscriminate indicators such as per capita R&D spending. The principal reason for caution in the use of such benchmarks is that countries differ significantly with respect to their size and their industrial structures. Such differences affect their propensity to invest in R&D. Differences with respect to areas of industrial specialization, inputs to the innovation process, trade patterns, technological specialization, and the institutional infrastructures that support innovation are all constitutive features of national systems of innovation, and, by extension, of the capacity to perform R&D. In fact R&D performance varies enormously between different industrial sectors and between firms of different size. A more accurate benchmark is a measure of R&D intensity that controls for both firm size and the industrial structure of the individual economy.[25]

This factor has long been recognized as relevant to any attempt to measure or evaluate Canada's R&D performance. A background paper prepared for the consultations on the S&T Review argued that among Canadian firms size rather than foreign ownership was a major determinant of the propensity to perform R&D,[26] while an earlier report to the Science Council of Canada concluded that roughly 40 per cent of Canada's underperformance of R&D in the business sector was accounted for by the industrial structure of the economy.[27] More recently, Jorge Niosi's analysis of Canada's national system of innovation depicted its distinctive industrial and sectoral patterns. It is stronger in 'upstream' areas of fundamental research, as

evidenced by the relatively large proportion of R&D performed in the higher education sector and the comparatively high level of publication by Canadian scientific
researchers. Furthermore, not only does the business sector in Canada perform less
R&D than the business sector in many of its industrial competitors, including the
United States, the Netherlands, Sweden, and Switzerland, but also the R&D performed is strongly concentrated, both in a relatively small number of firms and in
specific industrial sectors. Telecommunications, aerospace, engineering and scientific services, finance, insurance and real estate, electronic equipment, and phar-
maceuticals together account for more than half of all business expenditures on R&D
in Canada. Canada's R&D system also displays patterns of strong regional variation.[28]
Attempts to boost our R&D performance, or even develop a more adequate measure
of our relative performance, must take account of these distinctive features of the
'national system of innovation', yet there is little recognition of these aspects of it
in the leaked version of the Innovation White Paper.

THE INNOVATION SYSTEMS APPROACH

As was suggested above, the government's innovation policy would benefit from
making fewer commitments to broad objectives of dubious value to our innovation
performance and paying more attention to insights relevant to policy development
that are derived from the innovation systems approach. Innovation and technical
progress are generated by the complex interaction among the institutions that produce, distribute, and apply various kinds of knowledge. Countries vary in the extent
to which, and the sectors in which, they display a strong capacity to perform R&D
and introduce new products and processes, because they differ in the underlying
structures of their innovation systems. Firms are the main actors in the innovation
system, but their capacity to innovate is the product of their complex interactions
with other elements of the system, particularly their ability to adopt and use knowledge generated elsewhere in the system. The innovative performance of individual
countries is influenced by the effectiveness with which the elements of the innovation system interact in the creation and application of knowledge.

The innovation systems approach grows out of work by Christopher Freeman and
Bengt-Åke Lundvall. In his original study of the Japanese innovation system,
Freeman defined a national system of innovation as 'the network of institutions in
the public and private sectors whose interactions initiate, import, modify and dif-
fuse new technologies', and underlined the role of social and political institutions
in supporting the adoption and dissemination of scientific and technical knowledge.[29] Bengt-Åke Lundvall adopted a somewhat different approach, starting from
the premise that the most fundamental resource in the modern economy is knowledge, and, consequently, the most important process is learning. The learning
process is an interactive one, which must be understood in its institutional and cultural context. A significant aspect of his approach is the importance he attaches to
the patterns of interaction between firms, which constitute a collective learning

process, which leads in turn to the acquisition and use of new technical knowledge. This flows from his belief that innovation is increasingly tied to a process of interactive learning and collective entrepreneurship, especially with respect to the relationships between producers and users of new technology. For him 'a system of innovation is constituted by elements and relationships which interact in the production, diffusion and use of new, and economically useful, knowledge and . . . a national system encompasses elements and relationships, either located within or rooted inside the borders of the nation state'.[30]

The key elements that comprise the national innovation system include the internal organization of firms; the network of inter-firm relationships; the role of the public sector; the institutional set-up of the financial sector; the degree of R&D intensity; and the nature of R&D organization. The interactions among these elements of the innovation system are influenced by a variety of broader factors, which include the macroeconomic and regulatory environment, the system of corporate governance, the nature of the education and training system, the state of the communications infrastructure, and prevailing conditions in individual factor and product markets. Interactions among the various institutions and actors that comprise the national innovation system take a variety of different forms. The OECD representation of the pattern of interaction among these actors is shown in Figure 8.1.

The innovation system in a knowledge-based economy encompasses three key functions:

- Knowledge production—developing and providing new knowledge;
- Knowledge transmission—educating and developing human resources;
- Knowledge transfer—disseminating knowledge and problem-solving.

For most national innovation systems, the production, transmission, and transfer of knowledge have become more challenging in recent years. The role of the public sector in stimulating and sustaining innovative behaviour is critical. In most of the industrial countries, governments directly or indirectly fund between 40 and 50 per cent of the costs of R&D. Moreover, the public sector provides a vast array of infrastructure that is critical for the innovation process, in the form of the post-secondary educational system, public R&D facilities, and a wide range of institutions that support the process of technology transfer. The impact of public policies, such as the way in which public funding of R&D is administered, upon the private sector's capacity for innovation is a central aspect of the national system of innovation.[31]

The OECD has concluded that the study of national innovation systems offers new criteria for evaluating the effectiveness of government S&T policies. In the past, government policies have been oriented toward overcoming or compensating for *market* failures; however, the insights afforded by studies of the national innovation system also make it possible to study the nature of *systemic* failures. Applying the innovation systems approach enables policy-makers to identify sources of success and failure within the broader mix of institutions that facilitate or inhibit the process

Figure 8.1
National System of Innovation

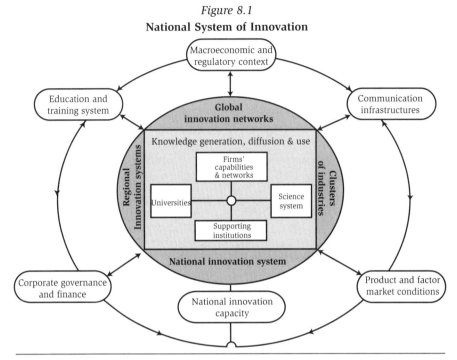

Source: Adapted from OECD, *Managing National Innovation Systems* (Paris, 1999), 23.

of innovation, as well as specific structural gaps in the innovation system. The results of this analysis may also prescribe a broader range of policies, which place greater emphasis on the role of social factors and institution-building than traditional approaches do.[32]

Recently, the focus of the work on innovation systems has shifted from the national level to the regional and local levels. This shift grows out of the recognition that innovative capabilities are sustained through local and regional communities of firms and supporting networks of institutions that share a common knowledge base and benefit from their shared access to a unique set of skills and resources. The regional level is critical for this process, because the factors of space and proximity contribute to the kind of tacit knowledge and the capacity for learning that support innovation. The regional innovation system, like the national one, can be conceived in terms of both the demand side and the supply side. On the supply side are located the institutional sources of knowledge creation in the regional economy. Closely linked to these are the institutions responsible for training and for the preparation of highly qualified labour power. The demand side of the system subsumes the productive sector—firms that develop and apply the scientific and technological output of the supply side in the creation and marketing of innovative products and processes. Bridging the gap between the two is a wide range of organizations, which play a role in the acquisition and diffusion of technological ideas and know-how. These may include technology centres, technology brokers, business innovation centres, organizations in the higher education sector that facilitate the interface with the private sector, and mechanisms of financing innovation, such as venture capital firms.[33]

This emphasis on the region as a locus of innovation, and on the value of geographic proximity for the learning process, also reflects the attention paid to the emergence of a number of dynamic clusters in key locales around the globe. Michael Porter defines a cluster as 'a geographically proximate group of interconnected companies and associated institutions in a particular field, linked by commonalities and complementarities'.[34] Clusters include concentrations of interconnected companies, service providers, suppliers of specialized inputs to the production process, customers, manufacturers of related products, and, finally, governmental and other institutions, such as national laboratories, universities, vocational training institutions, trade associations, and collaborative research institutes.

Clusters operate within the distinctive features of the national and regional innovation systems, and the process of cluster development is embedded within a complex set of economic, social, and institutional relationships at both the regional and national levels. Nowhere is this more apparent than in the cases of the most successful US clusters, such as Silicon Valley, Austin, or San Diego. They have benefited from the highly decentralized nature of the post-secondary education system, with complementary and interlocking roles for both the federal and state governments. Changes introduced in the 1970s and 1980s in capital gains rates and the tax treatment of stock options, as well as the rules governing investments in venture capital by pensions funds, stimulated the growth of the venture capital industry, a factor critical for the development of many clusters. The federal government also played a central role as the initial customer for many of the early products of the high-technology clusters, and, finally, as the most important source of funding for much of the critical research and development that underpinned their growth.[35]

CONCLUSION: IMPLICATIONS FOR CANADA'S INNOVATION POLICY

The lesson to be drawn from this analysis is that national policy can play a significant role in fostering local and regional economic development. The question is, what mix of policies is the most judicious means of enhancing this aspect of the national innovation system? There is little doubt that strong support for higher education and the funding of basic research, which has enjoyed a prominent position in recent federal initiatives, is critical to the overall performance of the innovation system. Keith Pavitt argues that one of the key features of the US innovation system has been the massive and pluralistic funding by government of institutions of high academic quality, and a willingness to make long-term investments in basic research that leads to the development of new, often multidisciplinary fields, such as biomedical- and information communications technology (ICT)-related areas of teaching and research. However, he also warns against relying exclusively on the linear, or informational, conception of the benefits that flow from this investment.[36] The measures introduced since 1997 to increase support for the performance of basic research in universities, research hospitals, and government laboratories have gone a certain way toward enhancing the capacity of Canada's research infrastructure, but as the Conference Board numbers indicate, we still have a long way to go to reach a level comparable with that of the most research-intensive economies.

Research institutions are a critical component of regional and local innovation systems, but they operate in the context of a broad array of other actors. A more comprehensive framework of policies to support the innovation system must recognize the interactive and interdependent nature of the roles played by these actors. As was noted above, the development of new innovative capabilities is often location-based—it occurs in a specific geographic locale and displays a strong regional component. What is essential for the effective upgrading of a system of innovation is the 'embedding' of the business sector into a broader subsystem that involves a greater complexity of interaction and stronger linkages between the actors that comprise it.[37]

Policies to enhance the national innovation system must be designed with an eye to the fact that their impact will occur at the local level within the context of industrial clusters and will be mediated through the intervening effects of the regional innovation system. Attempts to develop policy at the national level exclusively may founder on the diversity that characterizes the Canadian innovation system. A regional focus helps ground our understanding of the innovation process within these diverse realities.[38] A framework designed to accomplish this requires a broad mix of policies, including those that provide support for upgrading the innovative capabilities of firms across a range of sectors; infrastructure (both physical and technological) policies targeted at promoting the rapid diffusion of new technologies across a range of firms; policies to build the market for new technologies; and policies to support the growth of SMEs through increased networking and interaction. This framework must aim to stimulate both the supply of new knowledge (the technology base) and the demand for the technology (the capacity of firms to absorb and utilize the knowledge). Improving the innovation system involves the coordinated upgrading of both demand and supply in order to utilize the new resources provided by the technological infrastructure.[39]

Many of the essential elements for the enhancement of Canada's innovative capacity are currently in place. The research capacity of public sector research institutions, including universities, research hospitals, and government laboratories has been greatly strengthened in recent budgets. Yet federal policy toward research in the higher education sector continues to pretend that it operates in a vacuum, ignoring the fact that much of the rest of the operating funds for these institutions flows through the provincial governments and is strongly affected by other federal policies, such as the Canada Health and Social Transfer. A truly effective policy to support the research and technological infrastructure of the innovation system must adopt a more holistic approach to its funding and operation. An upgrading of the communications infrastructure is also critical to a promotion of the more rapid uptake and diffusion of new technologies, especially in the area of ICTs. Recent initiatives to support Government Online, CA*net4, SchoolNET, and the Community Access Program can contribute to this process, but they must also be coupled with a stronger role for government as a consumer of related products and services in order to stimulate their rapid diffusion through the private sector.

However, greater attention must also be paid to fostering the growth of dynamic, locally based clusters of innovative firms embedded in regional innovation systems. Recent support for the NRC's cluster strategy represents a valuable step in this direction, but again tends to focus primarily on the supply side of the cluster development process. The success of these new initiatives in stimulating the growth of clusters in various locales across the country depends, in part, on the capacity of local networks of firms to take up and utilize the knowledge outputs of these facilities. The availability of innovative financing is critical, especially in more disadvantaged regions, such as Atlantic Canada. In this respect, proposed measures to expand the venture capital activities of the Business Development Bank will prove helpful, but the effective operation of the venture capital market also requires that it be integrated with the broader capital markets to ensure that the venture capital can be recycled into new investments. Another federal program that has recently garnered praise from those in the investment field is the Canadian Community Investment Program, which links angel investors with entrepreneurs.[40] Federal policy should ensure that these various elements of the policy environment are well aligned.

In addition, a well-functioning innovation system requires that the federal government work with and through regional and local partners to stimulate the development of dynamic clusters at the local and community levels. In this respect, the recommendation in the leaked White Paper to provide smaller communities with funding to develop innovation strategies with the participation of local leaders from private, public, and academic sectors is most intriguing. A key virtue of this approach is the involvement of local actors in thinking about how to design effective innovation strategies within the framework of existing national and regional policies. Building trust among economic actors in a local or regional economy is a difficult process that requires a constant dialogue between the relevant parties so that interests and perceptions can be better brought into alignment. The need for social learning at the local and regional level is critical to the success of such efforts.[41] Recent experiments in both the United States and Europe may offer some useful lessons for regions and communities interested in stimulating innovation and cluster development. An invaluable asset in this process could be IRAP's network of 260 Industrial Technology Advisors across the country that enjoys strong linkages with existing networks of firms, research-intensive institutions, and community associations in their local and regional economies. IRAP is widely regarded as one of the most successful federal programs for diffusing technologies and adapting them to firm-specific uses.[42] Further expansion of its role could build on this strong foundation.

The challenge for the future of industrial and innovation policy in Canada is to learn from the best of alternative approaches at both the regional and the local levels in devising a means to overcome the traditional weaknesses of Canadian innovation policy. This will require an approach that builds from the bottom up and integrates the perspectives of all three levels of government in a coordinated fashion both to increase national capabilities and to reflect regional and local realities.

NOTES

The author is indebted to David Arthurs, Adam Holbrook, and Ezra Miller, as well as to the editor of this volume, for helpful comments on an earlier draft. Responsibility for any remaining errors or omissions is mine alone.

1 Government of Canada, *Speech from the Throne* (Ottawa, 30 Jan. 2001).
2 Hon. Paul Martin, Speech to the Toronto Board of Trade, Toronto, 14 Sept. 2000.
3 The Liberal Party of Canada, *Creating Opportunity: The Liberal Plan for Canada* (Ottawa, 1993), 7.
4 'Innovation Paper Sets the Stage for Wide Consultation Leading to New Strategy,' *Research Money* 15, 9 (28 Nov. 2001).
5 Andrew Stritch, 'An Innovative Economy: Science and Technology Policy', in Andrew F. Johnson and Andrew Stritch, eds, *Canadian Public Policy: Globalization and Political Parties* (Toronto: Copp Clark, 1997), 88–9.
6 Gilles Paquet and Jeffrey Roy, 'Prosperity Through Networks: The Bottom-Up Strategy That Might Have Been', in Susan D. Phillips, ed., *How Ottawa Spends 1995–96: Mid-Life Crises* (Ottawa: Carleton University Press, 1995), 138–9.
7 Government of Canada, *A New Framework for Economic Policy*, Agenda: Jobs and Growth (Ottawa: Department of Finance, 1994), 30.
8 Government of Canada, *Building a More Innovative Economy*, Agenda: Jobs and Growth (Ottawa: Industry Canada, 1994).
9 Paquet and Roy, 'Prosperity Through Networks', 146.
10 John de la Mothe, 'One Small Step in an Uncertain Direction: The Science and Technology Review and Public Administration in Canada,' *Canadian Public Administration* 39, 3 (Fall 1996): 415–16.
11 Government of Canada, *Science and Technology for the New Century: A Federal Strategy* (Ottawa: Supply and Services Canada, 1996), 6.
12 de la Mothe, 'One Small Step', 415–16.
13 Organisation for Economic Co-operation and Development, *Managing National Innovation Systems* (Paris, 1999), 15.
14 KBE/S Working Group, *Knowledge-based Economy/Society: Feasibility Study* (Ottawa, 1997), 1.
15 Andrei Sulzenko, 'Technology and Innovation Policy for the Knowledge-Based Economy: The Changing View in Canada', *OECD STI Review* 22 (1998): 294.

16 Canada. Department of Finance, *The Canadian Opportunities Strategy*, Budget 1998 (Ottawa, Feb. 1998).
17 Canada. Department of Finance, *Building a Strong Economy Through Knowledge and Innovation*, Budget 1999 (Ottawa, Feb. 1999).
18 Canada. Department of Finance, *Strengthening Health Care for Canadians*, Budget 1999 (Ottawa, Feb. 1999).
19 Hon. Paul Martin, Minister of Finance, *Budget Speech 2000*, Ottawa, February 28, 2000.
20 Statistics Canada, *Science Statistics*, Service Bulletin 25, 8 (Ottawa, Nov., 2001).
21 Hon. Jean Chretien, 'Address by the Prime Minister in Reply to the Speech from the Throne', House of Commons, Ottawa, 31 Jan. 2001.
22 The Conference Board of Canada, *Collaborating for Innovation: 2nd Annual Innovation Report* (Ottawa, 2000), v–vi, 4.
23 Minister of Finance, *The Budget Plan 2001* (Ottawa: Department of Finance, 21 Dec. 2001), 115–25.
24 'Innovation Paper Sets the Stage for Wide Consultation Leading to New Strategy', *Research Money* 15, 19 (Ottawa, 28 Nov. 2001): 7.
25 Keith Smith, 'Comparing Economic Performance in the Presence of Diversity', *Science and Public Policy* 28, 4 (Aug. 2001): 269–71; see also Jorge Niosi, with André Manseau and Benoit Godin, *Canada's National System of Innovation* (Montreal and Kingston: McGill-Queen's University Press, 2000), 11–15, for a similar but more extensive list of factors.
26 Adam Holbrook and Robert Squires, 'Does Foreign Ownership Affect R&D Performance,' *Science and Public Policy*, 23, 6 (1996).
27 Canada Consulting Group, 'Final Report on the Sectoral R&D Study', Presentation to the Science Council of Canada, Ottawa, June 1991.
28 Niosi, *Canada's National System of Innovation*, 57–73.
29 Christopher Freeman, *Technology Policy and Economic Performance: Lessons from Japan* (London: Pinter, 1987), 1.
30 Bengt-Åke Lundvall, *National Systems of Innovation: Towards a Theory of Innovation and Interactive Learning* (London: Pinter, 1992), 2.
31 Niosi, *Canada's National System of Innovation*, 8.
32 OECD, *Managing National Innovation Systems.*
33 For a fuller treatment of the different levels of the innovation system, see my 'From the National to the Local: Recent Lessons for Economic Development Policy,' in Caroline Andrew, Katherine Graham, and Susan Philips, eds, *Urban Affairs: Is It Back on the Policy Agenda?* (Montreal and Kingston: McGill-Queen's University Press, 2002).
34 Michael Porter, 'Clusters and Competition: New Agendas for Companies, Governments, and Institutions', in *On Competition* (Cambridge, MA: Harvard Business Review Books, 1998), 199.
35 David A. Wolfe, 'Social Capital and Cluster Development in Learning Regions', in J. Adam Holbrook and David A. Wolfe, eds, *Knowledge, Clusters and Learning Regions: Economic Development in Canada* (Kingston: School of Policy Studies, Queen's University, 2002).
36 Keith Pavitt, 'Public Policies to Support Basic Research: What Can the Rest of the World Learn from US Theory and Practice? (And What They Should Not Learn)', *Industrial and Corporate Change* 10, 3 (2001): 771. For a review of

the implications of this for Canada, see David A. Wolfe and Ammon Salter, 'The Socio-Economic Importance of Scientific Research to Canada', Discussion paper prepared for the Partnership Group for Science and Engineering, Ottawa, Oct. 1997.

37 Morris Teubal and Esben Andersen, 'Enterprise Restructuring and Embeddedness: A Policy and Systems Perspective', *Industrial and Corporate Change* 9, 1 (2000): 90.

38 J. Adam Holbrook and David A. Wolfe, 'Introduction: Innovation Studies in a Regional Perspective', in *Innovation, Institutions and Territory: Regional Innovation Systems in Canada* (Kingston: School of Policy Studies, Queen's University, 2000), 1–15.

39 Teubal and Andersen, 'Enterprise Restructuring', 96–101; Morris Teubal, 'Policies for Promoting Enterprise Restructuring in National Systems of Innovation', *OECD Sti Review* 22 (1998): 142–8.

40 Denzil Doyle, 'Believe It or Not, Canada Is Making Progress', *Silicon Valley North* 7, 3 (28 Nov. 2001).

41 For a broader discussion of this process, see Meric S. Gertler and David A. Wolfe, *Innovation and Social Learning: Institutional Adaptation in an Era of Technological Change* (Basingstoke: Palgrave, 2002).

42 Richard G. Lipsey and Kenneth Carlaw, ' Technology Policies in Neo-Classical and Structuralist Evolutionary Models', *OECD STI Review* 22 (1998): 57–61.

9

Biotechnology Policy in Canada:
The Broadening Scope of Innovation

MARKUS SHARAPUT

This chapter examines the evolution of biotechnology policy in Canada since the early 1980s. It outlines the various phases of development of this policy, with special attention to the incorporation of a new core issue as a central feature of each phase. What links the various phases of biotechnology policy development in Canada is the a priori characterization of biotechnology (particularly by the Liberal government) as innovative. Biotechnology has been characterized as an *enabling* technology—in short, as a technology whose application has tremendous potential for both economic growth and social transformation. Until recently, however, it was the potential for economic growth that was most closely associated with the formation of biotechnology policy. Biotechnology's potential for widespread application has led to its evolution into an inter-ministerial, horizontal policy file; ultimately, however, it is a file coordinated and governed by the characterization of biotechnology as an industrial sector. As a consequence, although the most recent stage of biotechnology policy formation has explicitly incorporated the consideration of socio-ethical issues, these issues are considered within a context that presupposes that innovation-led economic growth can be made (or is inherently) socially progressive. The public controversy this assumption prompts has made biotechnology something of a political hot potato. While many government agencies are involved in forming or administering biotechnology policy, few wish to be seen as responsible for that policy. To understand how this situation developed we must understand the broader context of biotechnology policy, including its place in the competitive strategy advocated by the Canadian government. A definition of the sector itself is also needed, and a historical analysis of the phases of policy formation, in order to show how the incorporation of socio-ethical concerns into biotechnology policy was governed by a pre-existing context oriented toward the commercial applications of biotechnology.

LIBERAL COMPETITIVE STRATEGY: COMPETITION AS INNOVATION

Since the beginning of its second mandate, the Liberal government has put forward a competitive strategy based on deriving competitive advantages for firms in Canada by encouraging the development of innovation-driven gains in productivity. Made explicit as early as 1994 with the release of the core document of the Jobs and Growth Agenda, *Building a More Innovative Economy* (BAMIE), the new strategy was characterized as the government's response to the increasingly competitive environment of globalization. The BAMIE document constituted an effort to transform policy in such a way as to take account of the effects of globalization, and it argued that competitive success now depended on ongoing productivity gains derived from innovation. It identified innovation as a market-oriented, commercial activity, and it noted the need to develop enabling technologies through the formation of an innovation system.[1] As a whole, the BAMIE report was a first step in identifying what Canada had to do to develop its innovation system.

This new 'innovative competition' strategy was formulated in a broader theoretical and policy context. This context was significant, in that it involved critical transformations in how competition was understood, both in terms of the role of government in competition, and in terms of how one was to compete successfully. Stemming from the work of authors such as Michael Porter, the new theories on competition argued that states (or rather, state economies) do not compete directly. Rather, economic competition is carried out by firms. The state's role was now generally considered to be one of facilitation; the state was expected to foster the development of conditions conducive to successful competition.

The theoretical underpinnings that have informed the even larger dynamics of globalization involve a general change in emphasis with respect to the role of the state. In the past, the spatial focus of state regulation was the state itself; states established tariffs to define the limits of their economic space, and devised strategic regulatory policies designed to promote the competitive success of the nationally defined economic unit. Globalization has been facilitated, however, by a regulatory project that undermines this approach. The gradual dismantling of tariffs through the GATT/WTO process has reduced the cost of trans-border economic activity, while the harmonization of economic policy through institutions such as the OECD and the various regional economic treaties, such as NAFTA, has reduced the differences between states with respect to the conditions under which internal economic activity operates. Government strategies for economic success have taken these transformations into account. Governments still promote competitive success for nationally resident economic actors, but since it is increasingly difficult to do so by separating or sheltering economies, they now do so by encouraging behaviour on the part of resident economic actors that is in tune with the new economic environment.[2]

A second consequence of the opening of national economies through globalization has been a shift in how economic actors compete. While national economic success in the past was often derived from the strategic exploitation of comparative factor endowments, such as natural resources, the increasing availability of such endowments on global markets has undermined the success of this strategy. Porter and others have argued that long-term competitive success must now be derived from ongoing improvements in productivity. While some productivity improvement can be achieved through the mobilization of labour, the most reliable source of ongoing productivity improvement is innovation.

Innovation, in this context, must be distinguished from invention and R&D in general. Technological innovation, as defined by the OECD's Frascati manual, consists of 'new products and processes and significant technological changes in products and processes. An innovation has been implemented if it has been introduced on the market (product innovation) or used within a production process (process innovation). Innovations therefore involve a series of scientific, technological, organizational, financial and commercial activities.'[3] Innovation is thus distinguished from invention in that it involves the successful adoption of technology in such a way as to change market-oriented activity; it can be deployed as a competitive strategy because of the market effects of innovation-derived productivity gains.

Innovation-driven competitive strategies focus on two key concepts, enabling technologies and innovation systems. Enabling technologies (such as biotechnology) are defined by their capacity to create new industrial sectors and, through cross-sector pollination, to act as motive forces for the continued expansion and growth of existing sectors. Many of these emerging technologies are, however, knowledge- and capital-intensive, to the extent that their widespread adoption requires a concerted, even coordinated effort on the part of industry, academy, and government. While innovative processes may offer new opportunities for growth, these opportunities exist only potentially.

Early attempts to analyse this potential tended to focus on the idea of measuring innovative capacity in quantifiable terms, such as the gross expenditure on research and development (GERD), expressed as a percentage of GDP. Recent efforts, however, have suggested that expenditure on R&D per se does not take into account the larger innovative process, and that the innovative potential offered by technology is best understood as realized through the processes of an innovation system. An innovation system's primary functions are the integration of component elements and the transmission of information among these elements and between the system and its environment. The idea of an innovation system thus involves more than innovative capacity or the process of innovation; it also incorporates the various systemic elements that support this process; an innovation system implies not just a way of doing (innovation), but a way of being (innovative).[4] Within any particular innovation system, the core elements we noted above (industry, academy, and government) are integrated in networked clusters with reflexive lines of communication, and are grounded in a structure that permits flows of information between this integrated structure and the market as a whole, so as to allow the system to respond quickly to market demands.[5]

Early arguments regarding innovation systems dealt with the idea at a national level.[6] Recently, however, many of those engaging the question of innovation have applied the general critique of the state associated with globalization to the idea of innovation systems. This critique states that globalization constitutes a challenge to national sovereignty, that state borders are more porous than before, and that economic activity within states increasingly consists of a constellation of regional zones of activity rather than a homogeneous, nationally characterized whole. This regional critique focuses on the disjuncture between the state and innovative spaces, suggesting that national economies are not integrated into global economic activity as a whole and, consequently, that efforts to deal with the interaction between the global/innovative world and the national space that focus on the national level of analysis tend to subsume the increasingly important regional variations characteristic of all economies. This argument does not necessarily suggest that the state, or national economic spaces, are irrelevant; rather, it suggests that the dominant institutional and organizational phenomena central to the idea of an innovation system are now resident within these regional spaces of activity. Regional innovation systems approaches thus attempt to map out the interrelationships between the regional, the national, and the global when analysing innovative activity and innovation systems.[7] While there is some validity to this critique, it is important to remember that innovation systems policy, that is, the deliberate attempt by a state to foster the development of an innovation system that will in turn foster competitive success, is strategic in nature and formulated at the level of national space. It consists of efforts by governments to adapt their policy strategies in the new environment of globalization so as best to foster the development of a competitive advantage for firms operating within the space of the state in question. The potential impact of the state on innovation has been commented on by authors such as Bob Jessop,[8] and was recognized as early as 1983 by the OECD's Scientific, Technological Policy Committee.[9]

BIOTECHNOLOGY POLICY IN THE CONTEXT OF INNOVATION-BASED COMPETITION

Biotechnology was identified by the Liberals as a component of Canada's competitive strategy in the 1994 *BAMIE* document, and has since been the focus of great attention, both within government and within public debate. In part, the attention paid to the emerging sector has been due to a combination of expectation and ignorance, both emerging from the enormous transformative potential of biotechnological applications. Biotechnology is expected to act as one of the enabling technologies that will drive economic growth in the new century; its potential applications cover a number of economic sectors, and its capacity for social transformation is enormous. As a result, biotechnology has become both a critical horizontal policy field and a potential political liability.

Biotechnology policy has brought together a wide array of ministries and governmental agencies, each with different and occasionally competing claims to regulatory authority (with Industry Canada emerging as the lead trans-ministerial coordinator). At the same time that the expected benefits prompt sharing responsibility for this file across ministerial boundaries, however, biotechnology has become a subject of public debate. Innovation has increasingly been identified with risk as well as opportunity, social as well as economic transformation. Moreover, as recent public opinion surveys indicate, biotechnology is a relatively new technology, and the public is still unfamiliar with it.[10] Consequently, while a ministry might become involved with biotechnology policy, such as the regulation of genetically modified food, in order to encourage or regulate its economic aspects, it quickly finds itself drawn into debates over the social and ethical implications of the application of biotechnology. While the government's engagement with biotechnology policy has broadened over time to incorporate a recognition of these wider issues, there are few government agencies that seek to be held responsible for their resolution in the public's mind. Biotechnology policy's wide application, transformative potential, and extensive links to innovative and competitive strategies have meant that it is evolving into a quintessential horizontal policy field at the same time that it is becoming recognized as a policy field for which ultimate responsibility is a liability; while many ministries have a hand in the bag, few wish to be caught holding it. An understanding of how this situation evolved requires, first, a sketch of the limits of the sector itself, followed by an examination of the various phases in the development of biotechnology policy. These phases are characterized by the incremental collection of core issues; while the initial phase of biotechnology policy was primarily concerned with the development of basic R&D capacity, later phases combined this focus with the goal of adapting R&D to commercial/innovative application, and the regulation of the emerging sector in accordance with emerging social and ethical concerns.

Sector Profile

The breadth of the applications of biotechnology can make it difficult to define the sector's specific parameters. Despite this challenge, the federal government has, since the mid-1990s, undertaken a series of statistical profiles of the sector, and of the application of biotechnology in the wider Canadian economy. The technology itself is generally defined by the government as 'the application of science and engineering in the direct or indirect use of living organisms or parts of organisms in their natural or modified forms in an innovative manner in the production of goods and services or to improve existing processes'.[11] Although biotechnology is often characterized as a new technology, this definition includes applications of biotechnology that have been used for millennia, such as the use of yeast in fermentation and baking. The expectation that biotechnology will function as an enabling technology, however, stems from the much more recent development of biotechnological techniques such as genomics, transgenics, and xenotransplantation.[12] By 1996, 14 per cent of Canadian firms used some form of biotechnology. The projected economic benefits of biotechnology are significant. The global market for biotechnology is expected to have grown from $20 billion to $50 billion between 1995 and 2005. Total employment in the Canadian biotechnology sector grew from 9,823 to an expected 15,800 between 1998 and 2001, with 1,899 positions still unfilled. Biotechnology activity in Canada in 1997 produced $1.017 billion in revenue and $413 million in exports, with the health and agri-food sectors accounting for almost 95 per cent of Canadian biotechnology sales and 97 per cent of exports.[13] Given government estimates that each $1 billion in exports generates 11,000 jobs in Canada, and the growth potential of the sector, it is unsurprising that biotechnology has been identified as a critical sector in the Jobs and Growth Agenda.

In 1997 there were 282 biotechnology firms operating across Canada, with 31 per cent located in Quebec, 25 per cent in Ontario, 20 per cent in British Columbia, 18 per cent in the other western provinces, and 6 per cent in the Atlantic region. The bulk of biotechnology firms (more than 70 per cent) are small (50 employees or less) and entrepreneurial, and tend toward regional specialization (Quebec, Ontario, and British Columbia specialize in health applications, the other western provinces in agriculture and resource applications, and Atlantic Canada in aquaculture, forestry, and biodiversity applications).[14]

Phase 1: Building R&D Capacity in Biotechnology

Although the federal government was paying attention to biotechnology by the late 1970s, the first phase of its prominence began in 1980, when the Minister of State for Science and Technology, John Roberts, formed a Biotechnology Task Force. Having identified biotechnology as a sector with enormous potential for growth, and having noted that an indigenous biotechnology industry scarcely existed, the Task Force took as its purpose advising the Minister on the possibility of developing such an industry in Canada, with particular reference to identifying potential areas of specialization, developing a strategy for the growth of research and development, consulting with industry, academy, and government stakeholders, and developing a plan of action incorporating specific policies and programs for recommendation to the Minister.[15] The Task Force reported in 1981, with a set of core recommendations that included government intervention to encourage the growth of the science base, R&D, and biotechnological human resources, and the formation of a set of appropriate industrial regulations. These recommendations were codified in 1983 with the establishment of the National Biotechnology Strategy (NBS).

The preliminary mandate of the NBS was to monitor international, federal, and provincial initiatives, and to advise the minister of industry on the evolution of Canada's science and technology infrastructure and on government policies and programs related to biotechnology. This mandate was focussed more on the development of R&D and invention than on commercial development and innovation. The NBS was given initial funding of $22 million between 1983 and 1985, and this level was confirmed at $11 million per year after 1985. These funds were supplemented by expenditures on the part of the National Research Council to develop research infrastructure for biotechnology, including the construction of two biotechnology research centres, one in Montreal and one in Saskatchewan. The facility in Saskatchewan was dedicated to research on plants, but the Montreal facility came under criticism for its lack of a coordinating research goal. This criticism was part of a growing concern about government efforts to develop biotechnological research to date; critics asserted that the focus on developing the industry had so far consisted primarily of a government-funded research push, without a complementary private sector pull.[16] This call for greater coordination between government expenditure and the market demands of the private sector was to become a defining feature of the second phase of biotechnology policy development.

Phase 2: Commercialization, Social Transformation, and the Formation of the NBAC

The mandate of the NBS was broadened in the late 1980s with the formation of the National Biotechnology Advisory Committee (NBAC). The NBAC's initial mandate was related to the revolutionary capacities of the new technology. The anticipated effects of biotechnology were those associated with other enabling technologies: prosperity as a result of the expansion of the sector itself, as well as spillover effects that would boost productivity in other sectors. The realization of these anticipated effects demanded the formation of a regulatory framework capable of anticipating and coordinating sector growth. By the end of NBAC's mandate, however, it was becoming clear that the application of biotechnology raised a series of questions that emerged from its transformative impact on social and ethical issues; biotechnology provided new capabilities, but it necessitated asking hard questions about how those capabilities should be employed. Finding answers to these questions necessitated the use of tools that lay outside the NBAC's mandate, which culminated in 1998 with the publication of its sixth report. This report made a series of recommendations covering issues of leadership, commercialization, technology and innovation, market access, and intellectual property. In addition, it noted the increasing importance of socio-ethical issues in biotechnology, and called for a renewal of the NBAC and its role.

The first recommendation in the NBAC's sixth report was relatively straightforward. In order for Canada to reach the sectoral growth target of having Canadian firms capture 10 per cent of the global market by 2005, the NBAC argued, an active leader was necessary for strategic coordination. It recommended that the minister of industry should take on this role. This recommendation was enthusiastically followed. Throughout the late 1990s, biotechnology was actively promoted by Industry Canada as a sector critical to Canada's competitive strategy. For example, biotechnology was mentioned in the federal Science and Technology Strategy, *BAMIE*, and the 1997 Speech from the Throne as one of the cornerstones of the Jobs and Growth agenda. The leadership role of Industry Canada was reinforced by later recommendations that it take on a coordinating position with regard to other ministries concerned with biotechnology issues.

Second, the Report recommended a series of policies that emerged from efforts to commercialize the sector. While the preliminary focus of the NBS had been on building up pre-commercial, basic R&D capacity in the sector, efforts to commercialize the results of this research (that is, to convert invention to innovation) were encountering difficulty. According to the Report, biotechnology products went through five stages of development: the initial research stage, followed by three stages of clinical trials, and the culminating stage, manufacturing. The small scale of most biotechnology firms meant that they generally did not have sufficient manufacturing capacity, and tended to form alliances with large multinationals through licensing arrangements, in order to produce biotechnological products. The further along the pipeline a biotechnology product was when it was licensed, the higher the returns a biotechnology firm could expect (returns ranged from 2 per cent to 5 per cent for research-stage licensing to 35 per cent and more for manufacturing-stage licensing).[17] The Report noted that many biotechnology firms were encountering difficulties with product development that forced them to license their work before they could recoup maximal returns.

These difficulties took many forms. First, while the employment potential of the sector was one of its most attractive features (the Report anticipated the creation of 10,000 new management and technology jobs by the year 2000), Canadian biotechnology firms encountered difficulties in finding sufficient numbers of qualified personnel. The Report recommended the creation of a private/public sector training network designed to meet long-term employment needs, and the adjustment of immigration policies and active recruitment (including the adjustment of tax policy to provide recruitment incentives) to meet short-term needs.

Second, firms were encountering serious capitalization difficulties. The Report recommended a series of policies to help firms overcome capitalization barriers, including a reassessment of tax policy (involving a review of R&D tax credits, the relaxation of tax barriers to strategic partnering, and the acceleration of capital-cost schedules), the simplification of securities and venture-capital regulations to allow for international partnering, and additional funding for biotechnology products to government programs such as Technology Partnerships Canada and the Industrial Research Branch.[18]

The NBAC sixth report's third recommendation was related to the commercialization barriers raised in its second, in that it focussed on the erosion of Canada's research capacity in the biotechnology sector. This was a critical barrier to the innovative role envisioned for biotechnology by the government, in that basic R&D formed the resource pool for the commercial (innovative) application of biotechnology in the Canadian economy. While it may be possible to import basic R&D resources for innovative development, the central role envisioned for biotechnology as an enabling technology (with Canada positioned as a world leader) prohibited reliance on derivative research, and demanded the security of having the basic resource pool resident in Canada.[19] The biotechnology sector in Canada, exposed as it was to competitive pressure, was generally focussed on commercially directed, innovative research rather than basic exploratory research, which in Canada was traditionally publicly funded through granting agencies and educational institutions.

The Report also argued that government cuts to universities and granting agencies in the 1990s (Canada's GERD has traditionally been lower than the G7 average, and in the years 1993 to 1997 federal R&D funding had been cut by 9.7 per cent) was undercutting the long-term viability of the biotechnology sector.[20] Although the Report noted that the government was taking some steps to overcome this erosion, notably through the formation of the Canada Foundation for Innovation and the development of the Networks of Centres of Excellence program, these organizational and institutional programs were insufficient, and reinvestment in the budgets of granting councils was necessary. The Report also recommended, in essence, the development of Canada's national innovation system through the building of institutional networks between universities, industry, venture capital, and business professionals, in order to facilitate technology transfer and efficient invention-innovation conversion. This latter series of recommendations included efforts to meet the long-term human resource needs of the innovation system. Cuts to university budgets and funding agencies had the effect of simultaneously undermining Canada's capacity to renew its pool of expertise and accelerating the drain of researchers to better-funded research locations. The Report recommended the development of virtual networks to facilitate shared-resource research projects, and funding to facilitate the recruitment of the next generation of biotechnology workers.

Fourth, the Report recommended a broad review of the regulatory environment for biotechnology. In part, this included bringing Canada's health, environmental, and safety regulations into harmony with international standards, both by internal change and by advocating the adoption of a common set of norms outside of Canada (the report specifically suggested lobbying Canada's trading partners to adhere to WTO standards). Differences in regulatory standards inhibited foreign market access for Canadian biotechnology, and inhibited inter-national networking and co-operation. The goal was to be realized in the short term through the expansion of joint product reviews involving Canadian and foreign regulatory agencies, and in the long term through the development of mutual recognition of regulatory standards and processes between Canada and its trading partners (including the development of common standards for handling genetically modified organisms and applications of human genome research). A second component of regulatory review involved the reassessment of Canada's intellectual property policies, building on recommendations filed by the NBAC in a 1991 report. The Report argued that Canada must adjust its intellectual property regime to meet WTO-mandated standards, particularly in the area of the patenting of higher life forms,[21] that it must either shorten regulatory delays or offer compensation in the form of patent-term restoration for biotechnology products,[22] and that it must develop effective procedures to inhibit the practice of non-utilitarian, speculative patenting. Finally, the Report recommended a review of Canada's regulatory process for biotechnological products, which would include the formation of regulatory networks incorporating advisory panels (which would inform the regulatory process in such a way that it could respond to the specific characteristics of biotechnology), and the harmonization of regulatory timelines for biotechnology with international benchmarks (to remove competitive barriers for those applying for regulatory approval in Canada).

The fifth and sixth recommendations of the NBAC's final report were particularly significant, in that they introduced the explicit incorporation of socio-ethical considerations in biotechnology policy (the defining feature of the next phase of that policy), and the renewal of the national biotechnology advisory structure, which would result in the formation of the agency that would be the primary source of advice in that phase, the Canadian Biotechnology Advisory Committee (CBAC). In part, concerns about socio-ethical issues stemmed from commercial motivations: the market for biotechnology depended, in part, on the presence of a consumer base knowledgeable about and comfortable with the technology. This required, in turn, the formation of methods to educate the public about biotechnology (especially its risks and rewards), the development of mechanisms within the sector such that social and ethical considerations were taken into account, and, finally, the development of public confidence in such mechanisms. To further this end, the NBAC recommended that it evolve into an advisory body with a broader membership, mandate, and public role. Furthermore, it recommended that this new body foster a general public discussion of biotechnology-related issues to ensure that public concerns were incorporated into the biotechnology policy-formation process.

The NBAC recommended that the mandate of its successor body take into account the direction and pace of biotechnology evolution, commercial applications of the technology, the effectiveness of the biotechnology strategy, alternative approaches taken by other countries, provincial biotechnology initiatives, federal initiatives related to but outside of the biotechnology strategy, public input, public awareness and discussion, and the development of formal mechanisms to incorporate social, ethical, economic, health and safety, and environmental perspectives. It recommended that the new body retain the independence experienced by the NBAC, but retain also a consultative relationship with relevant ministries (particularly Industry), in order to respond to governmental questions. It recommended the formation of inter-ministerial reporting relationships (again, spearheaded by Industry), and reporting relationships with other agencies that advise on issues related to biotechnology, such as the Advisory Council on Science and Technology (ACST). It recommended that the new body take on an oversight role in the implementation of the successor to the NBS, the Canadian Biotechnology Strategy (CBS). In order to make the new body capable of fulfilling this role, it recommended the granting of an independent budget and the formation of a supporting secretariat. Finally, it recommended that the new agency organize and fund public consultations, issue reports, and organize issue-specific working groups, which would incorporate expert non-members, to address emerging questions related to biotechnology.

The second phase of Canadian biotechnology policy was highlighted by an attempt to come to terms with the challenges of commercializing emergent technologies. It was characterized by a recognition of the relationship—and the tension—between processes of invention and processes of innovation, particularly the need for responsive and flexible regulation that is harmonized with international practices and norms. This period was concurrent with a broader discussion of the role innovation would play within the Canadian economy; consequently, it was informed by a general strategy to develop a Canadian innovation system, and to define the needs and role of enabling technologies within that system. Finally, it was characterized by a growing recognition of the consequences of making such technologies central to strategic economic planning, in that concern about the economic transformations such technologies prompted was increasingly matched by awareness that such transformations were not limited to economic conditions, and that the growth of sectors such as biotechnology necessitated the consideration of social and ethical implications as well.

Phase 3: The Canadian Biotechnology Strategy and
the Incorporation of Social and Ethical Concerns

In 1997, partly anticipating the recommendations of the NBAC's sixth report, the government undertook a series of broad-based stakeholder consultations, with a selection of Canadians, with sector and industry interests, and with the relevant government agencies and ministries.[23] The results of these consultations were incorporated into the renewal, in 1998, of the NBS as the Canadian Biotechnology Strategy (CBS). The new CBS incorporated a series of recommendations emerging from the consultative process. These included a mechanism for internal government coordination on biotechnology issues, the formation of a policy framework to govern the operation of the CBS, and the formation of the CBAC, as an arm's-length advisory group. These outcomes, while constituting an attempt to construct a coherent framework for biotechnology issues in Canada, were intended as only the first step in an ongoing process.[24]

The recommendation that there be a mechanism for internal coordination resulted in the formation of an inter-ministerial committee coordinated by the minister of industry, the Biotechnology Ministerial Coordinating Committee (BMCC). The BMCC was to be supported by a deputy ministerial committee and a group of assistant deputy ministers for day-to-day coordination and implementation, and was to be advised by the CBAC. The recommendation to form a biotechnology policy frame-work, building on the results of initial consultation, resulted in the formation of a common vision for biotechnology, to be realized through nine policy goals and ten core themes for action in the initial years of the new CBS.[25] These action themes were the development of public confidence through communication and awareness, research and development, health and environmental regulation, biotechnology for public health, intellectual property, technology commercialization, international issues, human resources, policy-relevant data collection and analysis, and sector strategies. Each theme was to incorporate a series of possible policy initiatives, and action on these initiatives was to be informed by advice from the CBAC.[26]

The advisory and monitoring mandate of the CBAC gave it a critical role in the new CBS. The CBAC consists of 20 members and a chairperson, chosen from a pool of applicants and nominations. The members have a broad range of expertise, includ-ing science, business, nutrition, law, environment, philosophy, ethics, and public advocacy, reflecting the expanded mandate of the agency. Members are part-time, are volunteers, and serve two- to three-year terms. The members were appointed in September 1999, and met for the first time in October 1999.[27]

In February 2000, the CBAC presented the BMCC with its program plan, a document that outlined the planning progress the CBAC had made since its inception. The pro-gram plan reconfirmed the broader, ongoing advising mandate of the CBAC, and out-lined the organizational model the agency had adopted. Within the CBAC, three standing committees had been formed, dealing with issues of stewardship (socio-ethical, legal, environmental, and regulatory issues raised by biotechnology), eco-nomic and social development (R&D contributing to biotechnological innovations, and their health, environmental, and economic applications), and citizen engage-ment (creating an ongoing discussion of the public policy implications of biotech-nological innovation), respectively. In addition to listing the standing committees, the program plan also set out the criteria that the CBAC would use to select its future activities. The core criteria included centrality to the CBAC mandate, feasibility, time-liness, complementarity (i.e., non-replication), CBAC alignment (degree of multi-dimensionality), and potential policy impact. The program plan also outlined the distinction between general activities of the CBAC, which related to its ongoing man-date, and special activities, which were limited in duration and directed by a steer-ing committee made up of representatives from each of the standing committees.[28]

In its first year of operation, the CBAC's general activities focussed on communi-cations, public outreach regarding biotechnology issues, and monitoring and report-ing. A cornerstone of its communications activity was the development of a com-munications strategy, which incorporated a Web site (where the minutes of CBAC meetings were to be posted), an on-line forum, and a toll-free number. Other com-munications activity involved the development of public education on biotechnol-ogy, the preparation of media releases and media conferences, and the development of a stakeholder contact list. The CBAC's outreach activities included member par-ticipation in conferences on biotechnology and the formulation of tentative plans for sponsoring both national biotechnology conferences and specific-issue workshops for the public. Its monitoring and reporting functions included networking with other relevant agencies, the review of external reports that related to the CBAC's mandate, and the publication of an annual report structured around the three CBAC standing committees. It also advised members of the BMCC on three specific issues: the terms of reference for the formation by the Royal Society of Canada (RSC) of an Expert Scientific Panel on the Future of Food Biotechnology, a review of international developments concerning genetically modified (GM) food prompted by proposals submitted to the G8 and OECD dealing with the health and environmental implications of GM food and crops, and the drafting of a memorandum advising on the on-going appeal process of the Harvard onco-mouse patent.[29]

In additional to these general activities, the CBAC also began planning five special projects, with two targeted for immediate implementation. The two immediate projects focussed on the regulation of GM food and the protection and exploitation of biotechnological intellectual property (BIP), specifically, the patenting of higher life forms. The projects planned for later implementation were concerned with incorporating socio-ethical considerations into the policy process, the use of genetically based interventions, and genetic privacy. Each special project was to be directed by a steering committee, while as part of its general mandate the CBAC planned a series of public consultations on each special project. For the three special projects scheduled for later implementation, preliminary plans, including the formation of initial project objectives and research questions, were outlined. For the first years of its mandate, however, the CBAC restricted the bulk of its activity to its primary project targets.

The GM food project was prompted by internal discussions regarding the efficacy of Canada's regulatory regime for biotechnology applications, and the high public profile of the GM food issue. The project focussed initially on three core elements of study: the science base underpinning regulation, the governance of regulatory systems, and the public concern regarding the socio-ethical and legal aspects of GM food regulation; however, as a consequence of the formation of the RSC Expert Committee, the project was later limited to the two latter topics. The project progressed in two stages, the first involving the clarification of research topics and the solicitation of studies, and the second incorporating the results of these studies (and other relevant reports) into public consultation documents, which in turn will be incorporated into a final report, with recommendations.[30]

The GM food project encountered controversy in this latter, public consultation stage. A number of the organizations contacted by the CBAC, including the Council of Canadians, the Canadian Environmental Network, and Greenpeace, abstained from the CBAC consultation process on the basis that the terms of reference for the consultation were too limited. They argued that CBAC had an inherent bias toward an industrial characterization of biotechnology, that is, that the issue of economic growth and development would be prioritized over socio-ethical issues.[31] For example, the Council of Canadians raised objections concerning the perceived conflicts

of interest between the role of industrial promotion and that of protection of public
health and safety, both of which fell under the aegis of the Canada Food Inspection
Agency (CFIA).[32] The CBAC responded with a letter noting that it was not responsible to the biotechnology industry; it was, rather, an independent, expert advisory
committee committed to providing evidence-based advice, taking into account the
views of Canadians.[33] The boycott of CBAC consultations by the NGO coalition illustrates the complexity that emerges when socio-ethical issues are taken into account
in the formation of biotechnology policy. When the CBAC, like other government
agencies, introduced socio-ethical issues, it did so in order to enhance an existing
policy project; it was assumed that the expansion of biotechnology had innovative
and progressive potential. The inclusion of these other issues raised the question of
how to ensure that biotechnology policy met the socio-ethical criteria of Canadians;
it presupposed, however, that the development of biotechnology applications will
meet those socio-ethical criteria; for many Canadians, however, this is still a matter
of debate.

Questions regarding the ethically acceptable limits of biotechnology application
also surfaced in the project dealing with the protection and exploitation of biotechnological intellectual property. This project was prompted in part by the immediacy
of such cases as that of the Harvard onco-mouse, the questions they raised, and the
attention the topic was receiving from such international organizations as the WTO,
which was assessing the topic as part of a review of its agreement on trade-related
aspects of intellectual property (TRIPS). The inclusion of socio-ethical issues in the
consideration of biotechnological intellectual property was unsurprising, in that the
patenting of higher life forms is one of the most volatile issues associated with
biotechnology. The project was also prompted by the apparent absence of the appropriate tools within existing Canadian intellectual property policy to deal with such
questions. A recurring theme of the various appeals in the onco-mouse case has
been the need for clear legislation outlining the limits in the treatment of bio-organ-
isms as intellectual property. Like the GM food project, the BIP project proceeded in
two phases, the first concerning itself with an internationally comparative study of
the relative merits of the Canadian intellectual property regime, and the second
dealing with the relative efficacy of that regime for the biotechnology sector, including its capacity to incorporate socio-ethical considerations. The BIP project was supplemented by a second steering committee dealing specifically with the higher life
form question.[34]

In addition to reporting on its internal activities, the CBAC outlined in its first
annual report developments that impinged on concerns raised by the NBAC in its
final report. The report described emerging biotechnological techniques, such as
genomics, the use of stem cells, cloning, and xenotransplantation; it also gave an
update on developments within the agri-food applications of biotechnology, and
profiles of federal initiatives to build Canada's scientific capacity in biotechnology
and of the development of the industry itself. Many of the initiatives addressed concerns raised by the NBAC with respect to commercialization and the maintenance of

the R&D resource base for biotechnological innovation. The initiatives included the incorporation of Genome Canada, with a budget of $160 million over three years; the formation of the Canadian Foundation for Innovation (intended to develop Canada's research infrastructure); the Canadian Research Chairs Program (budgeted at $650 million); $150 million in increased funding to Technology Partnerships Canada (TCP) (as of May 2000, TCP had invested $204 million in biotechnology, which is anticipated to leverage an additional $750 million from other sources of investment); the expansion of the Industrial Research Assistance Program to facilitate technology transfer; a reduced tax burden for small business in the 2000 federal budget; and the augmentation of the Canadian Intellectual Property Office staff to facilitate biotechnology patent applications.[35]

The activities of the CBAC since its inception indicate that the core issues associated with biotechnology policy, such as R&D development and successful commercialization, are still very much a part of that policy; these concerns have, however, been augmented by an engagement with the socio-ethical questions raised by biotechnology. In some cases this concern is overt (as in the upcoming CBAC special project), but it has also become a feature of the broader CBAC mandate, having been incorporated into its day-to-day advising, its (occasionally controversial) public consultation, and its other projects. To some extent, as we have noted, this new concern is prompted by the commercial impact of such issues; the market for GM food will be affected by the public's degree of knowledge about the technology and its capacity to assess the impact such foods might have. It seems clear, however, that the federal government and its biotechnology-related agencies are increasingly aware that the transformative characteristics of enabling technologies such as biotechnology are not limited to their economic impact alone.

CONCLUSIONS

Biotechnology is a transformative technology. As a consequence of both direct sector growth and potential spillover effects, its applications have the potential to function as an engine of economic growth and prosperity. At the same time, however, the new capacities biotechnology provides have the potential to transform axiomatic social assumptions and core Canadian values. The imminent possibility of human cloning, for example, raises interesting questions about the role of the individual in Canadian society, while the relative availability and the expense of bio-therapeutic techniques raises questions about the rights of the individuals whom these techniques might produce (the right to universal health care, for example). Early stages of the federal government's engagement with biotechnology were primarily concerned with the role to be played by biotechnology as an enabling technology, and the necessity of maintaining a balance between invention and innovation in the innovation system that supports such technologies. Recently it has become clear, however, that the transformative impact of enabling technologies such as biotechnology requires consideration of a broader range of issues, and the incorporation of public debate into the policy process in order to place socially acceptable limits upon biotechnology's transformative potential. A difficulty arises here, however, in that the incorporation of such debate into the policy process conditions that debate with the assumptions of that process, such as the assumption that biotechnology innovation is inherently progressive. As the controversy over GM foods indicates, not all Canadians are convinced that this is the case.

The case of biotechnology illustrates the challenges that enabling technologies pose, both as a technical problem of policy management and as a social problem of political management. The breadth of biotechnology applications and the role anticipated for the biotechnology sector in the Canadian competition strategy have meant the evolution of a horizontal policy file, which nevertheless displays the characteristics of its coordinating ministry; biotechnology policy is inter-ministerial, but is ultimately the responsibility of Industry. As a consequence, social and ethical considerations are incorporated into the formation of Canadian biotechnology policy as part of a project of competitive industrial development. This in turn creates friction and controversy with those elements of Canadian society that see the need to introduce social and ethical concerns into the biotechnology debate at an earlier stage. The characterization of biotechnology as an innovative, enabling technology is ultimately based on a definition of innovation that sees all technology-facilitated economic growth as progressive; in this framework, innovation is for everybody. As the growing controversy over biotechnology indicates, not all of Canadian society sees this form of innovation as an unproblematic process; in this framework, the question most often posed is 'Innovation for whom?'

NOTES

1 Industry Canada, *Building a More Innovative Economy* (Ottawa: Industry Canada, 1994).

2 Michael Porter, *Canada at the Crossroads: The Reality of a New Competitive Environment* (Ottawa: BCNI, 1991).

3 OECD, *Main Definitions and Conventions for the Measurement of Research and Experimental Development (R&D): A Summary of the Frascati Manual* (Paris: OECD, 1994), 4.

4 The idea that innovation depends on a mode of being is characteristic of other approaches than that of innovation systems. For example, Castells refers to a 'milieu of innovation'. By this Castells means a spatially associated cluster of synergistic factors that foster and encourage technological innovation. Castells maintains that innovation is not an isolated instance; rather it 'reflects a given state of knowledge, a particular institutional and industrial environment, a certain availability of skills to define a technical problem and to solve it, and economic mentality to make such application cost-efficient, and a network of producers and users who can communicate their experiences cumulatively.' Manuel Castells, *The Rise of the Network Society* (Oxford: Blackwell, 1996), 37.

The idea that innovation occurs within a dynamic convergence of actors and conditions has been described by a number of different terms. The systemic approach to innovation is, however, gaining predominance, and it is this approach that will concern us in this discussion.

5 For a preliminary survey, see Chris Freeman and Bengt-Ake Lundvall, eds, *Small Countries Facing the Technological Revolution* (New York: Pinter, 1988); Chris Freeman, ed., *The Economics of Innovation* (Brookfield: Edward Elgar, 1990); Bengt-Ake Lundvall, ed., *National Systems of Innovation: Towards a Theory of Innovation and Interactive Learning* (London: Pinter, 1992); Richard R. Nelson, ed., *National Innovation Systems: A Comparative Analysis* (New York: Oxford University Press, 1993); Philip Cooke, 'Introduction: Origins of the Concept', in Hans-Joachim Braczyk, Philip Cooke, and Martin Heidenrich, eds, *Regional Innovation Systems: The Role of Governances in a Globalized World* (London: UCL, 1998).

6 See Lundvall, *National Systems of Innovation*; Nelson, *National Innovation Systems*; and Charles Edquist, ed., *Systems of Innovation: Technologies, Institutions and Organizations* (Washington: Pinter, 1997).

7 See John de la Mothe and Gilles Paquet, 'National Innovation Systems and Instituted Process', in Zoltan Acs, ed., *Regional Innovation, Knowledge and Global Change* (New York: Pinter, 2000), 29–33; David Wolfe, *Social Capital and Cluster Development in Learning Regions* (unpublished working paper, 2000), 3.

8 See Bob Jessop, 'Towards a Schupetarian Workfare State? Preliminary Remarks on Post-Fordist Political Economy', *Studies in Political Economy* 40 (Spring 1993): 7–40.

9 De la Mothe and Paquet, 'National Innovation Systems and Instituted Process', 28.

10 Canadian Biotechnology Advisory Committee, *Canadian Biotechnology Advisory Committee Annual Report 1999–2000* (Ottawa: CBAC, 2000).

11 Industry Canada, *Economic Profile of the Canadian Biotechnology Sector* (Ottawa: Industry Canada, 2000), 6.

12 Genomics is defined as the study of how genetic information is structured, stored, expressed, and altered; transgenenics involves the splicing of new genes into existing organisms to derive a desired effect; and xenotransplantation involves the use of non-human organs in human medical procedures (such as transplanting a pig or baboon heart into a human patient when a suitable human donor is unavailable). These techniques are often combined, for example in efforts to transgenically implant human genes into pigs in order to create a source of xenotransplanted organs that have a lower risk of rejection.

13 See Chuck McNiven, *Canadian Biotechnology Statistics: In Support of the Implementation of the Canadian Biotechnology Strategy* (Ottawa: Statistics Canada, 1999); Industry Canada, *Economic Profile of the Canadian Biotechnology Sector*.

14 Industry Canada. *Economic Profile of the Canadian Biotechnology Sector*.

15 Terence McIntyre, 'Asleep at the Switch: The Federal Government, Environment, and Planning for High Technology: The National Biotechnology Strategy 1983–1993', diss., U. of Waterloo, 1990, 83–5.

16 Ibid., 92–4.

17 National Biotechnology Advisory Council, *NBAC Sixth Report, 1998: Leading the Next Millenium* (Ottawa: Industry Canada, 1998), 13; National

Biotechnology Advisory Committee, *Fact Sheet: National Biotechnology Advisory Committee Sixth Report.* See Web site: http://biotech.gc.ca (1998).

18 The Report also stressed the need to fund biotechnology applications that had not been sufficiently considered. For example, at the time the report was tabled, capital investment in health-related biotechnology outstripped investment in agri-food applications by a factor of 10:1, despite market projections of $2 billion to $3 billion for agri-food by the year 2000. The report argued that diversified funding and the development of strategic clusters in agri-food and natural resources were necessary in order to maximize their economic potential.

19 For example, the Medical Research Council estimated that for every $1 million in research funding, 62 direct and indirect jobs were created, with spillover economic effects emerging from the networking of those employees in broader innovation systems. See National Biotechnology Advisory Council, *NBAC Sixth Report, 1998: Leading the Next Millenium*, 33.

20 Ibid., 34.

21 For example, patent applications for the Harvard onco-mouse (a genetically modified mouse with enhanced susceptibility to certain cancers) were rejected by the Commissioner of Patents and the Federal Court on the basis that Canada had no policy covering the patenting of higher life-forms. The case of the Harvard onco-mouse was later taken up by the successor to the NBAC, the CBAC, and is still a focus of regulatory concern.

22 For a review of the federal biotechnology review process, see G. Bruce Doern, *Inside the Canadian Biotechnology Regulatory System: A Closer Exploratory Look* (Ottawa: CBAC, 2000), a report prepared for the CBAC.

23 The core ministries associated with biotechnology are the ministries of Industry, Agriculture and Agri-Food, Health, Environment, Natural Resources, Fisheries and Oceans, and Foreign Affairs and International Trade.

24 See Bio-Industries Branch, Industry Canada, *The Canadian Biotechnology Strategy Online: Building the Canadian Biotechnology Strategy.* See Web site: www.strategis.gc.ca 1998; Industry Canada, *The 1998 Canadian Biotechnology Strategy: An Ongoing Renewal Process* (Ottawa: Industry Canada, 1998).

25 The vision for Canadian biotechnology called for efforts to enhance the quality of life of Canadians in the areas of health, safety, the environment, and social and economic development by positioning Canada as a responsible world leader in biotechnology. The nine goals for the CBS were to ensure Canadian access to biotechnology, to ensure an effective scientific base by means of strategic investment, to position Canada as a leader in social and ethical biotechnology issues, to develop a sensitivity to the capacity of developing countries to develop and manage biotechnology, to improve the public's understanding of biotechnology, to solicit advice on biotechnology, to promote understanding of and improvement in the Canadian regulatory framework for biotechnology, to develop a human resources strategy to support the development of biotechnology in Canada, and to develop multi-stakeholder action plans. See Bio-Industries Branch, Industry Canada, *The Canadian Biotechnology Strategy Online: Building the Canadian Biotechnology Strategy.*

26 Bio-Industries Branch, Industry Canada, *The Canadian Biotechnology Strategy Online: Building the Canadian Biotechnology Strategy.*

27 Canadian Biotechnology Advisory Committee, *Canadian Biotechnology Advisory Committee Annual Report 1999–2000.*

28 Canadian Biotechnology Advisory Committee, *Program Plan 2000.* See Web site: www.cbaccccb.ca/english/, (2000).

29 See Canadian Biotechnology Advisory Committee, *Canadian Biotechnology Advisory Committee Annual Report 1999–2000*; Canadian Biotechnology Advisory Committee, *Program Plan 2000.*

30 Ibid.

31 See Canadian Environmental Network, *Letter to the Government of Canada: Ministers, CBAC Committee members, and Prime Minister* (Ottawa: CEN, 2001).

32 Council of Canadians, *Media Release: Council of Canadians Dismisses Biased Biotech Report.* See Web site: www.canadians.org, (2001).

33 A. Naimark, *CBAC Response to NGO.* See Web site: www.cbac-cccb.ca, (2001).

34 See Canadian Biotechnology Advisory Committee, *Canadian Biotechnology Advisory Committee Annual Report 1999–2000*; Canadian Biotechnology Advisory Committee, *Program Plan 2000.*

35 Canadian Biotechnology Advisory Committee, *Canadian Biotechnology Advisory Committee Annual Report 1999–2000.*

10

The Return of Directed Incrementalism: Innovating Social Policy the Canadian Way

MICHAEL J. PRINCE

A style of social policy innovation that was prominent from the 1940s to the early 1970s is returning to prominence in the current project of reforming Canada's social union. In the earlier period, the making of social policy was less about sweeping reform than about ordered change; not so much about disjointed incrementalism as about directed incrementalism, 'a sequence of actions by governments implemented one by one over time, but guided and connected by a general conception of, and policy agenda for, the social role of the state'.[1] It took about 30 years and over 10 federal government mandates for the vision of a comprehensive pan-Canadian system of social security to be realized, and many, though not all, of its constituent ideas to be implemented in one form or another. Program creation, expansion, and restructuring took place in child and family benefits, elderly and retirement benefits, hospital and medical insurance, social housing, and welfare assistance. This period of social program expansion was followed by 20 years of critique and crisis, budgetary restraint and policy retrenchment, well into the 1990s, as governments pursued agendas of reducing deficits and controlling debt loads. This period too was very much an example of incrementalism, but still anything but disjointed. Rather, these decades were marked by a relentless and stealthy process of restructuring tax and transfer benefits, with governments less forthcoming about the thinking and planning behind the changes than they appear to be now.

In the late 1990s and early 2000s, there are signs that directed incrementalism— the setting of bold goals and working toward them step by step over the medium to long term—is returning as a strategy for innovating social policy in Canada. Examples include the articulation of new policy visions in several policy sectors, such as disability, children and family, and Aboriginal affairs; significant changes to Canada's governance regime itself, including tax collection agreements in fiscal federalism and the approval of the Nisga'a Treaty; and new approaches to the restructuring of some major social programs, such as a partial funding of the Canada Pension Plan (CPP) and the development of income-tested child benefits (provincial as well as federal) through the National Child Benefit (NCB) reform.

As Heraclitus wrote 26 centuries ago, 'One cannot step twice into the same river'; directed incrementalism, as a style of social reform, has returned to a political community, an economy, and a society vastly different from those of earlier times. In the current post-deficit era, social policy development is on the agenda once again, spurred in part by the reassertion of an activist federal role with the emergence of budget surpluses, and in part by a clearer understanding at the executive level that the making of social policy contributes to economic policy and to national prosperity. But we are not stepping into the same river. This latest phase of policy innovation is occurring within a different configuration of power relations in the Canadian social union, with provinces and territories exercising relatively more influence over social policy, individually and collectively, than previously. The same can be suggested of Aboriginal communities, social movements, and clientele groups. Then, too, strong undercurrents of the restraint age remain, evident for example in the closed-ended nature of federal transfers to other governments, in contrast to the open-ended cost-shared agreements of the expansion age. Elements of stealth live on in the new period, including the non-indexation of provincial social assistance and child benefit rates. The long arm of the federal Finance Department still reaches out to social policy-making, wielding considerable force. Likewise, old ideas and visions collide with newer paradigms that view social policies more as investments in opportunity than as protections against risk. Simultaneously, older policy ideas are revived by the emergence of modern concerns about social capital and community cohesion.

INNOVATION AND SOCIAL POLICY: PROCESSES AND POLITICS

In the world of public affairs, innovation is usually equated with implementation, not invention. For most governments most of the time, policy innovations are not the result of a moment of total intellectual originality, a conceptual discovery that leads to the first application of a unique idea; they are, rather, the result of the adoption of a vision or major goal, a policy instrument, a rule of decision-making, a governance arrangement, or a resource commitment that is new to a particular jurisdiction, but that has originated elsewhere. Thus, innovation in public policy involves the diffusion of new approaches, the drawing of lessons by interested others, and the acceptance and adoption of new approaches in whole or in part. Innovations are significant departures in practice, changes that lead to policies and programs that are qualitatively different from the existing ones.

Innovation is but one approach, among several others, to making changes in social policies and programs. Various approaches are outlined and described in Table 10.1; they range from the elimination of programs, to the restoration of previously diminished programs and services, through to the introduction of new ideas, structures, and benefits to practices either new or existing. The changes at the two ends of the spectrum can be regarded as opposite kinds of innovation; both involve the implementation of new ideas and practices in the social union, but one moves in the direction of rolling back the social role of the state, whereas the other enhances and expands that role.

Each one of these approaches has been called a reform, an advance, or an improvement by one government or another—an example of the use of rhetoric to portray certain changes in a middle-of-the-road or even positive light, and proof that the direction of change is in the eye of the beholder. Not all policy changes are creative by design or progressive in their effects for low-income and marginalized Canadians. What one person or group may deem to be an innovation in social policy, others may well reject on the grounds that the change is harmful to a particular group or unsustainable by the public purse. What constitutes an innovation, then, is in large part a political question of values, and the position in society of the person making the judgment.

Innovation, as a process, is commonly described as involving a sequence of stages: the generation, conception, or discovery of a new idea or practice; the introduction or initial application of the new idea or practice by a pioneering organization or jurisdiction; its early acceptance and adoption by other organizations or jurisdictions; and the more widespread implementation of the new idea and practice in the activities and structures of various sectors.[2] This pattern of initial innovation, early diffusion by a few other jurisdictions, a period of 10 or 20 years during which it is adopted by still other jurisdictions, and, finally, some kind of policy convergence across the country, has been repeated numerous times in Canadian social policy, most notably perhaps in the fields of health care and income security.[3] This experience shows that social policy innovation is not a quick and simple process, but a multifaceted and longer-term one, which is quintessentially political, as it must be in a federal, liberal democratic state.

As a political course of action, policy innovation comprises several additional processes. These include defining problems and framing opportunities; capturing public attention and articulating a persuasive case for change; managing conflict, or resistance to the new ideas and practices; and bargaining to build consensus, secure acceptance, and exert influence among individuals and groups with

Table 10.1
Making Social Policy Changes

Type of Change	General Features	Recent Examples
Contractive Innovation	Sharp and perhaps sudden change that shrinks a previous policy role of government.	Abolition of the Canada Assistance Plan and four of its five conditions, and its replacement by the Canada Health and Social Transfer (CHST) in 1996.
Erosion or Stealth	Gradual and steady changes that wear away a policy or program through attrition.	Partial de-indexation and non-indexation of various direct expenditure and tax credit programs. A prominent technique used from the late 1980s through the 1990s, which continues today in some provincial programs and federal benefits.
Experimentation	Specific, time-limited actions undertaken to test and learn something of a policy intervention.	Self-sufficiency projects on single parents and social assistance conducted in New Brunswick and British Columbia.
Restoration	Reinstatement, in full or part, of resources or design features such as eligibility to a program or agency.	Full indexation of the personal income tax/transfer system in 2000, which marked a return to pre-1986 policy.
Extension	Partial changes to programs that supplement or enlarge existing scopes or benefits.	The doubling, in 2000/1, of the maximum duration of combined maternity and parental leave under Employment Insurance to 50 weeks leave for parenting.
Expansive Innovation	Creation of a wholly new policy or program or introduction of a basic structural change to an existing program.	National Child Benefit strategy since 1997. Changes to CPP in 1998 to allow partial funding and investment of funds in market.

different interests in and responses to a planned change. Policy innovations are political interventions. They have consequences for the role of the state in the economy, as with the new investment policy of the CPP; for the role of the state in the well-being of families, as with the Canada Child Tax Benefit (CCTB) and the National Children's Agenda; and for the respective roles of different orders of government, as with the recent tax collection agreements and the Nisga'a Treaty.

Policy Innovation and the Social Union

Social policy innovation is of central importance to current issues and developments in Canadian federalism. A secondary rationale for the introduction of the Canada Health and Social Transfer (CHST) in 1996 was to end the supposed intrusiveness of the Canada Assistance Plan (CAP), with its several conditions for cost-sharing, thereby enabling provinces to pursue their own innovative approaches to social service delivery and income assistance reform.[4] The primary reason for the introduction of the CHST was to cut federal transfers to the provinces at a time when the federal government was dramatically cutting its own direct expenditures. Moreover, the federal Finance Department wished to end open-ended cost-sharing arrangements like CAP. In a similar vein, part of the NCB strategy agreed to in 1998 by the federal and provincial governments (with the exception of the Quebec government, which abstained because of the Parti Québécois's decision to boycott federal-provincial negotiations) is that provinces and territories can reinvest the social assistance savings they realize through reductions in welfare expenditures on behalf of children, as Ottawa invests more funds into the CCTB, in a range of alternatives, including income-tested child benefits, earnings supplements, and social and health services for low-income families with children.

For the Social Union Framework Agreement (SUFA), signed by provincial, territorial, and federal first ministers (all except Quebec's) in 1999, what constitutes an innovation has implications for triggering certain intergovernmental rules of the game. In section four of the SUFA, governments agree to give each other advance notice prior to the implementation of a major change in a social policy or program that will likely substantially affect another government. Section five, on the federal spending power, provides for the federal government to give provinces at least three months notice and an offer to consult before launching new Canada-wide initiatives funded through direct transfers to individuals or organizations for health care, post-secondary education, social assistance, and social services. On intergovernmental social transfers to the provinces and territories, whether cost-shared or block-funded, the SUFA commits the federal government not to introduce new Canada-wide social initiatives without the agreement of a majority of provincial governments. This goes well beyond prior notice. From the perspective of provinces, which launched the process for establishing a set of rules for managing the social union, these are slender limitations on the federal government's spending power. Even these mild rules, some observers argue, have not been consistently followed by Ottawa.[5] From the Ottawa Liberal perspective, mild rules are justified, on the grounds that the federal spending power is constitutional, that it has enabled governments to introduce new and innovative programs, and that it is essential to the promotion of Canada-wide goals and citizenship.

Another policy debate over the social union concerns the equalization program and whether or not it is in need of innovation. Some premiers are calling for fundamental changes to the formula as well as for an increase in the level of payments, while Canada's Minister of Intergovernmental Affairs, arguing that 'it ain't broke', has advanced a case for the status quo.[6] This issue and others reveal that the meanings provinces ascribe to any given federal social policy innovation are diverse. For some provinces it is a welcome intervention; for others it constitutes unilateral meddling in provincial domains; and for Quebec governments of all political stripes, it is typically seen as a serious and unwanted invasion into areas of jurisdiction that are, under the constitution, exclusively provincial—even though Quebec usually takes the federal money.

DIRECTED INCREMENTALISM: THE ART OF MOVING FORWARD

In public policy circles, the concept and practice of incrementalism is customarily associated with marginal changes related to immediate problems, rarely with substantial reforms or with innovation that is focussed on future possibilities. Charles Lindblom, the writer most responsible for popularizing the concept and examining it theoretically, coined the term 'disjointed incrementalism', or 'the science of muddling through'.[7] Lindblom stressed the practical limitations of an approach to decision-making in the public domain that is comprehensive and rational, arguing that for the most part policy- and decision-making is unplanned, and informed by incomplete information and contested analyses; the changes that result are relatively small shifts from existing activities. Lindblom did allow that incremental decision-making need not necessarily be conservative, suggesting that a series of small steps could build up, over time, to a major and possibly innovative change in policy. Disjointed incrementalism may produce significant change, but as the result of an accumulation of small adjustments, not as the achievement of previously stated major aims. It is this latter phenomenon, change that is focussed upon a particular goal, that distinguishes directed or sustained incrementalism as a style of social policy reform from the disjointed variety.

Directed incrementalism, as a way of making and altering social policy, recognizes that by and large innovative policy is implemented step by step. This approach, while characterized by a succession of small, moderate steps, can occasionally include a larger one, which is sometimes timed to coincide with a general election.[8] In addition, directed incremental reforms are informed by goals, visions, and guiding principles. It is through this style of policy reform that the political art of moving toward a set of preferred results achieves success.

There is an explicit purposefulness to directed incrementalism; ideas and images of social policy play an important role in informing policy designs and implementation strategies. Concepts similar to directed incrementalism can be found in the policy literature. One of these is 'rolling reform', to describe a process of policy innovation 'distinguished from both "incremental" and "omnibus" reform, in that it projects long-term restructuring goals but reaches them in small and partial steps.'[9] Another author has spoken of 'goal-directed muddling through', in which policy-makers articulate a vision for change, with goals and objectives, and adhere to that vision while responding to social problems through step-by-step reforms.[10]

Ken Battle has proposed the phrase 'relentless incrementalism' to describe the dominant process by which Canadian social policy is restructured. 'Relentless incrementalism consists of strings of reforms, seemingly small and discrete when made,
that accumulate to become more than the sum of their parts. Relentless incrementalism is purposive and patterned, not haphazard and unintended'.[11] Such change
can occur even without a strong and open public statement of values and aims, as
was the case with many of the reforms in the 1980s and 1990s that were characterized by stealth, even though there was a purpose and a plan behind them.

These allied concepts underline the fact that directed incrementalism is planned
change, with policy reforms deliberately moving toward long-term goals. This is not
to suggest that change inevitably happens smoothly, in a single direction. Reforms
may be patterned—something always easier to see in hindsight—but they are not
always necessarily neatly arranged or preordained. Both the understanding of the
issues and the policy goals can shift. Major social policy innovations in Canada are
typically implemented in an adaptive, fluid, and varied manner, within existing
power structures and prevailing beliefs, a process marked by struggles and setbacks
as well as successes. Lindblom stressed the difficulties in clarifying and organizing
values and goals so as to guide policy choices. However, while dispute on values is
inevitable, this does not mean that agreement among governments and with other
sectors is impossible. When visions for the National Children's Agenda and a disability policy strategy were being articulated, a consensus was reached by a number of stakeholders concerning guiding principles and desired outcomes. This
process was no doubt aided by extensive consultation processes and by the prospect
of new expenditures' being committed to these policy fields; it was probably also
informed by new thinking and increases in the amount of research on these areas.

Directed incrementalism relies on the enunciation of an open statement of core
social values, ambitious goals and working principles, and the adoption of a relatively long time frame for implementing policy innovations. Neil Bradford has noted
concerning this long-term perspective, 'It is a truism of federal politics in Canada
that national parties have not been effective catalysts or carriers of policy innovation. Yet, lengthening our time horizon reminds us that there have been major shifts
in the course of Canadian economic and social policy.'[12] Bradford describes
Canada's style of policy innovation as 'incremental-technocratic', to stress the vital
role played by central agencies of government, supported on occasion by major
royal commissions, as sources of new ideas and strategic directions. Incremental
policy-making may produce changes that are variations on what has existed in the
past, but, given a dimension of goal-directedness, these changes can also be visions
of the future. In directed incrementalism, the past and the future speak simultaneously to the present.

THREE LEVELS OF SOCIAL POLICY INNOVATION

Policy innovation involves three levels of action:

- new ways of conceptualizing, justifying, and thinking about public interventions;
- new ways for governments to structure themselves and interrelate with each other and with other sectors and agencies in civil society; and
- new ways of designing, financing, and delivering services and benefits.

Paradigms, the polity, and programs, therefore, are the three key levels at which innovating social policy affects substance (the what) and clientele (the whom). Any particular innovation can have consequences for each of the three levels, but often in ways that vary from moment to moment, or over an extended period of time. An innovation that substantially and concurrently changes actions and beliefs at all three levels would truly be a transformational innovation, but such innovations occur rarely.[13] Policy innovations, including the directed incrementalist kind, usually concentrate on one level more than the others, at least initially. In other words, policy innovations are multifaceted, yet less than all-inclusive, because, in addition to refashioning their contexts, they are in some manner shaped by them.

Innovation in Policy Paradigms: Switching or Stacking Perspectives?
The relationship between ideas and innovation in Canadian social policy has of late been of considerable interest to community activists and policy academics, and has been given more and more attention by federal and provincial government officials; all of these groups are engaged in formulating new paradigms or frameworks of ideas for certain policy fields. Thomas Kuhn, who applied the concept of paradigm to the natural sciences to explain the structure of scientific revolutions, conceived of paradigms as research traditions, the commonly accepted ideas, assumptions, and practices held by a group of scholars in a given field of inquiry. Innovations or revolutions in science occur, according to Kuhn, as the result of a paradigm switch, a sudden event in which the prevailing paradigm in a field is totally rejected, and replaced by an alternative paradigm. For Kuhn, 'the transition between competing paradigms cannot be made a step at a time.'[14] A paradigm shift, in this view, is a non-incremental process marked by a sharp and radical change in goals, problem definitions, and program responses. For Kuhn, a paradigm switch occurs in the world of science when the prevailing paradigm has become less and less able to adequately explain events and new findings that have resulted from crises, inventions, and discoveries. Eventually, the tension caused by this widening gap between paradigm and practice triggers a change in paradigm.

   In Canadian political discourse, policy paradigms find expression in legislation, intergovernmental agreements, vision statements, and documents concerning guiding principles. Such sets of ideas include an accepted terminology or discourse, endorsed by at least a sub-set of the policy actors in a field, for labelling and talking about issues, for posing questions, and for expressing beliefs on the preferred scope and limits of potential actions. In the world of public policy, a paradigm switch can result from a buildup of crises and policy failures, the development of new and persuasive evidence, dramatically increased and sustained media and public attention on an issue, a shift in the roles and relationships of individuals and organizations in a policy field, or key judicial decisions with constitutional implications.[15]

Social policy innovation is characterized not so much by paradigm switches, or even quick paradigm shifts, as by paradigm stacking. In the directed incremental style of reform, change in policy paradigms is more gradual and mixed than sudden and total, and frequently takes place through negotiations among federal and provincial/territorial government officials, or between government officials and Aboriginal leaders or representatives of civil society organizations. By and large, old policy paradigms do not die off in the face of the quick triumph of new ones; changes in paradigms are more an evolutionary than a revolutionary process. Deep-rooted paradigms in policy fields coexist and interact with alternative ones, at times clashing and at other times complementing each other, sometimes over decades.[16] Table 10.2 presents examples of the reality of paradigm stacking in several fields of contemporary Canadian social policy.

In public policy toward Aboriginal peoples, contending world views are held by Canadian governments on the one hand and by Aboriginal communities on the other. Michael Howlett portrays the present-day period as one of contestation between the vision of self-determination, a 'new paradigm [that] has yet to be institutionalized in any meaningful way', and 'elements of the old assimilationist paradigm in the courts and various constitutional forums.'[17] Augie Fleras similarly argues that, despite the rhetoric of reform in recent years, it is premature to declare that an Aboriginal paradigm shift has taken place, because a bureaucratic and a

Table 10.2

Competing Paradigms in Selected Social Policy Fields

Policy Field	*Paradigms in Effect*
Aboriginal Affairs	• Assimilation/Extinguishment of Rights
Children and Families	• Family Responsibility • Investment in Children
Disability	• Worthy Poor Assistance • Bio-Medical Rehabilitation • Citizenship and Human Rights
Health Care	• Medical Treatment • Social Determinants • Federal vs Provincial vs National • Public vs Private Provision
Income Maintenance	• Universality vs Selectivity • Economic Liberalism • Social Protection • Cultural Recognition

decolonizing perspective continue to coexist; rather than a paradigm shift, we have 'competing paradigms and entrenched interests'—in short, a 'paradigm muddle'.[18]

Research by Caroline Beauvais and Jane Jenson regarding policy thinking about the respective responsibilities of families and governments for the well-being of children identifies two policy paradigms. The older, well-entrenched paradigm they term Family Responsibility. 'Its hallmark is that parents are almost solely responsible for making decisions about their children's well-being. The role of public policy is to facilitate their decision-making by allowing a range of options to emerge. However, finding the necessary money to support certain options is also the responsibility of families.'[19] Access to adequate money and to public policies depends on parents' participation in the paid labour force and their status within it. Beauvais and Jenson suggest that the following innovative policy actions are informed by this paradigm: 'the federal government's decision to substantially increase paid parental leaves within the Employment Insurance regime; Quebec's draft bill that would extend parental insurance to almost every working mother, as well as offer a separate paternity leave; and the extension of unpaid parental leave in most provinces from, for several, 17 or 18 weeks to 35 to 37 weeks and, in some cases, up to 52 weeks.'[20]

With changes in the labour market and family structures, the emergence of new evidence of early childhood development, and growing critiques of social assistance, the old paradigm has come under increasing scrutiny and challenge. A second, newer way of thinking about families, children's needs, and the role of the state has arisen, the 'Investing in Children' paradigm. 'The watchword of this paradigm is investment. Its policy instruments are designed to express this commitment to *investment*, seeking to spend money where it is most needed and where it will generate a positive return.' With a greater emphasis on generating positive outcomes for children, especially children at risk, the focus of policy shifts somewhat away from the parents to the children, but also to the community and to the important role for health and social programs. Beauvais and Jenson present signs that there is a paradigm shift from the old to the new, but conclude that the two paradigms currently exist beside each other and that, given that both paradigms have strengths and weaknesses, the strategy of policy-makers might be to 'retain the best of each paradigm in a mixed model, rather than forcing a choice between them.'[21]

In disability policy, three paradigms are at play: the centuries-old view of people with disabilities as being 'worthy poor' deserving of local charity and eventually state assistance; the bio-medical model that stresses physical and mental limitations and incapacities; and the more recent human rights and full citizenship perspective, which seeks to enable persons with disabilities to participate in and contribute to society in accordance with their aspirations and their status as members of a democratic political community. As the twenty-first century begins, all three paradigms are in effect, and are reflected in the mass media and public discourse, a situation that leads to complexities in program design and challenges in mobilizing the disability community for innovations in policy.[22]

A similar pattern of competing paradigms within a policy field is apparent in the other fields outlined in Table 10.2, as well as in policy fields beyond.[23] Paradigm stacking occurs because of the fragmentation and complexity of modern civil society in general, and of the Canadian state in particular. Different sets of policy ideas are embedded in, and implemented and defended by, the programs and practices of different organizations, professions, and levels of government. Even if a particular paradigm in a policy field is challenged and goes out of intellectual or political fashion, it continues to be used, because it serves the interests of some groups, at the same time as other groups advance an alternative paradigm. A genuine paradigm shift may take decades, because of institutionalized differences and mistrust among groups and governments, and the high financial or political costs of fundamental change.[24] Moreover, it may happen that paradigms are stacked because they are somewhat compatible in practice. Influential paradigms are malleable and open to different interpretations and to updating: what makes them popular and enduring is their susceptibility to generalization and their apparent power to explain things. As Beauvais and Jenson suggest in relation to child and family policy, competing paradigms may well have overlapping and complementary ideas. Some aspects of each may be relevant to the understanding of social issues and the designing of policy responses—a useful feature, considering that no single paradigm is exhaustively comprehensive of the human condition.

Even when two or more paradigms active in a policy field are in some ways complementary, some clashes in understanding and perspective may still occur. Such clashes generate tension and turbulence over governing ideas, possibly resulting, as in the case of Aboriginal affairs, in 'erratic policy experiments, unfocused initiatives and false starts.'[25] They can also result in gaps, overlaps, and, consequently, inequities in program design and service provision, as in children and family policy, thereby raising valid concerns about unevenness in the quality of citizenship experienced by Canadians. Having multiple paradigms in operation in a policy field can also shape the choice of policy instruments and the style of federalism. In disability policy, the worthy poor and bio-medical paradigms, with their emphasis on rehabilitation and on segregated services for special needs, are heavily inclined toward service provision and toward delivery systems staffed by professionals. This fits well with provincial responsibilities and activities. The human rights and citizenship paradigm, by contrast, places greater emphasis on the reform of laws and the use of tribunals, the Charter of Rights and Freedoms, and courts to adjudicate claims. This is a more pan-Canadian and federalist outlook. With three paradigms operating within disability policy, there is a need for collaboration among disability groups and among governments.

The Political Community: Changing Rules, Roles, and Relationships

A second level of policy innovation begins to operate when governments restructure themselves and interrelate in new ways with other political bodies. It is within this wider governance context that policy paradigms are expressed and debated and programs are formulated and delivered.

The Nisga'a Treaty

Emerging forms of Aboriginal self-government range from the 'public government' model of the new territory of Nunavut, through the regional public of Nunavik, to reserve-based First Nation governments, with varying levels of autonomy and funding arrangements, to visions of urban self-government. In addition, innovative composite forms of Aboriginal and public government have been created by modern treaties in Yukon and the Nisga'a territory. Our attention is on the governing and fiscal arrangements created by the Nisga'a Treaty.[26]

Ratified by the Nisga'a people and the provincial and federal legislatures in 1999 and 2000, the Nisga'a Treaty is the first modern-day treaty in British Columbia, the only province in Canada in which the majority of Aboriginal peoples have not signed treaties. The Nisga'a Treaty has a number of noteworthy features with respect to governance structure, jurisdictional model, and fiscal arrangements. First and foremost, the Indian Act no longer applies, a change that has both substantial and deeply symbolic consequences. Nisga'a lands are no longer reserves within the meaning of the Indian Act. Instead, they are owned communally by the Nisga'a nation, with title vested in the Nisga'a government. Second, the treaty is comprehensive, in that all potential jurisdictions are included, and it is constitutional, in that the rights therein receive section 35 protections in the Constitution Act, 1982. Third, while the federal-provincial division of powers remains intact, the Nisga'a government has the authority to make laws to preserve, promote, and develop Nisga'a culture and language, and can make laws that prevail over federal and provincial laws concerning Nisga'a lands and the operation of the Nisga'a government.

The governance structure is moving from a two-tier system, with a Tribal Council and four Indian bands, to a three-tier system, with the Nisga'a Lisims (or central) Government, four Village Governments, and three Urban Locals, for Nisga'a citizens who live off the territory. The new structure is a form of Aboriginal federalism, with both the central government and the village governments enjoying law-making powers in their own spheres of competence.

On fiscal matters, section 87 of the Indian Act will no longer apply to Nisga'a citizens in respect to sales taxes after the treaty has been in effect for eight years, and in respect to all other taxes it will no longer apply after 12 years. The Nisga'a Treaty also includes a Fiscal Financing Arrangement (FFA) to support program and service delivery in a range of fields. Every five years, or at other periods as Canada, British Columbia, and Nisga'a agree, a FFA will be negotiated. A localized version of the equalization principle, a cornerstone of Canadian fiscal federalism, is enshrined in the fiscal arrangements. A central purpose of the Nisga'a FFA is to enable the provision of agreed-upon public services and programs to Nisga'a citizens and, where

applicable, non-Nisga'a occupants of Nisga'a Lands, at levels reasonably comparable to those prevailing in northwest British Columbia.

The Nisga'a Treaty and other emerging forms of Aboriginal self-government illustrate relatively new institutional expressions of rights, identity, and governance. The
full realization of Aboriginal self-government will require significant revisions to fiscal and political federalism and some innovations yet to be identified. The emergence of an Aboriginal order of government is a slow-moving constitutional change,
of the sort that created and continues to shape the unwritten part of the Canadian
constitution. It is a form of directed incremental reform of the polity.

Federal-Provincial-Territorial Tax Collection Agreements

Along with intergovernmental transfer agreements and the allocation of revenue
and expenditure responsibilities between governments, tax collection agreements
(TCAs) are major components of fiscal federalism in Canada. With the exception of
Quebec, all provinces and territories have TCAs with the federal government for the
administration and collection of personal income taxes.[27] Until recent reforms, the
TCAs operated on a 'tax on tax' system, whereby provincial tax rates were computed
as a percentage of the basic federal tax. Since the late 1980s, however, provinces
have proposed further decentralization of the personal income tax system, to enable
them to assume more autonomy in the use of the tax system to design economic
and social programs.

In 1998, governments agreed to greater fiscal flexibility, allowing provinces and
territories the option of levying their personal income taxes on taxable income ('tax
on income') or remaining with the basic federal tax ('tax on tax') system. The agreement coincided with the arrival of surpluses in the federal budgets and the prospect
of federal tax cuts, which, under the 'tax on tax' model, would automatically result
in cuts in provincial revenues as well. To provinces that were reeling from federal
cuts to transfer payments under the CHST and from other federal restraint actions,
such as those affecting Employment Insurance, this was intolerable. If provincial tax
rates were decoupled from federal rates, provincial revenues would be insulated
from federal tax reductions and provinces would be able to design their personal
income tax systems independently of Ottawa's rate structure.

Over the past few years, all provinces have announced their move to a 'tax on
income' approach, which means that as of the 2001 tax year, each province calcu-
lates provincial income tax directly on taxable income, rather than as a percentage
of basic federal tax. With justification, this has been billed by politicians and academics as the biggest change in the TCAs and the personal income tax system in
Canada in nearly 40 years.[28] As a policy change, this is constructive innovation (see
Table 10.1), the introduction of a basic structural change to an existing intergovernmental arrangement. It is an incremental reform in that a common federal definition of taxable income, which ensures a common tax base, is maintained, as is a
shared system for the administration and collection of personal income taxes for
the nine provinces and three territories. Further, where federal definitions of

non-refundable tax credits exist, such as those for charitable donations, provincial and territorial credits will use the same definitions. These principles are aimed at ensuring a degree of administrative efficiency and economy, policy simplicity, and consistency in the personal income tax system, while allowing greater flexibility on the part of provincial and territorial governments.

The provinces and territories now possess augmented authority over the setting of the number of tax brackets, and the tax rates to go with the brackets; over any number of surtaxes and low-income reductions; over any number of refundable tax credits; and over a distinct block of non-refundable tax credits. With respect to federal expenditure-based credits, including the CPP, EI, tuition, medical expenses, and charitable donations, provinces and territories now have the ability to raise the level of the federal gross credit.[29] In the short term, these measures constitute a defensive move to protect provinces and territories from revenue losses due to unilateral tax policy changes and cuts by Ottawa. They also reflect a longstanding demand by provinces for greater control over their fiscal policies—for a 'provincialization' of tax policy. One scholar of Canadian federalism calls it 'an important growth of effective provincial power.'[30] In the longer term, the measures will likely produce further experimentation and divergence in economic and social policy-making through the use of various income tax instruments.

Policies and Programs: New Approaches to Financing
and Delivering Child Benefits

The National Child Benefit (NCB) has been hailed as the first new national social program in 30 years, representing a significant return of federal involvement in social policy-making, a return accompanied by innovative actions on income assistance for low-income families with children.[31] While the Canada Child Tax Benefit (CCTB), which constitutes the federal component of the federal-provincial NCB reform, is not entirely a new initiative—there has been a refundable income-tested child tax benefit in the federal social policy tool kit since the late 1970s—it has some important new features with respect to how Ottawa spends, on whom, and what amount. With the abolition of CAP and the move to the CHST in 1996, Ottawa moved significantly away from the role of sharing the cost of financial assistance to some low-income families provided through needs-tested social assistance programs offered, designed, and managed by the provinces. Under the old system of uncoordinated federal and provincial income support to low-income families with children, working poor families typically received only about half the level of child-related benefits provided to families on welfare. Through the CCTB, Ottawa has moved substantially toward equalizing the level of child benefits provided to all low-income families, whatever their sources of income. A core aim of the CCTB, as a social policy reform, is 'to raise child-related payments for poor families not on social assistance *up to* the level paid to social assistance families'.[32] While the federal government is substantially increasing its child benefits for low-income families, it has also made modest improvements in the level of benefits paid to non-poor families. The income-tested CCTB, while it pays its maximum amount to low-income families, is not targeted narrowly on the poor. It also covers modest-income and middle-income families, excluding only high-income families.

The NCB was developed jointly by Federal/Provincial/Territorial Ministers of Social Services and introduced in July 1998. The main goals of the NCB are to reduce the depth of child poverty and to increase the labour market attachment of adults on welfare.[33] Under the NCB, the federal government injects new funds into child benefits through the CCTB, and participating provinces, territories, and First Nations commit to reinvest the welfare savings into new or enhanced programs of their choosing, for low-income families and their children. These reinvestments cover a broad range of provincial initiatives, including child care, early childhood development, income-tested child benefits and earnings supplements, and supplementary health care. In 1999, the Federal/Provincial/Territorial Council of Ministers of Social Policy released a discussion paper, *A National Children's Agenda: Developing a Shared Vision*, that set out a common vision, with common goals and areas for action. Following extensive consultations and reactions, an amended vision statement was formulated and published in 2000, giving explicit recognition to the need for programs for children with different abilities and life circumstances.[34]

The CCTB has two parts: the 'basic Child Tax Benefit' for low- and middle-income families and the 'National Child Benefit Supplement' for low-income families, that is, families with net incomes in 2001 of $32,000 or less. As of 2000, the CCTB levels (both the base benefit and the supplement) and their family income thresholds are fully indexed to inflation. At present, about eight in ten families with children are eligible for the CCTB. Along with the CCTB, there are income-tested child benefits and earnings supplement programs in nine provinces and all three territories, most of which are administered by the Canada Customs and Revenue Agency on behalf of provinces and territories through the personal income tax system.[35]

Within the context of the National Children's Agenda and the NCB, the CCTB is an example of directed incrementalism at work in Canadian social policy: it is guided by an overall vision concerning children; it has been put in place by means of intergovernmental agreements; and a series of expenditure commitments and policy enhancements have been projected over a multi-year time frame. In the 1996 budget the federal government allocated an additional $250 million to the then Child Tax Benefit, and another $600 million in the 1997 budget. The CCTB was established in July 1998 with an initial $850 million 'down-payment', which was followed by a further $425 million in July 1999. In January 2000, the CCTB became indexed to the yearly inflation rate. In July 2000 another $425 million was allocated, and in July 2001 a further $740 million. Federal income support for families with children has grown from $5.1 billion in 1996/7 to approximately $7.8 billion in 2001/2. Over this period, the maximum CCTB payable to an eligible family with one child has increased from $1,020 in 1996/7 to $2,372 in 2001/2.

With increases in the base CTB and in its threshold for maximum benefits, and a lowering of the benefit reduction rate, the proportion of families with children who qualify for the CCTB will grow from around 80 per cent to 95 per cent or more by July 2004, effectively a return to universal coverage in federal family benefits. The Chrétien Liberal government has pledged to increase the CCTB maximum benefit to about $2,520 for a first child, $2,380 for a second child, and $2,311 for each subsequent child by July 2004. Thus, a low-income family with four children is projected to receive approximately $9,450 by 2004/5. This amount falls below the levels proposed by social policy think tanks and advocacy groups by several hundred to a few thousand dollars. Even by mid-decade, in several provinces some families on social assistance will still be receiving some child-related benefits through provincial welfare programs rather than fully by the CCTB.[36]

The CCTB and wider NCB affect families with children, social policy, and federalism in a number of ways. One effect is a 'federalization' of child benefits, with Ottawa playing a growing role relative to the provinces and territories. For parents of children still on provincial welfare, a larger proportion of their benefit income is coming from federal income-tested support and a smaller proportion from provincial needs-tested assistance. With this federalization comes a modernization of program delivery: compared to provincial welfare, the CCTB is neither as discretionary nor as stigmatizing, and it is also less complex. A second effect is the move back toward universality, with a return to the situation in which almost all families are eligible for federal child benefits, last in effect a decade and more ago. A third effect is the enrichment of child benefits, although, still far from adequate, they are far from meeting the vision of the National Children's Agenda.

That the removal of all children in Canada from welfare has not been achieved, and will not likely be achieved for many years, is a sobering reminder that the reform journey we are on is one of directed incrementalism.

CONCLUSION

Social policy innovations involve advancing particular ideas and visions; changing the rules, and the roles and relationships of governments and other policy actors; and altering in considerable ways the structure of program benefits and obligations within and across generations and social groups.

The style of setting bold goals and then working toward them step by step over the long term is shaped and supported by various political and social factors. Of course, there are the ever-present realities of incomplete knowledge, limited budgets, competing claims, resistance to change, and reluctance to change, possibly on the part of a host of public and private groups. Then too, there are the dynamics of Canadian federalism, the pressures on national unity, and our cultural, political, and geographical diversities.[37] Joined with these are the familiar political imperatives of balancing different policy objectives on a crowded government agenda, mediating different stakeholder interests, and rarely starting from scratch on an issue. These factors help explain the incremental tendencies, but what of the more substantial, goal-oriented, and longer-term side of policy innovation? Factors on this side include political party platforms and longstanding convention resolutions; activist social movements and court decisions that push governments to consider program and value shifts that would not otherwise have been of immediate concern; the hegemony in recent times of majority governments (although minority governments were instrumental in the 1960s and early 1970s), which have enjoyed multiple mandates and, for the Liberals at least, effective relations with the senior echelon of the public service—this political authority and continuity is reinforced by the concentration of power within offices of first ministers, cabinets, and central agencies in our parliamentary federal system of government.

More than an analytic method, directed incrementalism is a style of governing and reforming policy, with its own form of political rationality. This is apparent when one considers the political benefits to policy-makers of directed incrementalism as recently practised in Canadian social policy. By staging a major reform over a number of years and a number of budgets, this style supports federal control over financial commitments and maintains a degree of flexibility for the finance minister in managing debt reduction, tax relief, and budget surpluses. Moreover, it supports the Liberals' policy agenda of renewing social programs in response to population trends, public needs, expenditure capacity, and political priorities. Taking all these elements together, this approach helps the prime minister balance the somewhat competing interests of social Liberals and business Liberals within the cabinet and the government caucus. Making a series of modest changes over time can be a way of 'smuggling changes' into the political system, as Lindblom remarked. 'Incremental steps can be made quickly because they are only incremental. They do not rock the boat, do not stir up the great antagonisms and paralysing schisms as do proposals for more drastic changes.'[38] Other policy analysts similarly note that 'quiet innovations'— where a major change goes almost unnoticed—generate little political pain for governments and may help allay concerns of program administrators and clients that reforms will come too quickly for them to accept and adapt to them.[39]

A related reason for the political attractiveness of directed incrementalism is that it avoids looking like previous unsuccessful 'big bang' efforts at reforming social policy. The ambitious and comprehensive social security reviews of Lalonde in the mid-1970s, of Macdonald in the mid-1980s, and of Axworthy in the mid-1990s— covering multiple programs, intra-departmental and intergovernmental relations, numerous objectives, and huge amounts of spending—all yielded disappointingly minor results in social policy reform from the vantage point of government. By contrast, directed incrementalism, with a common vision of policy, sector by sector, is a middle-level approach to reform, informing a series of small, moderate, and, occasionally, large steps toward innovation. Because the scope and the time frame of any particular program of reform are not explicitly defined, the federal government is able to sidestep possible opposition accusations of returning to the free spending and large interventionist habits of earlier governments. And, certainly, chasing grand social visions has never been the style of Prime Minister Chrétien, who has been more appropriately characterized as the ultimate step-by-step pragmatist.[40]

NOTES

I would like to thank Ken Battle, Bruce Doern, David Good, Steve Kerstetter, and Jim Rice for their comments, support, and advice on an earlier version of this paper.

1 James J. Rice and Michael J. Prince, *Changing Politics of Canadian Social Policy* (Toronto: University of Toronto Press, 2000), 66.
2 See Eleanor D. Glor, ed., *Policy Innovation in the Saskatchewan Public Sector, 1971–82* (North York: Captus Press, 1997), 4; Neil Bradford, *Commissioning Ideas: Canadian National Policy Innovation in Comparative Perspective* (Toronto: Oxford University Press, 1998), 19.
3 Rice and Prince, *Changing Politics*, 40–1.
4 Paul Martin, Minister of Finance, *The Budget Plan 1995* (Ottawa: Public Works and Government Services Canada, 1995), 53. See also Department of Human Resources Development Canada, *Improving Social Security in Canada: A Discussion Paper* (Ottawa: Public Works and Government Services Canada, 1994).
5 See, for example, Alain-G. Gagnon and Hugh Segal, eds, *The Canadian Social Union Without Quebec: 8 Critical Analyses* (Montreal: Institute for Research on Public Policy, 2000).
6 A series of newspaper accounts by policy analysts, federal and provincial government ministers, and premiers appeared on this issue in July 2001. See, for example, Stephane Dion, 'If It Ain't Broke,' *The Globe and Mail* [Toronto], 13 July 2001, A15.
7 Charles E. Lindblom, 'The Science of Muddling Through', *Public Administration Review* 19, 2 (1959): 79–88.
8 Rice and Prince, *Changing Politics*, chapters 3 and 10. Besides directed incrementalism, there are other ways to achieve significant change and innovation in policy; these include unplanned drift, gradualism, imposition, and the 'great leap forward' or 'big bang'.
9 Arnold J. Heidenheimer, Hugh Heclo, and Carolyn Teich Adams, *Comparative Public Policy* (New York: St. Martin's Press, 1975), 55.
10 The term is credited to Trevor Hancock and is discussed in Brian Wharf, *Communities and Social Policy in Canada* (Toronto: McClelland and Stewart, 1992), 243.
11 Ken Battle, 'Relentless Incrementalism: Deconstructing and Reconstructing Canadian Income Security Policy', in Keith Banting, Andrew Sharpe, and France St-Hilaire, eds, *The Review of Economic Performance and Social Progress. The Longest Decade: Canada in the 1990s* (Montreal and Ottawa: Institute for Research on Public Policy and Centre for the Study of Living Standards, 2001), 224–5.
12 Bradford, *Commissioning Ideas*, 1.
13 See Rice and Prince, *Changing Politics*, chapters 5 and 6; Donald R. Stabile, *Community Associations: The Emergence and Acceptance of a Quiet Innovation in Housing* (Westport, CT: Greenwood, 2000); Peter A. Hall, 'Policy Paradigms, Social Learning and the State: The Case of Economic Policy Making in Britain', *Comparative Politics* 25, 3 (1993): 275–96.

14 Thomas S. Kuhn, *The Structure of Scientific Revolutions* (Chicago: University of Chicago Press, 1962), 149.

15 Michael Howlett and M. Ramesh, 'Policy Subsystem Configurations and Policy Change: Operationalizing the Postpositivist Analysis of the Politics of the Policy Process', *Policy Studies Journal* 26, 3 (1998): 466–81; Carter A. Wilson, 'Policy Regimes and Policy Change', *Journal of Public Policy* 20, 3 (2000): 247–74.

16 W.D. Coleman, G.D. Skogstad, and M.M. Atkinson, 'Paradigm Shifts and Policy Networks', *Journal of Public Policy*, 16, 3 (1996): 273–302; Coleman et al. describe the paradigm shift in their case study as innovation through 'cumulative change', that is, a gradual transition resulting from a series of negotiated adjustments and planned changes over a number of years.

17 Michael Howlett, 'Policy Paradigms and Policy Change: Lessons from the Old and New Canadian Policies Towards Aboriginal Peoples', *Policy Studies Journal* 22, 4 (1994): 640–1. See also Sally M. Weaver, 'A New Paradigm in Canadian Indian Policy for the 1990s', *Canadian Ethnic Studies* 22, 3 (1990): 8–18.

18 Augie Fleras, 'The Politics of Jurisdiction: Indigenizing Aboriginal-State Relations', in David Alan Long and Olive Patricia Dickason, eds, *Voices of the Heart: Canadian Aboriginal Issues* (Toronto: Harcourt Brace, 1996), 169.

19 Caroline Beauvais and Jane Jenson, 'Executive Summary', *Two Policy Paradigms: Family Responsibility and Investing in Children* (Ottawa: Canadian Policy Research Networks Inc., 2001), 1.

20 Ibid., 2.

21 Ibid., 3. The new paradigm is not all entirely new, especially in the area of child income benefits. Parental primacy is an old idea that still holds, since few argue that parents are not the chief payers and carers for their children. That society, via the state, has an interest in and responsibility for investing in families with children dates back to 1918, with the introduction of the children's tax exemption.

22 Michael J. Prince, 'Citizenship by Instalments: Federal Policies for Canadians with Disabilities', in Leslie A. Pal, ed,, *How Ottawa Spends 2001–2002: Power in Transition* (Toronto: Oxford University Press, 2001), 177–200.

23 On the interplay among economic liberalism, social protection, and cultural recognition paradigms, see Rice and Prince, *Changing Politics*, chapters 1 and 6. On health care, see Sholom Glouberman, *Towards a New Perspective on Health Policy* (Ottawa: Canadian Policy Research Networks, 2000). Also see Leslie A. Pal, 'Competing Paradigms in Policy Discourse: The Case of International Human Rights', *Policy Sciences* 28 (1995): 185–207.

24 Weaver, 'A New Paradigm', 9–10.

25 Ibid., 10.

26 The following discussion is based on Michael J. Prince and Frances Abele, 'Funding an Aboriginal Order of Government in Canada: Recent Developments in Self-Government and Fiscal Relations', in Harvey Lazar, ed., *Canada: The State of the Federation 1999/2000: Toward a New Mission Statement for Canadian Fiscal Federalism* (Montreal and Kingston: McGill-Queen's University Press, 2000), chap. 12; Frances Abele and Michael J. Prince, 'Alternative Futures: Aboriginal Peoples and Canadian Federalism', in Herman Bakvis and Grace Skogstad, eds, *Canadian Federalism: Performance, Effectiveness, and Legitimacy* (Toronto: Oxford University Press, 2002), chap. 12.

27 For corporate income taxes, which this chapter does not discuss, all provinces except Alberta, Ontario, and Quebec have TCAs with the federal government.

28 Paul Martin, Minister of Finance, 'Government Outlines Measures to Make Tax System More Flexible for Provinces and Territories', News Release, 2000–004 (Ottawa: Department of Finance, 25 Jan. 2000), 1; Geoffrey E. Hale, 'The Tax System and the Growing Decentralization of Canada's Personal Income Tax System', in Lazar, *Canada: The State of the Federation*, 235.

29 Provinces and territories would not, however, have the flexibility to introduce non-refundable tax credits that fall below the level of the gross federal credits. Also, while the two-tier credit structure for charitable gifts has been maintained, provinces and territories have the flexibility of crediting charitable donations below a threshold at their lowest non-zero tax rate and the balance at their highest tax rate. For details, see Martin, 'Government Outlines Measures'.

30 Harvey Lazar, 'In Search of a New Mission Statement for Canadian Fiscal Federalism', in Lazar, ed., *Canada: The State of the Federation*, 15.

31 Battle, 'Relentless Incrementalism'; Speech from the Throne to Open the First Session of the 37th Parliament of Canada (Ottawa, 30 Jan. 2001).

32 Battle, 'Relentless Incrementalism', 212.

33 The Government of Quebec, while sympathetic to the principles of the NCB, does not participate, because it wishes to retain control over income support for the children of Quebec. The same applies to the National Children's Agenda. Quebec residents benefit from the increased CCTB in the same way as other Canadians do. See Web site: www:socialunion.gc.ca

34 Michael J. Prince, *Governing in an Integrated Fashion: Lessons from the Disability Domain*, CPRN Discussion Paper No. F/14 (Ottawa: Canadian Policy Research Networks, June 2001), 38–9.

35 For a recent overview of these provincial and territorial child benefits and earnings supplement programs, see Ken Battle and Michael Mendelson, 'Benefits for Children: Canada', in Ken Battle and Michael Mendelson, eds, *Benefits for Children: A Four Country Study* (Ottawa: The Caledon Institute of Social Policy, 2001), 155–62.

36 Battle, 'Relentless Incrementalism', 187, 199; Battle and Mendelson, 'Benefits for Children'.

37 Tom Kent, *A Public Purpose: An Experience of Liberal Opposition and Canadian Government* (Kingston and Montreal: McGill-Queen's University Press, 1988). A key social policy advisor to the Pearson and Trudeau Liberals, Kent writes, 'It has become conventional to object to the Canadian welfare state as a confusing mishmash of programs with major inefficiencies. The characterization is correct. What is hard to comprehend is that anyone should be so naïve as to suppose that hard-fought social changes could be achieved in our confederation and with our cultural and political diversities, by any means except piecemeal programs' (360).

38 Charles E. Lindblom, 'Still Muddling, Not Yet Through', *Public Administration Review* 39, 6 (1979): 520.

39 Donald R. Stabile, *Community Associations*.

40 Jeffrey Simpson, *The Friendly Dictatorship* (Toronto: McClelland and Stewart, 2001).

11

The Liberals' 'Reinvestment' in Arts and Culture: From Patron to Patronage?

MONICA GATTINGER

On 2 May 2001, some of the most prominent members of Canada's arts and culture community gathered in a concert hall at the CBC Broadcasting Centre in Toronto to hear Prime Minister Jean Chrétien and Minister of Canadian Heritage Sheila Copps make a 'major announcement' about Canadian arts and culture. The new initiative that the Prime Minister and Minister Copps unveiled did not disappoint their audience; it was comprised of over $560 million in new arts and culture expenditures, an increase of some 20 per cent in federal funding for the sector. 'Tomorrow Starts Today', the energetically named initiative, distributes new funding across the entire spectrum of the artistic process, from creation, production, and distribution of the arts, to enjoyment and preservation. The package includes spending commitments for artists, for the cultural industries, for access to the arts, and for preservation of historic sites. It also supports the export of Canadian cultural products and services and the production of Canadian content for the Internet.

The government's infusion of some half a billion dollars into arts and culture marks a clear departure from the Liberals' many years of repeated funding cutbacks to the sector. In a very high-profile manner, the Liberals have seemingly moved arts and culture from the expenditure chopping block to the spending spotlight and have accorded culture a more prominent place on the government's agenda. This chapter traces the Liberals' shift in orientation toward the sector in the Chrétien era and examines the main elements and dominant themes of Tomorrow Starts Today.

One of the chapter's key findings is that while the new funding is arguably a 'reinvestment' in arts and culture, that is, a re-funding of nearly a decade's worth of cutbacks, the new moneys are not simply being returned to the original points of cutback. That is, Tomorrow Starts Today does not merely restore funding to the same program areas and agencies that sustained cutbacks during the Chrétien era. The principal beneficiary of Tomorrow Starts Today's funding is the Department of Canadian Heritage, and this, as will be contended in this chapter, raises the spectre of undesirable political influence in granting and in programming decision-making for arts and culture. Additionally, a substantial portion of the new funding supports larger Liberal policy themes, notably youth and the new economy, and this, as will also be argued in this chapter, could have negative consequences for other more traditional targets of arts and culture spending.

The chapter is divided into two parts. The first discusses the Liberals' record on arts and culture policy in the Chrétien era, an era in which the sector experienced repeated funding cutbacks and scant attention in government-wide plans and priorities in the first mandate, a gradual rise on the government's agenda in the second mandate, and a major investment and higher profile in the third mandate. This section identifies factors that may account for the Liberals' apparent about-face on arts and culture, including macro- and meso-level political and economic considerations. Given the confines of a single chapter, this first section's discussion of the Liberal record on arts and culture is admittedly brief and only addresses the issues in a very broad way. The second half of the chapter concentrates on Tomorrow Starts Today. It presents the initiative's main spending commitments, and examines the twin characteristics of the new funding: its departmental focus and its youth/new economy focus. This section describes how these characteristics may render the new funding susceptible to undesirable political influence and probes both the potential rationales and the possible implications of these policy trajectories. Conclusions follow.

INTO THE SPOTLIGHT:
ARTS AND CULTURE IN THE THIRD LIBERAL MANDATE

In the Chrétien Liberal era, arts and culture policy has experienced a reversal of fortune in two important respects. First, the sector has gone from the expenditure chopping block to the spending spotlight, and second, arts and culture policy's position on the government agenda has been transformed from one of veritable obscurity to one of relative prominence. This section briefly traces these shifts and suggests a number of factors that may account for the change.

Arts and Culture in the First and Second Liberal Mandates
In the first and second terms of the Chrétien government, the dominant theme for

arts and cultural expenditures was reduction and restraint. In the first Liberal mandate, Program Review hit arts and culture hard, as it did other government sectors. In 1995/6, federal arts and culture spending was slashed by some 7 per cent.[1] Furthermore, arts and culture, perhaps perceived as a policy luxury or frill, bore a disproportionate share of the cutbacks. The 1995/6 Main Estimates show that of thirteen budget categories, only three, Transportation Programs, Natural Resource Based Programs, and Social Programs, endured a greater percentage expenditure decline from 1994/5 levels than did Heritage and Cultural Programs.

But Program Review was neither the beginning nor the end of expenditure cutbacks for the sector. As John Meisel and Jean Van Loon note in regard to cultural policy, 'When belts have to be tightened, it is usually the arts that are first to engage in slimming.'[2] Indeed, the tightening of the arts and culture expenditure belt was already underway prior to Program Review. Virtually all organizations in the current Canadian Heritage portfolio sustained cutbacks in the years leading up to the Program Review exercise. Among the more severe cuts were those to the Canada Council for the Arts, the Canadian Film Development Corporation (Telefilm Canada), and the National Library of Canada, whose budgets shrank by 12 per cent, 24 per cent, and 24 per cent, respectively, from 1992/3 to 1995/6[3] (the appendix to this chapter shows federal arts and culture spending from 1992/3 to 2001/2).

In the years following Program Review, the funding cuts to arts and culture continued unabated. From 1995/6 to 1997/8, federal expenditures on arts and culture declined a further 5 per cent. This time, among the agencies hit the hardest were the National Film Board, the National Archives of Canada, and the Canadian Broadcasting Corporation (CBC), with budgetary contractions in these two years of 24 per cent, 21 per cent, and 19 per cent respectively. All in all, from 1992/3 to 1997/8 federal arts and culture funding plummeted by almost half a billion dollars, from $2.87 billion to $2.39 billion. This amounts to an average decline of 17 per cent in federal funding for the period 1993 to 1998, a period during which, it should be remembered, a number of new agencies and programs were added to the Canadian Heritage Portfolio (for example, the National Capital Commission, Status of Women Canada, and the National Battlefields Commission). Given the severity of the cuts across this period, it is understandable that Canada Council Chairman Jean-Louis Roux dubbed the years 1993 to 1998 'the dark period'.[4]

It was only in the Liberals' second mandate that the government began slowly to return some funding to the sector. Increases were slight, however, in comparison to the declines of the previous years, and with the Liberals' '50–50' plan in place,[5] expenditure restraint was clearly the order of the day. As noted in the first Speech from the Throne (SFT) of the second mandate, 'The Government will continue to be vigilant and responsible about keeping the financial affairs of the country in order.'[6] New funding for arts and culture promised in the Red Book was also quite narrowly targeted, directed primarily to the Canada Council, the CBC, and the publishing industry. The Canada Council received a $25 million increase in its annual budget and a one-time contribution of $10 million to commission works of art to celebrate the new millennium, while annual support for the CBC and the publishing industry grew by $60 million and $15 million respectively. Other increases accruing to the sector during the second mandate included support for Canadian content on the Internet ($75 million), for feature filmmaking ($50 million), for magazine publishing ($150 million), and for sound recording ($30 million).[7]

In the first and second Liberal mandates, arts and culture was not only on the expenditure chopping block, it also occupied a relatively low priority position on the government's agenda. The first Liberal Red Book, *Creating Opportunity: The Liberal Plan for Canada*,[8] replete with detailed policy commitments across a wide range of sectors, scarcely devoted passing attention to arts and culture. In the 112-page document, the Liberals dedicated barely a page to the topic, and, ironically, reneged on one of the few cultural commitments that they did make, stable multi-year financing to national cultural bodies such as the Canada Council and the CBC.[9] Commenting on their failure to honour this promise, the Liberals noted, in *A Record of Achievement: A Report on the Liberal Government's 36 Months in Office*, their report card on their own Red Book commitments, 'Given the severe fiscal restraints facing the government, which necessitated cuts in many programs important to Canadians, cuts to the CBC and other major cultural agencies were reluctantly imposed.'[10]

The Liberals continued the scant attention to arts and culture in their 1993 election platform with minimal consideration for the sector throughout the first mandate. In the 27 February 1996 SFT, for example, in a single paragraph at the end—what seemed more like a gesture of courtesy or an afterthought than a statement of strategy or intent—the government noted the importance of culture, and the Liberals' commitment to strengthen it.[11] The Speech mentioned no specific initiatives and made no funding commitments to the sector. Indeed, it was not until the Liberals' second mandate that arts and culture began its ascent on the government's agenda.

The second Red Book, *Securing Our Future Together: Preparing Canada for the 21st Century*, accorded greater attention to arts and culture than its 1993 predecessor, and, in retrospect, signalled the beginnings of a turnaround in the government's approach toward the sector.[12] Arts and culture netted a chapter of its own in *Securing Our Future* that included promises of new funding for artists, for the multimedia industry, and for the publishing sector. While on this occasion the funding commitments were upheld, in the first half of the second mandate arts and culture remained peripheral to government-wide plans and priorities. The first SFT of this mandate made only minimal reference to the sector, and did so primarily as part of the government's strategy for Canada in the global knowledge-based economy. Under the heading 'Investing in Knowledge and Creativity', it described the government's strategies for promoting Canada's success in the knowledge-based economy, and noted, 'Support for knowledge goes beyond support for university research. Increasing support for the arts makes it possible for Canadian culture to reach audiences at home and abroad.'[13] With this brief mention, the Liberals appeared to be positioning the arts as a means of enabling or supporting Canada's success in the new economy—an approach that emphasized the industrial-trade potential of arts and culture.

This industrial-trade policy approach was reiterated and broadened in the second SFT of the second mandate.[14] Under the heading 'A Dynamic Economy for the 21st Century', the 12 October 1999 SFT reiterated the government's belief in the industrial-trade potential of culture, identifying culture as one of the 'strategic sectors with high export potential', to which the government would direct increased trade promotion support. In addition, the Liberals broadened their economic focus on arts and culture, designating 'cultural infrastructure', along with knowledge, information, and physical infrastructure, as essential 'Infrastructure for the 21st Century'. Again, the emphasis was on arts and culture's role in supporting or enabling Canada's success in the knowledge economy: 'For Canada to generate jobs, growth and wealth, it must have a leading, knowledge-based economy that creates new ideas and puts them to work for Canadians. To do this, it is essential to connect Canadians to each other, to schools and libraries, to governments, and to the marketplace—so they can build on each other's ideas and share information. Achieving this objective will require new types of infrastructure.'[15] While the Liberals did not define what was meant by 'cultural infrastructure', it was apparent that the Internet was to be a central element of its development and strengthening. The SFT singled out the potential of information and communications technologies to bring Canadians closer to each other ('New technologies offer new opportunities to strengthen the bonds between Canadians'[16]), and commitments were geared to building and strengthening the country's *digital* cultural infrastructure. Among the initiatives were the establishment of a virtual museum, which, by connecting 1,000 institutions across Canada, was to make the collections of key institutions such as the National Archives and the National Library available on-line, and expanded support for the production of Canadian content using new media. The Speech also noted that the government would work to maintain domestic cultural policy-making capacity in the international trading realm, stating that the government would 'work to develop a new approach internationally to support the diversity of cultural expression in countries around the world'.[17]

Arts and Culture in the Third Liberal Mandate

While arts and culture was beginning to see the expenditure and the political light of day in the Liberals' second mandate, it was not until the third mandate that arts and culture moved more fully into the spending and agenda spotlight. The Liberals' third Red Book, *Opportunity for All: The Liberal Plan for the Future of Canada*,[18] the most recent SFT,[19] and Tomorrow Starts Today are evidence of the rise to prominence of arts and culture in the most recent Liberal mandate. Ironically, *Opportunity for All*, a 32-page document often referred to as the 'Red Booklet' because of its brevity and imprecision in comparison to its predecessors, delineated more specific plans for arts and culture than the Liberals' most comprehensive election platform, the first Red Book. Furthermore, it promised substantial increases in funding for the sector. The party continued to emphasize the importance of new information and communications technologies in *Opportunity for All*, with commitments to stimulate Canadian Internet content, establish a Canadian Internet portal, and support new media production, with funding of $209 million distributed over 2001/2 to 2004/5. The Liberals also promised to increase support for young artists, develop international markets for artists, and support the transition to the new economy by the book publishing and sound recording sectors, with funding of $20 million, $60 million, and $146 million respectively, allocated from 2001/2 to 2004/5. Given the specific commitments the Liberals made in *Opportunity for All*, their election victory in November 2000 suggested that a brighter future was in store for arts and culture.

The January 2001 SFT affirmed that arts and culture would acquire a more positive financial footing in the Liberals' third mandate and that the topic was ascending on the government's agenda.[20] An entire section dedicated to arts and culture, 'Vibrant Canadian Culture', affirmed the expenditure commitments of *Opportunity for All*, and announced increased support for the CBC, assistance to communities to develop arts and heritage programs, and work to strengthen cultural infrastructure in Canada. Prime Minister Chrétien reaffirmed this engagement with arts and culture in his Reply to the Speech from the Throne, stating, '[I]n this mandate, the government will provide significant new support to ensure that our cultural institutions, our performers, our artists can play the critical role of helping us know ourselves.'[21]

After the Liberals' election promises and subsequent commitments in the SFT, it was clear that the stage was set for a major spending initiative on arts and culture. The only remaining questions were *when* the new funding would be announced, *how much* new money would be made available, and on what the new moneys would be spent. At a gala concert evening on 2 May 2001 at the CBC Broadcasting Centre in Toronto, organized and hosted by the government, these questions were answered. The evening, referred to by the Prime Minister as 'the show',[22] featured a night of performances by some of Canada's emerging young performers and, to the delight of many members of Canada's arts and culture community, a major announcement concerning arts and culture in Canada. Prime Minister Chrétien and Minister of Canadian Heritage Sheila Copps launched Tomorrow Starts Today, an initiative promising more than $560 million of new funding for arts and culture. Before elaborating on the main elements and dominant themes of Tomorrow Starts Today, we will examine in the following subsection the principal factors that led to its creation.

Why the Turnaround?

A variety of macro- and meso-level economic, political-institutional, and political factors propelled arts and culture's move into the spotlight in the Chrétien era. Arguably of greatest significance was a macro-economic influence: the federal surplus. With the growth of the fiscal dividend during the Liberals' second mandate and its continuation into the beginning of the third, new funding for arts and culture became a genuine possibility. After years of cutbacks and restraint, there was now some room in the budget to reinvest in the sector.

But, of course, the availability of a surplus, although undoubtedly a necessary condition for significant new expenditures on arts and culture, was not a sufficient condition. Political will was also an essential requirement. A number of factors fostered the political will to reinvest. First, in the macro-environment, real and perceived technological, political, and institutional threats to domestic cultural policy-making capacity continued to grow. Information and communications technologies, for example, significantly weaken certain instruments of cultural policy. How does one regulate Canadian content on the Internet, for example, when the network knows no national borders? Along with technology, international trade disputes have also raised concerns about the state's cultural policy-making capacity. Trade disputes over Canadian cultural policies, most notably the notorious magazines case, in which certain aspects of Canadian cultural policy were struck down by the World Trade Organization,[23] have elevated arts and culture policy and concentrated strategic attention upon it. In the Red Booklet, it was apparent that the dual challenge of technology and trade were key drivers for cultural policy: 'Globalization and the borderless information age raise some difficult questions about the ability of countries to carve out a unique cultural presence. In a world dominated by American television, films, and Internet sites, our goal as Canadians is not to keep that influence out but to ensure that Canadians have Canadian choices.'[24]

The second factor generating political will was at the meso-departmental level, where an active Minister and Deputy Minister were working hard to raise arts and culture's profile and to foster renewed funding for the sector. Within the Department of Canadian Heritage and in the broader arts and culture community, Minister of Canadian Heritage Sheila Copps is known as a staunch advocate of arts and culture, with a solid commitment and dogged determination to support and promote the sector. Minister Copps's dedication of her energy and passion to the portfolio since becoming Minister of Canadian Heritage in January 1996 has afforded the department ministerial longevity and a tireless voice in Cabinet. But while the Minister was undoubtedly one of the key individuals propelling arts and culture into the spotlight, she needed the support of her Cabinet colleagues, Treasury Board, and Finance as well. A crucial player in building this support was Alex Himelfarb, the Deputy Minister of Canadian Heritage. The naming of Himelfarb, a former Assistant Secretary to the Cabinet (Social Development Policy) at the Privy Council Office and a former Associate Secretary of the Treasury Board Secretariat, as Deputy Minister of Canadian Heritage in June 1999 brought a strong and effective advocate to the department. With intimate knowledge of the inner machinery of government and personal connections with some its key players, Himelfarb was well positioned to work with Minister Copps to garner executive support for the new initiative. The Minister and the Deputy Minister successfully positioned arts and culture as supportive of broader government plans and priorities, notably youth and the new economy. But, as will be discussed in greater detail later in this chapter, positioning arts and culture in this way is a double-edged sword. On the one hand, it was likely a critical factor in securing funding for the sector, but on the other, marshalling arts and culture in support of broader government policy objectives may crowd out the pursuit of more fundamental arts and culture policy purposes.

The third set of factors, operating at the macro-political level, buoyed arts and culture on the government's agenda and motivated support for increased funding to the sector. One of these factors is probably the desire to leave a political legacy, on the part of Prime Minister Chrétien, who continues to hint at retirement, and on the part of Minister Sheila Copps, who wishes to leave a legacy of her tenure as Minister of Canadian Heritage.[25] In a similar vein, 'the show' mounted for Tomorrow Starts Today may have been an attempt to shine some light on Minister Copps as a potential contender for the Liberal leadership.[26]

THE MAIN EVENT: 'TOMORROW STARTS TODAY'

Tomorrow Starts Today's funding is distributed over three fiscal years, 2001 to 2003, and is in support of five core objectives:

- 'Encourage the growth, development and diversity of creative work in this country, notably among young people who are being called upon to project our traditions into the future; and promote access to the arts and heritage for all Canadians.'
- 'Provide Canadians with the means to protect their built heritage.'
- 'Increase the production of Canadian content for the Internet, which is fast becoming the most popular medium of communication among Canada's youth, and promote the development of the new media industry.'
- 'Ensure that our cultural industries, notably the book and sound recording sectors, are able to prosper in the new digital economy and to project a Canadian voice that is strong and original.'
- 'Encourage export of cultural products and services in partnership with the Department of Foreign Affairs and International Trade and explore new markets for our artists.'[27]

The main spending commitments and actions in support of each of the five objectives are summarized below.

Development of and participation in the arts ($288 million). This funding supports artists in their creative work and promotes the enjoyment of works of art by Canadians. Artists will receive support directly, through an increase in the budget of the Canada Council for the Arts ($75 million) and through funding to assist young Canadians training for arts careers ($13 million). Tomorrow Starts Today also seeks to strengthen Canada's cultural physical infrastructure by funding the repair and upgrade of arts and heritage facilities across the country ($80 million). In addition, the government will provide funding to strengthen the financial and administrative capacity of arts and heritage organizations ($63 million). To foster Canadians' participation in the arts, the government is allocating $57 million to support arts celebrations, festivals, and arts presenters (organizations that present artists' work to audiences in their communities).

Built heritage preservation ($24 million). Moneys allocated to built heritage preservation seek to engage other levels of government and organizations in the private and voluntary sectors in the preservation of historic sites, heritage buildings and monuments, archeological sites, and other historic places. To this end, the government is creating a register of historic places, developing conservation standards and guidelines, and establishing a process of certification. Once this framework is in place, the government plans to introduce financial incentives to encourage the private sector to conserve heritage property.

Internet content and new media ($108 million). To increase production of Canadian content for the Internet and to promote development of the new media sector, the government will fund the digitizing of key cultural content, foster the creation and use of new media and multimedia Canadian content, and enhance access to Canadian cultural products and historical information.

Book and sound recording sectors ($56 million). Tomorrow Starts Today's support for the book industry builds on existing funding to the sector, provided by the Book Publishing Industry Development Program (BPIDP). The government plans to allocate additional funds to the BPIDP to aid the industry in distribution, marketing and promotion, and transition (assisting book publishers to meet short-term business challenges). The government also anticipates allocating some of the book sector funding to strengthening the Department of Canadian Heritage's capacity for research on the book industry. In the sound recording sector, the government is creating the Canada Music Fund, a new fund for writers and composers, for the production and promotion of new recordings, for projects addressing issues that affect the entire industry, and for the preservation and digitizing of significant works of music.

Cultural trade ($32 million). In partnership with the Department of Foreign Affairs and International Trade, the Department of Canadian Heritage will develop initiatives to foster cultural exports and will create a new export readiness program to assist cultural businesses and organizations involved in cultural trade.

From this preliminary tour of Tomorrow Starts Today a number of observations emerge. First, the announcement represents a significant increase in federal funding for arts and culture. Tomorrow Starts Today's $568 million represents an increase of 19 per cent in federal funding for the sector, and this increase rises to 25 per cent if the CBC is excluded from the calculation (the CBC alone accounted for almost $1 billion of the $2.9 billion in federal spending in the 2001/2 Main Estimates). Indeed, Tomorrow Starts Today's spending commitments represent an unprecedented increase in federal arts and culture spending in Canada. As Prime Minister Jean Chrétien noted in his speech at the 2 May announcement, the new funding is the 'biggest new investment in the arts in Canada that any government has made since the creation of the Canada Council more than forty years ago.'[29]

Second, using expenditure as a measuring stick, the Liberals are clearly placing the emphasis on the first and the third of Tomorrow Starts Today's objectives. Close to 70 per cent of the more than half a billion dollars seeks to support artists and promote access to Canadian arts and heritage ($288 million), and to increase Canadian Internet content and promote the multimedia industry ($108 million). Spending on the other three objectives pales in comparison: $24 million toward built heritage preservation, $56 million to the book and sound recording sectors, and $32 million to cultural trade.[30] This is a point that will be expanded upon farther on in the chapter.

Third, the funding is distributed across the entire creative process—from creation, to production and distribution, to access and preservation. Artists receive support, for example, through increases in the budget of the Canada Council for the Arts, the federal government's principal arts funding agency, and through increased contributions to the National Arts Training Contribution Program, a program that supports nonprofit arts training institutions such as the Royal Winnipeg Ballet School. And as will be discussed below, a significant proportion of Tomorrow Starts Today's funding seeks to stimulate the creation of Canadian content for the Internet. Support for production and distribution of arts and culture is channelled mainly through additional funding for the book and sound recording sectors, the new media industry, and cultural trade. Funding to support Canadians' access to the arts includes repairing and upgrading arts and heritage facilities (museums, theatres, galleries, etc.) and funding for arts festivals, celebrations, and arts presenters. The primary spending initiative to preserve arts and culture is the commitment to work with other levels of government and the private and voluntary sectors to preserve historic places.

Tomorrow Starts Today: From Patron to Patronage?

Tomorrow Starts Today's new spending commitments are very similar in size to the cutbacks sustained by the arts and culture sector in the first and second Liberal mandates. As calculated previously in the chapter, some half a billion dollars was slashed from arts and culture from 1992 to 1998. But while Tomorrow Starts Today is also a half-billion-dollar package, it is by no means a 'reinvestment' in arts and culture in the strict sense that it returns funds in the same pattern as that in which they were eliminated. The new spending is distinguished from the cutbacks in two important ways, its mode of delivery and its main priorities. The following paragraphs describe these twin characteristics and flag a number of concerns that merit further scrutiny, most notably the extent to which the new funding may be vulnerable to undesirable political influence.

The first characteristic, the mode of delivery, refers to the funding model the government has implicitly adopted for the new funds. Given the delicate relationship between the government on the one hand and arts and culture on the other, arm's-length delivery mechanisms have invariably been integral to the arts and culture policy field. Artists must be free to express themselves, even when their expression runs counter to government interests, and a crucial component of maintaining artistic freedom is third-party delivery mechanisms that remove granting and programming decisions from political influence. The patron model has sought to protect against the instrumental use of arts and culture by the state or the government of the day, by, for example, organizationally insulating a public broadcaster from state influence. The Canadian Heritage Portfolio has always consisted of a mix of departmental and arm's-length delivery mechanisms, such as the Canada Council for the Arts, the National Gallery, the CBC, the National Film Board, and the Canadian Film Development Corporation (Telefilm Canada). But while all of these agencies sustained substantial cutbacks in the 1990s, the vast majority of Tomorrow Starts Today funding is directed to the Department of Canadian Heritage. Apart from the new funding for the Canada Council ($75 million) and the CBC ($60 million), over 70 per cent of the new expenditures, more than $400 million, accrue to the department. This departmental emphasis stands in stark contrast to the comparable percentage of federal arts and cultural expenditures on the department in the 2001/2 Main Estimates. As the table in the appendix shows, federal spending on the department accounted for only 33 per cent of total federal arts and culture spending. It borders on ironic, perhaps, then, that the Prime Minister stated that Tomorrow Starts Today is the biggest single government investment in the arts since the creation of the Canada Council, the independent crown corporation that is the main arts funding agency at the federal level.

This departmental focus warrants two cautionary notes. First, at the very least it may signal that the department is being 'beefed up' at the expense of the broader arts and culture community. Indeed, as the Canadian Conference of the Arts notes, there is 'a concern in the cultural community that new programs will mean an increase in staff at the departmental level, thus ensuring more of the money will be tied up with program delivery mechanisms rather than going directly to the sector.'[31] Intensifying this concern is the fact that the announcement in May appears to have taken place some six months earlier than Department of Canadian Heritage bureaucrats had expected. Although the reason for advancing the schedule remains unclear, it may have been prompted by concerns at the ministerial level about government-wide budgetary politics. If the initiative had been delayed another six months, it risked being caught up in a formal budget process, which might have jeopardized the funding or generated undesirable delays. Whatever the reason for the early announcement, however, it has had both positive and negative effects. On the positive side, if it had not been announced early, Tomorrow Starts Today would probably not have seen the light of day. Given the growing concerns about Canada's future economic prospects and the tragic terrorist attacks in the United States, the window for new expenditure commitments lacking direct relation to anti-terrorism appears to be closing.[32] So, in retrospect, if the announcement had not been made in May the initiative would probably have been delayed or shelved. On the negative side, moving the announcement up may have made the implementation of Tomorrow Starts Today a major challenge. This is particularly true for those components of the initiative involving the introduction of new programs. Departmental staff are working rapidly to get programs off the ground, but with six months less lead time than they had expected. Adding further to the challenge is the imperative of developing clear departmental grant administration and performance evaluation guidelines in the wake of the so-called 'HRDC scandal'. Taking these factors together, it remains unclear what proportion of the funds will find their way to the arts and culture sector, and what sorts of delays await recipients before funds can be released from the department.

Second, at the very worst, the departmental emphasis of Tomorrow Starts Today is of concern because it may leave the new funds exposed to undesirable political influence. As Flora MacDonald, a former minister of the arts and culture portfolio, has noted, the government is able to 'lengthen' or 'shorten' its arm's-length relationship with cultural agencies through funding increases or decreases.[33] By directing by far the greater part of the new funding to the department, the government retains more control over the planning, priorities, and programs the funds will support. While the Department of Canadian Heritage has always been very careful to avoid making decisions involving artistic content, the real danger may be that because the new moneys are channelled through the department, they become vulnerable to political prerogatives, whether narrowly partisan or, as will be discussed in the following section, in support of broader government-wide objectives. In brief, the new spending may be vulnerable to redirection, and perhaps even more so in the wake of the 11 September 2001 terrorist attacks in the United States, which have considerably altered the domestic policy agenda.

The second defining characteristic of Tomorrow Starts Today is its main priorities: youth and the new economy. The following paragraphs sketch the contours of these two themes, identify the government's possible rationales for targeting youth and the new economy, and examine the possible implications of these policy trajectories.

Youth. With the new funding, the Liberal government targets youth as creators of and audiences for the arts. At the 2 May 2001 announcement, the theme of youth was apparent in the evening's line-up of performers: virtually all of the performers were young Canadian artists. And youth are specifically mentioned in the text of the initiative's two most generously funded objectives: development of and access to the arts ($288 million), and the promotion of Canadian Internet content and the new media industry ($108 million). As artists, young Canadians 'are being called upon to project our traditions into the future', and, with respect to their role as audience, the government notes that the Internet 'is fast becoming the most popular medium of communication among Canada's youth'.[34] Specific program elements either directly or indirectly targeting youth include the $13 million commitment for 'the training of young up-and-coming artists';[35] the $75 million funding increase for the Canada Council, an increase that, the government notes, 'will also support creation by young Canadians';[36] the $57 million to establish the Arts Presentation

Canada program, which will fund community arts festivals and will involve 'a specific emphasis on audience development and outreach activities for young audiences';[37] and the $108 million to promote Canadian cultural content on the Internet, which seeks to 'ensure that Canadians, particularly youth, have access to Internet material' about Canada.[38] Indeed, as the following excerpts from Minister Copps's speeches demonstrate, the youth thrust of the new funding is unmistakable:

> We are investing in creativity and excellence with a focus on building new young audiences and new young artists.[39]
>
> We're investing in festivals because we believe in building young audiences. We will also invest $108 million in new media and in Internet content in all languages—Aboriginal languages, French and English. Most of these funds will specifically target young people.[40]

This distinctive focus on youth raises the question, why? Why are youth so important to arts and culture? First, youth are ostensibly part of the Department of Canadian Heritage's mandate.[41] The Department's most recent Departmental Expenditure Plan[42] states that the Department of Canadian Heritage Act confers upon the Minister of Canadian Heritage, along with the Secretary of State (Multiculturalism and Status of Women) and the Secretary of State (Amateur Sport), responsibility for policies and programs related to a broad range of sectors, one of which is youth. The department administers a wide variety of programs for youth, including Exchanges Canada, which supports cross-country exchanges for young Canadians, Young Canada Works, which helps youth gain work experience in the cultural sector, and the previously mentioned National Arts Training Contribution Program. In this way, the focus on youth fulfils the department's mandate. Second, the youth emphasis addresses a Canadian demographic reality. The aging of Canada's population is having an impact on arts and culture policy just as it is on other policy fields, such as health care and human resources development. Youth represent the artists and audiences of the future, and as the population grows increasingly grey the support given to youth becomes integral to a long-term sustainable cultural development strategy.

A third rationale for focussing on youth, one that may be cause for concern in the broader arts and culture community, is the marshalling of arts and culture to address 'youth at risk'. This phrase, to which there is no widely agreed-upon definition, is becoming ever more topical at the Department of Canadian Heritage.[44] Broadly speaking, the phrase 'youth at risk' refers to the subgroup of youth who are marginalized, underprivileged, or disadvantaged in some way (for example, by belonging to immigrant or racial minorities, by growing up in disadvantaged areas, or by having suffered child abuse), and therefore at risk of social dislocation through, for example, crime, dropping out of school, substance abuse, or single-parenthood. The department first targeted youth at risk in a new initiative called First Works, a program to support young Canadians as artists, audiences, and cultural workers, one component of which was to give 'youth (including youth at risk) the chance to experience the creative process'.[45]

Two cautionary notes should be sounded about this emerging departmental priority. First, while supporting underprivileged youth may be a laudable goal, it must be remembered that engaging youth at risk is fundamentally a goal of social policy, not of arts and culture policy. To the extent that a focus on youth at risk crowds out more traditional forms of artistic and cultural development, this emerging priority may have unintended negative consequences. Second, because the majority of Tomorrow Starts Today funding was allocated to the Department of Canadian Heritage, there is a risk that expenditures initially intended for youth writ large (that is, youth as emerging artists, cultural workers, audience participants, and the like) may be redirected and more narrowly targeted to youth at risk. If this takes place, Tomorrow Starts Today may be funding youth at risk at the expense of fostering young talent, cultural labour force renewal, or audience development.

The New Economy. With Tomorrow Starts Today, the government placed a very solid emphasis on the new economy, specifically the Internet and the program content of the cultural industries. The new funding dedicates $108 million to developing Canadian Internet content and supporting the multimedia sector, and an important portion of the $56 million in new funding for the book and sound recording sectors is intended to assist these sectors in their transition to the digital economy. The rationales for this approach are three-fold.

First, as mentioned previously, Tomorrow Starts Today notes that the Internet is becoming the most popular means of communication among Canada's youth. The focus on the Internet, therefore, underpins the emphasis on youth discussed above. Second, the focus on the new economy supports the Liberal government's broader goal of supporting Canada's success in the new economy. Indeed, one of the four goals in the Liberals' 2000 election platform was to make Canada a 'smart country', a leader in the new economy.[46] Tomorrow Starts Today's investment in the multimedia industry, an indisputable new economy sector, supports this goal, and funding for the book and sound recording industries, which supports their efforts to 'take advantage of the opportunities in the new economy'[47] and to 'compete in a global, Internet-driven economy',[48] also champions this objective. Third, Tomorrow Starts Today's funding for Canadian Internet content supports the Liberal government's Connecting Canadians agenda, which includes increasing access to the Internet, building Internet infrastructure, facilitating electronic commerce, and delivering government information and services on-line.[49]

Tomorrow Starts Today's focus on the new economy merits critical reflection. Of notable cause for concern are the stated priorities for the Internet content funding. These include digitizing existing cultural collections such as those of the CBC and the National Film Board, putting reference materials on Canada on-line, developing tools to assist French content creation and navigation, and assisting on-line content initiatives such as the Virtual Museum of Canada, which connects museums across the country.[50] The funding does not seek to stimulate Canadian creators directly to express themselves artistically and culturally with digital media, but rather it hints at the development of *government-defined* Canadian culture on the Internet. Indeed, the Canadian Alliance Culture Critic stated that '[t]he problem with [Tomorrow Starts Today] is that the culture is being defined by the government.'[51] While only time will tell whether this perception is accurate, much will likely depend on what sort of program administration guidelines the Department of Canadian Heritage puts in place for this new funding. It will be critical for the department to consult widely with the arts and culture community to further refine and define the priorities listed above. It would also be prudent to include members of the community on granting juries and other bodies making crucial funding decisions.

CONCLUSION

This chapter examined Tomorrow Starts Today, the federal government's new funding initiative for arts and culture in Canada. Following a brief tour of federal funding for arts and culture in the Chrétien Liberal era, the chapter traced the sector's gradual rise to prominence on the government's agenda, from virtual obscurity in the first half of the 1990s, to relative prominence in the late 1990s, to a much higher profile in the early years of the twenty-first century. Several macro- and meso-level factors driving this reversal of fortunes were identified, including the availability of federal surpluses, the ascendance of youth and the new economy on the government's agenda, real and perceived threats to domestic cultural policy-making capacity, and the strength and effectiveness of the current Minister and Deputy Minister of Canadian Heritage. The second half of the chapter focussed on Tomorrow Starts Today, the new program that commits over half a billion dollars of new federal funding to arts and culture over three years. This section highlighted two of the key details of the new spending, and sounded several related cautionary bells. First, the bulk of the funding increases accrue to the Department of Canadian Heritage, and it is as yet unclear what proportion of the new moneys will be consumed by program delivery mechanisms at the expense of arts and culture recipients. Furthermore, the decision to maintain majority departmental control over the new expenditures increases the vulnerability of the new funding to co-option by the government to be applied to broader government plans and priorities or narrow partisan purposes. Second, the chapter probed two of the dominant themes of Tomorrow Starts Today, youth and the new economy, arguing that the government's rationale for focussing on these two themes was ultimately related to broader Liberal policy-making priorities and themes, and, when combined with the departmental focus of the new funding, raises the spectre of undesirable political influence on the development of Canadian Internet content, and that of targeting programming for youth at risk at the expense of more broadly based youth programming. This chapter has recommended that departmental decision-making processes involve members of the arts and culture community to the greatest extent possible, in order to minimize the new funding's vulnerability to political prerogatives.

NOTES

I would like to thank the many individuals who generously gave of their time to meet with me to discuss Tomorrow Starts Today, and arts and culture policy in general. While interviews were conducted on a confidential and anonymous basis, I would like to acknowledge the assistance of these insightful and dedicated individuals. I am also grateful to Bruce Doern for his helpful comments. The views expressed in this chapter are my own and do not necessarily represent the views of the government of Canada or any other organization. Any errors in fact or interpretation are mine alone.

1 Canada, *1995–1996 Main Estimates* (Ottawa: Public Works and Government Services, 2000).
2 John Meisel and Jean Van Loon, 'Cultivating the Bushgarden: Cultural Policy in Canada', in Milton C. Cummings, Jr., and Richard S. Katz, eds, *The Patron State: Government and the Arts in Europe, North American and Japan* (New York: Oxford University Press, 1987), 282.
3 Canada, *1995–1996 Main Estimates* (Ottawa: Public Works and Government Services, 1995), and Canada, *1992–1993 Main Estimates* (Ottawa: Public Works and Government Services, 1992).
4 See Chairman's Report, *Canada Council for the Arts 43rd Annual Report 1999–2000* (Ottawa: Canada Council for the Arts, 2000).
5 The '50–50' plan, part of the Liberals' 1997 election platform, committed the government to dedicating one-half of budget surpluses to program funding increases and the other to paying down the debt and reducing taxes.
6 *Speech from the Throne to Open the First Session Thirty-Sixth Parliament of Canada* (Ottawa, 23 Sept. 1997), 3.
7 Prime Minister's Office, 'Throne Speech 2001: A Vibrant Canadian Culture', Fact Sheet (Ottawa, 30 Jan. 2001). See Web site: www.pm.gc.ca
8 Liberal Party of Canada, *Creating Opportunity: The Liberal Plan for Canada* (Ottawa, Sept. 1993).
9 This is not to say that the Liberal government was inactive in this policy field during its first mandate, but rather that arts and culture were peripheral to government-wide plans and priorities. For an analysis of policy developments in the communications and cultural sector in the first Liberal mandate, see Vincent Mosco, 'Marketable Commodity or Public Good: The Conflict Between Domestic and Foreign Communications Policy', in Gene Swimmer, ed., *How Ottawa Spends 1997–98: Seeing Red: A Liberal Report Card* (Ottawa: Carleton University Press, 1998), 159–78.
10 Liberal Party of Canada, *A Record of Achievement: A Report on the Liberal Government's 36 Months in Office* (Ottawa, 1996), 89.
11 *Speech from the Throne to Open the Second Session Thirty-Fifth Parliament of Canada* (Ottawa, 27 Feb. 1996), 3. See Web site: http://www.parl.gc.ca/english/hansard/001_96-02-27/001GO1E.html
12 Liberal Party of Canada, *Securing Our Future Together: Preparing Canada for the 21st Century* (Ottawa, 1997).
13 *Speech from the Throne to Open the First Session Thirty-Sixth Parliament of Canada* (Ottawa, 23 Sept. 1997) 12.

14 *Speech from the Throne to Open the Second Session of the Thirty-Sixth Parliament of Canada* (Ottawa, 12 Oct. 1999).

15 Ibid, 7.

16 Ibid, 8.

17 Ibid, 13.

18 Liberal Party of Canada, *Opportunity for All: The Liberal Plan for the Future of Canada* (Ottawa, 2000).

19 *Speech from the Throne to Open the First Session of the 37th Parliament of Canada* (Ottawa, 30 Jan. 2001). See Web site: www.sft-ddt.gc.ca/ sftddt_e.htm

20 Ibid.

21 Address by Prime Minister Jean Chrétien in Reply to the Speech from the Throne (Ottawa, 31 Jan. 2001). See Web site: www.pm.gc.ca

22 Charles Gordon, 'The Arts Community Must Keep Biting the Hand That Feeds It', *The Ottawa Citizen*, 5 May 2001, B5.

23 For a comprehensive review of the magazines case and other trade disputes over culture in North America, see Keith Acheson and Christopher Maule, *Much Ado About Culture: North American Trade Disputes* (Ann Arbor: Michigan Press, 1999).

24 Liberal Party of Canada, *Opportunity for All*, 9.

25 'Chrétien: Culture's New Best Friend?' *The Globe & and Mail* [Toronto], 3 May 2001, R4.

26 Opinion expressed by a prominent member of Canada's arts and culture community in an interview with the author. See also John Geddes and Julian Beltrame, 'Who Would Be Caesar?' *Maclean's*, 25 June 2001, 31–32.

27 Department of Canadian Heritage, 'Major Investment in Canadian Culture', News Release (Toronto, 2 May 2001). See Web site: www.pch.gc.ca/ tomorrowstartstoday

28 Canada, *2001–2002 Main Estimates* (Ottawa: Public Works and Government Services, 2001).

29 'Address by Prime Minister Jean Chrétien Announcing a Major New Government of Canada Investment in Canadian Arts and Culture' (Toronto, 2 May 2001). See Web site: www.pm.gc.ca

30 The Canadian Broadcasting Corporation also receives additional funding of $60 million under Tomorrow Starts Today. The new moneys for the CBC are the only part of the Tomorrow Starts Today commitment to be disbursed as a lump sum rather than over three years.

31 Canadian Conference of the Arts, 'Major Influx of Federal Funding to Cultural Sector: Part II', Bulletin (31 May 2001) 3. See Web site: http://www.ccarts.ca/ eng/01news/bulletins_3/1701.html

32 See Joan Bryden, 'Economy Woes Could Stall PM's Plans: Initiatives for Aboriginal Poverty, Environment Likely Delayed: Officials', *The Ottawa Citizen*, 10 Sept. 2001; Eric Beauchesne, 'Control Spending, Canada Warned: Global Think-tank Urges Continued Debt and Tax Cuts, Less Social Generosity', *The Ottawa Citizen*, 7 Sept. 2001; James Baxter, Joan Bryden, and Tim Naumetz, 'War Effort to Cost Billions: Much of $7.2B Surplus Expected to Go to Military, Police, CSIS, Customs', *The Ottawa Citizen*, 26 Sept. 2001, A1-2.

33 Flora MacDonald, 'The Development of Cultural Policy: Some Cautionary

Notes', in Thomas J. Courchene and Arthur E. Stewart, *Essays on Canadian Public Policy: Proceedings of the Inaugural Conference of the School of Policy Studies Held in 1989* (Kingston: Queen's University, 1991), 65–90.

34 Department of Canadian Heritage, 'Major Investment in Canadian Culture'.

35 Department of Canadian Heritage, 'Government of Canada to Focus on Partnerships in a New Approach to Ensure the Vitality of the Arts', News Release (Vancouver, 25 May 2001). See Web site: www.pch.gc.ca/ tomorrowstartstoday

36 Ibid.

37 Ibid.

38 Department of Canadian Heritage, 'Fact Sheet—I Components of Canadian Culture On-Line', News Release (Montreal, 19 June 2001). See Web site: www.pch.gc.ca/tomorrowstartstoday

39 Speaking Notes for The Honourable Sheila Copps, Minister of Canadian Heritage, Announcement of the Government of Canada's Investment in the Canadian Book Industry (Winnipeg, 1 June 2001), 2.

40 Speaking Notes for The Honourable Sheila Copps, PC, MP, Minister of Canadian Heritage, for a Regional Announcement about the Historic Places Initiative of the 'Tomorrow Starts Today' Program (Edmonton, 8 June 2001), 3.

41 I use the word 'ostensibly' here because Section 4(2) of the *Department of Canadian Heritage Act*, which lists the powers, duties, and functions of the Minister of Canadian Heritage, does not list youth as part of the minister's jurisdiction, nor do previous Departmental Expenditure Plans list youth as one of the policy and program responsibilities of the department. The practice of including youth in the list of policy and program responsibilities of the ministry appears to have originated in the department's 2000/1 Departmental Expenditure Plan.

42 Department of Canadian Heritage, *2000–2001 Estimates, Part III: Report on Plans and Priorities* (Ottawa: Minister of Public Works and Government Services, 2000).

43 I use the word 'ostensibly' here because Section 4(2) of the *Department of Canadian Heritage Act*, which lists the powers, duties, and functions of the Minister of Canadian Heritage, does not list youth as part of the minister's jurisdiction, nor do previous Departmental Expenditure Plans list youth as one of the policy and program responsibilities of the department. The practice of including youth in the list of policy and program responsibilities of the ministry appears to have originated in the department's 2000/1 Departmental Expenditure Plan.

44 Many individuals interviewed by the author for this chapter noted the rise of 'youth at risk' on the department's policy and program agenda.

45 Department of Canadian Heritage, *2000–2001 Estimates, Part III: Report on Plans and Priorities*, 13. The nature and objectives of First Works have considerably altered since the Department's 2000/1 Report on Plans and Priorities; it has changed from a youth program to something more akin to a policy coordination unit within the department for youth initiatives.

46 Liberal Party of Canada, *Opportunity for All*, 2.

47 Department of Canadian Heritage, 'Fact Sheet—VI Books: Bringing Authors to Readers in a Digital Age', News Release (Toronto, 2 May 2001). See Web site: www.pch.gc.ca/tomorrowstartstoday

48 Department of Canadian Heritage, 'Fact Sheet—VII Sound Recording: From Creators to Audience: A Transition to the Digital Economy', News Release (Toronto, 2 May 2001). See Web site: www.pch.gc.ca/tomorrowstartstoday

49 For more information on the full range of federal programs in this field, see the Connecting Canadians Web site: www.connect.gc.ca

50 Department of Canadian Heritage, 'Fact Sheet—I Components of Canadian Culture On-line', News Release (Montreal, 19 June 2001). See Web site: www.pch.gc.ca/tomorrowstartstoday

51 Peter Mansbridge, 'Jean Chrétien Pledges Millions for the Arts in Canada', Broadcast Transcript, *The National* (CBC-TV), (2 May 2001).

Appendix
**Federal Arts and Culture Funding
1992/3 to 2001/2 ($ millions)**

Canadian Heritage Portfolio	1992/3	1993/4	1994/5	1995/6	1996/7	1997/8	1998/9	1999/2000	2000/1	2001/2
Department of Canadian Heritage[1]	1152.1	1033.4	1128.3	966.9	918.0	995.0	908.8	732.5[2]	831.4	952.2
Departmental Agencies										
Canadian Radio-television and Telecommunications Commission	37.8	34.8	21.5	21.2	3.3[3]	3.8	4.6	5.9	4.5	8.4
National Archives of Canada	62.4	59.4	59.4	58.3	49.8	46.2	45.0	45.2	46.8	50.8
National Battlefields Commission[4]			4.9	4.8	2.3	6.4	6.2	8.4	8.9	8.0
National Film Board of Canada	81.7	82.6	81.7	75.9	65.2	57.7	55.9	59.5	59.6	60.6
National Library of Canada	45.5	46.0	37.3	34.4	31.5	29.7	29.5	30.4	32.7	36.2
Parks Canada Agency[5]								347.2	345.7	368.0
Status of Women Canada[6]				15.2	16.6	17.1	17.0	17.0	17.6	21.2
Crown Corporations										
Canada Council for the Arts	108.4	99.3	98.4	95.9	90.8	88.7	112.0	116.5	114.5	124.2
Canada Science and Technology Museum	16.5	16.1	15.4	20.6	19.6	19.2	18.6	19.7	20.3	22.9
Canadian Broadcasting Corporation	1112.4	1089.5	1091.1	1064.6	963.2	857.9	844.0	903.9	901.1	923.0
Canadian Film Development Corporation (Telefilm Canada)	145.1	132.4	122.3	109.8	91.3	81.0	78.2	78.7	79.4	125.5
Canadian Museum of Civilization	40.7	39.1	38.1	46.2	44.1	45.6	44.5	46.3	47.5	49.7
Canadian Museum of Nature	19.5	18.8	18.1	25.0	24.1	20.6	19.5	20.5	21.1	23.7
National Arts Centre	22.5	22.3	21.7	19.3	17.4	19.6	19.5	21.5	21.5	23.9
National Capital Commission[7]			89.8	82.9	76.2	71.1	68.7	61.2	77.1	84.7
National Gallery of Canada	29.9	28.7	27.7	33.4	31.8	32.5	31.6	32.5	33.3	36.2
TOTAL	2874.5	2702.4	2855.7	2674.4	2445.2	2392.1	2303.6	2546.9	2663	2919.2

Sources: Canada, *1992–1993 to 2001–2002 Main Estimates* (Ottawa: Public Works and Government Services, 1992–2001).
1 Includes payments to Canada Post Corporation for publications distribution. Departmental expenditures for 1992/3 and 1993/4 include funding to Multiculturalism and Citizenship Canada and the Secretary of State, which were amalgamated with the Department of Canadian Heritage in 1993. Secretary of State funding for the Canada Student Loans Program excluded because the program was transferred to Industry Canada.
2 Funding decrease resulted largely because the Parks Canada Program became a separate agency (Parks Canada).
3 The $16.7 million dollar budget decrease resulted from the introduction of vote netting of some broadcast licence fees.
4 Joined the Canadian Heritage Portfolio in 1994/5.
5 See note ii.
6 Joined the Canadian Heritage Portfolio in 1995/6.
7 Joined the Canadian Heritage Portfolio in 1994/5.

12

Getting Greener in the Third Mandate? Renewable Energy, Innovation, and the Liberals' Sustainable Development Agenda

DEBORA L. VANNIJNATTEN

The 2000 budget, launched in an election year, indicated that environmental protection might assume a higher profile in a third Liberal term. In the Budget Speech, Finance Minister Paul Martin declared that 'for Canadians of all ages, protecting the environment is not an option—it is something we simply must do. It is a fundamental value—beyond debate, beyond discussion.'[1] The Minister announced that the federal government would establish a Sustainable Development Technology Fund, at a cost of $100 million, to help companies develop and bring to market 'green' technologies. Then, in the January 2001 post-election Speech from the Throne, the Liberal government stated that it would spend $4 billion over four years to promote 'leading edge' research in areas such as new environmental technologies. Martin noted that such research can deliver 'new solutions to environmental challenges, such as climate change'. In particular, the government announced its intention to support the development of fuel cell and other renewable energy technologies.

This chapter argues, first, that the higher profile accorded to environmental and particularly renewable energy technologies can be explained not as a sudden change of heart, but as the gradual outgrowth of the Liberal domestic policy agenda, cross-border Canada-US policy dialogue, and shifts within the energy industry.

Three pillars of the Liberal policy agenda—innovation, sustainable development, and addressing climate change—have become increasingly intertwined over the course of the Liberals' tenure, and the importance that they have assumed suggests that renewable energy programs will take on a more significant role. Second, the vilification of fossil fuels in recent debates over air quality policy in both Canada and the United States, especially within the context of binational negotiations on an 'Ozone Annex' to the Canada-United States Air Quality Agreement, has encouraged governments to think twice about their energy choices. Finally, major players within the domestic energy industry have begun to show more interest in, and put investments into, renewable energy developments.

Indeed, an examination of renewable energy policies and programs over the course of the Liberals' reign (effectively 1994–2001) reveals that, while the resources provided were not directly proportional to the government's policy rhetoric, support for renewable energy did increase modestly over the Liberals' first two mandates, even as Program Review ran its course and departmental budgets were significantly decreased. The more recent economic downturn and the events of September 11 have grasped the attention—and budgets—of federal policy-makers, and observers have already sounded the death knell for program spending. However, it is argued here that the policy context that has given rise to greater support for renewables is unlikely to unravel so quickly.

THE LIBERALS' ENVIRONMENTAL RECORD 1994–2000

A quick glance at the Liberals' first two mandates shows few environmental policy initiatives or, for that matter, successes, but the pre-election 2000 budget indicated a possible change of direction. The Liberals did fulfil some 1993 election promises in their first mandate: they created a Commissioner of the Environment and Sustainable Development in the Office of the Auditor General, and among their initiatives were the Greening of Government Operations, and Action 21, an environmental public awareness program. Possible barriers to 'environmentally sound practices' within the tax system were analysed, and changes were made to encourage investment in non-conventional energy projects. Income tax deductions for contributions to environmental trusts were extended and there was minor investment in programs promoting energy efficiency and renewable energy development. Yet, as Juillet and Toner have argued, environmental initiatives in the Liberals' first mandate 'were "sideswiped" by the Liberals' growing fascination with fiscal issues, job creation, economic growth, and national unity.'[2]

Indeed, beginning in 1994, the Liberals, determined to put the nation's finances—which were in worse shape than they had previously believed—in order, administered sizable budget cuts to government departments, especially those considered to house 'economic programs'. For example, Environment Canada absorbed cuts amounting to 32 per cent from 1995/6 to 1997/8 (from $737 million to $503 million) and lost one quarter of its staff (1,400 of 5,700).[3] The department was left with reduced policy capacity and fewer resources, to implement a continually expanding mandate. Natural Resources Canada (NRCan) underwent even greater cuts; departmental spending was reduced by close to 60 per cent between 1994/5 and 1998/9,[4] and many programs were pared back or eliminated altogether.

In the Liberals' second mandate, revisions to the Canadian Environmental Protection Act were completed, but environmentalists and the House of Commons Standing Committee on Environment and Sustainable Development pronounced the revised act a disappointment. In 1998, in a move denounced by environmentalists as a 'downloading' of federal responsibility for environmental protection to the provinces, the federal government signed on to the Canada-Wide Accord on Environmental Harmonization, an intergovernmental agreement designed to eliminate duplication in federal and provincial environmental policies and to facilitate cooperative standard-setting. Moreover, the Liberals had moved toward 'voluntary' pollution control initiatives by industry in areas such as toxic substance management and greenhouse gas (GHG) reductions, with little positive effect. Attempts to enact federal legislation protecting endangered species were unsuccessful: there were two attempts, two failures.

Throughout their first two mandates, the Liberals maintained a rhetorical commitment to the principles of sustainable development. Yet the Liberal record has received considerable critical attention, both at home and abroad. One of the keenest observers of the federal government's performance has been the Environmental Commissioner, who was, ironically, installed by the Liberals. Reports emanating from the Commissioner's Office, which are much anticipated—with trepidation in those bureaucratic quarters where programs are under review—have highlighted weaknesses in federal policy capacity and enforcement on a variety of fronts, including toxic substance management, air pollution, and water pollution. Some of the Commissioner's reports have detailed the shortcomings of the delivery instruments favoured by the Liberals, including intergovernmental (federal-provincial) agreements and voluntary initiatives, while others have focussed attention on the inability of Canada to meet its international environmental commitments, especially with regard to GHG reductions. Moreover, American environmental groups and even government officials have criticized Canada's lack of action on air pollution and on endangered species protection. The Organization for Economic Co-operation and Development, in an evaluation of Canada's environmental performance released in the fall of 2000, concluded that the country had mismanaged the Atlantic fishery; fallen short on toxic substance and water resource management; fumbled its response to climate change; given some of the most generous subsidies in the world to resource industries, as opposed to cleaner, high technology sectors; and relied too heavily on voluntary, poorly monitored initiatives by industry as environmental protection delivery mechanisms.[5]

When the 2000 budget was presented, it appeared that such criticisms had hit their mark. In addition, the government's financial situation was looking brighter. A Sustainable Development Technology Fund was to be established, at a cost of

$100 million, to help companies develop and bring to market green technologies. The government also promised to create a Canadian Foundation for Climate and Atmospheric Sciences, to link researchers studying climate change and air pollution; to provide additional funding for the Climate Change Action Fund; to formulate a National Strategy on Species at Risk, as well as a Great Lakes Action Plan; and to support municipal investments in water conservation and waste management.[6] As noted above, the January 2001 post-election Speech from the Throne then promised a considerable amount of new moneys for environmental technologies. And, in February, the federal Minister of the Environment, David Anderson, unveiled a $120-million package of regulatory, research, and monitoring initiatives to address air pollution problems.

This brief accounting of policy and programs seems to indicate a sudden change of direction in 2000 toward a more activist environmental approach. However, as will be discussed below, the evolution of the policy context that has influenced the Liberals' environmental agenda has in reality been more gradual.

WHY FOCUS ON RENEWABLES?

Renewable energy development and application represents, in many ways, a 'hard test' of the Canadian government's commitment to protect the environment, in a way that other programs, such as those promoting energy efficiency, do not. Renewable energy technologies, including wind, solar, earth (geothermal), biomass, and fuel cells technologies, present considerable implementation challenges. With few exceptions, renewable energy generation is not yet competitive with conventional energy generation under current cost structures, which focus on initial start-up rather than life-cycle costs and which do not engage in 'full-cost pricing', that is, taking environmental impacts into account. Thus, significant government support is necessary, in the form of both up-front technology development and intervention in energy markets to encourage application.

Moreover, fossil fuel extraction is key to the economic health of several provinces, most notably Alberta, but also Saskatchewan, Nova Scotia, and Newfoundland, and any moves to redirect energy generation to renewable forms on environmental grounds are likely to cause federal-provincial tensions, in an area where relations are already strained. Not surprisingly, the fossil fuel lobby also is an influential policy actor, whose presence is felt at all levels of government, particularly in natural resource departments. In addition, provincial utilities, which have traditionally held monopolies over power generation, have been stubborn supporters of large-scale thermal (coal-burning) and hydro generating stations. Finally, the Canadian public generally has not been aware of renewable energy alternatives that can save them money and make a contribution to the environment.

Yet, while the obstacles to renewable energy development in Canada are significant, its environmental benefits are considerable, especially when compared with conventional (fossil fuel) energy production. Air pollutants such as sulphur oxides, nitrous oxides, carbon dioxide, carbon monoxide, and particulate matter, all of which are by-products of the burning of fossil fuels, can be greatly reduced, or eliminated altogether, when green power sources are employed. This, in turn, reduces such problems as smog, acid rain, and global warming, as well as the effects on human health, and other environmental effects, such as damage to vegetation and crops, associated with poor air quality. Moreover, the environmental damage that occurs throughout the life cycle of fossil fuels, from exploration, to extraction and transport, to use and disposal, can be avoided with renewable energy technologies.

To reap these environmental benefits, Canadian governments must carefully set out a policy framework for renewable energy development and application, and adequately fund associated programs over the medium to longer term. Renewable energy sources—as with nuclear, large-scale hydro, oil sands, and clean-coal technologies—will not develop to the scale necessary for cost-effectiveness without government intervention. And, given the legacy of generous government subsidies for these other energy technologies, renewables have a great deal of catching up to do. At present, renewable and alternative energy sources make up a mere 6 per cent of Canada's primary energy supply, and most of that is derived from burning biomass.[7]

TOWARD A POLICY CLIMATE THAT FAVOURS RENEWABLES

The Domestic Policy Agenda
The innovation and sustainable development paradigms have been central pillars of the Liberal domestic policy agenda. Both foresee a leadership role for the federal government, both are science and technology (S&T)-focussed, and both have placed an increasing emphasis on meeting the challenge posed by global climate change, a third Liberal policy focus. In addition, the programs and goals connected with these three pillars—innovation, sustainable development, and addressing climate change—have become increasingly intertwined and entrenched over the course of the Liberals' tenure. Moreover, this intertwining has pointed the way toward increased federal support for renewable energy development.

In Liberal policy documents from the 1993 Red Book (which outlined the party's campaign platform) to the 1994 *Building a More Innovative Economy* (BAMIE) report, through successive reports on federal S&T, and, finally, in consecutive budgets, the major focus for Liberal economic policy has been 'innovation'. These documents have emphasized that in a global, knowledge-based economy the advantage goes to those countries that are innovative. It is innovation that spurs both productivity and high-wage job creation, and that enables Canadian companies to carve out a place in competitive, international markets. Further, government has a role to play in fostering innovation, as the BAMIE document pointed out, by regulating 'smarter'; by helping to accelerate the commercialization of new products and processes; and by supporting S&T. This agenda was supported by the 1995 review of federal S&T, which called for a strategy whereby Canada would pursue a more systematic approach to S&T, and focus on commercialization.[8]

At the same time, the Liberals pledged their commitment to the principles of sustainable development. The 1993 Red Book declared that '[p]reventive environmental care is the foundation of the Liberal approach to sustainable development'.[9] The 1994 Throne Speech reiterated the Liberals' commitment to integrating sustainable development into government decision-making. Under the legislation creating the Office of the Commissioner of the Environment and Sustainable Development, enacted shortly thereafter, all federal departments were required to submit to Parliament annual sustainable development strategies, which would then be used by the Commissioner to judge their environmental performance. Environment Canada's own strategies, like those of other departments, emphasized in-house S&T activities as their contributions to pollution prevention.

In government discussions and documents, the connection between innovation and sustainable development has been made continually, with S&T as the linkage mechanism. The 1994 BAMIE document argued that a healthy environment 'is essential for sustained growth, prosperity, and job creation', and that technology must be harnessed to support environmental goals.[10] The 1996 *Science and Technology for a New Century: A Federal Strategy* noted that '[s]cience and technology are key to achieving sustainable development. Protecting and conserving the environment . . . will require increased innovation in all sectors of society.'[11] Then *Minding Our Future*, the first report on implementation of the S&T strategy, released in late 1997, declared in its introduction,

> A productive national system of innovation can generate the knowledge that society needs to make environmentally sustainable decisions. . . . Because of the close connection between the success of the innovation system and the need to achieve sustainable development, the various players, many of whom have been adversaries in the past, need to form partnerships.[12]

The second implementation report, *Building Momentum*, included sustainable development as a 'key science and technology file', and identified global climate change as an emerging policy challenge: 'Canada's signing of the Kyoto Protocol on greenhouse gas emissions has focused attention on how federal science and technology activities can best contribute to an understanding of, and help to mitigate, global climate change.'[13] Finally, *Forging Ahead*, the 1999 implementation report, announced significant new investments of $1.8 billion in S&T, and contained a detailed description of co-operative S&T activities designed to address GHG reductions, much of it coordinated by NRCan, which had assumed lead responsibility for the climate change file. The report argued for 'the need to set new targets [for reduction] and develop even more advanced technologies that will lead to the stabilization of atmospheric greenhouse gas concentrations and co-beneficial improvements in other air issues such as urban smog and acid rain.'[14]

The Liberals' increasing emphasis on S&T programs as a way of addressing climate change occurred even as (or perhaps because) the government seemed unable to formulate a concrete GHG reduction strategy. An early attempt by the Liberals to formulate a national GHG reduction plan in their first mandate by means of a national consultation process was unsuccessful and, instead, the Voluntary Challenge Registry, which encouraged industry to reduce its emissions voluntarily, was established. After the Liberals signed on to the 1997 Kyoto Protocol, which committed Canada to a 6-per cent reduction in GHG emissions from 1990 levels by 2012, a national Climate Change Secretariat was established, and another large-scale consultation process was initiated to examine the impacts, costs, and benefits of implementing Kyoto. Sixteen multi-stakeholder issue tables formulated a series of options papers between 1998 and 2000 that served as the basis for the Action Plan 2000 on Climate Change. S&T issues figured prominently in the work of the issues tables and in Action Plan 2000, which is designed to take Canada one-third of the way to achieving the Kyoto target.

Policies designed to encourage renewable energy development and application exist quite comfortably at the apex of the three policy objectives discussed above: fostering innovation, working toward sustainable development, and addressing the climate change imperative. Renewable energy development and application represents the type of high technology, high-wage sector with job creation potential that is so dear to the hearts of those currently implementing the innovation paradigm across the federal government. In addition, the way that energy is produced, supplied, and consumed in Canada is probably the most important factor determining the ability of the federal government to achieve its sustainable development goals. Renewable energy represents an alternative to conventional energy sources—an alternative that can help policy-makers meet the needs of the present without compromising the ability of future generations to meet their own needs. At the same time, employing renewable energy technology can significantly reduce GHG emissions, which lead to climate change.

Canada-United States Cross-Border Policy Spillage

The pervasive American influence on Canadian environmental policy is well documented and stems from the close environmental and economic relationship between the two countries. With respect to the issues discussed here, cross-border policy dialogue and developments in two interrelated arenas—air quality and energy politics—have moved Canada in the direction of a more integrated air quality management regime and, in turn, greater debate about the merits of fossil fuel-based energy generation vs that from 'greener' power sources.

Canada-US air quality relations have been characterized by increasing interaction and co-operation over the past two decades, with accelerating activity in the mid- to late 1990s. The Canada-US Air Quality Committee (AQC), established under the 1991 Canada-US Air Quality Agreement, broadened the scope of cross-border interaction with respect to acid rain research, monitoring, and policy initiatives in the early to mid-1990s. In 1996, the AQC initiated efforts to move the two countries toward negotiating an 'Ozone Annex' to the Air Quality Agreement to reduce smog-causing emissions. In the run-up to and during actual negotiations, in 1999 and 2000, much critical attention was focussed on Canada's, especially Ontario's, high-emission, coal-fired power sector. Canadian federal officials and environmentalists, quite publicly and in various media, worried that Ontario's weak air pollution controls might jeopardize the negotiations, because the United States had just instituted new federal emission reduction requirements on its own coal-fired plants in the Midwest and wanted similar controls instituted in Canada.[15]

In the final agreement, made official in early 2001, the Canadian and Ontario governments agreed to make power sector emission reductions and to match more stringent American standards for transportation and recreational vehicles. As the Annex provisions are implemented over the coming years, Canadian and Ontario air quality policy-makers will be prompted to be more activist and to consider emission reduction alternatives. Environmental groups have launched a campaign questioning Ontario's whole approach to power generation, and have argued that the coal-fired plants could be phased out at a relatively low cost.[16] Interestingly, Ontario has already announced that some of Ontario Power Generation's coal-fired units will be retrofitted to burn cleaner natural gas.

In tandem with these developments, various air quality problems—acid rain, ground-level ozone, GHGs, and mercury—have converged in policy discussions in both countries, especially with regard to utilities powered by fossil fuel. The United States is ahead of Canada with respect to such thinking and has been in the process of moving beyond a regulatory strategy of addressing one air pollutant at a time (that is, SO_2, then NO_x, then CO_2, and so on) to a 'multi-pollutant' approach to reducing power sector emissions. Such a strategy would involve the simultaneous establishment of annual emission caps and national emissions trading regimes for each pollutant. In Canada, the Canadian Council of Ministers of the Environment held stakeholder consultations in January of 2001 on the possibility of formulating a Multi-Pollutant Emission Reduction Strategy for the power sector and other sectors (such as pulp and paper, iron and steel, and base metals smelting). This more integrated manner of looking at air quality management also has served to highlight the disadvantages of fossil fuel energy generation for a range of air quality problems.

Moreover, policy discourse about fossil fuel reliance and air pollution in Canada have overlain related discussions about the environmental impacts of energy deregulation in the provinces. Environmental groups, such as Energy Probe in Ontario, have long argued that electricity deregulation and the break-up of provincial utility monopolies would allow smaller-scale, greener energy concerns—including co-generation and renewable energy projects—to gain a foothold in electricity markets. In both Ontario and Alberta, deregulators were encouraged to move in the direction taken by many US states—which have also been engaged in electricity deregulation—by adopting minimum renewable electricity standards (or quotas), establishing renewable energy funds (charging a small fee on electricity sold, to support renewable energy development), mandating net metering (which allows customers who themselves generate electricity to feed it back into the system and benefit financially), and requiring electricity providers to disclose on electricity bills the fuel mix and the environmental impact of their products (in order to increase consumer awareness).[17] Three states—Connecticut, New Jersey, and Massachusetts—have adopted all four of these policies, while New York, Maine, Illinois, and Pennsylvania have adopted three of the four. While provinces thus far have not been as activist, they may feel pressure to consider such alternative instruments more carefully as they attempt to gain increased access to US energy markets, especially in the Northeast.

The air quality-energy nexus has come into even clearer focus in the debates over President George W. Bush's National Energy Plan (NEP). Bush's NEP called for an increase in the domestic and continental energy supply, mainly through increased oil and gas exploration and development, but also through the increased use of coal. As a consequence, both Houses of Congress have been embroiled in divisive debates about drilling for oil in the Arctic National Wildlife Refuge (ANWR), in the Florida Gulf, under the Great Lakes, and on federally protected lands. However, Bush's NEP has had the effect of mobilizing angry environmental and conservation groups, and has accelerated study into the relative impacts of different types of energy production and different technologies. Discussions about energy conservation and renewable energy, which had been given a slight push forward after the implications of Kyoto sank in, have thus been accorded even higher profile, with environmental interests marshalling their arguments against reliance on fossil fuel.

Private Sector Developments
At the same time as policy developments in Canada and across the Canada-US border have focussed on the links between pollution levels and energy choice, Canadian energy companies have begun to show more interest in renewable energy development. As NRCan's Director, Renewable and Electrical Energy Division, has noted, one of the most important changes over recent years has been a shift in industry attitudes toward renewable energy sources.[18] This shift has been spurred not only by competitive instincts (given that European governments currently provide generous incentives for their companies to develop wind and solar power technologies that can then be sold abroad) but also, probably, by the need for some 'green PR' in the wake of debates about GHG reductions (especially in regard to new oil sands development) and flaring practices in Alberta's oilfields. In 1998, renewable energy sources, particularly wind power, were identified as the fastest growing energy sources in the world.[19]

One of the more interesting developments on the Canadian scene has been the formation of the Clean Air Renewable Energy (CARE) coalition, in which energy companies such as Transalta, Westcoast Energy, BP Canada, and Shell Canada have teamed up with environmental groups such as the Pembina Institute, Friends of the Earth, and Pollution Probe to lobby the federal government for expanded tax credits for renewable energy sector R&D as well as credits for consumers who buy energy generated from renewable sources.[20] Moreover, Transalta has undertaken a project with the Canadian Wind Energy Association to encourage the Alberta government to increase its wind-generating capacity. Also, Suncor Energy Inc. has struck a deal with Europe's EHN, a group of renewable energy companies, to develop wind energy projects in Canada. In addition, the soon-to-be-privatized Ontario Power Generation has recently made investments in wind turbine technology, and it has also announced its participation in an $18-million fuel cell project, the largest in the world, for delivering heat and electricity to buildings.

Given this policy context, in which domestic, cross-border, and private sector developments have come to point in the same direction, it is perhaps not surprising that the government has responded substantively. While it would certainly be diffi-cult to argue that the resources allocated have matched policy rhetoric, there has been a gradual increase in government support for renewable energy development and application, which is in keeping with the confluence of policy agendas described above.

THE LIBERAL TRACK RECORD ON RENEWABLES

Budget and Speeches

The Liberals' Red Book had declared, 'We want to promote, not hinder, the research, development, and implementation of clean and energy efficient technologies; [and] renewable energy use', and 'A Liberal government will work with provincial and urban governments to improve energy efficiency and increase the use of renewable energies.'[21] In the January 1994 Throne Speech, the Liberals reiterated their com-mitment to sustainable development and highlighted the positive relationship between pollution prevention, the development of 'green industries', and job creation.

The February 1994 budget was geared toward setting out a firm deficit reduction strategy, which would rely on expenditure cuts to federal programs to achieve its targets. Yet, the budget did announce the creation of a Task Force on Economic Instruments and Disincentives to Sound Environmental Practices, which was to study the barriers to environmentally friendly investment practices. The Task Force, comprised of academics, government officials, and business and environmental rep-resentatives, proposed, in a November report, a series of measures that could be taken immediately, and also recommended that a baseline review of the environ-mental impacts of taxes, grants, and subsidies be undertaken.[22] The environment received little attention in the 1995 budget, which merely announced that the income tax treatment of energy efficiency, renewable energy, and non-renewable energy investments would continue to be reviewed.

The 1996 budget was more ambitious. The Finance Minister's 1996 Budget Plan declared that '[t]he development of renewable energy sources will better position Canada in meeting its long-term energy demands and its international commitment to reduce CO_2 levels.'[23] Citing the Task Force's work, the Budget announced the creation of a new Canadian Renewable Energy and Conservation Expenses (CRCE) category in the tax system. With the CRCE, a new class of 'intangible' expenditures for renewable energy development, similar to development costs incurred to determine the existence, location, extent, or quality of non-renewable resources such as oil and natural gas, would be created.[24] Expenditures eligible for CRCE treatment would be fully deductible and could be carried forward indefinitely. Thus, taxpayers investing in renewable energy projects would receive more rapid deductions for expenditures that would otherwise be capitalized by developers in the early stages. Flow-through share (FTS) financing for the renewable energy sector was also extended, thereby allowing it access to financing similar to that available for junior oil, gas, and mining companies.[25] At the same time, FTS arrangements for the non-renewable sector were tightened. Together, these measures were intended to provide 'an essentially level playing field between certain renewable and non-renewable energy investments'[26] and to encourage investment in the preproduction phases of renewable energy projects. They were also included in the budget as 'reallocations to high-priority areas'. Finally, the 1996 budget announced the creation of Technology Partnerships Canada, a $250-million fund to encourage the development of high technology products and processes, including environmental technologies.

The 1997 budget proceeded to stay the course in terms of program spending reductions, and the focus on technological innovation continued. The CRCE definition was modified slightly to include, for example, the costs of acquiring and installing test wind turbines, and to reduce the qualification threshold for photovoltaic systems. This budget also earmarked $20 million per year over three years to promote investments in energy efficiency and renewable energy for commercial buildings.[27] Some of these funds would be spent under the auspices of a new Climate Change Action Fund.

The 1998 budget was the first balanced budget since 1969/70, and focussed on tax relief as well as on helping Canadians adapt to the new 'knowledge economy'. This budget addressed the environment in technological terms: $34 million was allocated to foster innovation by small and medium-sized businesses and to implement state-of-the-art technologies for preventing pollution as well as for using energy, water, and natural resources more efficiently. The 1999 budget heralded new investments in health care, more tax cuts, and continued moderate support for innovation programs.

The 2000 budget represented continuity with respect to policy focus but also change with respect to funding. The budget announced $700 million worth of initiatives to develop new environmental technologies and improve environmental practices between 1999/2000 and 2002/3. The Finance Minister declared that

[t]he development, dissemination and use of environmental technologies are essential as Canada makes the transition to a more environmentally benign information economy. To help Canada remain a world leader in environmental technology, the Government will establish a Sustainable Development Technology Fund at an initial level of $100 million. This fund will stimulate the development

and demonstration of new environmental technologies, particularly those aimed at reducing greenhouse gas emissions such as fuel cells, wind turbines and advanced materials.[28]

The budget also announced new funding totalling $210 million for the CCAF and for federal energy efficiency and renewable energy programs. Moreover, changes would be made to federal procurement policy to favour environmentally friendly energy generation, thereby stimulating market demand for green power. In this budget, then, the innovation, sustainable development, and climate change agendas appeared to be coming together even more explicitly, with environmental technologies, including renewable energy technologies, as the beneficiary. As the Finance Minister noted in his budget speech,

> The unequivocal fact is that climate change—indeed, the entire environmental spectrum—will provide challenges, but for an innovative economy it presents many more opportunities. Indeed, those nations that demonstrate how to truly integrate environmental and economic concerns will forge new tools and develop new technologies that others will have to adopt. Tremendous awards await those nations that get there first, for those which do it best.[29]

The May 2001 Economic Update, provided at the beginning of the Liberals' third mandate and in lieu of a regular budget, noted that a slowdown in the global economy and a weaker US economy was having an effect on Canada. The Finance Minister declared that the government would continue to hold the line on program spending, continue with tax cuts, and continue to invest in innovation. According to the Update, moneys allocated for new environmental technologies and practices were considered part of the government's 'stimulus package.'[30]

Departmental Activity
It is NRCan that has lead responsibility for renewable energy development and application at the federal level, with Environment Canada and Industry Canada playing supporting roles. NRCan's Energy sector, which is the focus here, is one of four line sectors in the department and accounts for approximately one-third of departmental expenditures and 15 per cent of its personnel. NRCan has been forced to administer significant cuts to its departmental budget and to the Energy sector especially; between 1994/5 and 1998/9, the Energy sector lost approximately three-quarters of its budget and one-quarter of its personnel.[31]

Throughout the ongoing deep budget cuts and the restructuring brought about by Program Review, sustainable development and addressing climate change have taken on a higher profile among departmental priorities. A comparison of the Energy Sector Business Plans for 1996–9 and 1998–2001 shows this shift, particularly with regard to the climate change imperative. Moreover, renewables have fared relatively well, thanks both to the policy context and to the support of then Natural

Resources Minister Anne McLellan. Renewable and alternative energy programs were taken out from under the umbrella of the existing Efficiency and Alternative Energy Program in the Office of Energy Conservation, which had focussed primarily on energy efficiency, and given a higher profile within a new Renewable and Electrical Energy Division (REED). Renewables programs also received a slight increase in funding and personnel, despite deep cuts to other programs.[32] In fact, renewables programs were consciously sheltered throughout the ongoing evaluation and restructuring exercises. Moreover, an official in the Minister's Office was designated as an 'assistant for renewable energy' and communicated frequently with personnel in the new Division with respect to the contributions renewables could make to the department's sustainable development and GHG reduction policies.[33]

In October of 1996, McLellan announced the release of NRCan's Renewable Energy Strategy, based on 'three pillars': enhancement of investment conditions through the use of the tax system; technology initiatives in the area of research and development; and market development initiatives to reduce market barriers and create demand. The Strategy was designed to establish a more sustainable energy mix; to contribute to economic growth and job creation in a 'rapidly expanding "green" industry'; to limit GHG emissions; and to address air pollution problems such as acid rain and urban smog. The Strategy declared that '[t]he Government of Canada believes that renewable energy sources must play an increasingly important role in Canada's future energy mix.'[34]

The 1996 post-budget period saw considerable follow-up activity at the departmental level in relation to the tax changes. In June, the ministers of Finance and Natural Resources released a discussion paper on the implementation of the new tax measures and sought stakeholder input into the definition of allowable expenses under the newly created CRCE category. In September, the two departments released a study examining the impact of Canada's tax system on a range of energy investments. *The Level Playing Field: The Tax Treatment of Competing Energy Investments* focussed on the 'uplift', or the percentage of the capital costs of a project covered by incentive provisions of the tax system (that is, the higher the uplift, the greater the relative advantage provided by the tax system). The report concluded that 'while the playing field is not level, the variation in tax support is not large and does not indicate a bias among most renewable and non-renewable energy investments.'[35] While conventional oil and gas investments received relatively modest support from the tax system, in the range of 5 to 10 per cent, renewable energy projects received tax support of a comparable nature at 5 to 15 per cent (somewhat higher if deductions could be applied against income, as would be the case with the 1996 budget changes). In December, a detailed definition of the CRCE, based on stakeholder input, was released, and implementation followed shortly thereafter. As noted above, the CRCE was broadened in the following budget. More recently, there has been some musing about the possibility of 'tilting' tax incentives more aggressively toward renewables in order to energize their development, likely in response to lobbying by the CARE coalition.

NRCan also supports a wide array of renewable energy technology programs. In 1995/6, REED's expenditures on renewables R&D amounted to $8 million; by 1999/2000 this figure was approximately $10 million.[36] Most of these expenditures are used to support private sector activities, with NRCan providing technical expertise when required, and they are aimed at lowering the cost and improving the reliability of renewable energy technologies. Some work is conducted at NRCan's own laboratories, such as the CANMET Energy Technology Centre in Ontario (photovoltaics) and the Energy Diversification Research Laboratories in Quebec (biomass). The Renewable Energy Technologies Program supports renewable energy technology development and field trials by Canadian industry with a view to accelerating domestic and international market penetration. As is evident from the discussion in the previous section, these programs and expenditures do not include a variety of renewable-related technology activities that are conducted interdepartmentally or by other departments. NRCan also manages the Program of Energy Research and Development, which coordinates and allocates funding to interdepartmental energy R&D activities, and it runs an Energy Technology Futures Project focussed on longer-term R&D to meet mainly climate change goals.

NRCan's renewable energy market development initiatives, while modest, have focussed on assessing markets and boosting consumer awareness. In 1995/6, NRCan spent close to $1 million on market development initiatives,[37] which grew to almost $5 million by 1999/2000.[38] The Renewable Energy Deployment Initiative provides technical and financial support to municipal governments, businesses, and public institutions for the implementation of renewable energy heating and cooling systems in their buildings. Also, REED conducts market assessments for the renewable energy industry in order to identify new and emerging markets.

Finally, NRCan and Environment Canada have been involved in Green Power (electricity generated from renewable energy sources) pilot projects, whereby the departments have committed to buying 15 to 20 per cent of their electricity needs from green power sources (which would match the amount of energy generated by fossil fuel that the federal departments currently use). Ontario, Alberta, and Saskatchewan have been selected as sites for green power pilot projects. The longer-term goal of those pushing the Green Power concept is to have the program transferred to Public Works, where it can be implemented across government.

Much of this activity is being driven by the climate change imperative, and measures designed as incentives for renewable energy development have increasingly become intertwined with the federal government's climate change agenda. In 1996, Natural Resources Minister Ann McLellan had declared that '[r]enewable energy and energy conservation are key components of the federal government's climate change and sustainable development priorities.'[39] As NRCan's 1998–2001 Energy Sector Business Plan states, 'Our biggest challenge over the planning period—climate change—will be a key test for sustainable development and for the concept of the horizontal management of issues within our sector, the department and beyond.'[40] The Action Plan 2000 on Climate Change highlights the role that ongoing renewable energy programs will have on GHG reductions. The Plan targets key sectors that account for over 90 per cent of Canada's GHG emissions, and in those sectors constituting the largest sources of GHG emissions, including transportation, oil and gas, and electricity generation, renewable energy and alternative fuels projects are among the chosen implementation instruments.[41]

Thus, NRCan is being driven more than ever before by the need to show leadership on GHG reductions. GHG emissions have continued to increase over the mid- to late 1990s, and there can be no doubt that the climate change issue is a thorn in the Liberals' collective side. The country's lack of progress in reducing emissions, as well as its insistence in international negotiations that it be allowed to employ less stringent implementation instruments, have left it increasingly marginalized—and lumped in with the 'bad boy' of climate change politics, the United States—on the world stage. As one NRCan official has observed, Canada's GHG emissions outlook,[42] carefully pieced together in preparation for the Action Plan 2000 on Climate Change, has become *the* major influence in the calculations of energy forecasters.[43]

PROSPECTS FOR RENEWABLES IN THE THIRD MANDATE

There can be no doubt that the events of 11 September 2001 have changed political calculations and policy priorities. In the wake of the terrorist attacks in New York and Washington, politicians and government officials in the United States have turned their attention to borders, national security, and waging 'a different kind of war'. The deterioration of the economic situation, which predated the autumn attacks but has since become worse, also has changed the political context. Massive government spending has been approved by Congress for an economic stimulus package and domestic security projects, and for military manoeuvres in the Middle East. Environmental and other nongovernmental organizations have chosen, at least for the time being, to suspend their campaigns criticizing the policies of the Bush administration, for fear of appearing 'unpatriotic' in a time of national crisis. New environmental initiatives, including the multi-pollutant air quality bill, will be difficult to move forward, and some Republicans in Congress are using the current situation to argue for accelerated energy development, of the conventional variety, in ANWR and on federally protected lands.

As Chapter One has shown, the Canadian federal government has had to take a similar path regarding security and border measures, and Finance Minister Paul Martin's December 2001 budget has put other priorities on hold. Martin has vowed time and again that he will not put the 'fiscal integrity' of the government in danger. At first glance, then, it appears that the door that was just beginning to open on environment-related spending is once again swinging shut. Certainly, there can be no doubt that the resolve of those in Liberal ranks calling for increased spending of any kind will be sorely tested in the coming year.

However, the forces that have pushed environmental, and particularly renewable, energy programs upward on the political agenda remain firmly in place. Certainly, international actors will continue to watch Canada's performance with respect to reducing GHG, especially in light of the recently signed Kyoto implementation agreement. In the United States, one should not underestimate the momentum generated by existing air quality programs and policies; even the administration of Bush Sr continued with its groundbreaking clean air initiatives in the early 1990s, despite military engagement in the Middle East. American actors that are currently complying with green power requirements or overseeing compliance with them or with the new US federal air emission standards—the most demanding since those initiated by Bush Sr—will look to ensure that Canadian counterparts do not gain a competitive edge. Moreover, recent private sector investments in renewables, some of which were announced after September 11, are an important indicator of increased industry interest.

Perhaps most importantly, the resources directed toward renewable energy technology and application projects are linked to the fulfilment of a complex of policy objectives—connected to innovation, sustainable development, and GHG reduction—that has become entrenched over the course of the Liberals' first two mandates. The existing policy regime, in which renewables have a place, has emerged out of the steady evolution of policy discussions, an intertwining of programs, and substantive policy change; it is unlikely to unravel. That which the Liberals have joined together will not likely be easily torn asunder.

NOTES

1 Paul Martin, Minister of Finance, *Better Finances, Better Lives: The Budget Speech 2000* (Ottawa: Public Works and Government Services Canada, 2000), 13.

2 Luc Juillet and Glen Toner, 'From Great Leaps to Baby Steps: Environment and Sustainable Development Under the Liberals', in Gene Swimmer, ed., *How Ottawa Spends 1997–98: Seeing Red: A Liberal Report Card* (Ottawa: Carleton University Press, 1997), 194.

3 Glen Toner, 'Environment Canada's Continuing Roller Coaster Ride', in Gene Swimmer, ed., *How Ottawa Spends 1996–97: Life Under the Knife* (Ottawa: Carleton University Press, 1996), 111.

4 Paul Martin, Minister of Finance, *Budget in Brief 1996* (Ottawa: Public Works and Government Services Canada, 1996), 10, Chart 2.

5 Martin Mittelstaedt, 'Environment Report Ranks Canada Near Bottom of OECD', *The Globe & Mail* [Toronto], 11 Apr. 2001. See Web site: http://www.theglobeandmail.com

6 Paul Martin, Minister of Finance, *The Budget Plan 2000* (Ottawa: Public Works and Government Services Canada, 2000).

7 Natural Resources Canada, *Renewable Energy Strategy: Creating a New Momentum* (Ottawa, Oct. 1996), 3.

8 Government of Canada, *Summary Report of the Interdepartmental Task Force on Science and Technology Review* (Ottawa, 1995).

9 The Liberal Party of Canada, *Creating Opportunity: The Liberal Plan for Canada* (Ottawa, 1993), 63.

10 Industry Canada, 'Building a More Innovative Economy: Principles and

Approach'. See Web site: http://www.ic.gc.ca/cmb/welcomeic.n... d6629f852565d7005b965e!OpenDocument Accessed 09/11/2001.

11 Government of Canada, *Science and Technology for a New Century: A Federal Strategy*. See Web site: http://strategis.ic.gc.ca/pics/te/e-strat96.pdf Accessed 27/10/01, 26–29.

12 Government of Canada, *Minding Our Future: A Report on Federal Science and Technology—1997*. See Web site: http://strategis.ic.gc.ca/SSG/te01167e.html Accessed 27/10/01, 1–2.

13 Government of Canada, *Building Momentum: A Report on Federal Science and Technology—1998*. See Web site: http://strategis.ic.gc.ca/SSG/te01436e.html Accessed 09/08/2001. See '4.0 Emerging Policy Challenges'.

14 Government of Canada, *Forging Ahead: A Report on Federal Science and Technology—1999*, 'Message from the Minister of Industry'. See Web site: http://strategis.ic.gc.ca/cgi-bin/a...or percent20product percent20contains percent20'004') percent20 Accessed 09/08/2001. See '3.1.5 Future Challenges'.

15 Debora L. VanNijnatten, 'Negotiating the Canada-U.S. Ozone Annex: A Case Study in Transboundary Environmental Relations', Global Affairs Institute Transboundary Case Program, Maxwell School, Syracuse University, 2001.

16 See, for example, Ontario Clean Air Alliance, *Countdown Coal* (Toronto, Apr. 2000).

17 S. Clemmer, B. Paulos, and A. Nogee, *Clean Power Surge: Ranking the States* (Cambridge, MA: Union of Concerned Scientists, Apr. 2000), 5.

18 Interview with David Burpee, Director, Renewable and Electrical Energy Division, Natural Resources Canada, 31 Aug. 2001.

19 Worldwatch Institute, 'Wind Power Sets New Record', News Release, 1998. http://www.worldwatch.org/alerts/981229.html. Accessed on 11/25/2001.

20 Matthew MacKinnon, 'Tax Breaks Proposed for Green Consumers', *The Globe and Mail* [Toronto], 27 Dec. 2000. See Web site: http://www.globeandmail.com

21 The Liberal Party of Canada, *Creating Opportunity*, 64, 70.

22 G. Toner, 'Environment Canada's Continuing Roller Coaster Ride', 110.

23 Paul Martin, *The Budget Plan 1996* (Ottawa: Public Works and Government Services Canada, 1996), 170.

24 Natural Resources Canada, 'Backgrounder: Canadian Renewable and Conservation Expense', News Release 96/74 (a).

25 The allocation through the CRCE and FTS changes was approximately $20 million from 1997/8 to 1998/9. Department of Finance Canada, *Budget in Brief 1996* (Ottawa: Public Works and Government Services Canada, 1996), 19, Table 3.

26 Paul Martin, *The Budget Plan 1996*, 52.

27 Paul Martin, Minister of Finance, *The Budget Plan 1998* (Ottawa: Public Works and Government Services Canada), 117.

28 Paul Martin, Minister of Finance, *The Budget Plan 2000* (Ottawa: Public Works and Government Services Canada).

29 Paul Martin, Minister of Finance, *The Budget Speech 2000* (Ottawa: Public Works and Government Services Canada), 13.

30 Paul Martin, Minister of Finance, *Economic Update* (Ottawa: Public Works and Government Services Canada), 11–13.

31 Natural Resources Canada, *Expenditure Plan for FY 96/97* (Ottawa), 1–2.
32 The new Division received an additional $500,000 in operations funding and one additional FTE.
33 Interview with David Burpee.
34 Natural Resources Canada, *Renewable Energy Strategy: Creating a New Momentum* (Ottawa, Oct. 1996), 14.
35 Natural Resource Canada and Finance Canada, 'Level Playing Field Study Released.' Joint News Release: 96/89, 5 Sept. 1996. The study noted two exceptions to this overall conclusion: ethanol, which benefits from extremely generous tax treatment, and investments in direct heating from renewable sources (such as solar walls, district heating), which are disadvantaged by the tax system.
36 Interview with David Burpee.
37 Natural Resources Canada, *Renewable Energy Strategy*, 10.
38 Interview with David Burpee.
39 Natural Resources Canada, 'New Tax Measures for Renewables and Energy Conservation', News Release 96/74, 27 June 1996.
40 Natural Resources Canada, *Energy Sector Business Plan 1998-2001*. See Web site: http://www.nrcan.gc.ca:80/es/new/bp98e.htm
41 Government of Canada, *Action Plan 2000 on Climate Change* (Ottawa: Supply and Services Canada, 2000).
42 National Climate Change Process Analysis and Modelling Group, *Canada's Emissions Outlook: An Update* (Ottawa, Dec. 1999).
43 Interview with Neil McIlveen, Director, Analysis and Modelling Division, Natural Resources Canada, 31 Aug. 2001.

Appendix A

CANADIAN POLITICAL FACTS AND TRENDS

Canadian Political Facts and Trends presents a snapshot of key political developments between April 2001 and January 2002, particularly those events that are related to chapters in this year's edition. It was compiled and written by Rachel Laforest.

2001

3 April: The federal government orders the first major review of the public service since the 1960s, to be headed by the deputy minister of Public Works and Government Services, Janice Cochrane.

4 April: Federal Minister of Fisheries Herb Dhaliwal announces a reduction of the cod quota off southern Newfoundland this year from 20,000 tonnes to 15,000 tonnes.

5 April: Justice Minister Anne McLellan and Solicitor General Lawrence MacAulay introduce legislation against organized crime.

6 April: Prime Minister Jean Chrétien announces the creation of a new cabinet committee on energy, chaired by Foreign Affairs Minister John Manley and including Justice Minister Anne McLellan and Natural Resources Minister Ralph Goodale.

6 April: Health Minister Allan Rock unveils new rules for the medical use of marijuana.

11 April: The federal government launches a new national organ donation program with the creation of the National Council on Organ and Tissue Donation and Transplantation.

19 April: The Canada Customs and Revenue Agency announces that provisional duties of 5 per cent to 96 per cent will be applied to hot-rolled steel sheets and strips imported from a dozen countries. The duties take effect immediately.

23 April: Prime Minister Jean Chrétien signs a free trade agreement with Costa Rican President Miguel Rodriguez.

24 April: Transport Minister David Collenette approves Canada 3000's takeover of Halifax-based CanJet Airlines.

3 May: The Commons Standing Committee on Health begins hearings into draft legislation that will form the basis for Canada's first law on reproductive technology. The Commons committee is to report back to Health Minister Allan Rock on the proposed legislation by the end of January 2002.

10 May: In a public letter, federal Privacy Commissioner George Radwanski urges Information Commissioner John Reid to stop trying to obtain and release the Prime Minister's agendas for the past five years.

15 May: Prime Minister Jean Chrétien announces a $15-billion reduction in the national debt—the largest payment ever.

15 May: Eight Canadian Alliance MPs break ranks and demand Stockwell Day's resignation as leader of the party. They refuse to formally leave the caucus, claiming allegiance to the party's grassroots and its principles. Those calling for Mr Day's resignation are former house leader Chuck Strahl and MPs Gary Lunn, Jim Gouk, Val Meredith, Art Hanger, Jay Hill, Grant McNally, and Jim Pankiw.

16 May: In the British Columbia election, the Liberal party wins 77 seats, the New Democrats, two.

17 May: The five parties in the House of Commons unanimously back a motion to create a committee with a broad-ranging mandate to study solutions to the use of banned narcotics.

17 May: Canadian Alliance communications advisor Ezra Levant tenders his resignation after he and three members of Stockwell Day's communications office threaten to sue rebel MP Chuck Strahl for accusing the leadership of 'dishonest communications'.

17 May: The federal official languages commissioner, Dyane Adam, wins the right to defend Quebec's English minority in a court challenge of the province's amalgamation plans for Montreal.

18 May: Minister of Foreign Affairs John Manley and Minister of Industry Brian Tobin argue that Canada should sever its links with the monarchy and that a Canadian should fulfil the constitutional role of head of state instead of the Queen.

22 May: Denise Tremblay, Mr Chrétien's special representative in St Maurice, who helped secure controversial government grants and loans for the Grand-Mère Inn in his riding, has been appointed to the federal Veterans Review and Appeal Board.

24 May: The RCMP contact Canadian Alliance party executives about $50,000 paid to former MP Jim Hart, who gave up his seat for Stockwell Day. It is illegal for an MP to accept money or a reward to quit Parliament, and an offence to give money or a reward for that purpose.

25 May: The Canadian Alliance's ruling council, after a vote in a closed session, suspends Rick Anderson, who was a strategic adviser to former Reform leader Preston Manning. If Mr Anderson wishes to return to the 44-member council, he must sign an undertaking to cease criticizing the leader.

25 May: Consumer affairs ministers from the federal, provincial, and territorial governments agree to update and harmonize consumer protection legislation as it applies to Internet transactions.

29 May: A government-appointed commission recommends a 20-per cent wage hike for MPs and senators.

30 May: The government's Web site for electronic tendering calls for bids on assigning a dollar value to Canada's vast water assets.

30 May: A human resources committee tables a report in the House of Commons stating that further reforms are needed, to ease Employment Insurance eligibility rules, to extend coverage to more people, and to revamp the way benefits are calculated.

30 May: Prime Minister Jean Chrétien appoints Sheila Fraser as Canada's first female auditor general.

7 June: The federal government introduces a motion to fast-track a bill that would give MPs an average salary increase of 20 per cent.

11 June: Natural Resources Minister Ralph Goodale, Environment Minister David Anderson, and Transport Minister David Collenette release plans to reduce pollutants and to fund research into fuel-efficient cars, an initiative that will cost $110 million.

19 June: The federal government announces a package of benefits for the shipbuilding industry, including low-interest loans for domestic and foreign buyers, access to government research and development funds, and money for job retraining.

25 June: Another Canadian Alliance member, Andy Burton, leaves the party caucus, further dividing MPs and bringing the number of dissidents closer to the 12 needed for official party status in the House of Commons.

28 June: The Supreme Court of Canada rules that the town of Hudson in Quebec has the right to prohibit pesticide use.

29 June: Justice Robert Cairns rules that spending limits on third-party advertising during elections violates the Charter of Rights.

4 July: The federal government announces new official regulations that will govern marijuana possession and production in Canada.

5 July: Justice Minister Anne McLellan announces $145 million in new funding over the next four years for a national, community-based crime prevention program.

12 July: Agriculture Minister Lyle Vanclief announces $854,700 in federal funding for the creation of a national centre for organic agriculture, associated with Nova Scotia's Agricultural College.

12 July: Deborah Grey resigns from the Canadian Alliance party's executive committee over the question of Stockwell Day's leadership.

17 July: Stockwell Day announces he well step aside 90 days before a leadership election, which will be held on a date to be determined by the party's National Council.

18 July: The Assembly of First Nations issues an ultimatum giving the federal government 30 days to join talks on revamping the Indian Act.

1 August: Canada's premiers and territorial leaders begin their annual meeting in Victoria to discuss health care, infrastructure, energy, and agriculture.

6 August: New regulations come into effect governing the medical use of marijuana. The rules allow terminally ill people, as well as people who are in severe chronic pain, to possess and grow marijuana.

20 August: Minister Herb Dhaliwal issues a temporary licence to the Burnt Church Mi'kmaq, making the fishery legal for seven days, with several restrictions.

27 August: Federal Fisheries Minister Herb Dhaliwal announces that the temporary fishing licence issued on 20 August will be extended until October 20.

29 August: Finance Minister Paul Martin announces the promotion of Nicholas Le Pan, currently deputy superintendent of financial institutions, to superintendent.

30 August: The federal government officially merges the Canada Information Office and the Communications Co-ordination Services Branch into Communications Canada.

30 August: Federal Fisheries officers confiscate dozens of Native lobster traps laid near New Brunswick's Burnt Church reserve.

11 September: Terrorist attacks occur in the United States: two hijacked airliners crash into the twin towers of the World Trade Center, a third crashes into the Pentagon, and a fourth crashes near Pittsburgh.

16 September: Shots are fired on the waters of Miramichi Bay during a confrontation between Native and non-Native fishermen.

16 September: Transport Minister David Collenette announces the introduction of new safety measures for all domestic and international flights.

16 September: Minister of Foreign Affairs John Manley announces that Canada will 'unambiguously' join US military action in striking back at terrorism.

25 September: Transport Minister David Collenette tells Air Canada that it will not be bound by legislation that prevents it from laying off employees until March of next year.

1 October: A new cabinet committee on domestic security and terrorism, chaired by Foreign Affairs Minister John Manley, is created to coordinate the federal government's response to the September 11 terrorist attacks in the United States.

2 October: Transport Minister David Collenette announces $160 million in emergency aid to help Canada's airlines recover losses incurred in the days immediately following the September 11 terrorist attacks.

10 October: Foreign Affairs Minister John Manley announces that Canada will spend an extra $250 million on security and anti-terrorism measures in the next six months.

12 October: Immigration Minister Elinor Caplan announces new immigration measures to combat terrorism.

15 October: Justice Minister Anne McLellan introduces new anti-terrorism legislation aimed at giving police more authority to crack down on terrorists and to cut off fundraising for suspected terrorist groups.

19 October: Solicitor-General Lawrence MacAulay and Defence Minister Art Eggleton announce an extra $47 million for the Canadian Security Intelligence Service (CSIS) and the Communications Security Establishment (CSE), to fight terrorist threats. MacAulay announces that the RCMP will be getting an additional $54 million as well.

19 October: The World Trade Organization rules against a $1.7 billion low-interest loan given by the Canadian government to Air Wisconsin to enable it to buy 150 aircraft from Bombardier.

20 October: The federal government approves a constitutional amendment that will change the name of the province of Newfoundland to Newfoundland and Labrador.

23 October: Transport Minister David Collenette announces that Ottawa will scrap the current restriction that prevents individual Canadian investors from owning more than 15 per cent of Air Canada's stock. However, the limit of 25 per cent on individual foreign ownership of the airline will not be changed.

2 November: Indian Affairs Minister Robert Nault cuts off the funds to the First Nations Governance Institute, which was created in March to explore Native self-governance.

6 November: Public Service Alliance of Canada members ratify a three-year contract with the federal government that will give them an 8.5 per cent wage increase over the life of the deal.

14 November: Industry Minister Brian Tobin announces $20 million to promote tourism across Canada.

20 November: Justice Minister Anne McLellan presents amendments to Bill C-36 that ease most of the concerns of Liberal and Canadian Alliance MPs.

22 November: The federal government unveils a second wide-ranging anti-terrorism bill. In all, the bill amends 19 acts of Parliament and introduces a new law to implement the Biological and Toxin Weapons Convention.

27 November: The Liberals invoke closure on Bill C-36 after the proposed legislation was returned to the House for debate, with amendments agreed to in committee.

28 November: Bill C-36 is approved by a vote of 190 to 47.

28 November: A $400-million class action lawsuit against the federal government is filed alleging that the Canada Pension Plan discriminates against people in same-sex relationships.

30 November: Federal and provincial housing ministers sign a framework agreement that opens the way for Ottawa to spend $680 million on affordable housing construction.

30 November: Finance Minister Paul Martin and Human Resources Minister Jane Stewart announce new cuts to Employment Insurance premiums.

3 December: Lane MacAdam, president and chief executive officer of the Canada Games Council, is appointed director-general of Sport Canada.

4 December: Auditor General Sheila Fraser issues a report on federal departments and services.

6 December: Canada's Business Council on National Issues (BCNI) announces that it will adopt a new name and a broader mandate. Canada's pre-eminent big business lobby will be known as the Canadian Council of Chief Executives (CCCE).

10 December: The federal budget is tabled.

19 December: Agriculture and Agri-Food Minister Lyle Vanclief announces that the Spring Credit Advance Program will be renewed for the 2002 growing season.

19 December: Justice Minister Anne McLellan announces an extension of the amnesty on illegal firearms until 31 December 2002.

2002

7 January: Defence Minister Art Eggleton announces that a 750-member battle group will join American forces hunting al-Qaeda fighters in southern Afghanistan.

7 January: Stockwell Day announces that he will be a candidate to win back the leadership of the Canadian Alliance at its leadership vote.

9 January: Alberta's Advisory Council on Health, headed by Don Mazankowski, former federal Conservative deputy prime minister, issues a report calling for more competition and for a larger role for the private delivery of health services. It also calls for the appointment of an expert panel to determine whether coverage for some medical services should be eliminated.

10 January: It is announced that the House of Commons Committee on Foreign Affairs will hold coast-to-coast hearings into the future of Canada-US relations. The committee is chaired by Bill Graham, MP for Toronto Centre-Rosedale.

11 January: Statistics Canada announces that in December 2001 Canada's unemployment rate had increased from 7.5 per cent to 8.0 per cent, a figure it had not reached since the spring of 1999.

14 January: Industry Minister Brian Tobin announces his resignation from politics for personal reasons, a move that surprises pundits and that alters the dynamics of the possible leadership race to succeed Prime Minister Jean Chrétien.

15 January: Prime Minister Jean Chrétien announces a major Cabinet shuffle, promoting John Manley to Deputy Prime Minister, bringing in several new faces from the backbenches, and shifting more than a dozen ministers, in the wake of the sudden resignation of Brian Tobin.

16 January: Newly appointed federal Health Minister Anne McLellan states in her first day as minister that public health care should not be 'frozen in time', and that she is 'open' to changes in the Canada Health Act.

Appendix B

FISCAL FACTS AND TRENDS

This appendix presents an overview of the federal government's fiscal position, and includes certain major economic policy indicators for 1990–2001, as well as some international comparisons.

Facts and trends are presented for federal revenue sources, federal expenditures by ministry and by type of payment, the government's share of the economy, interest and inflation rates, Canadian balance of payments in total and with the United States in particular, and other national economic growth indicators. In addition, international comparisons on real growth, unemployment, inflation, and productivity are reported for Canada, the United States, Japan, Germany, and the United Kingdom.

The figures and time series are updated each year, providing readers with an ongoing current record of major budgetary and economic variables.

Table B.1

Federal Revenue by Source

1991/2 to 2000/1

As a Percentage of Total

Fiscal Year	Personal Tax[a]	Corporate Tax	Indirect Taxes[b]	Other Revenue[c]	Total Revenue	Annual Change
1991/2	62.8	7.7	20.6	8.9	100.0	2.2
1992/3	63.0	6.0	21.7	9.4	100.1	-1.4
1993/4	60.1	8.1	23.0	8.8	100.0	-3.8
1994/5	61.0	9.4	22.0	7.6	100.0	6.0
1995/6	60.4	12.2	20.4	7.0	100.0	5.4
1996/7	59.0	12.1	20.7	8.3	100.0	7.5
1997/8	58.5	14.7	20.1	6.7	100.0	8.0
1998/9	59.0	13.9	20.2	7.0	100.0	1.6
1999/2000	59.1	14.0	19.8	7.1	100.0	6.1
2000/1	56.6	15.8	20.2	7.4	100.0	7.2

Revenue by Source is on a net basis.

(a) Employment Insurance contributions are included in the total.

(b) Consists of total excise taxes and duties.

(c) Consists of non-tax and other tax revenue.

Source: Department of Finance, *Fiscal Reference Tables* (Sept. 2001), Table 3.

Figure B.1

**Sources of Federal Revenue as a
Percentage of Total, 2000/1**

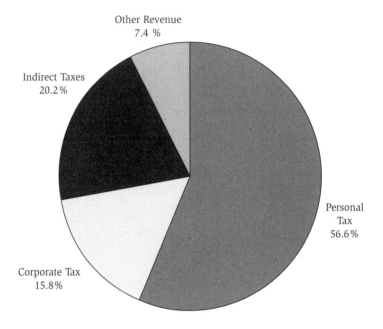

Other Revenue
7.4 %

Indirect Taxes
20.2%

Personal
Tax
56.6%

Corporate Tax
15.8%

Source: Department of Finance, *Fiscal Reference Tables* (Sept. 2001), Table 3.

Figure B.2
Federal Expenditures by Ministry
2001/2 Estimates

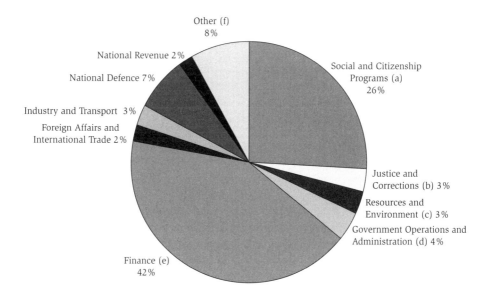

(a) Social and Citizenship programs include departmental spending from Canadian Heritage, Citizenship and Immigration, Human Resources Development, Veterans Affairs, Health, and Indian Affairs and Northern Development.

(b) Justice and Corrections includes spending from the Department of Justice and the Solicitor General.

(c) Resources and Environment includes departmental spending from Agriculture and Agri-Food, Environment, Fisheries and Oceans, and Natural Resources.

(d) Government Operations and Administration Spending includes that from Public Works and Government Services, the Governor General, Parliament, the Privy Council, and the Treasury Board.

(e) Finance expenditures include, but are not limited to, spending on public interest charges and many major social transfers to the provinces.

(f) Other includes the consolidated specified purposes account (Employment Insurance).

Source: Department of Finance, *Main Estimates, Budgetary Main Estimates by Standard Object of Expenditure*, Part II, 2001–2002, 1–24 to 1–29.

Figure B.3
Federal Expenditures by Type of Payment
1996/7 to 2003/4

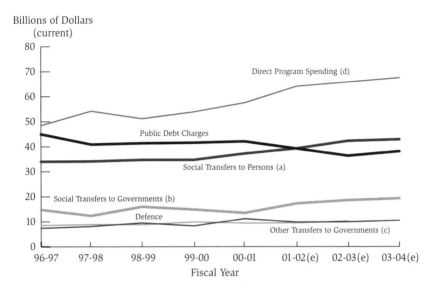

(a) Includes elderly benefits, Employment Insurance benefits, and relief for heating expenses.
(b) Consists of the Canada Health and Social Transfer (CHST). Prior to the CHST, two separate social transfers existed: Established Program Financing for health and post-secondary education expenditures, and the Canada Assistance Plan for welfare and welfare services. The CHST figures include cash transfers to the provinces, and do not include the value of the tax point transfer.
(c) Includes fiscal equalization and transfers to Territories, statutory subsidies, and recoveries under the Youth Allowance program.
(d) Includes all operating and capital expenditures, including defence.
(e) Figures for these years are budgetary estimates.
(f) Includes program spending and public debt charges. It is not a summation of the reported program categories.

Source: Department of Finance, *Budget Plan 2001*, Table 1.4 and Table 7.7; Public Accounts of Canada, Vol. I, External Expenditures by Type, various years.

Figure B.4

**Federal Revenues, Program Spending, and Deficit/Surplus as Percentage of GDP
1993/4 to 2003/4**

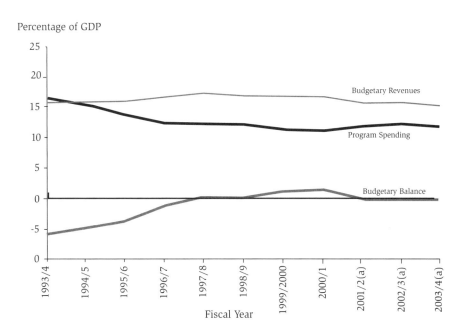

(a) Figures for these years are estimates.

Note: Budgetary revenue and program spending are based on fiscal years, while GDP
is based on the calendar year. Revenues, program spending, and the deficit/surplus
are on a net basis. Program spending does not include public interest charges. GDP
is nominal GDP.
    Beginning in 1997/8, the budget deficit trend line changes to indicate a
budgetary surplus as a percentage of the GDP.

Source: Department of Finance, *Fiscal Reference Tables* (Sept. 2001), Table 2;
Department of Finance, *Budget Plan 2001*, Table 1.4.

Table B.2
Federal Deficit/Surplus
1992/3 to 2000/3

Billions of Dollars (current)

Fiscal Year	Budgetary Revenue	Total Expenditures	Budgetary Deficit/Surplus	As % of GDP
1992/3	120.4	161.4	-41.0	5.9
1993/4	116.0	158.0	-42.0	5.8
1994/5	123.3	160.8	-37.5	4.9
1995/6	130.3	158.9	-28.6	3.5
1996/7	140.9	149.8	-8.9	1.1
1997/8	153.2	149.7	3.5	0.3
1998/9	155.7	152.8	2.9	0.3
1999/2000	165.7	153.4	12.3	1.3
2000/1[a]	173.7	161.9	11.8	1.2
2001/2[a]	174.5	166.3	8.2	0.8
2002/3[a]	178.4	170.8	7.6	0.6

(a) Figures for these years are estimates.

Note: While revenue, expenditures, and deficit categories refer to fiscal years, nominal GDP is based upon a calendar year. Total expenditures include program spending and public debt charges.

Source: Department of Finance, *Fiscal Reference Tables* (Sept. 2001), Tables 1 and 2; Department of Finance, *Economic Statement and Budget Update 2000* (18 Oct. 2000), Table 1.4.

Figure B.5
Federal Revenue, Expenditures, and the Deficit
1994/5 to 2003/4

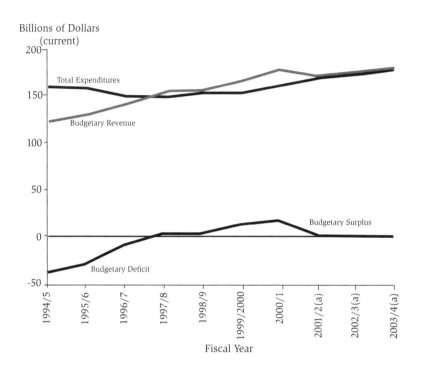

(a) Figures for these years are estimates.

Note: Expenditures include program spending and public interest charges on the debt.

Source: Department of Finance, *Fiscal Reference Tables* (Sept. 2001), Tables 1 and 2; Department of Finance, *Budget Plan 2001*, Table 1.4; *Public Accounts of Canada*, Statement of Revenues and Expenditures, various years.

Figure B.6
Growth in Real GDP
1992–2001

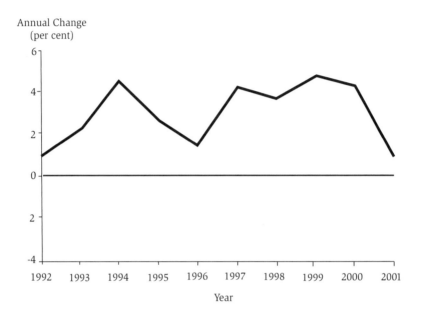

Source: Statistics Canada, *The Daily*, cat. #13–001, various years.

Figure B.7
**Rates of Unemployment and Employment Growth
1992–2001**

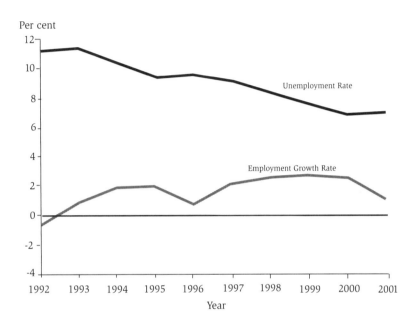

Note: Employment growth rates and the unemployment rate apply to both sexes, 15 years and older, and are seasonally adjusted.

Source: Statistics Canada, *Historical Labour Force Statistics* (71–201), various years.

Figure B.8

Interest Rates and the Consumer Price Index (CPI)

1992–2001

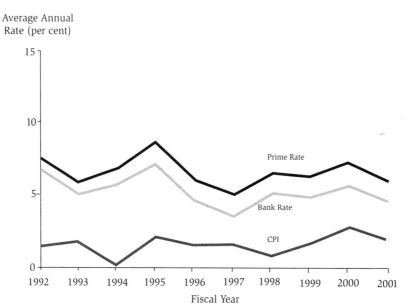

Note: The CPI is not seasonally adjusted. The Prime Rate refers to the prime business interest rate charged by the chartered banks, and the Bank Rate refers to the rate charged by the Bank of Canada on any loans to commercial banks.

Source: *Bank of Canada Review*, Table F1, various years; Statistics Canada, *The Consumer Price Index*, cat. #62–001, various years.

Figure B.9
Productivity and Costs
1991–2000

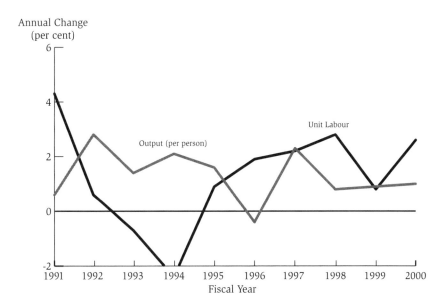

(a) Output per person hour is the real GDP per person hour worked in the business sector, and is a measure of productivity. This trend shows the annual percentage change of this indicator. Real GDP is based on constant 1986 prices.
(b) Unit Labour cost in the business sector is based on the real GDP, in constant 1986 prices. This trend shows the annual percentage change in this indicator.

Source: Statistics Canada, cat. #15–204, various years.

Figure B.10
Balance of Payments
1991–2000

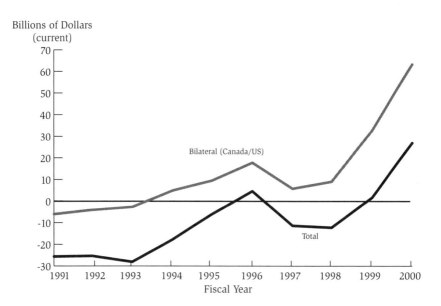

Source: Statistics Canada, cat. #67–001, various years.

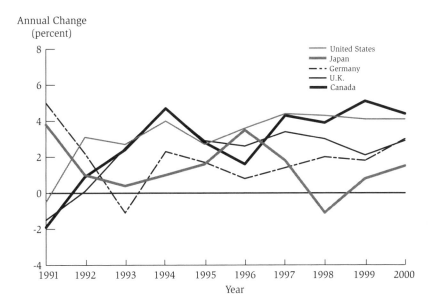

Figure B.11
Growth in Real GDP
Canada and Selected Countries
1991–2000

Source: Organization for Economic Cooperation and Development (OECD), *Economic Outlook*, no. 70 (Dec. 2001), Annex Table 1.

Figure B.12
Unemployment Rates
Canada and Selected Countries
1991–2000

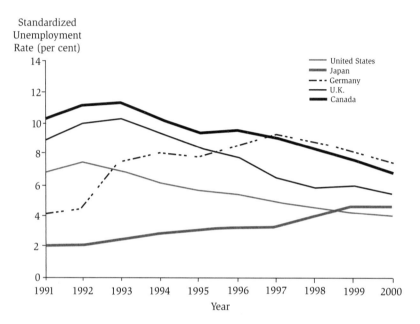

Source: *OECD Economic Outlook*, no. 70 (Dec. 2001), Annex Table 22.

Figure B.13
Annual Inflation Rates
Canada and Selected Countries
1991–2000

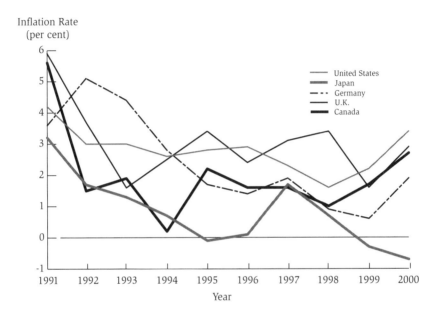

Source: *OECD Economic Outlook*, no. 70 (Dec. 2001), Annex Table 16.

Figure B.14
Labour Productivity
Canada and Selected Countries
1991–2000

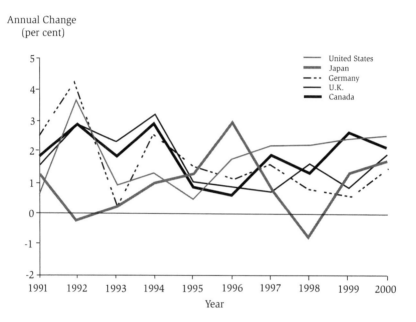

Note: Labour productivity is defined as output per unit of labour input. The data is for labour productivity growth in the business sector. The series on total economy unit labour cost was dropped because inclusion of the public sector was thought to be a distorting influence.

Source: *OECD Economic Outlook*, no. 70 (Dec. 2001), Annex Table 13.

Table B.3
International Comparisons
1991–2000

Percentage Change from Previous Year

Growth in Real GDP

	1991	1992	1993	1994	1995	1996	1997	1998	1999	2000
Canada	-1.9	0.9	2.4	4.7	2.8	1.6	4.3	3.9	5.1	4.4
US	-0.5	3.1	2.7	4.0	2.7	3.6	4.4	4.3	4.1	4.1
Japan	3.8	1.0	0.4	1.0	1.6	3.5	1.8	-1.1	0.8	1.5
Germany	5.0	2.2	-1.1	2.3	1.7	0.8	1.4	2.0	1.8	3.0
UK	-1.5	0.1	2.5	4.7	2.8	1.6	4.3	3.9	5.1	4.4

Unemployment Rates

	1991	1992	1993	1994	1995	1996	1997	1998	1999	2000
Canada	10.3	11.2	11.4	10.3	9.4	9.6	9.1	8.3	7.6	6.8
US	6.8	7.5	6.9	6.1	5.6	5.4	4.9	4.5	4.2	4.0
Japan	2.1	2.2	2.5	2.9	3.1	3.4	3.4	4.1	4.7	4.7
Germany	4.2	4.5	7.6	8.1	7.9	8.5	9.4	8.9	8.2	7.5
UK	8.9	10.0	10.3	9.4	8.5	7.9	6.5	5.9	6.0	5.5

Labour productivity

	1991	1992	1993	1994	1995	1996	1997	1998	1999	2000
Canada	1.8	2.9	1.8	2.9	0.8	0.6	1.9	1.3	2.6	2.1
US	0.4	3.7	0.9	1.3	0.4	1.8	2.2	2.2	2.4	2.5
Japan	1.3	-0.2	0.2	1.0	1.3	3.0	0.8	-0.8	1.3	1.7
Germany	2.6	4.3	0.2	2.7	1.5	1.1	1.6	0.8	0.5	1.4
UK	1.5	2.8	2.3	3.2	1.0	0.8	0.7	1.6	0.8	1.9

Source: *OECD Economic Outlook*, No. 70, December 2001, Annex Tables 1, 13, 22.

ABSTRACTS/RÉSUMÉS

Gerard W. Boychuk
Federal Spending in Health: Why Here? Why Now?

Ottawa's attempts to assume a leadership role in health care have been sharply constrained. For the most part this has resulted from Ottawa's simultaneously reducing its fiscal transfers to the provinces and defining its main role in the field to be to enforce the Canada Health Act's prohibitions against user fees and privatized service delivery. Apart from this role and, in part, because of it, federal involvement in health care has been limited to a number of small, but important and innovative, initiatives that are unlikely to produce the kind of visibility that the federal government would like to achieve, given its fiscal commitment in this area. A number of recent moves strongly suggest a pending major federal repositioning in the field. Despite conventional wisdom, which casts it as the defender of the principles of the Canada Health Act, Ottawa may relax its insistence on some of these principles in order to establish a more direct and visible role for itself in major new programs, such as home care, pharmacare, or the provision of health technology.

Les tentatives du gouvernement fédéral d'assumer un rôle prépondérant dans les soins de santé ont été sérieusement limitées du fait qu'Ottawa définit son rôle principal comme celui de faire respecter les interdictions de la Loi canadienne sur la santé relatives aux frais d'utilisation et à la privatisation de la prestation de services en même temps qu'il réduit ses transferts fiscaux vers les provinces. En dehors de ce rôle et, en partie, à cause de celui-ci, la participation fédérale aux soins de santé a été limitée à un certain nombre d'initiatives innovatrices, de petite envergure mais significatives, peu susceptibles de produire la sorte de visibilité recherchée par le gouvernement vu son engagement fiscal dans ce domaine. Certaines initiatives récentes suggèrent un repositionnement majeur de la part du gouvernement. Malgré son image stéréotypée de défenseur des principes de la Loi canadienne sur la santé, Ottawa va peut-être moins insister sur certains de ceux-ci afin de se donner un rôle plus direct et visible dans de nouveaux programmes importants tels que les soins à domicile, le régime d'assurance-médicaments ou la prestation de technologies de la santé.

Monica Gattinger
The Liberals' 'Reinvestment' in Arts and Culture: From Patron to Patronage?

The federal government's infusion of a half-billion dollars into arts and culture marks a clear departure from the many years of funding cutbacks to the sector. With Tomorrow Starts Today, the Liberals seem to have moved arts and culture from the expenditure chopping block to the spending and agenda spotlight. This chapter traces the Chrétien Liberals' shift in orientation toward the sector and examines the main elements and dominant themes of Tomorrow Starts Today. It argues that the fact that the Department of Canadian Heritage is the principal beneficiary of the new moneys raises the spectre of undesirable political influence in arts and culture granting and program decision-making. In addition, a substantial portion of the new funding supports larger Liberal policy themes, notably the new economy and youth, which could have negative consequences for more traditional targets of arts and culture spending. The chapter recommends that, in order to minimize the new funding's vulnerability to patronage, members of the arts and culture community be involved in departmental decision-making.

L'infusion d'un demi-milliard de dollars fédéraux dans les arts et la culture marque une nette réorientation par rapport aux nombreuses années de réductions de financement dans ce secteur. Avec le programme un avenir en art les libéraux ont apparemment décidé de mettre fin aux compressions du passé et de privilégier les arts et la culture dans leurs dépenses et leur programme. Ce chapitre retrace cette nouvelle orientation et examine les éléments principaux et les thèmes dominants d'un avenir en art. Nous soutenons que puisque le nouveau financement profite surtout au ministère du Patrimoine canadien, cela soulève le spectre d'une influence politique indésirable dans les processus de prises de décision en matière de subventions et de programmes. De plus, une partie importante du nouveau financement soutient des thèmes libéraux plus généraux tels que la jeunesse et la nouvelle économie, ce qui pourrait avoir des conséquences négatives pour les cibles plus traditionnelles des dépenses sur les arts et la culture. Ce chapitre recommande, afin de minimiser la vulnérabilité au patronage, que l'on fasse participer les membres de la communauté artistique et culturelle aux processus décisionnels au sein du ministère.

Geoffrey Hale

Innovation and Inclusion: Budgetary Policy, the Skills Agenda, and the Politics of the New Economy

The 2001 federal budget reflects the federal government's ongoing efforts to balance adaptation to structural economic change, fiscal sustainability, and old-fashioned distributive politics. Its longer-term agenda emphasizes continuing to invest in basic and applied research in order to promote Canada's competitiveness in the North American and global economies, while fostering human capital and 'inclusion' in the new economy. This chapter examines the context for the innovation and skills agendas, which are central to the government's strategy for economic and social renewal, and the incremental steps taken to implement these agendas since the last election amid the fiscal and political constraints arising from the events of 11 September 2001 and the cyclical downturn in the North American economy.

Le budget fédéral de 2001 reflète les efforts continus du gouvernement fédéral de concilier l'adaptation au changement économique structurel, la durabilité fiscale ainsi que la bonne vieille politique distributive. Le programme à long terme met l'accent sur des investissements continus dans la recherche fondamentale et appliquée pour promouvoir la compétitivité du Canada dans les économies nord-américaine et mondiale tout en favorisant le capital humain et l'inclusion dans la nouvelle économie. Ce chapitre examine le contexte des programmes en matière de compétences et d'innovation qui jouent un rôle essentiel dans la stratégie gouvernementale pour le renouvellement économique et social ainsi que les mesures prises graduellement pour mettre ces programmes en oeuvre depuis les dernières élections et dans le cadre des contraintes fiscales et politiques découlant des événements du 11 septembre 2001 et du ralentissement cyclique de l'économie nord-américaine.

Michael Hart and Brian Tomlin
Inside the Perimeter: The US Policy Agenda and Its Implications for Canada
An examination of the ways policy priorities in Canada are profoundly shaped, both directly and indirectly, by the public policy agenda in the United States, the chapter begins with a description of the US policy process, particularly the setting of the policy agenda and the president's role in this process. The policy agenda that was being developed by the Bush administration prior to the terrorist attacks on New York and Washington on 11 September 2001 is described, and the immediate and medium-term implications of the attacks for that agenda are identified. The chapter then turns to an examination of the effects of the Bush agenda, before and after 11 September, on Canadian policy priorities, and the policy process in Canada.

Nous examinons les façons dont les priorités en matière de politiques sont profondément influencées au Canada, directement et indirectement, par les politiques gouvernementales des États-Unis. Ce chapitre commence par décrire le processus politique américain, en particulier l'établissement du programme d'action et le rôle du président dans ce processus. Nous décrivons le programme d'action que l'administration Bush était en train d'élaborer avant les attentats terroristes sur New York et Washington du 11 septembre 2001 et nous identifions les répercussions immédiates et à moyen terme de ces attentats sur ce programme d'action. Nous examinons ensuite les effets du programme Bush, avant et après le 11 septembre, sur les priorités en matière de politiques au Canada ainsi que sur le processus politique au Canada.

Luc Juillet and Gilles Paquet
The Neurotic State
For a number of years a vicious circle has been at play in Ottawa: growing distrust and a critical attitude of citizens toward the state has led the public service and the government to fear the consequences of information disclosure, and to centralize control of decisions and information, which in turn reinforces citizens' distrust, and promotes aggressive calls for more transparency. The result has been a drift toward a neurotic governance regime. Using a framework proposed by Kets de Vries and Miller to analyse 'organizational neuroses', the authors identify the dominant neurotic style of the Canadian state, illustrate the dynamics at work through an analysis of the recent debates concerning the Access to Information Act, and explore some of the consequences of these dynamics.

Depuis quelques années, un cercle vicieux est en opération à Ottawa: en réponse à la méfiance croissante et à l'attitude critique des citoyens à l'égard de l'État, la Fonction publique et le gouvernement en sont venus à craindre les conséquences politiques du partage de l'information et à préconiser un contrôle central accru sur les processus décisionnels, ce qui en retour tend à renforcer la méfiance des citoyens et à leur faire revendiquer de façon agressive une plus grande transparence. Le résultat est un style de gouvernance marqué par la méfiance et la paranoïa. À l'aide d'un cadre d'analyse proposé par Kets de Vries et Miller pour analyser les « névroses organisationnelles », les auteurs identifient le style dominant de névrose de l'État canadien, illustrent la dynamique en jeu à travers une analyse des débats récents autour de la Loi sur l'accès à l'information, et explorent certaines des conséquences de cette dynamique.

Michael J. Prince

The Return of Directed Incrementalism: Innovating Social Policy the Canadian Way

Directed incrementalism proceeds by setting bold goals and working toward them step-by-step over the medium to long term. A style of social policy innovation prominent from the 1940s to the early 1970s, directed incrementalism is returning as a notable method of reforming Canada's social union. Examples examined in the chapter include new policy visions in disability, children and family, and Aboriginal affairs; significant changes to Canada's tax collection agreements and the approval of the Nisga'a Treaty; and new approaches to developing income-tested child benefits through the National Child Benefit reform. The author contends that social policy innovation is characterized not so much by switching or even quickly shifting paradigms as by stacking them. In the directed incremental style of reform, change in policy paradigms is more gradual and mixed than sudden and total, and frequently takes place through negotiations among federal and provincial/territorial government officials and between government officials and Aboriginal leaders or representatives of civil society organizations.

Le gradualisme dirigé consiste à établir des objectifs audacieux et à s'en approcher étape par étape à moyen ou à long terme. Ce style d'innovation en matière de politique sociale a dominé depuis les années 1940 jusqu'au début des années 1970, et fait un retour à l'heure actuelle comme méthode notable de réformer l'union sociale canadienne. Dans ce chapitre nous examinons, entre autres, les exemples suivants: les nouvelles visions stratégiques concernant les personnes handicapées, les enfants et la famille; les affaires autochtones; les changements significatifs aux accords canadiens en matière de perception fiscale; la signature du traité avec les Nisga'a; les nouvelles approches en vue d'élaborer des prestations pour enfants fondées sur l'étude du revenu dans le cadre de la Réforme de la prestation nationale pour enfants. Nous soutenons que cette innovation en matière de politique sociale consiste moins à subsister ou même à modifier les paradigmes qu'à les entasser. Dans la réforme selon le style du gradualisme dirigé, la modification des paradigmes se fait de façon plutôt graduelle et partielle que soudaine et totale et elle repose fréquemment sur des

négociations parmi les représentants des gouvernements fédéral et provinciaux ou
territoriaux ou bien sur des négociations entre les représentants gouvernementaux et
les dirigeants autochtones ou les représentants des organisations de la société civile.

James J. Rice
Being Poor in the Best of Times
This chapter examines the federal government's failure to significantly reduce child
poverty in Canada during the emergence of what many have called the 'new economy'. While the reduction of child poverty stands as an enormous challenge to any
government, it seemed on the edge of possibility given the federal government's
success in essentially eliminating poverty for the elderly. Although members of the
House of Commons 'promise[d] to eliminate child poverty by the year 2000', things
did not turn out well for poor children. In fact, in six out of eight years in which the
United Nations voted Canada 'the best place in the world to live', child poverty
increased. These years can be thought of as bitter years for children. This chapter
explores some of the reasons for these failures.

Ce chapitre examine l'échec des tentatives du gouvernement fédéral de réduire de
façon significative la pauvreté infantile au Canada au cours de l'émergence de ce que
plusieurs ont appelé la croissance de la "nouvelle économie". Si la réduction de la
pauvreté infantile représentait un défi énorme pour tout gouvernement, celle-ci sem-
blait être sur le point de se réaliser vu l'élimination essentielle réussie par le gou-
vernement fédéral de la pauvreté chez les personnes âgées. Même si la promesse
d'éliminer la pauvreté infantile dès l'an 2000 venait des députés de la Chambre des
communes, tout n'a pas bien fini pour les enfants pauvres. En fait, pendant six des
huit années de la période où l'ONU déclarait que le Canada était "le meilleur pays
où vivre" la pauvreté infantile a augmenté. Ces années ont été pénibles pour les
enfants. Ce chapitre explore certaines raisons de cet échec.

Markus Sharaput
Biotechnology Policy in Canada: The Broadening Scope of Innovation
Biotechnology has emerged as a core sector within the Liberal government's strategy for economic competition. The role played by biotechnology is based on its
characterization as an enabling technology; such a technology has enormous potential for innovative application, with a consequent potential for economic growth and
social transformation. Biotechnology policy in Canada has emerged as a key horizontal policy file; although coordinated by Industry Canada, the file is inter-ministerial, reflecting the breadth of applications for the technology, both existing and
anticipated. It has also emerged as a layered policy; initial phases of policy development dealt with the growth of R&D capacity in the sector, and the commercialization of that capacity for economic gain. The most recent phase has been characterized by the incorporation of socio-ethical considerations into the policy formation
process. The incorporation of these issues has not been without controversy,

however, in that a number of non-governmental organizations have begun to question whether such issues can be a part of biotechnology policy formation, or whether they must be debated prior to the formation of that policy.

La biotechnologie s'avère un secteur clef dans la stratégie de compétition économique du gouvernemental libéral. Le rôle joué par la biotechnologie repose sur la caractérisation de celle-ci comme technologie habilitante; une telle technologie offre un énorme potentiel d'applications innovatrices, et donc un potentiel dans le domaine de la croissance économique et de la transformation sociale. La politique canadienne en matière de biotechnologie s'est avérée un dossier horizontal clef en matière de politiques; bien que coordonné par Industrie Canada, ce dossier est interministériel et reflète donc toute la gamme d'applications, existantes et anticipées, de cette technologie. Elle s'est avérée également multidimensionnelle; au début de l'évolution de cette politique, il s'agissait d'assurer la croissance de la capacité en recherche et développement au sein du secteur, ainsi que la commercialisation de cette capacité afin de récupérer des gains économiques. La phase la plus récente de l'évolution de la politique en matière de biotechnologie a été caractérisée par l'incorporation de considérations socioéthiques dans le processus d'élaboration des politiques. L'incorporation de ces questions ne s'est pas passée sans controverse, cependant, en ce sens qu'un certain nombre d'organisations non gouvernementales ont commencé à demander si de telles questions peuvent faire partie de l'élaboration des politiques en matière de biotechnologie ou si elle ne doivent pas être plutôt débattues avant l'élaboration de cette politique.

Allan Tupper
Toward a New Beginning? The Chrétien Liberals and Western Canada
This chapter examines the relationship between the government of Canada and the four western Canadian provinces in the aftermath of the 2000 general election. It examines the renewal of the federal Liberals' interest in western Canada as the region diversifies economically and becomes heavily urbanized. The chapter notes a nascent Liberal strategy for increasing support in western Canada that stresses greater federal visibility, increased recognition of western resource industries as national strengths, and an emphasis on federal measures that promote 'new economy' initiatives in western Canada. Also noteworthy are Ottawa's efforts to establish strong relationships with the government of Alberta. The chapter argues that, contrary to conventional wisdom, Liberal prospects are relatively good in western Canada, because of a decline in western Canadian regionalism and a diminished role for provincial governments as vehicles for regional protest. Ottawa's strategy faces hurdles, but a Liberal renaissance is possible.

Ce chapitre examine les relations entre le gouvernement du Canada et les quatre provinces de l'Ouest au lendemain des élections de l'an 2000. Nous examinons le regain d'intérêt des libéraux fédéraux pour l'Ouest au moment où cette région se diversifie économiquement et s'urbanise fortement. Ce chapitre note l'apparition d'une stratégie libérale pour rehausser l'appui du parti dans l'Ouest qui met l'accent sur une visibilité fédérale accrue, une plus grande reconnaissance des industries primaires de l'Ouest comme des forces nationales ainsi que l'introduction de mesures fédérales qui favorisent les initiatives de la "nouvelle économie" dans l'Ouest. Il faut mentionner également les efforts d'Ottawa pour établir de bonnes relations avec le gouvernement de l'Alberta. Ce chapitre soutient que, contrairement aux idées reçues, les libéraux ont de bonnes perspectives d'avenir dans l'Ouest vu le déclin du régionalisme de l'Ouest canadien ainsi que le rôle réduit des gouvernements provinciaux en tant que véhicules de la protestation régionale. La stratégie d'Ottawa fait face à certains obstacles mais une renaissance libérale est bien possible.

Debora L. VanNijnatten

Getting Greener in the Third Mandate? Renewable Energy, Innovation, and the Liberals' Sustainable Development Agenda

The federal government indicated in its 2000 budget that environmental protection would assume a higher profile in a third Liberal term. This chapter argues that the higher profile accorded to the environment, particularly to technologies related to renewable energy, emerged as a result of three factors: the Liberal domestic policy agenda (with its focus on innovation, sustainable development, and addressing climate change), cross-border Canada-US policy dialogue, and shifts within the energy industry. An examination of federal policy since 1993 reveals that support for renewable energy did indeed increase modestly over the Liberals' first two mandates, even as Program Review ran its course and departmental budgets were significantly decreased. The more recent economic downturn and the events of September 11 have grasped the attention of federal policy-makers and have been reflected in decreased program spending. Still, the three factors in the policy context remain operative, and therefore federal support for renewable energy technologies is unlikely to unravel quickly.

Le gouvernement libéral fédéral a indiqué dans son budget de l'an 2000 que la protection de l'environnement jouerait un rôle plus important au cours d'un troisième mandat libéral. Ce chapitre soutient que cette importance accrue donnée à l'environnement, en particulier à des technologies reliées à l'énergie renouvelable, a apparu à la suite de trois facteurs: le programme de politique intérieure des libéraux (mettant l'accent sur l'innovation, le développement durable et les problèmes du changement climatique), le dialogue transfrontalier entre le Canada et les Etats-Unis au sujet des politiques, ainsi que les changements survenus dans l'industrie énergétique. Un examen de la politique fédérale depuis 1993 révèle que l'appui accordé à l'énergie renouvelable a bien augmenté de façon modeste au cours des deux premiers mandats des libéraux, alors même que l'Examen des programmes suivait son cours et que les budgets des ministères étaient réduits de façon considérable. La baisse économique récente et les événements du 11 septembre ont saisi l'attention des décisionnaires fédéraux en matière de politiques et se reflètent dans les dépenses diminuées en matière de programmes. Il n'en reste pas moins que les trois facteurs du contexte politique continuent d'opérer et que l'appui fédéral accordé aux technologies relatives à l'énergie renouvelable est peu susceptible de disparaître d'ici peu.

David A. Wolfe
Innovation Policy for the Knowledge-Based Economy: From the Red Book to the White Paper

The need to accelerate Canada's transition to a knowledge-based economy and to increase our investment in research and development has been a prominent theme of the Liberal government since 1993. The commitment to move Canada from fifteenth to fifth place in R&D spending was a central plank in the Liberal platform in the federal election of 2000. The December 2001 budget and the Innovation White Paper were expected to implement this policy priority, but early indications are that they fall short of what is expected. Progress toward realizing the commitment has been undermined, during the first mandate, by the priority on a balanced budget, and, more recently, by the new security agenda. This chapter reviews the government's analyses of Canada's innovation performance and its prescriptions to remedy the shortcomings. It evaluates the effectiveness of the current policy mix and questions whether the deployment of new funds without a better understanding of the nature of the innovation system in this country will suffice to achieve the government's stated goal.

La nécessité d'accélérer la transition du Canada vers une économie du savoir et d'augmenter nos investissements en recherche et développement est un thème dominant du gouvernement libéral depuis 1993. L'engagement de faire avancer le Canada du 15e au 5e rang dans les dépenses en recherche et développement a été un article central du programme électoral des libéraux en l'an 2000. Le budget de décembre 2001 ainsi que le livre blanc sur l'Innovation devaient mettre cette priorité politique en oeuvre, mais tout porte à croire, à l'heure actuelle, que ceux-ci ne répondent pas aux attentes. Les progrès en vue de la réalisation de cet engagement ont été entravés par la priorité accordée à un budget équilibré au cours du premier mandat, et, plus récemment, par la nouvelle stratégie en matière de sécurité. Ce chapitre examine les analyses faites par le gouvernement de la fiche du Canada en matière d'innovation ainsi que les prescriptions de celui-ci pour remédier aux défaillances. Nous évaluons l'efficacité de la gamme actuelle de politiques et nous exprimons un doute que l'utilisation de nouveaux fonds, en l'absence d'une meilleure compréhension de la nature du système d'innovation au pays, suffise pour atteindre l'objectif déclaré du gouvernement.

CONTRIBUTORS

Gerard W. Boychuk is an Assistant Professor of Political Science at the University of Waterloo.

G. Bruce Doern is a Professor of Public Policy and Administration at Carleton University, and holds a joint Research Chair in Public Policy in the Politics Department at the University of Exeter.

Monica Gattinger is a Ph.D. candidate in Public Policy in the School of Public Policy and Administration at Carleton University.

Geoffrey E. Hale is an Assistant Professor of Political Science at the University of Lethbridge.

Michael Hart is the Simon Reisman Professor of Trade Policy in the Norman Paterson School of International Affairs at Carleton University.

Luc Juillet is an Assistant Professor of Political Science and a Fellow of the Centre on Governance at the University of Ottawa.

Gilles Paquet is a Professor of Economics and Governance in the Faculty of Administration and a Fellow of the Centre on Governance at the University of Ottawa.

Michael Prince is the Lansdowne Professor of Social Policy and an Associate Dean in Social Development at the University of Victoria.

James Rice is a Professor of Social Policy in the School of Social Work at McMaster University.

Markus Sharaput is a Ph.D. candidate in Political Science at York University.

Brian Tomlin is a Professor in the Norman Paterson School of International Affairs at Carleton University.

Allan Tupper is a Professor in the Department of Political Science at the University of Alberta.

Debora L. VanNijnatten is an Assistant Professor in the Department of Political Science at Wilfred Laurier University.

David A. Wolfe is a Professor of Political Science and Co-Director of the Program on Globalization and Regional Innovation Systems in the Centre for International Studies at the University of Toronto.

THE SCHOOL OF PUBLIC POLICY AND ADMINISTRATION
at Carleton University is a national centre for the study of public
policy and public management.

The School's Centre for Policy and Program Assessment provides research services and courses to interest groups, businesses, unions, and governments in the evaluation of public policies, programs, and activities.

The *How Ottawa Spends* Series

How Ottawa Spends 2001–2002: Power in Transition
edited by Leslie A. Pal

How Ottawa Spends 2000–2001: Past Imperfect, Future Tense
edited by Leslie A. Pal

How Ottawa Spends 1999–2000: Shape Shifting: Canadian Governance Toward the 21st Century
edited by Leslie A. Pal

How Ottawa Spends 1998–99: Balancing Act: The Post-Deficit Mandate
edited by Leslie A. Pal

How Ottawa Spends 1997–98: Seeing Red: A Liberal Report Card
edited by Gene Swimmer

How Ottawa Spends 1996–97: Life Under the Knife
edited by Susan D. Phillips

How Ottawa Spends 1995–96: Mid-Life Crises
edited by Susan D. Phillips

How Ottawa Spends 1994–95: Making Change
edited by Susan D. Phillips

How Ottawa Spends 1993–94: A More Democratic Canada . . . ?
edited by Susan D. Phillips

How Ottawa Spends 1992–93: The Politics of Competitiveness
edited by Frances Abele

How Ottawa Spends 1991–92: The Politics of Fragmentation
edited by Frances Abele

How Ottawa Spends 1990–91: Tracking the Second Agenda
edited by Katherine A. Graham

How Ottawa Spends 1989–90: The Buck Stops Where?
edited by Katherine A. Graham

How Ottawa Spends 1988–89: The Conservatives Heading into the Stretch
edited by Katherine A. Graham

How Ottawa Spends 1987–88: Restraining the State
edited by Michael J. Prince

How Ottawa Spends 1986–87: Tracking the Tories
edited by Michael J. Prince

How Ottawa Spends 1985: Sharing the Pie
edited by Allan M. Maslove

How Ottawa Spends 1984: The New Agenda
edited by Allan M. Maslove

How Ottawa Spends 1983: The Liberals, The Opposition & Federal Priorities
edited by G. Bruce Doern

How Ottawa Spends Your Tax Dollars: National Policy and Economic Development 1982
edited by G. Bruce Doern

How Ottawa Spends Your Tax Dollars: Federal Priorities 1981
edited by G. Bruce Doern

Spending Tax Dollars: Federal Expenditures, 1980–81
edited by G. Bruce Doern